Online Resources

Included with your purchase are multiple online resources. This includes the practice tests in an interactive format and a convenient study timer to help you manage your time.

Instructions for accessing these resources can be found on the last page of this book.

Praxis 7001 Elementary Education Multiple Subjects Study Guide
4 Practice Tests and Exam Prep
[Includes Detailed Answer Explanations]

A. T. Segura

Copyright © 2025 by Webster's Test Prep

All rights reserved. No part of this publication may be reproduced, distributed, or transmitted in any form or by any means, including photocopying, recording, or other electronic or mechanical methods, without the prior written permission of the publisher, except in the case of brief quotations embodied in critical reviews and certain other noncommercial uses permitted by copyright law.

Written and edited by Webster's Test Prep.

Webster's Test Prep is not associated with or endorsed by any official testing organization. Webster's Test Prep is a publisher of unofficial educational products. All test and organization names are trademarks of their respective owners. Content in this book is included for utilitarian purposes only and does not constitute an endorsement by Webster's Test Prep of any particular point of view.

ISBN 13: 9781637758687

Table of Contents

Online Resources *1*

Welcome *1*

Quick Overview *2*

Test-Taking Strategies *3*

Introduction *7*

Study Prep Plan *9*

Math Reference Sheet *12*

Reading *13*

   Phonological Awareness *13*

   Phonics and Decoding *20*

   Vocabulary and Fluency *32*

   Comprehension of Literature and Informational Texts *41*

   Written Expression *76*

   Practice Quiz *98*

   Answer Explanations *99*

Mathematics *100*

   Numbers and Operations *100*

   Algebraic Thinking *116*

   Geometry & Measurement, Data, Statistics, and Probability *127*

   Practice Quiz *167*

   Answer Explanations *168*

Social Studies *169*

   United States History, Government, and Citizenship *169*

   Geography, Anthropology, and Sociology *180*

Table of Contents

   World History and Economics *188*

   Practice Quiz *196*

   Answer Explanations *197*

Science ***198***

   Earth Science *198*

   Life Science *216*

   Physical Science *242*

   Practice Quiz *256*

   Answer Explanations *257*

Practice Test #1 .... ***258***

   Reading and Language Arts *258*

   Mathematics *271*

   Social Studies *279*

   Science *287*

Answer Explanations #1 .... ***295***

   Reading and Language Arts *295*

   Mathematics *303*

   Social Studies *309*

   Science *315*

Practice Tests #2, #3, & #4 .... ***322***

Index ***323***

Online Resources ***335***

Welcome

Dear Reader,

Welcome to your new Webster's Test Prep study guide! We are pleased that you chose us to help you prepare for your exam. There are many study options to choose from, and we appreciate you choosing us. Studying can be a daunting task, but we have designed a smart, effective study guide to help prepare you for what lies ahead.

Whether you're a parent helping your child learn and grow, a high school student working hard to get into your dream college, or a nursing student studying for a complex exam, we want to help give you the tools you need to succeed. We hope this study guide gives you the skills and the confidence to thrive, and we can't thank you enough for allowing us to be part of your journey.

In an effort to continue to improve our products, we welcome feedback from our customers. We look forward to hearing from you. Suggestions, success stories, and criticisms can all be communicated by emailing us at support@testprepbooks.com.

Sincerely,
Webster's Test Prep Team

Quick Overview

As you draw closer to taking your exam, effective preparation becomes more and more important. Thankfully, you have this study guide to help you get ready. Use this guide to help keep your studying on track and refer to it often.

This study guide contains several key sections that will help you be successful on your exam. The guide contains tips for what you should do the night before and the day of the test. Also included are test-taking tips. Knowing the right information is not always enough. Many well-prepared test takers struggle with exams. These tips will help equip you to accurately read, assess, and answer test questions.

A large part of the guide is devoted to showing you what content to expect on the exam and to helping you better understand that content. In this guide are practice test questions so that you can see how well you have grasped the content. Then, answer explanations are provided so that you can understand why you missed certain questions.

Don't try to cram the night before you take your exam. This is not a wise strategy for a few reasons. First, your retention of the information will be low. Your time would be better used by reviewing information you already know rather than trying to learn a lot of new information. Second, you will likely become stressed as you try to gain a large amount of knowledge in a short amount of time. Third, you will be depriving yourself of sleep. So be sure to go to bed at a reasonable time the night before. Being well-rested helps you focus and remain calm.

Be sure to eat a substantial breakfast the morning of the exam. If you are taking the exam in the afternoon, be sure to have a good lunch as well. Being hungry is distracting and can make it difficult to focus. You have hopefully spent lots of time preparing for the exam. Don't let an empty stomach get in the way of success!

When travelling to the testing center, leave earlier than needed. That way, you have a buffer in case you experience any delays. This will help you remain calm and will keep you from missing your appointment time at the testing center.

Be sure to pace yourself during the exam. Don't try to rush through the exam. There is no need to risk performing poorly on the exam just so you can leave the testing center early. Allow yourself to use all of the allotted time if needed.

Remain positive while taking the exam even if you feel like you are performing poorly. Thinking about the content you should have mastered will not help you perform better on the exam.

Once the exam is complete, take some time to relax. Even if you feel that you need to take the exam again, you will be well served by some down time before you begin studying again. It's often easier to convince yourself to study if you know that it will come with a reward!

Test-Taking Strategies

1. Predicting the Answer

When you feel confident in your preparation for a multiple-choice test, try predicting the answer before reading the answer choices. This is especially useful on questions that test objective factual knowledge. By predicting the answer before reading the available choices, you eliminate the possibility that you will be distracted or led astray by an incorrect answer choice. You will feel more confident in your selection if you read the question, predict the answer, and then find your prediction among the answer choices. After using this strategy, be sure to still read all of the answer choices carefully and completely. If you feel unprepared, you should not attempt to predict the answers. This would be a waste of time and an opportunity for your mind to wander in the wrong direction.

2. Reading the Whole Question

Too often, test takers scan a multiple-choice question, recognize a few familiar words, and immediately jump to the answer choices. Test authors are aware of this common impatience, and they will sometimes prey upon it. For instance, a test author might subtly turn the question into a negative, or he or she might redirect the focus of the question right at the end. The only way to avoid falling into these traps is to read the entirety of the question carefully before reading the answer choices.

3. Looking for Wrong Answers

Long and complicated multiple-choice questions can be intimidating. One way to simplify a difficult multiple-choice question is to eliminate all of the answer choices that are clearly wrong. In most sets of answers, there will be at least one selection that can be dismissed right away. If the test is administered on paper, the test taker could draw a line through it to indicate that it may be ignored; otherwise, the test taker will have to perform this operation mentally or on scratch paper. In either case, once the obviously incorrect answers have been eliminated, the remaining choices may be considered. Sometimes identifying the clearly wrong answers will give the test taker some information about the correct answer. For instance, if one of the remaining answer choices is a direct opposite of one of the eliminated answer choices, it may well be the correct answer. The opposite of obviously wrong is obviously right! Of course, this is not always the case. Some answers are obviously incorrect simply because they are irrelevant to the question being asked. Still, identifying and eliminating some incorrect answer choices is a good way to simplify a multiple-choice question.

4. Don't Overanalyze

Anxious test takers often overanalyze questions. When you are nervous, your brain will often run wild, causing you to make associations and discover clues that don't actually exist. If you feel that this may be a problem for you, do whatever you can to slow down during the test. Try taking a deep breath or counting to ten. As you read and consider the question, restrict yourself to the particular words used by the author. Avoid thought tangents about what the author *really* meant, or what he or she was *trying* to say. The only things that matter on a multiple-choice test are the words that are actually in the question. You must avoid reading too much into a multiple-choice question, or supposing that the writer meant something other than what he or she wrote.

Test-Taking Strategies

5. No Need for Panic

It is wise to learn as many strategies as possible before taking a multiple-choice test, but it is likely that you will come across a few questions for which you simply don't know the answer. In this situation, avoid panicking. Because most multiple-choice tests include dozens of questions, the relative value of a single wrong answer is small. As much as possible, you should compartmentalize each question on a multiple-choice test. In other words, you should not allow your feelings about one question to affect your success on the others. When you find a question that you either don't understand or don't know how to answer, just take a deep breath and do your best. Read the entire question slowly and carefully. Try rephrasing the question a couple of different ways. Then, read all of the answer choices carefully. After eliminating obviously wrong answers, make a selection and move on to the next question.

6. Confusing Answer Choices

When working on a difficult multiple-choice question, there may be a tendency to focus on the answer choices that are the easiest to understand. Many people, whether consciously or not, gravitate to the answer choices that require the least concentration, knowledge, and memory. This is a mistake. When you come across an answer choice that is confusing, you should give it extra attention. A question might be

confusing because you do not know the subject matter to which it refers. If this is the case, don't eliminate the answer before you have affirmatively settled on another. When you come across an answer choice of this type, set it aside as you look at the remaining choices. If you can confidently assert that one of the other choices is correct, you can leave the confusing answer aside. Otherwise, you will need to take a moment to try to better understand the confusing answer choice. Rephrasing is one way to tease out the sense of a confusing answer choice.

7. Your First Instinct

Many people struggle with multiple-choice tests because they overthink the questions. If you have studied sufficiently for the test, you should be prepared to trust your first instinct once you have carefully and completely read the question and all of the answer choices. There is a great deal of research suggesting that the mind can come to the correct conclusion very quickly once it has obtained all of the relevant information. At times, it may seem to you as if your intuition is working faster even than your reasoning mind. This may in fact be true. The knowledge you obtain while studying may be retrieved from your subconscious before you have a chance to work out the associations that support it. Verify your instinct by working out the reasons that it should be trusted.

8. Key Words

Many test takers struggle with multiple-choice questions because they have poor reading comprehension skills. Quickly reading and understanding a multiple-choice question requires a mixture of skill and experience. To help with this, try jotting down a few key words and phrases on a piece of scrap paper. Doing this concentrates the process of reading and forces the mind to weigh the relative importance of the question's parts. In selecting words and phrases to write down, the test taker thinks about the question more deeply and carefully. This is especially true for multiple-choice questions that are preceded by a long prompt.

9. Subtle Negatives

One of the oldest tricks in the multiple-choice test writer's book is to subtly reverse the meaning of a question with a word like *not* or *except*. If you are not paying attention to each word in the question, you can easily be led astray by this trick. For instance, a common question format is, "Which of the following is...?" Obviously, if the question instead is, "Which of the following is not...?," then the answer will be quite different. Even worse, the test makers are aware of the potential for this mistake and will include one answer choice that would be correct if the question were not negated or reversed. A test taker who misses the reversal will find what he or she believes to be a correct answer and will be so confident that he or she will fail to reread the question and discover the original error. The only way to avoid this is to practice a wide variety of multiple-choice questions and to pay close attention to each and every word.

10. Reading Every Answer Choice

It may seem obvious, but you should always read every one of the answer choices! Too many test takers fall into the habit of scanning the question and assuming that they understand the question because they recognize a few key words. From there, they pick the first answer choice that answers the question they believe they have read. Test takers who read all of the answer choices might discover that one of the latter answer choices is actually *more* correct. Moreover, reading all of the answer choices can remind you of facts related to the question that can help you arrive at the correct answer. Sometimes, a misstatement or incorrect detail in one of the latter answer choices will trigger your memory of the subject and will enable you to find the right answer. Failing to read all of the answer choices is like not reading all of the items on a restaurant menu: you might miss out on the perfect choice.

11. Spot the Hedges

One of the keys to success on multiple-choice tests is paying close attention to every word. This is never truer than with words like *almost*, *most*, *some*, and *sometimes*. These words are called "hedges" because they indicate that a statement is not totally true or not true in every place and time. An absolute statement will contain no hedges, but in many subjects, the answers are not always straightforward or absolute. There

are always exceptions to the rules in these subjects. For this reason, you should favor those multiple-choice questions that contain hedging language. The presence of qualifying words indicates that the author is taking special care with his or her words, which is certainly important when composing the right answer. After all, there are many ways to be wrong, but there is only one way to be right! For this reason, it is wise to avoid answers that are absolute when taking a multiple-choice test. An absolute answer is one that says things are either all one way or all another. They often include words like *every*, *always*, *best*, and *never*. If you are taking a multiple-choice test in a subject that doesn't lend itself to absolute answers, be on your guard if you see any of these words.

12. Long Answers

In many subject areas, the answers are not simple. As already mentioned, the right answer often requires hedges. Another common feature of the answers to a complex or subjective question are qualifying clauses, which are groups of words that subtly modify the meaning of the sentence. If the question or answer choice describes a rule to which there are exceptions or the subject matter is complicated, ambiguous, or confusing, the correct answer will require many words in order to be expressed clearly and accurately. In essence, you should not be deterred by answer choices that seem excessively long. Oftentimes, the author of the text will not be able to write the correct answer without offering some qualifications and modifications. Your job is to read the answer choices thoroughly and completely and to select the one that most accurately and precisely answers the question.

13. Restating to Understand

Sometimes, a question on a multiple-choice test is difficult not because of what it asks but because of how it is written. If this is the case, restate the question or answer choice in different words. This process serves a couple of important purposes. First, it forces you to concentrate on the core of the question. In order to rephrase the question accurately, you have to understand it well. Rephrasing the question will concentrate your mind on the key words and ideas. Second, it will present the information to your mind in a fresh way. This process may trigger your memory and render some useful scrap of information picked up while studying.

14. True Statements

Sometimes an answer choice will be true in itself, but it does not answer the question. This is one of the main reasons why it is essential to read the question carefully and completely before proceeding to the answer choices. Too often, test takers skip ahead to the answer choices and look for true statements. Having found one of these, they are content to select it without reference to the question above. The savvy test taker will always read the entire question before turning to the answer choices. Then, having settled on a correct answer choice, he or she will refer to the original question and ensure that the selected answer is relevant. The mistake of choosing a correct-but-irrelevant answer choice is especially common on questions related to specific pieces of objective knowledge.

15. No Patterns

One of the more dangerous ideas that circulates about multiple-choice tests is that the correct answers tend to fall into patterns. These erroneous ideas range from a belief that B and C are the most common right answers, to the idea that an unprepared test-taker should answer "A-B-A-C-A-D-A-B-A." It cannot be emphasized enough that pattern-seeking of this type is exactly the WRONG way to approach a multiple-choice test. To begin with, it is highly unlikely that the test maker will plot the correct answers according to some predetermined pattern. The questions are scrambled and delivered in a random order. Furthermore, even if the test maker was following a pattern in the assignation of correct answers, there is no reason why the test taker would know which pattern he or she was using. Any attempt to discern a pattern in the answer choices is a waste of time and a distraction from the real work of taking the test. A test taker would be much better served by extra preparation before the test than by reliance on a pattern in the answers.

Introduction

Function of the Test

The Praxis Elementary Education: Multiple Subjects exam is one of the Educational Testing Service's (ETS's) Subject Assessment tests. The Subject Assessment tests are intended to measure knowledge of more than ninety specific subjects taught by educators in kindergarten through twelfth grade classrooms. These tests also aim to teach skills and knowledge in those subject areas. The tests are offered worldwide but are primarily used in the United States mostly as a required part of the certification and licensing procedure in certain individual states. They are also used as part of the licensing process by some professional associations and organizations.

The Elementary Education: Multiple Subjects exam covers four individual subjects: Reading and Language Arts, Mathematics, Social Studies, and Science. States that require the test typically require that a test-taker reach a minimum passing score on each of the four sub-tests in order to pass and receive the license or certification sought. Individuals taking the test are usually beginning teachers, either freshly out of college, having recently decided to seek a particular license or certification, or having recently moved to a state where the test is required or preferred.

Test Administration

The test is administered by computer through an international system of testing centers, including Prometric centers, some colleges and universities, and a variety of other locations. Although it is primarily used in the United States, the test is available at locations throughout the world. However, the test is not available at all times. Instead, there is a window of approximately two weeks per month during which the test may be taken. The individual subtests can be taken separately, but the fee for taking them together offers a significant discount from the combined cost of the four individual tests.

Accommodations for test-takers meeting the requirements of the Americans with Disabilities Act include extended testing time, additional rest breaks, a separate testing room, a writer/recorder of answers, a test reader, and large print test materials. Alternate forms of the test are available in sign language, Braille, or audio format.

Test takers may opt to retake the test at any time after twenty-one days have passed from the initial attempt. An individual wishing to retake one of the four tests that comprise the Multiple Subjects exam must also wait twenty-one days from the initial attempt of that exam.

Test Format

All questions are selected response (in which the test-taker chooses from multiple choice options or chooses a particular word, sentence or part of a graphic), and numeric entry (in which the test-taker gives a numeric answer). In all cases, the test-taker will receive a question from the computer and be prompted to select a response from the options on the screen or enter a number. Questions may be answered in any order, and test takers may mark questions to return to them later.

The four sub-tests of the exam break down as follows:

Subject	Minutes	Questions
Reading and Language Arts	90	80
Mathematics	65	50
Social Studies	50	55
Science	50	50
Total	255	235

Scoring

Raw scores are based on the number of correct responses with no penalty for incorrect answers or guesses. The raw scores are then converted to a scaled score from 100 to 200. The required passing scaled score varies from state to state and from sub-test to sub-test. On the Reading and Language Arts sub-test, the required score ranges from a low of 154 to a high of 165 with most states requiring at least a 157. The median score in 2015 was a 169. On the Mathematics sub-test, the required score ranges from a low of 143 to a high of 171 with most states requiring at least a 157. The median score in 2015 was a 170. On the Social Studies sub-test, the required score ranges from a low of 142 to 166 with most states requiring at least a 155. The median score in 2015 was a 163. Finally, on the Science sub-test, the required score ranges from a low of 144 to 170 with most states requiring at least a 159. The median score in 2015 was a 167.

ETS also offers a "Recognition of Excellence" to test takers who perform exceptionally well on the exam. The award is typically given to test takers whose scores fall in the top 15 percent of scores on the exam.

Study Prep Plan

1 **Schedule** - Use one of our study schedules below or come up with one of your own.

2 **Relax** - Test anxiety can hurt even the best students. There are many ways to reduce stress. Find the one that works best for you.

3 **Execute** - Once you have a good plan in place, be sure to stick to it.

One Week Study Schedule	
Day 1	Reading
Day 2	Mathematics
Day 3	Social Studies
Day 4	Science
Day 5	Practice Tests #1 & #2
Day 6	Practice Tests #3 & #4
Day 7	Take Your Exam!

Two Week Study Schedule			
Day 1	Reading	Day 8	Science
Day 2	Literature and Informational Texts	Day 9	Physical Science
Day 3	Writing, Speaking, and Listening	Day 10	Practice Test #1
Day 4	Mathematics	Day 11	Practice Test #2
Day 5	Geometry & Measurement...	Day 12	Practice Test #3
Day 6	Components of the Coordinate Plane	Day 13	Practice Test #4
Day 7	Social Studies	Day 14	Take Your Exam!

Study Prep Plan

One Month Study Schedule

Day 1	Reading	Day 11	Solving Problems Involving Measurement	Day 21	Practice Quiz
Day 2	Literature and Informational Texts	Day 12	Practice Quiz	Day 22	Practice Test #1
Day 3	Practice Quiz	Day 13	Social Studies	Day 23	Answer Explanations #1
Day 4	Writing, Speaking, and Listening	Day 14	Geography, Anthropology...	Day 24	Practice Test #2
Day 5	Language	Day 15	World History and Economics	Day 25	Answer Explanations #2
Day 6	Practice Quiz	Day 16	Practice Quiz	Day 26	Practice Test #3
Day 7	Mathematics	Day 17	Science	Day 27	Answer Explanations #3
Day 8	Algebraic Thinking	Day 18	Life Science	Day 28	Practice Test #4
Day 9	Geometry & Measurement...	Day 19	Regulation and Behavior	Day 29	Answer Explanations #4
Day 10	Perimeter, Area, Surface Area...	Day 20	Physical Science	Day 30	Take Your Exam!

Build your own prep plan by visiting the Online Resources page.

Instructions and a QR code can be found on the last page of this guide.

As you study for your test, we'd like to take the opportunity to remind you that you are capable of great things! With the right tools and dedication, you truly can do anything you set your mind to. The fact that you are holding this book right now shows how committed you are. In case no one has told you lately, you've got this! Our intention behind including this coloring page is to give you the chance to take some time to engage your creative side when you need a little brain-break from studying. As a company, we want to encourage people like you to achieve their dreams by providing good quality study materials for the tests and certifications that improve careers and change lives. As individuals, many of us have taken such tests in our careers, and we know how challenging this process can be. While we can't come alongside you and cheer you on personally, we can offer you the space to recall your purpose, reconnect with your passion, and refresh your brain through an artistic practice. We wish you every success, and happy studying!

Math Reference Sheet

Symbol	Phrase
+	added to, increased by, sum of, more than
-	decreased by, difference between, less than, take away
×	multiplied by, 3 (4, 5 . . .) times as large, product of
÷	divided by, quotient of, half (third, etc.) of
=	is, the same as, results in, as much as
x, t, n, etc.	a variable which is an unknown value or quantity
<	is under, is below, smaller than, beneath
>	is above, is over, bigger than, exceeds
≤	no more than, at most, maximum; less than or equal to
≥	no less than, at least, minimum; greater than or equal to
√	square root of, exponent divided by 2

Geometry	Description
$P = 2l + 2w$	for perimeter of a rectangle
$P = 4 \times s$	for perimeter of a square
$P = a + b + c$	for perimeter of a triangle
$A = \frac{1}{2} \times b \times h = \frac{bh}{2}$	for area of a triangle
$A = b \times h$	for area of a parallelogram
$A = \frac{1}{2} \times h(b_1 + b_2)$	for area of a trapezoid
$A = \frac{1}{2} \times a \times P$	for area of a regular polygon
$C = 2 \times \pi \times r$	for circumference (perimeter) of a circle
$A = \pi \times r^2$	for area of a circle
$c^2 = a^2 + b^2; c = \sqrt{a^2 + b^2}$	for finding the hypotenuse of a right triangle
$SA = 2xy + 2yz + 2xz$	for finding surface area
$V = \frac{1}{3}xyh$	for finding volume of a rectangular pyramid
$V = \frac{4}{3}\pi r^3; \frac{1}{3}\pi r^2 h; \pi r^2 h$	for volume of a sphere; a cone; and a cylinder

Radical Expressions	Description
$\sqrt[n]{a} = a^{\frac{1}{n}}; \sqrt[n]{a^m} = (\sqrt[n]{a})^m = a^{\frac{m}{n}}$	a is the radicand, n is the index, m is the exponent
$\sqrt{x^2} = (x^2)^{\frac{1}{2}} = x$	to convert square root to exponent
$a^m \times a^n = a^{m+n}$	multiplying radicands with exponents
$(a^m)^n = a^{m \times n}$	multiplying exponents
$(a \times b)^m = a^m \times b^m$	parentheses with exponents

Property	Addition	Multiplication
Commutative	$a + b = b + a$	$a \times b = b \times a$
Associative	$(a + b) + c = a + (b + c)$	$(a \times b) \times c = a \times (b \times c)$
Identity	$a + 0 = a; 0 + a = a$	$a \times 1 = a; 1 \times a = a$
Inverse	$a + (-a) = 0$	$a \times \frac{1}{a} = 1; a \neq 0$
Distributive		$a(b + c) = ab + ac$

Data	Description
Mean	equal to the total of the values of a data set, divided by the number of elements in the data set
Median	middle value in an odd number of ordered values of a data set, or the mean of the two middle values in an even number of ordered values in a data set
Mode	the value that appears most often
Range	the difference between the highest and the lowest values in the set

Graphing	Description
(x, y)	ordered pair, plot points in a graph
$y = mx + b$	slope-intercept form; m represents the slope of the line and b represents the y-intercept
$f(x)$	read as f of x, which means it is a function of x
(x_2, y_2) and (x_2, y_2)	two ordered pairs used to determine the slope of a line
$m = \frac{y_2 - y_1}{x_2 - x_1}$	to find the slope of the line, m, for ordered pairs
$Ax + By = C$	standard form of an equation, also for solving a system of equations through the elimination method
$M = (\frac{x_1 + x_2}{2}, \frac{y_1 + y_2}{2})$	for finding the midpoint of an ordered pair
$y = ax^2 + bx + c$	quadratic function for a parabola
$y = a(x - h)^2 + k$	quadratic function for a parabola with vertex
$y = ab^x; y = a \times b^x$	function for exponential curve
$y = ax^2 + bx + c$	standard form of a quadratic function
$x = \frac{-b}{2a}$	for finding axis of symmetry in a parabola; given quadratic formula in standard form
$f = \sqrt{\frac{\Sigma(x - \bar{x})^2}{n - 1}}$	function for standard deviation of the sample; where $\bar{x}$ = sample mean and n = sample size

Proportions and Percentage	Description
$\frac{gallons}{cost} = \frac{gallons}{cost}$: $\frac{7 \text{ gallons}}{\$14.70} = \frac{x}{\$20}$	written as equal ratios with a variable representing the missing quantity
$\frac{y_1}{x_1} = \frac{y_2}{x_2}$	for direct proportions
$(y_1)(x_1) = (y_2)(x_2)$	for indirect proportions
$\frac{change}{original\ value} \times 100 = $ percent change	for finding percentage change in value
$\frac{new\ quantity - old\ quantity}{old\ quantity} \times 100$	for calculating the increase or decrease in percentage

Reading

Phonological Awareness

Well before children are able to read and write, they begin to develop basic listening skills and gradually begin to imitate and produce the sounds they hear. Since **language** is used to communicate one's needs, react to situations, share experiences, and develop an understanding of the surrounding world, these beginning stages form the foundation of a child's literacy development. Before a child reaches the preschool years, they begin to develop the ability to recognize and manipulate the sounds in their environment.

Phonological awareness is the ability to identify and manipulate specific units of oral language, including words, syllables, onsets, and rimes. The beginning stages of phonological awareness occur when a child is able to listen to and understand spoken and written words, and can recognize the various sounds within those words. Phonological awareness is also defined as the ability to sound out various words by connecting the sounds heard to familiar sounds and to manipulate those sounds in order to create new sounds and words. A child demonstrates phonological awareness when they do the following:

- Appropriately recognize and apply words that rhyme—*cat, bat, sat*
- Identify initial letters—the *c* in *cat*
- Identify middle letters—the *a* in *cat*
- Identify ending letters—the *t* in *cat*
- Separate simple words into their individual sounds or phonemes—c/a/t *cat*

There are many strategies educators can use to strengthen a child's phonological awareness. One effective strategy to strengthen a child's awareness of word units is clapping out the number of syllables in a word. Familiar and enjoyable songs, such as "Bingo," help children to identify individual phonemes within a word and strengthen their spelling skills, listening comprehension, and rhythm. Other strategies may include word games that challenge children to think of rhyming words or words that share the same initial, middle, or ending sounds. Creating fun and engaging ways for children to strengthen their phonological awareness will build the framework for future literary success.

Some classroom strategies to strengthen phonemic awareness may include:

- Introduction to nursery rhymes and word play
- Introduction to speech discrimination techniques to train the ear to hear more accurately
- Repeated instruction connecting sounds to letters and blending sounds
- Use of visual images coupled with corresponding sounds and words
- Teaching speech sounds through direct instruction
- Comparing known to unfamiliar words
- Practicing pronunciation of newly introduced letters, letter combinations, and words
- Practicing word decoding
- Differentiating similar sounding words

Teaching Phonological Awareness

Phonemes, Syllables, Onsets, and Rimes

A **phoneme** is commonly referred to as a sound or a group of sounds that differentiate one word from another in a spoken language. Phonemes are language-specific sound units that do not carry inherent meanings but are simply known as the smallest unit in a language. For example, there are phonemes unique to the English language that do not necessarily exist in other spoken languages. In English, although there are only twenty-six letters, there are forty-four phonemes:

Forty-Four Phonemes in English			
Consonant Sounds		**Vowel Sounds**	
/b/	boy	/a/	bat
/d/	desk	/e/	head
/f/	fall	/i/	dish
/g/	game	/o/	rock
/h/	hand	/u/	muck
/j/	joy	/a/	bake
/k/	king	/e/	meet
/l/	life	/i/	like
/m/	map	/o/	moat
/n/	nail	/yoo/	cube
/p/	park	/e/	alarm
/r/	run	/oo/	doom
/s/	sock	/oo/	nook
/t/	tail	/ou/	mouse
/v/	veil	/oi/	toy
/w/	water	/o/	call
/y/	yawn	/u/	herd
/z/	zebra	/a/	hair
/ch/	chalk	/a/	star
/sh/	shallow		
/th/	thorn		
/wh/	whale		
/zh/	leisure		
/ng/	sing		

Mastery of all forty-four phonemes in oral and written communication is a strong predictor of future reading readiness.

Syllables are defined as one complete unit of pronunciation. Every syllable contains only one vowel sound that can be created by one or more vowels. Syllables can consist of vowels that stand alone or combine with consonants. Studying syllables and how they operate will help children become stronger readers and aid in spelling proficiency. Educators will often introduce new words that contain more than one syllable by teaching children to say and write the syllable. Segmenting a word into its individual syllables, as well as blending syllables into whole words, allows children to see the key parts of a word and provides opportunities for them to strengthen their reading skills.

In the English language, there are six different types of syllables, four of which are syllable combinations:

- Closed syllables: syllables that end in a consonant, as in *bat*, or *it*
- Open syllables: syllables that end with a vowel, as in *he*, *she*, or *we*
- Vowel-consonant-e syllables: syllables that end with a silent *e*, as in *ate*, *wife*, or *mile*
- Vowel team syllables: syllables that work in combination to create a new sound, as in *mouth* or *join*
- Consonant + le syllables: syllables that contain a consonant and end with an *le*, as in *turtle*

- R-Controlled syllables: syllables that contain a vowel followed by the letter *r*, where the *r* controls how the vowel is pronounced, as in *bird* or *word*

A word is broken up into two pieces: onset and rime. The **onset** is the initial phonological unit of any word, whether it is a consonant or a consonant cluster. The **rime** is the string of letters that follows the onset, usually consisting of a vowel or variant vowels along with one or more consonants. Many words in the English language share common features or patterns. These **word families** often share the same letter combinations that form the same or similar sounds. When introducing word families, educators will often initiate activities involving onsets and rimes to help children accurately recognize, read, and spell simple words. The study of onsets and rimes has shown to improve a child's overall literacy skills, increase reading fluency, and strengthen spelling skills. The following word family list illustrates words separated into onset and rime:

Word	Onset	Rime
sun	s	un
sunny	s	unny
sunshine	s	unshine

Blending, Segmenting, Substituting, and Deleting Phonemes, Syllables, Onsets, and Rimes

The ability to break apart a word into its individual phonemes is referred to as **segmenting**. Segmenting words can greatly aid in a child's ability to recognize, read, and spell an entire word. In literacy instruction, **blending** is when the reader connects segmented parts to create an entire word. Segmenting and blending practice work together like pieces of a puzzle to help children practice newly-acquired vocabulary. Educators can approach segmenting and blending using a multi-sensory approach. For example, a child can manipulate letter blocks to build words and pull them apart. An educator may even ask the child to listen to the word being said and ask him or her to find the letter blocks that build each phoneme, one at a time:

/m/ /u/ /g/

/b/ /a/ /t/

/r/ /u/ /n/

Once children are able to blend and segment phonemes, they are ready for the more complex skill of blending and segmenting syllables, onsets, and rimes. Using the same multi-sensory approach, children may practice blending the syllables of familiar words on a word wall, using letter blocks, paper and pencil, or sounding them out loud. Once they blend the words together, students can then practice segmenting those same words, studying their individual syllables, letters, and sounds. Educators may again read a word out loud and ask children to write or build the first syllable, followed by the next, and so on. The very same practice can be used to identify the onset. Children can work on writing and/or building this sound followed by the word's rime. Word families and rhyming words are ideal for this type of exercise so that children can more readily see the parts of each word. Using words that rhyme can turn this exercise into a fun and engaging activity.

Once children have demonstrated the ability to independently blend and segment phonemes, syllables, onsets, and rimes, educators may present a more challenging exercise that involves **substitutions** and **deletions**. As these are more complex skills, children will likely benefit from repeated practice and modeling. Using word families and words that rhyme when teaching this skill will make the activity more enjoyable, and it will also greatly aid in a child's overall comprehension.

Substitution and Deletion Using Onset and Rime

Word	Onset Deletion	Rime Deletion	Onset Substitution	Rime Substitution
run	un	r	fun	rat
bun	un	b	gun	bat
sun	un	s	nun	sat

Substitution and Deletion Using Phonemes

Word	Phoneme substitution	Phoneme deletion
sit	sat	si
bit	bat	bi
hit	hat	hi

Substitution and Deletion Using Syllables

Word	Syllable substitution	Syllable deletion
cement	lament or, cedar	ce
moment	statement, or motive	mo
basement	movement, or baseball	base

Rhyme and Alliteration

Teaching a child to recognize **rhymes** within words is one of the basic levels of phonological awareness. A child must closely pay attention to the word's different sounds. By teaching them to pay attention to the individual sounds, children also learn that words can be made up of multiple, different parts. They should listen to the sounds within different words and determine if they are similar, meaning they have rhyme, or if they are different, meaning they do not have rhyme.

Alliteration is when two or more words in a phrase begin with the same sound or sound group. For example, the phrase *chunky chocolate chips* includes the 'ch' sound at the beginning of each word.

Teaching a child to recognize alliteration in words is similar to teaching them to recognize rhyme. Not only is it another early, basic level of phonological awareness, but it helps the child to recognize patterns within words. Having children listen to the individual word sounds helps reinforce that words are broken up into multiple parts.

Expressive and Receptive Language Skills

English language skills can be broken down into two categories: expressive (talking skills) and receptive (listening skills). Students need different types of encouragement at every stage to develop their language skills.

Receptive language is defined as when students are able to understand words and can begin to follow instructions but aren't necessarily able to use words to communicate yet. Educators can encourage this stage in literacy development by providing the student with many opportunities to interact on a social level with peers. Educators should also consider starting a personal dictionary, introducing word flashcards, and providing the student with opportunities to listen to a story read by another peer, or as a computer-based activity. One of the simplest and best ways to develop receptive language skills is through reading aloud to students and asking basic comprehension questions.

Expressive language is defined as when students can express themselves with either words or gestures. It often comes after a solid understanding of receptive language. There are many ways to build upon expressive language, which vary depending on the child's literacy level.

When a child begins to communicate to express a need or attempt to ask or respond to a question, the child is said to be at the **early intermediate literacy stage.** Educators should continue to build vocabulary knowledge and introduce activities that require the student to complete the endings of sentences, fill in the blanks, and describe the beginning or ending of familiar stories.

When a child begins to demonstrate comprehension of more complex vocabulary and abstract ideas, the child is advancing into the **intermediate literacy stage**. It is at this stage that children are able to challenge themselves to meet the classroom learning expectations and start to use their newly acquired literacy skills to read, write, listen, and speak. Educators may consider providing students with more advanced reading opportunities, such as partner-shared reading, silent reading, and choral reading.

When a child is able to apply literacy skills to learn new information across many subjects, the child is progressing toward the early **advanced literacy stage**. The child can now tackle complex literacy tasks and confidently handle much more cognitively demanding material. To strengthen reading comprehension, educators should consider the introduction to word webs and semantic organizers. Book reports and class presentations, as well as continued opportunities to access a variety of reading material, will help to strengthen the child's newly acquired literacy skills.

Concepts of Print

Concepts of Print
Print awareness includes the understanding that:

1. **Words** are made of letters, spaces appear between words, and words make sentences.

2. **Print** is organized in a particular way (e.g., read from left to right and top to bottom, read from front to back, etc.), so books must be tracked and held accordingly.

3. Different types of print serve specific purposes (magazines, billboards, essays, fiction, etc.).

Print awareness provides the foundation on which all other literacy skills are built. It is often the first stage of reading development. Print awareness helps students develop skills such as word reading, reading comprehension, and letter-sound correspondence. For this reason, a child's performance on tasks relevant to their print awareness is indicative of the child's future reading achievement.

The following strategies can be used to increase print awareness in students:

1. A teacher can read aloud to students or conduct shared reading experiences. In order to maximize print awareness within the student, the reader should point out the form, function, orientation, and sounds of letters and words.

2. Utilize shared reading experiences as a tool for building one-to-one correspondence. **One-to-one correspondence** is the ability to match written letters or words to a spoken word when reading. This can be accomplished by pointing to words as they are read. This helps students make text-to-word connections. Pointing also aids **directionality**, or the ability to track the words that are being read.

3. Use the child's environment. To reinforce print awareness, teachers can make a child aware of print in their environment, such as words on traffic signs. Teachers can reinforce this by labeling objects in the classroom.

4. Instruct students about book organization during read-alouds. Students should be taught the proper orientation, tracking, and numbering conventions of books. For example, teachers can differentiate the title from the author's name on the front cover of a book.

5. Let students practice. Allowing students to practice book-handling skills with wordless books, predictable text, or patterned text will help to instill print awareness.

Return Sweep

Return sweeping refers to a reader moving their eyes from the end of one line on the right side of the page back to the left side of the page to begin a new line. The return sweep can be taught by modeling pointing to the words when reading to your child. Your child will learn to do this as they begin reading independently, and physically moving their finger from the end of one sentence to the beginning of the next will help train their eyes to follow this same process.

Parts of a Book

It is important to teach a new reader the different parts of a book, as each part contains its own valid and useful information. While there are simpler ways to reduce this list, here is an extensive list of the different parts/components of a standard book.

(1) Front Matter

  (a) Title

  (b) Copyright information

  (c) Dedication (if applicable)

  (d) Table of Contents

  (e) Foreword (if applicable)

  (f) Acknowledgments

  (g) Preface or Introduction (if applicable)

  (h) Prologue (if applicable)

(2) Body Matter

(a) This is the content of the book

(3) Back Matter

(a) Epilogue (if applicable)

(b) Appendix (if applicable)

(c) Glossary (if applicable)

(d) Bibliography (if applicable)

(e) Index (if applicable)

(f) Author's biography

The Form and Function of Print
Fostering print awareness also entails making sure the reader understands what books are used for and how a book actually works. This means that the reader needs to know how to turn a page, how to navigate the page (numbers and chapters), and how to distinguish the different parts of the book.

Included in this is also making sure the reader knows that print is typically organized from left to right and that there should be spaces between words. In order to help a new reader develop stronger print awareness and understanding of the form and function of print, environmental intervention is necessary. This means that parents and peers and any other influential members in the reader's life should make it a point to point out print. They should not only point out print but also make it a point to point out the different forms within print (i.e. line spacing, capitalization, page layouts, etc.)

Identifying Upper- and Lower-Case Letters

Recognizing Uppercase and Lowercase Letters
Among the skills that are used to determine reading readiness, letter identification is the strongest predictor. **Letter recognition** is the identification of each letter in the alphabet. Letter recognition does not include letter-sound correspondences; however, learning about and being able to recognize letters may increase student motivation to learn letter sounds. Also, the names of many letters are similar to their sounds, so letter recognition serves as a gateway for the letter-sound relationships that are needed for reading to occur. Similarly, the ability to differentiate between uppercase and lowercase letters is beneficial in determining where a sentence begins and ends.

To be fluent in letter identification, students should be able to identify letter names in and out of context with automaticity. In order to obtain such familiarity with the identification of letters, students need ample experience, acquaintance, and practice with letters. Explicit instruction in letter recognition, practice printing uppercase and lowercase letters of the alphabet, and consistent exposure to printed letters are essential in the instruction of letter recognition.

Research has revealed that the following sequencing guidelines are necessary to effectively promote letter naming and identification:

1. The initial stage includes visual discrimination of shapes and curved lines.

2. Once students are able to identify and discriminate shapes with ease, then letter formations can be introduced. During the introduction of letter shapes, two letters that share visual (*p* and *q*) or auditory (/a/ and /u/) similarities should never be presented in back-to-back.

3. Next, uppercase letters are introduced. Uppercase letters are introduced before lowercase letters because they are easier to discriminate visually than lowercase letters. When letter formations are first presented to a student, their visual system analyzes the vertical, horizontal, and curved orientations of the letters. Therefore, teachers should use think-alouds when instructing how to write the shape of each letter. During think-alouds, teachers verbalize their own thought processes that occur when writing each part of a given letter. Students should be encouraged to do likewise when practicing printing the letters. Continuous consonant sounds and vowel sounds (like /s/, /a/, and /f/) should be taught before stop consonant sounds (like /t/, /p/, and /k/). Short vowel sounds should be taught before long vowel sounds.

4. Once uppercase letters are mastered, lowercase letters can be introduced. High-frequency lowercase letters (*a, e, t*) are introduced prior to low-frequency lowercase letters (*q, x, z*).

5. Once the recognition of letters is mastered, students need ample time manipulating and utilizing the letters. This can be done through sorting, matching, comparing, and writing activities

Phonics and Decoding

Phonics is the study of sound-letter relationships in alphabetic writing systems, such as the English language, and it is paramount to a child's future ability to read and write. Phonics helps children recognize and identify letter symbols and translate these symbols into their corresponding sound units, phonemes. The study of phonics concerns itself with the **Alphabetic Principle**—the systematic relationships that exist between letters and sounds—as well as with **Phonemic Awareness**—the understanding that letters correspond with distinct sounds and that there are specific rules governing the placement of letters in the English language.

As children become more familiar with recognizing the names and shapes of each letter, called **graphemes**, they begin to verbally practice their corresponding sounds—the phonemes. Although this sounds straightforward, it can pose significant challenges to both the children and teachers.

For example, when children learn that the letter *y* is pronounced /wigh/, but that it can make other various sounds, including /ee/, /i/, and /igh/—depending on letter placement—it may take repeated practice in order for children to pronounce and read this one letter accurately. Some examples would be the words, *happy, gym,* and *cry*. Although each word contains the same vowel, *y*, the placement of the *y* in each word differs, which affects the letter's pronunciation.

For this reason, there is an ongoing debate in literacy circles regarding the appropriate instructional approach for teaching phonics. Should educators teach letter shapes with their corresponding names or letter shapes with their corresponding sound or sounds? Is it possible to combine instruction to include shapes, names, and sounds, or should each of these skills be taught in isolation with a cumulative approach—shape, sound/s, and name? Some experts believe that when children are introduced to letter names and shapes in isolation of their corresponding sounds, children can become quickly confused, which can delay reading acquisition. Therefore, the answer to what approach to take lies with a keen understanding of a student's background knowledge in English and each child's specific needs. In order to create effective phonics instruction and help students strengthen literacy development, it is strongly suggested that educators are sensitive and aware of these unique challenges to English language acquisition.

It is widely accepted that letter-sound relationships are best taught systematically, introducing one relationship at a time and gradually increasing in complexity. Effective instruction in the initial stages of phonics awareness involves explicit introduction of the most important and the most frequently used letter-sound relationships. For instance, short vowels should be introduced and practiced ahead of long vowels, and lower-case letters should be introduced ahead of upper case as they occur the most often. Letters that frequently appear in simple words, such as /a/, /m/, and /t/ would be logical starting points.

The following guide offers an introduction of phonics instruction:

Introduction	Examples
Initial consonants	s, t, m, n, p
Short vowel and consonant	-it, -in, -at, -an
Consonant blends	-st, -bl, -dr
Digraphs	-th, -ph, -sh, -ch
Long vowels	ear, eat, oar, oat
Final (silent) e	site, mine, lane
Variant vowels and diphthongs	-au, -oo, -ow, -ou, -oi
Silent letters and inflectional endings	-kn, -gn, -wr, es, s

Effective phonics instruction begins with focusing on the overall literacy experiences of the students and connecting these experiences to further their literacy development. Best practices in teaching will work to establish a student's prior phonics knowledge, if there is any at all. Educators can differentiate their instruction based on their students' unique needs and background knowledge of phonics. Creating phonics activities that ensure students are actively engaged and motivated is key to overall success in literacy development.

Once children have mastered the relationship that exists between the names, shapes, sounds of letters, and letter combinations, educators may begin a more implicit instructional approach by incorporating the children's current phonics awareness with simple basal readers that focus on basic monosyllabic words. Grouping monosyllabic words according to their initial sounds continues to be an effective approach to instruction as the students advance in their understanding and application of phonics. When educators combine or further this practice with that of identifying the names of the initial letters in the words, children are likely to have more success with overall literacy development. A word wall with simple consonant-vowel-consonant words in alphabetical order acts as a visual reference to help strengthen a child's literacy development:

Reading

Word Wall

A	B	C
add	ball	car
age	bean	clean
ant	black	cub

At this stage, educators begin laying the foundation for reading readiness. Children begin listening to others read and start to recognize familiar sounds within the words being read. They independently practice sounding out words and will soon learn how to independently segment, blend, and manipulate the individual sounds in each newly acquired word.

When a child demonstrates phonological awareness and a clear understanding of how phonics works, they are ready to further their literacy development with **word analysis**. Word analysis is an effective study that helps students acquire new vocabulary. **Morphemes** are words that are broken down into their smallest units of meaning. Each morpheme within words carry specific meanings, therefore adding to children's understanding of entire words. When children begin to recognize key morphemes—especially prefixes and suffixes—they are beginning to demonstrate word analysis skills, which is a critical foundation in literacy development.

Word analysis helps children to read and comprehend complex reading materials, including informational texts. It is essential for vocabulary development. Word analysis skills also help children clarify the meaning of unknown words, figurative language, word relationships, and nuances in word meaning with the use of context clues.

Some effective instructional strategies to teach word analysis skills include **Universal Design for Learning** (UDL), studying words according to a subject theme, using diagrams and graphic organizers, and pre-teaching and reviewing new vocabulary on a regular basis. UDL involves the modeling of how to analyze new words by breaking them down into their individual morphemes and studying each morpheme separately. Once each morpheme in a given word has been identified and defined, students put the morphemes back together in order to understand the word in its entirety. The following is a word analysis study of the word *astronaut*:

Word	Morpheme 1	Morpheme 2	Word Meaning
astronaut	astro—Greek origin, roughly translates to anything relating to the stars and outer space	naut—Greek origin, roughly translates to "sailor"	a sailor of outer space

Studying words according to a shared theme is another effective word analysis strategy. For instance, when studying mathematics, educators may focus on words that contain the same prefix, such as *kilometer*, *kilogram*, and *kilowatt*. Common suffixes in science include *microscope*, *telescope*, and *macroscope*.

Diagrams and graphic organizers provide students with visual clues to contrast and compare word meanings. From organizational charts and mind maps to Venn diagrams and more, visual aids help students readily see and analyze the similarities and differences in various word meanings.

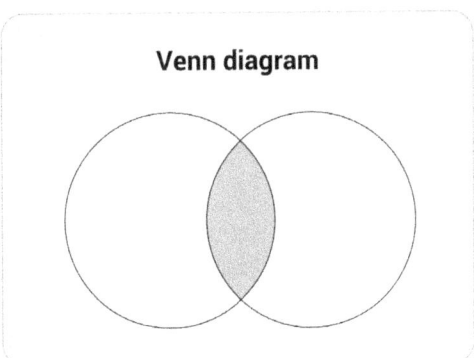

With the introduction to new topics of discussion or a new theme to any subject area, it is likely that there will also be an introduction to new, unfamiliar words. Both educators and students will benefit from a formal introduction to these new words prior to the lesson. Pre-teaching new vocabulary increases vocabulary acquisition and allows children to become comfortable and familiar with new terms ahead of the lesson. Pre-teaching new vocabulary has also been shown to reduce unnecessary stress and time that would otherwise be taken to stop lessons in order to explain unfamiliar words.

Phoneme-Grapheme Correspondences

Phoneme-grapheme correspondence or the **alphabetic principle** refers to a child's ability to recognize the correspondence between letter sounds (phoneme) and the visual representation of that letter (grapheme).

Some techniques for teaching phoneme-grapheme correspondence include:

- The teacher could say the phoneme and have the student write the grapheme, either in the air or on paper. Prior to the student being able to write, the teacher could say the phoneme and the student could just identify the grapheme from a small group of letters.
- The teacher could have the student choose a graphic from a set of images that begins with the same sound said by the teacher.
- The teacher can write a word, choose a letter sound, and ask the student to identify the matching grapheme. For example, a teacher can ask "Where is the /c/ in cat?" and have the student point to the letter C.
- The teacher can point out the visual features of letters, like the curves and lines that students can use to help identify the letter, while saying the phonemic sound associated with it.

When children begin to learn the various letter-sound correspondences, also known as phoneme-grapheme correspondence, their phonemic awareness begins to overlap with their awareness of orthography and reading. One of the widely accepted strategies to employ when introducing children to letter-sound correspondences is to begin with those correspondences that occur the most frequently in simple English words. In an effort to help build confidence in young learners, educators are encouraged to introduce only a few letter-sound combinations at a time and provide ample opportunities for practice and review before introducing new combinations. Although there is no formally established order for the introduction of letter-sound correspondences, educators are encouraged to consider the following general guidelines. However, they should also keep in mind the needs, experiences, and current literacy levels of the students. The following is intended as a general guide only:

1. a	6. n	11. g	16. l	21. x
2. m	7. c	12. h	17. e	22. v
3. t	8. d	13. i	18. r	23. y
4. p	9. u	14. f	19. w	24. z
5. o	10. s	15. b	20. k	25. j
				26. q

As a generally accepted rule, short vowels should be introduced ahead of long vowels, and lowercase letters should be mastered before the introduction of their upper-case counterparts.

Spelling conventions in the English language are primarily concerned with three areas: mechanics, usage, and sentence formation.

Mechanics

For primary students who are just beginning to master the alphabetic principle, educators should first concentrate on proper letter formation, the spelling of high-frequency words and sight words and offer classroom discussions to promote the sharing of ideas. When children begin to write in sentences to share their thoughts and feelings in print, educators may consider the introduction of an author's chair, in which students read their writing out loud to their classmates.

Although the phonetic spelling or invented spelling that primary students employ in these early stages may not be the conventional spelling of certain words, it allows primary students to practice the art and flow of writing. It works to build their confidence in the writing process. This is not the time for educators to correct spelling, punctuation, or capitalization errors as young learners may quickly lose interest in writing and may lose self-confidence.

One strategy to employ early on to help students with proper spelling is to ensure there is an easily accessible and updated word wall that employs high-frequency words and sight words. Students should be encouraged to refer to the word wall while they write.

Usage

Usage concerns itself with word order, verb tense, and subject-verb agreement among other areas. As primary children often have a basic knowledge of how to use oral language effectively in order to communicate, this area of spelling conventions may require less initial attention than the mechanics of spelling. During read-aloud and shared reading activities, educators may wish to point out punctuation marks found in print, model how to read these punctuation marks, and periodically discuss their importance in the reading and writing process.

When children begin to engage in writing exercises, educators may wish to prompt self-editing skills by asking if each sentence begins with a capital and ends with a period, question mark, or exclamation point.

Sentence Formation

Verbs, nouns, adverbs, and adjectives all play significant roles in the writing process. However, for primary students, these concepts are fairly complex to understand. One instruction approach that may prove effective is to categorize a number of simple verbs, nouns, adverbs, and adjectives on index cards by color coordination. Educators can then ask one child to choose a noun card and another student to choose a verb card. The children can then face the class and read their words starting with the noun and then the verb. The students can even try reading the verb first followed by the noun. A class discussion can follow, analyzing whether or not the sentences made sense and what words might need to be added to give the sentence more meaning.

Teaching Phonics Systematically, Explicitly, and Recursively

Teaching phonics **systematically** simply means that phonics instruction is built gradually, one phonics sound at a time. It provides a structure for teaching phonics in an orderly, step-by-by step approach that starts at the basics and builds upon student knowledge with each new skill. Systematic instruction also involves plenty of review to ensure that students don't forget previous phonics knowledge and skills. In systematic phonics instruction, it's important that the teacher focuses on one letter-sound at a time, waiting until students master each sound to move forward to the next.

Teaching phonics **explicitly** means that each part of the lesson is teacher-led and modeled to ensure that students are taught phonics in an accurate and detailed way. The teacher leads every part of the lesson and does not expect for students to simply learn letter sounds through reading or other methods. Explicit phonics instruction involves repetition, direct instruction, and consistency. A teacher who teaches phonics explicitly might do so by writing the letter B on the board and saying, "B says /b/ as in bin, bee, and bat". The students then look at the B and chorus the /b/ sound.

Teaching phonics systematically and explicitly has been proven, through research, to be more effective than teaching phonics implicitly, or **recursively**. Implicit phonics focuses on teaching from the whole word to its parts, rather than from its parts to the whole word, as done with explicit phonics. It is more student-led, requiring the student to use context to try and figure out what a word might be, rather than using the part-to-whole approach of sounding it out.

Teaching Common Phonics Patterns and Rules

Decoding and encoding are **reciprocal phonological skills**, meaning that their steps are opposite of each other.

Decoding is the application of letter-sound correspondences, letter patterns, and other phonics relationships that help students read and correctly pronounce words. Decoding helps students to recognize and read words quickly, increasing reading fluency and comprehension. The steps of the decoding process are as follows:

1. The student identifies a written letter or letter combination.

2. The student identifies the sound of that letter or letter combination.

3. The student understands how the word's different letters or letter combinations fit together.

4. The student verbally blends the letter and letter combinations together to form a word.

Encoding is the spelling of words. In order to properly spell words, students must be familiar with letter/sound correspondences. Students must be able to put together phonemes, digraphs or blends, morphological units, consonant/vowel patterns, etc. The steps of encoding are identified below:

1. The student understands that letters and sounds make up words.

2. The student segments the sound parts of a word.

3. The student identifies the letter or letter combinations that correspond to each sound part.

4. The student then writes the letters and letter combinations in order to create the word.

Because the stages of decoding and encoding are reciprocal skills, phonics knowledge supports the development of reading and spelling. Likewise, the development of spelling skills reinforces phonics and decoding. In fact, the foundation of all good spelling programs is alignment with reading instruction and students' reading levels. Phonics instruction begins with simple syllable patterns and then progresses toward more complex patterns, the sounds of morphemes, and strategies for decoding multisyllabic words. Through this process, new vocabulary is developed. Sight word instruction should not begin until students are able to decode target words with automaticity and accuracy. Spelling is the last instructional component to be introduced.

After students master letter-sound correspondences, consonant sounds, and short vowel sounds, they should begin learning VC and CVC words. After mastery of VC and CVC words, students should learn consonant blends and digraphs, including CCVC words. Then, students should learn long vowel sounds, including CVCV words, followed by diphthongs.

Consonant Digraphs
Consonant digraphs are simply two or more consonants put together to represent a single sound. For example, in the word "tough," the "g" and "h" form "-gh," which can represent the sound /f/. A similar example would be the "p" and "h" in "digraph," also representing the sound /f/. Some other common consonant digraphs include: *ch, ck, kn, mb, ng, sh, th, wh,* and *wr*.

A teacher should introduce digraphs after students have mastered CVC words. Teachers should first introduce the concept of digraphs by explaining to students that a digraph is when two letters work together to make a single sound. Then, show examples of the digraph or digraphs they are first introducing, for example /ch/ and /sh/. Explain the letters C and H make the /ch/ sound, like in the word *chip*, and that the letters S and H make the /sh/ sound, like in the word *ship*. Break words into parts to identify the digraph, for example, the word chop can be broken into /ch/ /o/ /p/, students should then be able to identify the /ch/ sound as the digraph.

Blends
A **consonant blend** is similar to a consonant digraph in that it involves two or more consonants put together. However, blends are different than digraphs in that each consonant that is "blended" still has its own sound, they don't make a new sound like a digraph does. For example, think of the "s" and "t" in "star." Or you could think of the "c" and "l" in "clock". In this example, the "c" and "k" at the end would be an example of a consonant digraph as opposed to the "c" and "l" at the beginning which are a consonant blend.

Like digraphs, consonant blends can be taught after mastery of CVC words and should be taught explicitly, with many examples provided. It's important to note the most common consonant blends, which are s-blends, l-blends, and r-blends. S-blends are consonant blends that start with the letter "s", which can be at the beginning (e.g., space) or ending (e.g., mist) of a word. L-blends and r-blends include either an "l" or "r" as the second letter of the blend (e.g., place, slice, frown, and frost).

Diphthongs
A diphthong is formed when two vowel sounds combine to form a single syllable. There are eight diphthongs within the English language, examples of which are listed below. It's generally best to teach diphthongs after mastery of CVC words, blends, and digraphs.

Diphthong	Example	Diphthong	Example
"aw"	Straw, claw, law, saw, crawl	"au"	Haul, author, cause, pause, sauce

"ew"	Chew, blew, few, new, stew	"oo"	Food, shampoo, soon, room, balloon
"oi"	Point, join, coin, noise, spoil	"oy"	Boy, toy, joy, deploy, oyster
"ow"	Cow, how, brown, crown, flower	"ou"	House, cloud, round, ouch, found

Teachers should explicitly teach all eight diphthongs and have students practice identifying them within words. One great way to have students practice is by pairing cards that have pictures (e.g. moon, spoon, food) with a card that has that diphthong listed ("oo").

Schwa Sound

The **schwa** sound is a sound that any vowel could make. The simplest way to characterize the schwa sound is to say that the vowel is making the short /u/ sound, or the /ŭ/ sound. This would sound like "uh." For example, words like *above*, *camel*, and *freedom* contain the short /u/ sound. In *above*, the "a" and the "o" make the schwa sound. In *camel*, the "e" makes the sound. In *freedom*, the "o" makes the sound.

Word Families

Word families are words that share the same pattern or feature. This could look like the same combinations or letters and/or having similar sounds. See the chart below for a representation of word families.

ake	ate	ick	est	ay	ight	ing	ock	uck	ice
awake	create	sick	best	away	light	bring	clock	duck	dice
brake	date	chick	rest	day	fight	swing	block	yuck	mice
make	late	kick	test	clay	night	ring	knock	truck	nice
snake	mate	lick	vest	okay	right	sting	shock	tuck	slice
rake	skate	trick	nest	play	sight	spring	dock	chuck	twice

Teaching word families helps students to learn to spell words and furthers their connection of letters and sounds. By learning familiar word families, students can identify new words more easily because of their understanding of sounds. The best way to explain word families is to start simple (e.g., -at, -an, -it) and increase the difficulty as students' progress.

Roots and Affixes

The study of **morphology** concerns itself with the segmenting of words into their respective affixes and roots. It also involves the studying of a word's origins. Children who study morphology expand their vocabulary knowledge as they begin to understand that words are connected by similar spelling patterns and similar meaning.

Affixes

Affixes are parts of words that are bound to the root word either in front, following, or in the middle of the word itself. Since affixes do contain meanings, they are considered morphemes, but they are unable to exist without being attached to the root words.

Prefixes are affixes that appear in front of root words, such as *dis*appear or *un*able. Generally speaking, prefixes denote negation, direction, or intensity. For example, in the word *disappear*, the prefix *dis* means *not* or *opposite of*. Therefore, *disappear* can be defined as *to not appear*. In the word *inject*, the prefix *in* refers to *inside* or *towards*, and in the word *excruciate*, the *ex* works as an intensifier referring to the pain as being *thorough*.

Suffixes are affixes that appear at the end of root words. There are two types of suffixes: inflectional and derivational. **Inflectional suffixes** can change the number, tense, or degree of the word, such as the word *loud* changing to *loudest*. **Derivational suffixes** change the parts of speech of a given word. The word *slow* functions as an adjective in this sentence: *The slow turtle walks*. When the suffix -*ly* is added to the end of *slow*, the part of speech is automatically changed to an adverb: *The turtle walks slowly*.

Infixes—affixes that appear in the middle of a word—are the least conventional and most rare of all affixes. An example is the word *cupful*. This consists of the root word, *cup*, and the suffix, -*ful*. In order to pluralize this word, an *s* would need to be strategically placed directly following the letter *p* to form *cupsful*. The *s* acts as an infix, inserting itself and its meaning in the middle of the word.

Roots and Base Words

Root words are referred to as free morphemes that can stand alone and carry an independent meaning without the need of any affixes. Some examples are the root words *help*, *kind*, and *shy*, which clearly hold their own meaning, but can also be attached to affixes, as in *helpful*, *unkind*, and *shyness*.

Base words are very similar to root words. In fact, they are nearly indistinguishable. However, a base word is the word that can stand on its own. This is different from root words because not all root words are readable on their own.

When students are invited to become word detectives, the study of root words and affixes is of prime importance. There are several instructional approaches to the study of root words and affixes, including a multi-sensory guided approach in which children can physically pull apart the affixes to be left with the root word and then manipulate the root word by playing with a variety of suffixes and prefixes. The following table begins with the original word containing both a prefix and suffix. The word is pulled apart into its individual components—root, prefix, and suffix. Then, it is given a new prefix and suffix to form a new word, carrying a completely new meaning:

Original Word	Root Word	Prefix	Suffix	New Prefix	New Suffix	New Word
inactive	act	in	ive	de	ate	deactivate
disbelieving	believe	dis	ing	un	able	unbelievable
unbearable	bear	un	able	for	ing	forbearing

Effective instruction for root, prefix, and suffix study should involve the active exploration of words, with ample opportunity for children to read the words in meaningful context. Typically, a formal study of root words and affixes is introduced by the 4th grade, but it may be introduced earlier, depending on the students' understanding of basic phonics and spelling patterns. It is important for educators to keep in mind that new vocabulary terms, verb forms, plurals, and compound words may present a challenge for some students.

A formal study of root words, prefixes, and suffixes strengthens a child's knowledge of word meanings, expands vocabulary knowledge, and advances their understanding and application of various spelling patterns. Children will learn more about how affixes affect the spelling of the root word and can completely alter its meaning, which ultimately strengthens their ability to read, write, and spell accurately and effectively. As children become familiar with various affixes, they will begin to decipher the meaning of unfamiliar words that share the same affixes and roots.

Syllabication Patterns

Syllabication is the process of separating a word into its individual syllables. It is an essential skill in learning how to accurately pronounce words. Syllabication involves learning various syllabic patterns and rules in the English language; therefore, repeated practice is best. Since every syllable has one vowel sound, the study of syllabication must be preceded with a firm understanding of how English vowel sounds operate. For instance, short vowels sound much different than long vowels, and some vowel sounds are formed using more than one vowel, as in the sounds *ou* or *oi*.

To help children master syllabication, educators will need to introduce and practice the various **syllabication patterns**:

Rule/Pattern	Examples
1. Monosyllabic words are never divided.	house, car, eat, run
2. Compound words are divided between the individual words that make up the compound word.	base/ment; up/stairs; out/side
3. Divide a word directly after its prefix.	pre/view; de/text; un/seen
4. Divide a word directly before its suffix.	ac/tion; trac/tion
5. If a word ends in a consonant + le, divide directly before this consonant.	tur/tle; cy/cle
6. If there are two consonants directly in the middle of the word, divide between the consonants.	rab/bit; sis/ter
7. Keep consonant blends and digraphs together.	fast/ing; bun/ches
8. In words containing the letter combinations ck or the letter x, syllables are generally divided directly before the ck or the x.	ni/ckel; ta/xi
9. If a single consonant is positioned between two vowels and the first vowel is short, divide directly after the consonant.	nev/er; hab/it
10. If a single consonant is positioned between two vowels and the first vowel is long, divide directly before the consonant.	ma/jor; lat/er;

Rule/Pattern	Examples
11. When two vowels in a word make individual sounds, divide between the two vowels.	ri/ot; li/on

While these syllabication patterns are helpful in order to gain a clearer understanding of how syllables operate, they are by no means exhaustive. As children gradually strengthen their awareness and application of syllables, educators may introduce them to more complex patterns.

Distinguishing High-Frequency Sight Words from Decodable Words

Beginning readers enter primary school years with many challenges involving literacy development. Tackling the alphabetic principle and phonemic awareness helps children to recognize that specific sounds are usually comprised of specific letters, or a combination thereof, and that each letter or combination of letters carries a specific sound. This process is called **decoding**. However, these young readers are also faced with the challenge of sight word mastery. **Sight words** do not necessarily follow the alphabetic principle and appear quite often in primary reading material. Some sight words are decodable, but many are not, which requires the additional challenge of memorizing correct spelling. Some of these non-decodable sight words include words such as *who*, *the*, *he*, *does*, and so on. There are approximately one hundred sight words that appear throughout primary texts.

The goal for primary teachers is to help emergent readers to recognize these sight words automatically, in order to help strengthen reading fluency. One effective instructional approach is to provide children daily opportunities to practice sight words in meaningful contexts and to establish a clearly visible, large print word wall that children can freely access throughout the day. **Dr. Edward William Dolch** was a well-known and respected children's author and professor who, in the late 1940s, published a list of sight words he believed appeared most frequently in children's literature for grades kindergarten through second grade.

Now known as the **Dolch Word List**, these sight words are still widely used in primary classrooms throughout the United States. Organized by grade and frequency, the Dolch Word List consists of 220 words in total, with the first one hundred known as the "Dolch 100 List." **Dr. Edward Fry**, a university professor, author, and expert in the field of reading, published another commonly used high-frequency word list approximately a decade later. Although similar in many ways to the Dolch List, the Fry Word List primarily focuses on sight words that appear most frequently in reading material for third to ninth grade. Other high-frequency word lists now exist, but the Dolch and Fry word lists are still widely used in today's elementary classrooms. The debate, however, is whether to teach high-frequency sight words in isolation or as part of the integrated phonics program.

Unlike many sight words, **decodable words** follow the rules of phonics and are spelled phonetically. They are spelled precisely the way they sound—as in words like *dad* and *sit*. When a child has mastered their phonics skills, these decodable words can also be easily mastered with continued opportunities to practice reading. Activities involving segmenting and blending decodable words also help to strengthen a child's decoding skills. Some educators will find that it is beneficial to integrate lessons involving decodable words and high-frequency sight words, while others may see a need to keep these lessons separate until children have demonstrated mastery or near mastery of phonemic awareness. Some activities that encourage the memorization of sight words and strengthen decoding skills involve the use of flash cards, phonemic awareness games, air writing, and card games, such as *Bingo* and *Go Fish*.

Both Dolch and Fry word lists are organized according to frequency and grade level. It is widely accepted that educators follow a cumulative approach to reading instruction, introducing high-frequency sight words that are also phonetically decodable. Should words appear in the lesson that are not phonetically decodable, educators may wish to use this as an opportunity to evaluate the children's phonemic awareness skills and determine whether or not students are ready for lessons that integrate non-decodable sight words. For instance, an educator might challenge a student to study the parts of the non-decodable sight word by asking whether or not there are parts of the word that are phonetically decodable and parts that are not. This approach gives students the opportunity for guided word study and acts as a bridge between phonemic awareness skills and sight word memorization.

Determining what lists of words to introduce to students varies greatly and depends on an initial and ongoing spelling assessment of each child to determine their current spelling and reading levels. Effective instructional approaches also involve the intentional selection of words that demonstrate a specific spelling pattern, followed by multiple opportunities to read, spell, segment, and blend these word families. Students will benefit the greatest with ongoing formative and summative assessments of their decoding skills as well as their ability to apply their word knowledge to and memorize non-decodable sight words.

With the reinforcement of high-frequency word walls, daily opportunities to read, write, and engage in meaningful word games and activities, children will gradually begin to develop their reading and spelling skills and learn to become more fluent and capable readers.

Multisensory Approaches to Support Recognition of Non-Decodable Words

Traditionally, **non-decodable** or **irregular words** have been taught as whole words through visual memory and flashcards. However, not all students learn best this way. A **multisensory approach** provides alternative ways to learn by engaging other senses. Engaging different senses activates different parts of the brain, which makes content accessible for a greater variety of learners.

Writing, tracing, or building irregular words helps to increase recall, particularly if the student names the letters while writing or placing them in the correct order. **Rainbow writing**, or repeatedly tracing over the letters in a word with different colors of pencils or crayons, provides variety and fun. So does writing words with different types of letters (for example, bubble letters or fancy letters). Writing need not be limited to paper, though. Other options include writing on white boards or chalkboards, writing in sand or shaving cream, and writing in the air with a pointer finger. Alternatively, words can be built with letters on various media including paper letters, rubber stamps, letter tiles, magnetic letters, letters written on cubes or blocks, or letter beads. Letters can also be created using based modeling clay, or even posable wax sticks.

Flash cards provide a repetitive visual review of irregular words. They can also be used to create interactive games that further reinforce learning in a more kinesthetic and interactive way. The games bingo, Memory Match, and Go Fish are all easy to set up, explain, and play.

Worksheets can help to reinforce learning of irregular words. Teachers can create coloring sheets that have words in different sections; each word corresponds to a particular color, as in a color-by-number drawing. Read It, Write It, Build It worksheets display an irregular word with spaces in which the student can write the word and also build it with paper letters, rubber stamps, or other media. Students should also be given the opportunity to read and construct sentences containing the irregular words.

When repeating words and their spellings, using different sounds and gestures can make them memorable. For example, say "g-o, go" while pointing away from yourself, or spell "w-h-a-t" and then draw out the question "whaaaat?" while raising your arms in a questioning posture and tilting your head to the side. Chanting is another vocal and auditory way to reinforce words through repetition. There are also educational songs available online that reinforce the learning of particular sight words.

Finally, students may benefit from kinesthetically engaging with irregular words. Ask a student to jump to the card containing a particular sight word among those laid out on the floor. Alternatively, you can write the words on sticky notes and place them on the wall; have students jump to tap the appropriate word. You can also lay the cards on a table and have students swat them with a fly swatter.

Vocabulary and Fluency

Build, Expand, and Use Expressive and Receptive Vocabulary

Students have both an expressive and receptive vocabulary, meaning the words they use to talk (expressive) and the words that they understand (receptive). Both their expressive and receptive vocabularies need to be built and expanded upon to improve in their overall English skills. The best way to improve students' expressive and receptive vocabularies is by explicitly teaching new words, their definitions, and having students practice spelling and using those new words.

New vocabulary words should be chosen based on how relevant they are to what students are learning and reading at the time. When choosing which words to teach, it may be helpful to consider a word's tier. Tier one words are used commonly in speech and usually learned through oral language. Tier two words are used in many subjects, and tier three words are specific to particular subjects. Generally, vocabulary words taught through literacy falls within tier two.

To teach a new vocabulary word, start by saying the word and having students repeat it. Ask students to reflect on and discuss whether they're familiar with the word or its meaning. When possible, link the word with previously learned words or concepts.

Work with students and use appropriate resources (such as dictionaries) to help them develop a definition that plainly captures meaning in a way that is accessible to them. Use a vocabulary word in a sentence and ask students to do the same. Display vocabulary words, their definitions, and even related pictures on a word wall or in a graphic organizer.

Next, read aloud or have students read a level-appropriate text that includes the new vocabulary words. If reading aloud, stop to point out the vocabulary words as you read them. Walk through your thinking process of decoding the word and remind students of its meaning in this context. If students are reading independently, have them find and highlight new vocabulary words and review their definitions before they read the text.

Reinforce the learning of new vocabulary words with games like bingo, charades, and Pictionary. Challenge students to use the new words as much as they can when they're talking and writing and praise them when they do.

Teaching Vocabulary in Multiple Contexts

The key to embedding a vocabulary word in students' long-term memory is to expose them to the word multiple times in different contexts including various texts, images, audio, and multimedia. Teachers should use engaging and varied instruction to teach and reinforce new vocabulary words.

Maximize how often and in what ways students are exposed to vocabulary words by including definitions and examples as well as illustrations and anecdotes that make the words more memorable and meaningful for students. Gestures or miming can be used to physically engage students in the representation of a word.

In addition to having the teacher represent the word in auditory, visual, and kinesthetic ways, it is particularly beneficial to have students make their own personal connections to the word, thereby maximizing the likelihood that they will remember its meaning. Encouraging students to think-pair-share with a partner can help to stimulate thinking.

Other ways of encouraging students to make personal connections to words include using semantic maps to provide images, examples, synonyms, and even song lyrics or other attributes to help students categorize vocabulary words and connect them with prior knowledge. Alternatively, students can use sticky notes or pictures to add their visual or word-related (for example, synonyms, antonyms) impressions to a word wall.

It is important to vary the ways in which students practice their new vocabulary words. Flash cards with words on one side and definitions or related visuals on the reverse are helpful for students who learn through repetition. Alternatively, students can sort words into categories (for example, parts of speech; people, places, things; or categories of the students' choosing). Teachers can provide samples with vocabulary words used incorrectly and ask students to correct the mistakes. Finally, writing or speaking assignments in which students are tasked with correctly using new vocabulary words can also reinforce their learning.

Match an Instructional Method to Word Complexity

Texts should not be too hard or too easy for students. But how can teachers evaluate text complexity to ensure that they are giving their students appropriate materials? There are quantitative and qualitative methods of determining a text's level.

Quantitative measures attempt to objectively calculate the difficulty of a text. The most common quantitative measures are **readability formulas**, or mathematical equations that strive to calculate the difficulty of a text.

Fry's formula is a common readability formula that requires teachers to count the number of sentences and syllables in three random passages of one hundred words each. They then average each number and chart the two numbers on a Fry graph. The **Fry graph** uses the numbers to produce a suggested grade level for the text. While this method is a useful tool for estimating a text's complexity, teachers should take it with a grain of salt; Fry's formula does not account for variation within grade levels and the text's qualitative factors.

Fry Graph

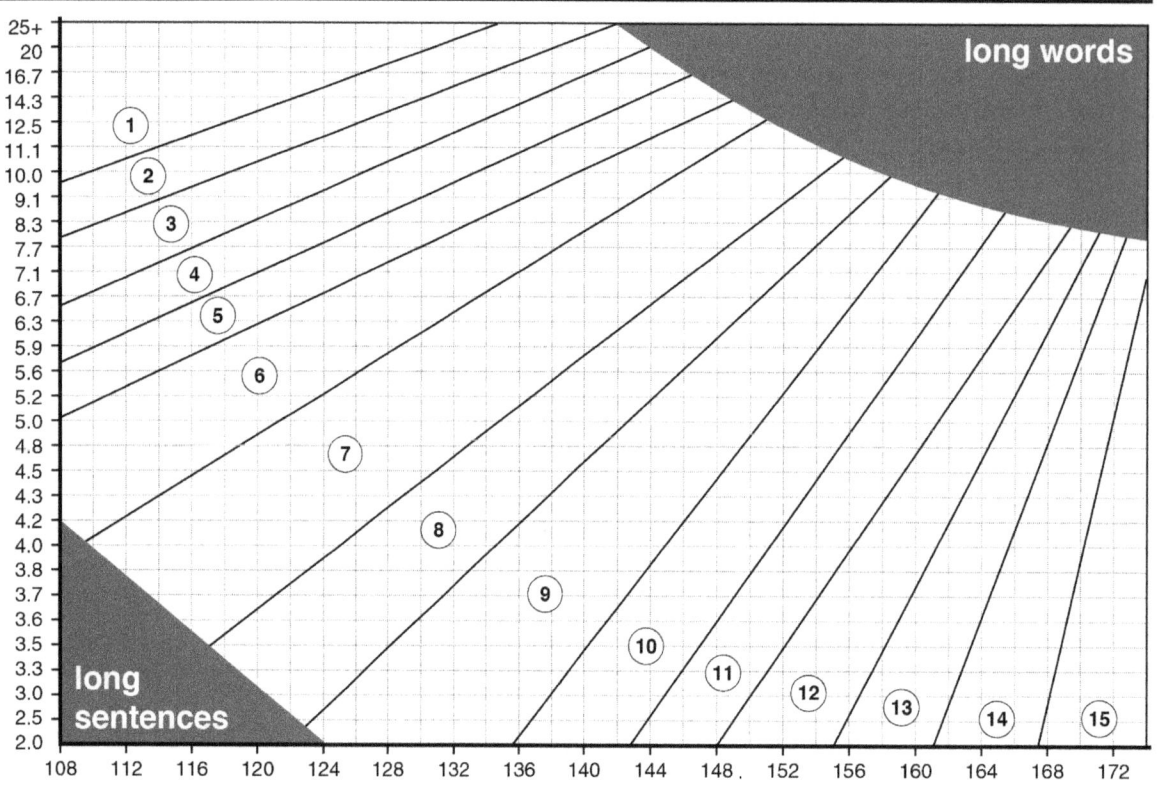

The other common quantitative measures are **Lexile text measures**. Like Fry's formula, these measures rate texts based on sentence length and word complexity. However, the Lexile method uses a database of text rankings instead of having teachers do the math themselves. It also gives texts a numerical rating from 0L to 2000L (L stands for Lexile) instead of a grade level. The most common way to test for a students' Lexile Reading Level is by having them take the Scholastic Reading Inventory, which sets the students' Lexile score level and identifies areas where the student excels and struggles in reading.

Another common way to determine student reading levels is through a Developmental Reading Assessment (DRA). The DRA is an individually administered standardized assessment of student reading skills. It generally consists of each student reading a teacher-selected passage or book, and then retelling the story to the instructor to assess for comprehension. While the student reads, the teacher should take notes of words that the student struggles with and any issues they have in accuracy, fluency, and prosody.

Qualitative measures identify subjective elements that affect the text's complexity. Below are some qualitative criteria that teachers can use to determine complexity.

- **Predictable structures** make texts easier to grasp, and they are especially useful in material intended for young children. For example, many fairy tales and children's books repeat questions and phrases. These predictable elements make the text less complicated, as children get into the pattern of the story and do not have to approach each repetition as an entirely new element.

- **Vocabulary** also determines a text's difficulty, and it cannot always be detected by quantitative measures. For example, the word "daft" consists of just one syllable, but it is clearly a more obscure word than "cat." However, Fry's formula would count the two words as the same level. Hence, teachers should skim the material to ensure the vocabulary is at an appropriate level. While texts should include some vocabulary words that will be new to students, an excess of new vocabulary renders reading so frustrating that students are likely to lose interest.

- Teachers should also consider the level of **background knowledge** required to understand a text. If easily learned background information is required (for example, basic historical context), teachers can present it to students before they begin to read a book. But if the background knowledge is complicated or far above the students' grade level, the book is not a good fit.

- Lastly, the **level of meaning** refers to how much abstract thought a text requires. Some texts only require students to understand the literal events of the book. More complex books, however, demand that students use abstract thought to make inferences and evaluate events. High levels of symbolism and abstract thought will be too difficult for younger students, while books that require only literal interpretation will likely seem boring to more mature students.

When educators go a step further in their planning by considering the needs of their individual students, reading instruction will be more effective. Educators should consider the various reader variables, such as level of reading fluency, the number of reluctant and motivated readers in the classroom, and the degree of home support for reading.

All of these factors combined significantly impact the type of text, level of complexity, and the tasks children are given to accomplish based on the reading material. Considering these factors that measure text complexity will also assist educators in choosing instruction and evaluation techniques.

Features of Text-Leveling Systems

For educators to apply quantitative, qualitative, and reader and task considerations effectively prior to introducing a reading assignment, they must first understand and consider the unique features of text-leveling systems:

Quantitative Measures	Qualitative Measures	Student and Task Measures
Total word count	Text predictability	Reluctant readers
Number of different words	Text structure and organization	Motivated readers
Number of high-frequency words	Visual aid, illustration, and info graphics support	Struggling readers
Number of low-frequency words	Background knowledge of topic	Interest in topic
Sentence length	Single theme vs. multi-themes	
Sentence complexity		

Teaching Word Solving

Context Clues

When using **contextual strategies**, students are introduced to new words indirectly within a sentence or paragraph. Contextual strategies require students to infer the meaning of a word by utilizing semantic and contextual clues.

Appositives and parenthetical elements can be very effective contextual strategies. **Appositives** are words that define or add meaning to a term that directly precedes them. An example of a sentence that includes apposition is: "Strawberries, heart-shaped and red berries, are delicious when eaten right off of the vine." In this sentence, the definition of strawberries ("heart shaped and red berries") directly follows the term and is introduced with and closes with a comma.

Parenthetical elements are specific types of appositives that add details to a term but not necessarily a definition. For example: "My cat, the sweetest in the whole world, didn't come home last night." In this sentence, the parenthetical element ("the sweetest in the whole world") further describes the cat but does not provide a definition of the word "cat."

Syntax

There is a certain order to the way in which words are placed in a sentence. For instance, many English sentences follow the pattern of noun + verb + object. The more acquainted children become with syntax, the stronger their ability to recognize parts of speech and how they are interrelated.

Structural Analysis

Structural analysis skills are beneficial in the pronunciation of new words. When readers use **structural analysis**, they recognize affixes or roots as meaningful parts within a word. When a new word doesn't contain parts that are recognized by a student, the reader can use phonic letter–sound patterns to divide the word into syllables. The word parts can then be combined to yield the proper pronunciation.

Word maps are visual organizers that promote structural analysis skills for vocabulary development. They may require students to provide definitions, synonyms, antonyms, and pictures for given vocabulary terms. Alternatively, **morphological maps** may be used to relate words that share a common morpheme.

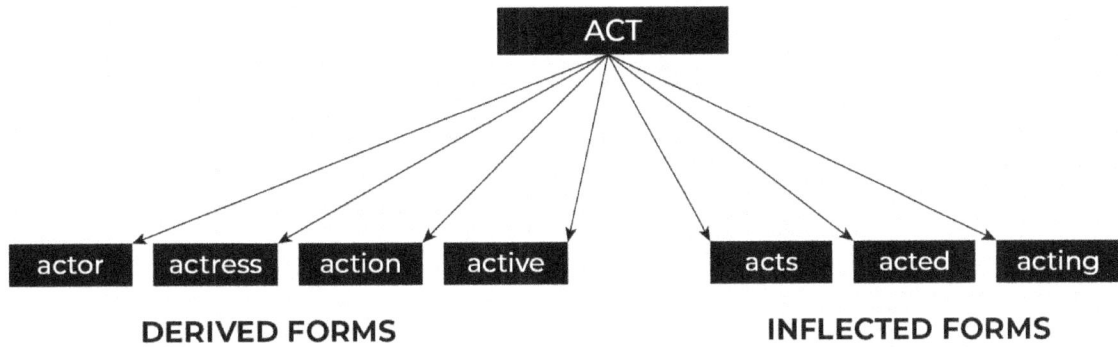

Similarly, **word webs** are used to compare and classify a list of words. Word webs show relationships between new words and a student's background knowledge. The main concept is in the center of the word web while secondary and tertiary terms stem off from it.

The table below identifies additional ways in which teachers can help students independently define unfamiliar words or words with multiple meanings:

Strategy	Examples
By Definition: Look up the word in a dictionary or thesaurus. Helps students realize that a single word can have multiple meanings.	Her favorite fruit to eat was a date. He went on a date with his girlfriend.
By Example: Invite students to offer their own examples, or to state their understanding following your own examples.	A myth is a story attempting to explain a natural phenomenon, such as the story of Prometheus to understand fire.
By Synonym: Understand that words have many different meanings. Some words are better synonyms than others.	She was very happy that day; her face was *radiant* with joy.
By Antonym: Teach student to look for words that have opposite meanings if the context of the sentence calls for its opposite.	Hannah was not happy that day; she was, in fact, very *depressed*.
By Apposition: **Apposition** is when the definition is given within the sentence.	The mango, a round, yellow, juicy fruit with an enormous seed in the middle, was ripe enough to eat.
By Origin: Identify Greek and Latin roots to figure out meanings of words.	In the word *hypertension*, the root "hyper" is a Greek word meaning "above" or "over."
By Context: Identifying what a word means by the surrounding text.	Water evaporates when it becomes hot, and the liquid turns into gas.

As children advance in their reading fluency, written material will likewise become more complex. Students transition from reading works in which the meaning is literal and direct, to works that require a more critical thinking approach. Educators can facilitate this transition by modeling and demonstrating how to use context clues, syntax, roots, and suffixes to derive meaning from texts.

Guide Students to Understand a Wide Variety of Words through Direct Instruction and Independent Vocabulary Learning

Common
Common words are also called tier one words. They are the basic words that are used in everyday conversations that are often heard regularly. Most of the time, common words won't need to be taught through direct, explicit instruction. Students will usually have a basic knowledge of tier one words, and that knowledge can be built upon through regular use and spelling instruction. Students will grasp many common words independently through independent or shared reading, conversations with peers and family, and in other non-academic settings.

Contextual
Tier two words are also referred to as contextual vocabulary because they are more complex and can mean different things in different contexts. They are generally longer and more difficult to spell than common words, but not as difficult as content-specific words. Contextual words should be taught explicitly and directly and are best taught as spelling or vocabulary words. They're the types of words that are usually seen in academic

settings, however they aren't specific to a certain field like content-specific words are. It's best to present contextual words to students in a variety of settings to help encourage understanding, memorization, and use.

Content-Specific
The top level of words that students will need to be taught are **content-specific, or tier three,** terms which students will need to commit to memory and understanding. They are words that apply to specific lessons, concepts, or ideas that are generally at a higher level. Some examples include *monarchy, isosceles,* and *quagmire.*

It is important as an instructor to use content-specific language when it's part of a lesson to build familiarity for the students hearing that language. However, tier three words don't need to be taught explicitly (as in vocabulary/spelling words) and should be covered naturally as the new concepts are learned. Students may also learn content-specific words independently through their own reading and studies.

Instructional Methods to Foster Automaticity

Reading fluency has been traditionally defined as a student's ability to read accurately, quickly, and with appropriate expression. This definition only accounts for reading aloud, however, so it has been expanded to include silent reading. **Silent reading fluency** is the ability to read more than one word at a time without having to vocalize one's reading. If readers are able to derive the accurate meaning and message from a reading passage without involving too much labor of reading mechanics, they are said to be reading with fluency. Reading fluency is automatic, with less attention and effort spent on decoding, allowing the reader to concentrate fully on reading comprehension. When a reader reaches the fluency stage, reading becomes much more of an enjoyable activity.

Generally, fluent readers do not require the need to reread passages for understanding and have developed a fairly large inventory of sight-word vocabulary. Fluent readers are usually able to self-correct and employ a number of reading strategies. Signs that a child is having difficulty with reading fluency include reading slowly, focusing on only one word at a time, needing to reread the passage for understanding, and stopping often to decipher and decode unknown words. There are three main focus areas that relate to reading fluency: accuracy, rate, and prosody. When children read accurately with steady, consistent speed and appropriate expression, reading comprehension is likely to strengthen.

Accuracy
Accuracy refers to the frequency of pronunciation errors a student might make when reading. When students make frequent pronunciation errors while reading, guess at the pronunciation of unknown words, or ignore words altogether, they are showing signs of **dysfluency**. Reading accurately requires the reader to read words correctly with minimal to no errors. When errors do occur, readers who read with accuracy are generally able to self-correct and continue reading without interrupting the flow of the reading.

Rate
Reading rate refers to a student's ability to recognize words automatically without having to spend any time on decoding them. This manifests in their ability to read texts at a steady and consistent rate. Both accurate reading and reading at a consistent rate greatly strengthen a reader's overall reading comprehension.

Prosody
Prosody refers to appropriate expression when reading—showing emotions, such as excitement, panic, or sorrow that accurately matches the intended emotions of the text. Readers may be able to read texts with accuracy and at a steady and consistent rate, but if they are unable to vocalize any expression in their reading or if the expression used does not match the intended expression of the text, their overall comprehension will be

negatively affected. Readers who engage in an emotional or personal level with the text will experience greater reading comprehension and fluency.

Methods of Supporting Fluent Reading Behaviors at Multiple Levels

Phoneme Level

Phonemic awareness is the ability to understand the individual sounds (phonemes) that make up words. Being able to identify and manipulate phonemes is a foundational skill for those learning to read. Although phonemic awareness is auditory and does not directly involve reading, it is vital in establishing a strong connection to language.

By breaking words down into their smallest units, readers gain an essential understanding of how letters relate to sounds. Phonemic awareness is often used as a predictor for future success with reading. Once a student reaches the point of phonemic awareness, it is much easier to learn about phonics and the visual component of printed words. The student will be able to approach new words with the skills necessary to sound them out.

It is important for teachers to explicitly teach phonemes, one phoneme at a time. There are 44 phonemes, which are composed of the 26 letters of the alphabet. In many cases, phonemes have multiple different **graphemes** (or spellings). Without strong instruction, it is not uncommon for students to struggle with understanding basic word structure, phonics, and reading. Thus, the phoneme level is the initial base that is crucial in supporting fluent reading behaviors and setting students up for success.

Teachers can choose which phoneme to start with, but some good options include letters that make only one continuous sound which is included in the letter's name, like /s/, /m/, and /f/. Take care to not introduce letters that look or sound alike (e.g., d and b, /a/ and /u/).

Word Level

At the word level, instructors can focus on teaching word recognition and word identification. **Word recognition** is the ability to correctly and automatically recognize words at sight, without needing to use strategies. Word recognition is a prerequisite for fluent reading and reading comprehension. Practicing sight words is a great way to encourage automatic word recognition because it teaches the student to recognize the words at sight. While automatic word recognition can't necessarily be taught, it can be encouraged through regular interaction with print (e.g., independent and teacher-led reading/matching games/etc.

Word identification is the ability to recognize spoken or written words using letter patterns, context clues, knowledge of sight words, or other strategies. The best way to teach word identification is through thoroughly covering phoneme-grapheme correspondence, decoding strategies, and basic word structure.

To help with vocabulary, teachers might consider putting up a word wall with words relevant to the students' reading levels. This promotes word consciousness (an awareness of words) and provides visual reinforcement.

Passage Level

Reading aloud has been proven effective in strengthening reading fluency. Whisper-reading accompanied by teacher monitoring has also proven effective for students who do not yet display automaticity in their decoding skills.

Timed reading of sight phrases or stories also improves fluency with respect to rate. During a **timed reading** exercise, the number of words read in a given amount of time is recorded. Routinely administering timed readings and displaying the results in graphs and charts has been shown to increase student motivation.

Timed-repeated readings, where a student reads and re-reads familiar texts in a given amount of time, is a commonly used instructional strategy to increase reading speed, accuracy, and comprehension. Students read and re-read the passage until they reach their target rate.

Impact of Fluency on Comprehension

In reading fluency, specific instructional strategies will help strengthen a student's ability to read text accurately, at a consistent rate, and with appropriate expression. This helps strengthen reading comprehension. When students experience dysfluency in their reading, their overall comprehension will be negatively impacted. With an inability to make connections in their reading, children are unable to grasp the meaning in the text. When children are more focused on decoding individual words rather than on comprehending the text's message, much of their cognitive efforts are spent on deciphering the pronunciation of individual words, with little left to devote to comprehension of the text itself.

As children's reading fluency strengthens, they are able to interact on a much higher level with a variety of texts. It is important for educators to recognize that reading fluency acts as a bridge to reading comprehension and that time devoted to the individual components of reading fluency benefits a child's overall reading comprehension.

Difficulty with reading also affects also other types of schoolwork. For example, a long-form question on a science test may be difficult to comprehend without a solid understanding of vocabulary. Likewise, without fluency, it will be difficult for a student to comprehend what they are reading. The correlation is so strong that reading fluency is often used as a predictor for later comprehension skills. Once fluency is developed, readers can tackle longer texts at a higher level. This expanded fluency leads to an expanded vocabulary as they learn new words.

There are many strategies to assist readers with learning these skills. To help with fluency, oral reading repetition may prove useful. This allows students to become comfortable with the text and practice reading aloud. Reading orally helps students connect reading to their speech, which improves the speed at which they read and the expression they give to the words.

Comprehension of Literature and Informational Texts

Support Students' Listening Comprehension

Listening comprehension is an important aspect of learning and a skill that can be developed with time and effort. It can be enhanced by first activating students' background knowledge about the topic to be discussed; that way, they have some existing ideas to link the new information with. Having students preview a few questions about the topic before listening gives them guidance on what information to focus on. Pausing throughout a listening exercise to ask students questions or have them summarize what they've heard so far also promotes comprehension.

Students can practice listening comprehension through a variety of activities including conversing, following directions, and listening to stories. Teachers can help to build stamina in listening to stories by starting with reading shorter passages aloud and slowly increasing the amount students are expected to listen and absorb information.

Games are another great way to increase listening comprehension. The classic telephone game, in which each person takes a turn repeating to the next person what they heard from the previous person, is a great listening exercise. For another game, read a passage or story and then read it again with some changes to the details; have students identify the changes. In barrier games, two players sit on opposite sides of a visual barrier with identical materials in front of them. The players take turns describing how they are manipulating the materials, and the goal is to have identical setups at the end of the game.

<u>Listening Comprehension in Relation to Reading Comprehension</u>
Listening and reading are both learned, receptive language skills that use the same areas of the brain. They are interconnected with writing and speaking, which are productive language skills, so working on any one of these skills also improves the others.

Gough and Tunmer's "simple view" of reading breaks it into two parts: **decoding** (recognizing and sounding out words) and **language comprehension** (the ability to understand language and the meaning of the words read). Everyone first learns to comprehend language by listening, a necessary base skill for reading and reading comprehension. Therefore, students can better understand complex language and connections by listening first rather than by reading first. Exposing them to different vocabulary words through listening also provides a foundation for reading comprehension once they can decode words.

Early reading education focuses on decoding, but as students become more fluent decoders, the goal shifts to learning through reading: the ability to make sense of what is read.

Reading comprehension is notably affected by both students' vocabulary and background knowledge. Listening exercises can be used to develop language skills that are critical to reading comprehension. Language skills include the ability to:

- Recall literal descriptions, facts, and details
- Decipher the meaning of unknown words using context in the passage
- Connect text using inferences and prior knowledge
- Identify the main idea
- Summarize text

As younger students work to build their reading skills, non-print sources of information allow them to access technical language and topics better than they can through reading, and the non-print sources don't require them to expend mental energy decoding text. **Non-print sources** might include things like pictures or physical representations of associated words. The same is true of technical texts in older grades (for example, scientific writing). Therefore movies, performances, read-alouds, podcasts, and audiobooks are all good approaches to building listening comprehension, background knowledge, connections between existing and new knowledge, and vocabulary development that will strengthen students' reading comprehension. Students can also read along in a book or script while listening to an audio version, which enhances decoding and comprehension, particularly in struggling readers and English learners (ELs). All these auditory activities can be enhanced by asking students to make predictions and summarize information.

Another activity for bridging listening comprehension and reading comprehension is to have students act out a story they've listened to. The teacher can assign parts and provide scripts. Students work individually and in groups to increase their fluency and comprehension by practicing reading their parts, with support from peers, teachers, or parents, as necessary. After several days of practice, the whole class can perform the story together with scripts in hand.

Support Students' Speaking and Listening Skills as they Discuss Texts

Students learn best when they can share their thoughts on what they've read or written and receive feedback from their peers and instructors. For example, after reading a short story or poem, the teacher may ask a guiding question and have students discuss their answers with a partner. An effective method for this is think-pair-share, in which students *think* about a question the teacher poses about the text, then *pair* up with a partner or small group, and finally *share* their thoughts with their partner(s). It's important to circulate the room to monitor conversations, reminding students to give others time to speak before responding, thus reinforcing their speaking and listening skills.

It's important to explicitly teach the concept of active listening to students. Active listening means paying attention to the person who is speaking, understanding what they are saying, and reflecting on and remembering the information. Some techniques for improving students' active listening include directed drawings, games like telephone or Simon Says, and by modeling it for students by actively listening when they're speaking.

For writing, conferencing is frequently done in the revision stage. Conferences can be done in a one-on-one setting, typically between a student and instructor, or in a small group of students with guidance from the instructor. They are useful in that they provide an atmosphere of respect where a student can share their work and thoughts without fear of judgment. Conferences also allow the instructor to provide immediate feedback or prompt students for deeper explanations of their ideas. The most successful conferences have these characteristics:

- Have a set structure
- Focus on only a few points—too many are confusing or distracting
- Are solution based
- Allow students to both discuss their thoughts/works and receive/provide feedback for others
- Encourage the use of appropriate vocabulary
- Provide motivation and personal satisfaction or pleasure from reading and writing
- Allow a time where questions can be asked and immediately answered

Utilizing Background Knowledge

Background knowledge, or knowledge related to a text's topic, comes from readers' experiences as well as what they have learned by reading and listening. It allows readers to make connections that enhance their ability to read, summarize, decipher word meaning, and comprehend the text.

Using background knowledge makes it easier for students to make inferences about the meaning of a text by using their knowledge to build on the information explicitly provided in the text. It also helps readers interpret literary devices like metaphors and idioms, and it helps them interpret increasingly technical, subject-specific topics in informational texts.

A student's background knowledge, including the associations and categories of concepts in their mind, is also called their **schema**. Children who have greater exposure to life events have greater schemas. Thus, students who bring extensive background knowledge to the classroom are likely to experience easier automation when reading.

Readers' growth and development therefore critically rely on building background knowledge and activating it. Building background knowledge is not simply teaching students facts; instead, it involves strategically building interconnected webs of concepts that promote future learning. It's important for teachers to be aware of the diverse backgrounds of their students before they begin a text. This can help them identify areas of background knowledge that should be supplemented before reading.

One way to build and activate background knowledge across the curriculum is to give students time to read about and conduct in-depth research on a single topic using a variety of media. Teachers can pair fiction and nonfiction books on the same topic. Various media can be used to build and activate students' knowledge of different settings and cultures. Videos and virtual field trips can expose children to information that they will build on while reading a book set in an unfamiliar place or culture.

Activating students' background knowledge before they read a text helps them make connections to what they already know about a topic. One pre-reading strategy that works well with books that have many illustrations is a **picture walk**. Before reading, teachers draw students' attention to the cover, read the title aloud, and asking them to say what the story might be about. Flipping through the pages and stopping at illustrations, the teacher can ask questions about characters, plot, setting, and predictions (for example, "Who is this character?" "Where does the story take place?" "What do you think will happen next?") Picture walks activate background knowledge while also providing context that allows students to better decode vocabulary words.

Before and during reading, teachers can model behaviors that encourage students to make connections between what they are reading and their past experiences (text-to-self), other things they have read (text-to-text), and what they know about the world (text-to world). Students may share these connections verbally or through writing or drawing. While displaying the cover of a book, the teacher may say aloud, "This reminds me of the time I..." or "This book reminds me of the one we read....". By doing so, the teacher is modeling to students how to activate their background knowledge before reading a text.

Methods for Teaching Comprehension

Reading comprehension involves the reader's use of prior knowledge, experience activation, prediction, text decoding, summarizing, and identification of the text's purpose to construct an understanding of the text's meaning.

Activating background knowledge before reading a new book can help students to recognize and decode new vocabulary words. Teachers may also ask students to predict what might happen in the reading based on the title, cover art, and illustrations (if there are illustrations). This is one of the first steps towards comprehension because it gets students thinking and developing an understanding of the overall meaning of the text.

Comprehension is best achieved through fluent reading. Phonics skills and decoding abilities both affect fluency, as does vocabulary knowledge. Students should be reading books at the appropriate level, or the level at which they can read at least 90 percent of the words. Harder texts disrupt the flow of their reading because the student will stop at unfamiliar words, which interferes with comprehension.

Having students slow down their reading speed also improves reading comprehension by giving them more time to process what they're reading. Reading aloud is one way to help students naturally slow down their reading speed. Further, rereading familiar texts facilitates decoding, enabling the student to read quickly and smoothly, which further increases comprehension.

Discussion, or verbal processing, of text before, during, and after reading helps students to remember what they've read and create meaning and connections that enhance comprehension. Ask guiding questions about what is happening in the book, what might happen next, and how the book relates to the students' experiences or other books they've read.

Similarly, teach students to pause and monitor their understanding of texts that they read independently, and teach them to reread sections that they don't understand. Using a journal or sticky notes, they can write down questions they have and words they don't understand. They can enhance understanding by defining vocabulary words they don't know and restating a passage in their own words, either independently or in a think-pair-share activity with a peer. They can also use what they've learned to predict what will happen next in the story and then read on to see if their prediction was accurate. Another way to reinforce understanding while reading is to ask students to create a mental picture of the story.

Graphic organizers are great tools to help enhance comprehension; they do this by organizing information and highlighting main ideas and relationships in a text. For example, **storyboards** show the order of events in a book, **flow charts** show cause-and-effect relationships among events in a story, and **Venn diagrams** compare and contrast. **KWL charts** (the acronym stands for *know, want, learn*) encourage the students to identify what they know about a topic (background knowledge), what they want to know about it, and what they've learned from reading a passage. Older students can be introduced to a variety of graphic organizers and then encouraged to use the type that works best for them.

After reading a story, students should be able to summarize it, discerning which information is important enough to include among the main ideas. Using **a five-finger retell activity** is an easy way to summarize; the five fingers are associated with five aspects of the text: characters, setting, plot, ending, and favorite part. Another simple way to summarize is to have students identify what happened in the beginning, middle, and end of the text.

Comprehension questions (who, what, where, why, how) also help to gauge students' understanding after reading and assist them in making meaning of the text. Teachers can also have students write their own comprehension questions, which indicates whether they were able to accurately pull the main ideas from the text.

To accommodate students of various learning styles, teachers can vary the medium through which students exhibit their understanding of a text. Nontraditional media include comic strips, collages, skits, alternate endings, trivia, illustrated timelines, and oral presentations.

Using Metacognition for Comprehension and Analysis

Metacognition is an awareness of one's own thoughts and thinking process. This awareness can be especially useful during reading because it helps the student to constantly be considering *how* they are thinking about the text. A metacognitive learner is aware of their thinking process and can identify areas in which they need additional information or teaching.

When approaching reading instruction, teachers can encourage metacognitive thinking by guiding students to use phrases such as *I'm noticing, I'm thinking,* and *I'm wondering*.

Another strategy is to have students verbally respond as they read a passage. Students may quietly say, "hm" when they struggle to understand something, "oh" or "wow" when they learn something new, or "oops" if they realize they misunderstood something. Using verbal cues to keep students aware of their own thought processes is a great way to encourage metacognition.

A metacognitive reader needs to be able to ask themselves what they are reading about and what a passage is trying to say. Before reading a passage, the reader can enhance their ability to comprehend material by previewing the text for clues. This may mean making careful note of any titles, headings, graphics, notes, introductions, important summaries, and conclusions. The reader may make physical notes regarding these elements or highlight anything they think is important before reading. Often, a reader will be able to gain information just from these elements alone, but close reading is required to fill in the details.

In general, one of the best ways to encourage metacognition is through verbal cues. Reminding students verbalize what they are thinking and how they got to that conclusion helps them understand their own thinking processes. Ultimately, a student who is aware of their own thinking process is better equipped to recognize what they need to improve their comprehension.

Guiding Students' Self-Selection of Appropriate Texts

It's important as an instructor to give students the independence to self-select texts to encourage independent reading and comprehension. However, teachers can guide students in the self-selection process in a few different ways. First, it's important to set aside a time daily for self-selected, independent reading. In many schools, this is called DEAR (drop everything and read) time. It's also important to have a large classroom and school library that is stocked with books on multiple levels covering many different cultures and backgrounds.

To help students self-select books to read, the teacher can test for and provide them with an AR (Accelerated Reader) level (or an alternative reading program). The teacher can have students self-select books within their AR level to ensure that the difficulty of the text isn't too difficult or too simple.

Another method for self-selection is the five finger rule. With this method, students will select a book they want to read and turn to a random page and read it. While reading, they'll put up a finger for each word that they don't know. Once they finish the page, they'll see how many fingers they're holding up to judge the book's difficulty. If they have no fingers up, or just one, the book may be too easy. Two to three fingers is a good level of difficulty. Four or five fingers is too difficult for independent reading.

Differentiating Instruction, Tasks, and Materials for All Learners

Personalize Learning Experiences for Students of Different Needs

Differentiated instruction acknowledges that, while a group of students may be learning the same subject, the way each student learns and processes the subject is different. Differentiation involves looking at the different learning methods and reading areas and identifying which of them students respond to. Educators can then tailor, or differentiate, lessons to build on these skills and expedite the learning process.

There are three main areas in which teachers can differentiate instruction: content, process, and product.

The first method of differentiated instruction involves grouping students based on their ability levels and modifying the content to fit their different abilities. For example, the teacher can make assignments more challenging to engage higher level students and provide easier assignments to lower-level students. This helps keep learners engaged because higher level students won't lose interest due to lack of difficulty, and lower-level students won't become frustrated by assignments that are too difficult.

To find out a student's ability level in a certain skill, teachers can do informal or formal assessments. For example, to evaluate students' reading comprehension skills, the teacher may assign a formal reading assessment to the entire class that consists of reading a text selection and answering multiple choice questions about the passage. Afterward, the teacher will compare student assessment scores along with any other relevant data to group students based on their reading comprehension abilities.

Another way that teachers can modify instruction is through the process of instruction. This means giving students the option to learn in ways that work for them. For example, providing visual aids like posters and charts is a way of differentiating instruction for visual learners, who respond best to pictures and shapes rather than words. Kinesthetic learners do best when they're actively engaged in the learning process, which usually includes moving around, simulating relevant scenarios, or role play activities that allow for active learning (like reading and acting out parts in a play).

Finally, teachers can also modify the product during differentiated instruction, which includes offering students the choice in how they complete assessments. For example, a student may be able to submit their choice of an essay, a visual depiction or art project, a song, or a speech rather than simply having only one option. This allows learners to demonstrate their knowledge in a way that is engaging and inclusive to their learning style.

Choosing Materials that are Culturally Responsive to All Learners

In terms of materials, teachers should have texts in the classroom library that are bilingual and appropriate for English learners (ELs). Choose authors with various ethnic backgrounds rather than only including the most popular books. When possible, find authors who have similar cultures to the students in the classroom.

Students at different learning stages will require different materials. Teachers should have difficult books for advanced students and appropriate books for the students who still struggle with reading. Students will have greater motivation to read if they can easily understand and relate to the message of the text.

Use of Graphic and Semantic Organizers to Support Comprehension

Make Lessons Visual by Using Graphic Organizers

Visual aids are great tools that can help develop students' creativity and support their comprehension of text. **Graphic organizers** include webs, anchor charts, Venn diagrams, story boards, KWL charts, spider maps, and charts, all of which help students organize information and develop higher-level thinking.

Diagrams and graphic organizers provide students with visual clues to contrast and compare word meanings. From organizational charts and mind maps to Venn diagrams and more, visual aids help students readily see and analyze the similarities and differences in various word meanings.

Venn diagrams are a visual way of comparing two topics to find their similarities and differences. The student should list the two topics above each of the circles, and list details about each topic (differences) within its corresponding circle. Details that are true about both topics (similarities) should be listed in the middle.

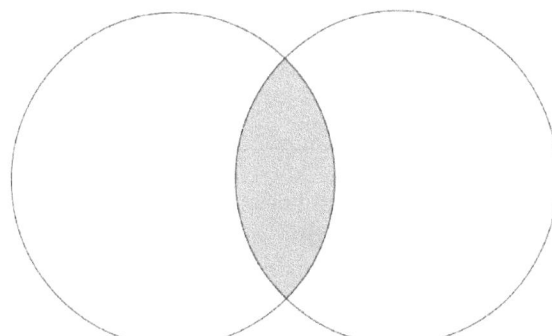

A KWL Chart includes three boxes, or sections, and is usually started before reading a passage or other texts. In the first box, the student will write what they know about a given topic or idea, and in the second box they will write what they want to know. Then, the class will together, or students will independently, read the text considering their preconceptions of the topic and thinking about what they wanted to know. Afterwards, the students will revisit the KWL chart for the last section, to add what they learned from reading the text. At this time students should revisit their K and W sections to note whether what they knew was true, and whether or not they learned what they wanted to know.

K-W-L Chart		
What I **K**now	What I **W**ant to know	What I **L**earned

There are many different types of charts, but the most common type are T-charts, which consist of two columns. T-charts are usually used to categorize two different ideas or concepts and highlight the differences or the relationship between the two. For example, students can use a T-chart to categorize the cause-and-effect relationships in a piece of text. In one column, the student can write the cause of something and then add the corresponding effect in the second column.

T-CHART

TOPIC:	TOPIC:

Semantic Organizers
To strengthen reading comprehension, educators should consider the introduction to word webs and **semantic organizers**. Semantic organizers are maps of words that visually depict the meaning and relationship between

words, phrases, and concepts. They can be as complex as the example below, or as simple as writing the word in the center of a paper and drawing lines to all of its synonyms and related phrases.

Genres, Structures, and Features of Literary Texts

A **genre** is a category of literature that possesses similarities in style and in characteristics. Based on form and structure, there are four basic genres:

Poetry
Poetry is fiction in verse that has a unique focus on the rhythm of language and focuses on intensity of feeling. It is not an entire story, though it may tell one; it is compact in form and in function.

Rhyme typically goes hand and hand with the study of poetry and involves the repetition of similar sounds. Sounds may rhyme at the end of every two or more lines, referred to as **end rhyme**, or may rhyme in the middle of a line, referred to as **internal rhyme**. The following offers examples of both:

> I went to school *today*,
>
> Not wanting to leave the *house*,
>
> And as I passed the *day*,
>
> I remained as quiet as a *mouse*.

In rain or *shine*, your house or *mine*,

We'll meet *again*, my dear *friend*.

The first poem demonstrates the example of end rhyme. The second example demonstrates internal rhyme.

Meter is the rhythm of the syllables within a poem. Each type of meter equates to the specific number of syllables and, possibly, the way the syllables are stressed. There are five basic meters: *iambic, trochaic, spondaic, anapestic,* and *dactylic*. Recognizing the meter within poetry helps readers understand the poem's rhythm and guides the reader in how to read the poem with the poet's intended emphasis. Meter also helps poets develop and maintain the structural elements within the poem.

Prose
Prose consists of fictional works written in standard form with a natural flow of speech and without poetic structure. Fictional prose primarily utilizes grammatically complete sentences and a paragraph structure to convey its message.

Drama
Drama is fiction that is written to be performed in a variety of media, intended to be performed for an audience, and structured for that purpose. It might be composed using poetry or prose, often straddling the elements of both in what actors are expected to present. Action and dialogue are the tools used in drama to tell the story. **Comedy** is any drama designed to be funny or lighthearted. **Tragedy** is any drama designed to be serious or sad.

Literary Nonfiction
Literary nonfiction is prose writing that is based on current or past real events and/or people. It includes straightforward accounts as well as those that offer opinions on facts or factual events. Nonfiction has the following subgenres:

- **Informational Text:** This is text written to impart information to the reader. It may have literary elements such as charts, graphs, indexes, glossaries, or bibliographies.

- **Persuasive Text:** This is text that is meant to sway the reader to have a particular opinion or take a particular action.

- **Biographies and Autobiographies:** These texts that tells intimate details of someone's life. If an author writes the text about someone else, it is a **biography**. If the author writes it about himself or herself, it is an **autobiography**.

- **Communicative Text:** This is text used to communicate with another person. It includes such texts as emails, formal and informal letters, and social media posts. This content often consists of two-sided dialogue between people.

Story Elements
There are five key elements to every story: characters, setting, plot, conflict, and resolution. Each story must have these elements to flow smoothly and maintain its structure. The characters of a story are who the story is about, the setting is where it takes place, the plot is the events that take place, the conflict is the major problem that needs to be solved often at the climax of the story, and the resolution is way that the conflict is resolved. Each of these concepts should be explained explicitly and in detail, and teachers should have students practice identified each of the five story elements in every text that they read.

Reading

Analysis of Characters, Setting, and Plot
When it comes to the study of stories or literary texts, it is important for children to gain an understanding and awareness of text structures and organization. All literary texts involve various story elements, including characters, setting, and plot. Being able to identify these elements and show their relationship to one another is key to understanding the story.

Characters
Characters are the story's figures that assume primary, secondary, or minor roles. **Central or major characters** who are those integral to the story—the plot cannot be resolved without them. A central character can be a **protagonist** or hero. There may be more than one protagonist, and they don't always have to possess good characteristics. A character can also be an **antagonist**—the force against a protagonist.

Character development is when the author takes the time to create dynamic characters that add uniqueness and depth to the story. **Dynamic characters** are characters that change over the course of the plot's timeline. *Stock* characters are those that appear across genres and embrace stereotypes—e.g., the cowboy of the Wild West or the blonde bombshell in a detective novel. A **flat character** is one that does not present a lot of complexity or depth, while a *rounded* character does. Sometimes, the **narrator** of a story or the **speaker** in a poem can be a character—e.g., Nick Carraway in F. Scott Fitzgerald's *The Great Gatsby* or the speaker in Robert Browning's "My Last Duchess." The narrator might also function as a character in prose, though not be part of the story—e.g., Charles Dickens's narrator of *A Christmas Carol*.

A story may have both main characters and minor characters, but all characters, regardless of their level of importance, work to provide the story's framework. Therefore, it is important for students to be able to list and describe all characters that appear throughout a story.

The following questions aid students in this endeavor:

- What do the characters look like?
- How old are they?
- What language or languages do they speak?
- What is their personality like?
- How do they relate to one another?
- Do you know of anyone like this in your life?
- Have you come across a similar character in another story?
- How are they the same?
- How are they different?

The more children identify with various characters in a story, the stronger their overall comprehension will be.

Setting
The **setting** is the time, place, or set of surroundings in which the story occurs. It includes time or time span, place(s), climates, geography—man-made or natural—, or cultural environments Emily Dickinson's poem "Because I could not stop for Death" has a simple setting—the narrator's symbolic ride with Death through town towards the local graveyard. Conversely, Leo Tolstoy's *War and Peace* encompasses numerous settings within settings in the areas affected by the Napoleonic Wars, spanning from 1805 to 1812.

The setting is very important to a story's framework and may even change periodically as the story unfolds. Understanding when and where a story takes place helps children visualize the various scenes and relate the story's setting to a time and place in their own lives or to a similar setting in another story. Questions that aid in the understanding of setting include the following:

- What country are the characters in?
- What year or era is it?
- Does the story take place in a suburban, urban, or rural location?
- Is the setting similar or different to where you live?
- How is it similar?
- How is it different?
- Does this setting remind you of a setting in another story?
- How are the settings similar? How are they different?
- Would you like to visit this setting? Give clear reasons why or why not.

A story's setting is critical to helping children make sense of a character's language, dress, attitude, relationships with others, and character traits. Building a stronger understanding of each character within a story will assist young readers in their overall text comprehension.

Plot, Conflict, and Resolution

The **plot** is what happens in the story. Plots may be singular, containing one problem, or they may be very complex, with many sub-plots. All plots have an exposition, a conflict, a climax, and a resolution. The **conflict** drives the plot and is something that the reader expects to be resolved. The plot carries those events along until there is a **resolution** to the conflict.

Educators build a bridge that strengthens students' story comprehension by helping children connect the story's plot to a familiar scenario in another story or by helping children connect the problem in the text with a problem they have encountered in their own lives. For instance, the plot can involve dealing with a bully, battling the elements of nature, or learning to overcome personal obstacles. The more children are able to relate to a story's plot, the greater their comprehension and appreciation of the story will be.

When teaching children about the various elements in literary texts, the use of visual aids, such as story maps, can provide invaluable assistance to a child's overall understanding:

Author's Point of View

An important reading comprehension skill is identifying the points of view that exist in literature. The **point of view** refers to the lens through which readers see the story unfold. Readers are often able to understand the overall story more fully when they can determine from what angle the story is told. The point of view of the main character or of several characters helps readers interpret character traits, understand how each character relates to the other, and determine how those relationships relate to the story's plot. In literary works, there are four main points of view to consider:

- Third person omniscient
- Third person limited
- First person
- Objective

First Person
Regarded in literature as the most intimate approach to point of view development, **first person** is written in first-person singular, using the pronouns *I*, *me*, and *my*. When authors apply this point of view, readers develop a clear understanding of the true inner feelings of that particular character and strengthen their understanding of how the character relates to the story's plot and to supporting characters.

Poetry often uses first person, e.g., William Wordsworth's "I Wandered Lonely as a Cloud." Two examples of prose written in first person are Suzanne Collins's *The Hunger Games* and Anthony Burgess's *A Clockwork Orange*.

Second Person
The **second-person point of view** is when the writer uses the pronoun *you*. It is not widely used in prose fiction, but as a technique, it has been used by writers such as William Faulkner in *Absalom, Absalom!* and Albert Camus in *The Fall*. It is more common in poetry—e.g., Pablo Neruda's "If You Forget Me."

Third Person
Third-person point of view is when the writer utilizes pronouns such as him, her, or them. It may be the most utilized point of view in prose as it provides flexibility to an author and is the one with which readers are most familiar. Third person refers to the use of the third person singular in writing, as in *he* or *she*. There are two main types of third person used in fiction.

Third-person omniscient uses a narrator that is all-knowing, relating the story by conveying and interpreting thoughts/feelings of all characters. Omniscient is defined as all knowing. When the author employs third-person omniscient, each character's perspective is revealed, allowing readers to consider and evaluate the points of view of all the characters within a story.

In **third-person limited**, the narrator relates the story through the perspective of one character's thoughts/feelings, usually the main character, thereby creating a more intimate impact on the reader and leaving the points of view of other characters a mystery to uncover. This point of view also employs the third person singular forms of *he* and *she* when speaking directly about a specific character.

Objective
The **objective point of view** reveals no feelings, thoughts, or opinions of characters; it remains void of emotional elements. This point of view focuses on facts, data, historical information, and quotations for reference. Authors who write in the objective point of view write as outside observers describing events as they happen.

To help students develop an awareness of which point of view the author is applying, educators may wish to model the thinking process required to locate point of view evidence. Beginning with a character analysis in chart form, for instance, educators and students can list all characters within a story and discuss the character traits of each one. Teachers may then ask the students why they believe characters possess certain traits and may then facilitate this understanding by referring to specific areas in the story that reveal these traits.

Using various excerpts from familiar stories to develop a character analysis also helps children strengthen point-of-view awareness. Working as literary detectives, students should be prompted to look for the pronouns *he*, *she*, and *I* and then focus on the key vocabulary surrounding these pronouns. The ability to identify key vocabulary used to evoke emotion, as well as vocabulary used to simply state facts, will be very useful in developing a student's ability to recognize points of view within a story:

Emotional Vocabulary	**Factual Vocabulary**
Fear: apprehensive, cautious, concerned, hesitant, uneasy, watchful	Facts: details, knowledge, information, proof
Anger: annoyed, cranky, critical, frustrated, irritated	Data: as evidenced by statistics
Sadness: disappointed, heartbroken, gloomy, depressed	Historical Information: recorded, an account of
Happy: amused, inspired, joyful, pleased	Quotations: testimony, witness, verification, affidavit

Tone

The **tone** of a story reflects the author's attitude and opinion about the subject matter of the story or text. Tone can be expressed through word choice, imagery, figurative language, syntax, and other details. The emotion or mood the reader experiences relates back to the tone of the story. Some examples of possible tones are humorous, somber, sentimental, and ironic.

Identifying Similarities and Differences

By taking character analysis one step further, students can compare and contrast the similarities and differences between the points of view of two or more characters in a story. The ability to consider various points of view helps children strengthen their critical thinking skills in both academic and social settings.

Educators should consider using a variety of instructional approaches when comparing and contrasting points of view. One strategy educators can implement is a class debate or partner debate. A debate brings students to center stage as they learn to defend the point of view of various characters within a story while listening to classmates defend the points of view of other characters. Friendly debating has been proven to strengthen a student's ability to reason, apply logic, communicate with self-expression, listen to others, and organize thoughts and opinions. Debating also helps children develop an appreciation for opposing points of view and, therefore, works to build stronger bonds both in and out of the classroom. By taking on the point of view of a character in a story with the added responsibility of defending that point of view with evidence, students broaden their own thought processes and challenge the world around them in more depth.

Visual aids are another strategy that educators use when comparing and contrasting points of views, especially when examining characters in stories. Venn diagrams are especially effective as they provide a clear space for unique perspectives, with a common overlapping section for similarities. There are several visual aids available for use in the classroom depending on the age and ability of the students. From the earliest of primary education to the upper-level high school grades, visual aids continue to be a powerful instructional tool. The visual aid below demonstrates opposing and shared characteristics of characters:

Literary Devices

Figurative Language

Figurative language is a specific style of speaking or writing that uses tools for a variety of effects. It entertains readers, ignites imagination, and promotes creativity. Instead of writing in realistic terms or literal terms, figurative language plays with words and prompts readers to infer the underlying meaning. Figurative language uses words in ways that are different than their original meaning, often using devices such as simile, metaphor, hyperbole, personification, or allusion to enhance one's writing. **Creative writing** tends to employ more non-literal expressions than academic or informative writing. Educators should give students ample time to experiment with different kinds of figurative language, especially when switching from creative to more academic writing.

Figurative language can be used to give additional insight into the theme or message of a text by moving beyond the usual and literal meaning of words and phrases. It can also be used to appeal to the senses of readers and create a more in-depth story. This is often seen in more descriptive writing.

It is also considered a rhetorical device in that figurative language is used to play on the *meanings* of words as well as the *sounds* of words. These kind of literary devices are more likely found in poetry but may also be found in non-fiction writing like speeches.

Figurative language, including metaphor, simile, hyperbole, personification, allusion, puns, onomatopoeia, oxymoron, idiom, litotes, alliteration, and synecdoche should all be taught through direct instruction and explained in great detail. Students should be well-versed in identifying each example of figurative language and note how they differ from one another. Another way to encourage understanding of figurative language is to read books that contain plenty of figurative language, and to identify where it's used throughout the text.

There are seven types of figurative language:

Type	Definition	Example
Personification	Giving animate qualities to an inanimate object	The tree stood tall and still, staring up at the sky.
Simile	The comparison of two unlike things using connecting words	Your eyes are as blue as the ocean.
Metaphor	The comparison of two unlike things without the use of connecting words	She was in the twilight of her years.
Hyperbole	An over-exaggeration	I could eat a million of these cookies!
Alliteration	The patterned repetition of an initial consonant sound	The bunnies are bouncing in baskets.
Onomatopoeia	Words that are formed by using the very sound associated with the word itself	"Drip, drip, drip" went the kitchen faucet.
Idioms	Common sayings that carry a lesson or meaning that must be inferred	That math work was a piece of cake!

Interpretation
Since idioms and hyperboles are commonly used in everyday speech, educators may wish to introduce them early.

>I'm so tired that I could sleep forever! — Hyperbole

>He's not playing with a full deck! — Idiom

Other forms of figurative language can be found in poetry and in children's stories. As educators come across figurative speech, they can prompt children's critical thinking skills by asking what they think the author meant by those words or that particular sentence. Giving concrete examples of each style and challenging children to attempt writing their very own creative sentences will strengthen their understanding and application of figurative language.

Nuance of Words
Nuances are the small differences that words can have in meaning depending on their context, often referred to as "shades of meaning." For example, although "lovely" and "good" mean nearly the same thing literally, they have two very different nuances. A reader will picture a "lovely chair" much differently than a "good chair" despite having the same definition.

This is because words can convey different levels of intensity or emotion despite meaning the exact same thing. Nuance can be taught with plenty of examples of words that mean the same thing but have two different nuances (like "lovely" and "good," "cheerful" and "elated," or "small" and "petite").

The words authors choose to use must always be well thought out. Although words carry specific meanings, they also carry **connotations**—emotional feelings that are evoked by the words. Connotation creates the tone of the writing. Some words can be said to be loaded words or trigger words that ignite strong emotional responses in readers. These two sentences offer examples:

> My grandfather is a robust, elderly man.
>
> My grandfather is a chubby, old man.

In the first sentence, the adjectives used to describe the grandfather instill positive emotions in the reader. However, in the second sentence, the adjectives instill negative emotions. The **mood** of a writing piece refers to the emotions—positive or negative—the reader feels during and after reading. **Tone** refers to the author's purposeful choice of words, designed to evoke those feelings.

Alliteration

Alliteration refers to the repetition of the first sound of each word. Alliteration can be used to build emotion in a piece, to cause the reader to slow down, or to add rhythm and structure to a piece. Recall Robert Burns' opening line:

> My love is like a red, red rose

This line includes two instances of alliteration: "love" and "like" (repeated *L* sound), as well as "red" and "rose" (repeated *R* sound). Next, assonance refers to the repetition of vowel sounds and can occur anywhere within a word (not just the opening sound). Here is the opening of a poem by John Keats:

> When I have fears that I may cease to be
>
> Before my pen has glean'd my teeming brain

One great way to teach alliteration to students is through tongue twisters like "Peter Piper picked a peck of pickled peppers". Most students enjoy getting the chance to try and repeat tongue twisters, making them a fun and memorable activity. Engaging in different types of instruction will help students form deeper mental connections to what alliteration is. Another way to teach alliteration is through poetry and song lyrics. Using engaging material, teachers should have students identify the examples of alliteration they can find within popular lyrics or poetry.

Strategies for Supporting Readers as they Construct Literal and Inferential Meaning

Literal Comprehension

Literal comprehension refers to the reader's ability to understand the actual meaning of texts. This is not meant to be complicated. It means literally understanding the facts, setting, plot, etc. of what is being read.

To bolster literal comprehension, show students how to ask pertinent questions. When they are reading stories, children should learn to ask who the characters are, what happened, where the story is taking place, and in what order the events occurred. Teachers can use graphic organizers like KWL charts and Venn diagrams to have students identify things they learned in the story. Teachers can also check for literal comprehension by conducting an assessment after reading with questions from the text.

Inferential Comprehension

Inferential comprehension requires students to understand the hidden context or unstated meaning of a text. They should be able to explain why an action occurred and what they think will happen next. This also referred to as "making inferences," when a student reads a selection of text and is able to understand a further meaning that isn't directly stated.

When it comes to inferential comprehension, children need to recall the facts that occurred in the story and what those facts represent. They should ask the following questions:

- Why did this happen?
- How might the characters feel?
- What might happen next?
- How important is "X" character?

Teachers can encourage students' inferential comprehension by modeling it while reading, making inferences aloud, and pointing out when students make inferences while reading. It's also important that the concept of making inferences is taught within direct instruction, and teachers should ask guiding questions to help students make inferences throughout the text, like those listed above.

Inferences Based on Textual Evidence

Although related to predictions and the finding of factual information, **inferences** refer to the ability to make logical assumptions based on contextual clues. People of all ages make inferences about the world around them on a daily basis but may not be aware of what they are doing. Even young children may infer that it is likely cold outside if they wake up and their bedroom is chilly or the floor is cold. While being driven somewhere on the highway and a child notices a person at the side of the road with a parked car, that child will likely infer that the individual is having car problems and is awaiting some assistance. Therefore, the challenge for educators is not necessarily teaching children how to infer, but rather demonstrating how this skill they already use can be transferred into the study of various texts.

One effective introductory strategy may be to set up scenarios within the classroom and challenge the children to infer what is happening. For instance, the educator may arrive at school pretending to have a cold without saying anything. By placing a personal box of tissues on the desk along with a nasal spray and frequently sneezing, the teacher is challenging the students to infer that he or she not feeling well.

Once the children begin to understand that making inferences is indeed similar to detective work by collecting key evidence, the educator can now introduce more inanimate objects like photographs, pictures, or diagrams void of explanatory language. The children's task would be to study the visual aids to try to infer what the subject is about. Educators can assist the children initially by asking questions aloud, modeling how to arrive at a logical inference. For example, the teacher might hold up a picture of a school in which all children are gathered in the playground and grouped according to their classes. Upon closer examination, the children might spot a fire truck parked at the side of the road and may infer that the school had a fire drill or an actual fire.

As the children progress in their ability to infer based on picture clues, it is time to transfer their new skill to texts. Educators may wish to begin with inference challenges in which students are prompted to write short stories about specific events—without directly mentioning the event. For instance, if a child is interested in swimming, they may write about the ideal temperature of the water, backstroke, freestyle, full laps, and so on without ever mentioning the word *swimming*. Other children in the class will then be prompted to read the short story and infer what the text is about. The children must examine the clues in the text, make an inference, and support the inference with evidence from the text:

In the second paragraph, it says that the water was relatively warm, so it was easy to finish a full lap. This must mean that the person was swimming in the water.

The more initial practice children receive before moving into more complicated texts, the most success they will have in making accurate inferences and, in turn, the more fun they will have acting as text detectives.

Literary analysis of a fictional text involves the study of character development, setting, mood, plot, point(s) of view, figurative language, and other literary elements. The **study of informational text** involves nonfictional elements, such as the author's purpose, major ideas or concepts, and more. All of these individual components in a text often interrelate and form the text's overall theme or message. Some common universal themes found in literature include disappointment, courage, overcoming obstacles, loneliness, and good triumphing over evil. In informational texts, the themes or messages vary greatly, but they usually involve subjects that pertain to the natural or social world. When children reach the stage in their literacy development that allows them to begin literary analysis exercises, they are beginning to take their reading comprehension beyond the surface details to arrive at an even deeper understanding of the text by studying these individual themes and messages.

When first introducing literary analysis, it is important for educators to select texts that carry themes children can relate to. Educators are encouraged to consider themes that depict similar life experiences or interests. Although many themes in texts are universal in nature, the younger the students are, the more important it is to choose texts that have themes with which they can identify, that appeal to their interests, and that inspire discussion and debate. As children progress and strengthen their literacy skills, they will be able to apply these skills to a wider variety of themes.

An ideal strategy to introduce literary analysis is to hold class discussions at the beginning and ending of texts, as well as periodically throughout the reading of a given text. Educators may prompt these class discussions with key questions that help students to make connections between the events and characters in a fictional text and the students' life experiences. Class discussions allow children to hear multiple ideas, which works to strengthen overall comprehension and build an appreciation of alternate points of view. These key questions also prompt children to consider their own feelings as they read the text, helping them to connect on a personal or emotional level, which strengthens overall comprehension. Class discussions should also challenge children a little further by asking them to explain why they feel a certain way about a message in the text. Once children have had ample opportunity to practice and master this skill, the next step is to teach children how to support their thoughts, feelings, and ideas by finding textual evidence that supports their views.

Learning to find supporting evidence within a text is a very complex skill that can initially cause some confusion and frustration. One strategy to employ that may assist children in learning how to find key information is the introduction of graphic organizers. The following is an example of a graphic organizer that is split into three sections:

Student Answer	Text Evidence (quotation and page number)	Explanation

Searching for supportive evidence involves more than merely finding a quotation. The above graphic organizer guides students to connect the specific quotation(s) to their interpretation and further provides students the opportunity to explain, in their own words, how their answers and the quotations are connected. Forming credible and logical responses to questions and supporting those responses with appropriate quotations from the text are considered very advanced literary skills, which take students to a much deeper understanding of literature.

Summarization of Information

While summarizing information from a text seems like an easy concept at first, it is more complex than one thinks. **Summarizing** involves the ability to extract the most important elements in writing, to eliminate elements of lesser importance, to reorganize the information, to rewrite information in one's own words, and, finally, to condense the writing into a significantly smaller text than that of the original. Thus, learning to summarize consists of many individual skills that all converge and overlap. There are two forms of summary: (1) summaries that aid the reader in understanding the text and (2) summaries that aid others in their understanding of the text.

Summarizing should be explicitly taught beginning in the primary school years with continual reinforcement and gradual introduction to more complex texts as students progress. In order to summarize effectively, children need to demonstrate the following abilities:

- Text comprehension
- Identification of main idea
- Elimination of inconsequential information
- Ability to condense
- Ability to paraphrase
- Ability to organize writing in a logical order

Personal Summaries

Educators are encouraged to first assist children in summarizing texts as a means to strengthen personal comprehension. For instance, when children are able to identify a text's main idea, state that idea in their own words, and back up that main idea with supporting evidence, they are learning to summarize, and their comprehension undoubtedly strengthens.

Summarizing for oneself is also an invaluable tool for studying and memorizing, which children will use throughout their academic careers. When students summarize for themselves, the goal is to strengthen overall comprehension of the text, arrive at the author's point of view, and isolate the main idea. Since the summary is intended to be only for the student, there is no need to pay particular attention to spelling, grammar, or sentence structure. Students are learning to make personal notes for the purpose of comprehension strengthening and, possibly, memorization for upcoming tests.

Summaries for Others

Once children have demonstrated a clear ability to summarize a variety of texts for their own understanding, educators may begin to introduce them to the skill of **summarizing for others**. This involves a more complex approach to summarization. Now that students have ownership of the given text, they inherit the challenge of explaining the text's meaning to an audience. In addition to extracting the main idea, eliminating unimportant text elements, reorganizing and condensing the text, and paraphrasing, students must now pay close attention to the summary's length, the mechanics of writing, and the audience. For example, are students writing to classmates to help them better understand the text? Are they writing the summary for their teacher, in an effort to demonstrate their ability to summarize? Since this type of summarization involves a polished finish, children must also employ proofreading and revision skills.

Educators who are introducing summarization for the first time should focus on less complex texts that involve familiar subject matter, and the texts should be well organized, with titles, possible subtitles, and easily identifiable main ideas. Allowing children to refer to the text as often as possible while learning to summarize is also an important teaching strategy. Children at the early stages of summarizing should not be expected to have memorized and clearly understood what they have read. Sometimes children need to reread the same text several times before beginning a summarization. By explicitly teaching children how to recognize signaling devices, educators help them summarize and isolate a text's main idea. Some signaling devices may be found in an introductory or summary statement or specific words or phrases that have been placed in italics, bold print, or are underlined.

The more advanced students become with summarizing texts, the greater their comprehension and ability to apply what they learn will be.

Types, Structures, and Features of Informational Texts

Informational text provides readers with factual information and is designed to lead the reader to a central idea or conclusion. It is important that students understand the different types, structures, and features of informational text.

As early as kindergarten, children are encouraged to read a variety of informational texts. Placing an assortment of texts in the classroom library, hanging posters on classroom walls that promote a wide range of topics, and providing children with ample time and opportunity to explore any number of subjects, has shown to have a very positive impact on reading comprehension and overall literacy skill development. Informational texts provide children an opportunity to explore and develop a better understanding of the world around them. Taking this one step further, by allowing children to choose topics of informational texts that pique their curiosity, educators help children develop a more positive attitude toward reading and writing.

Informational Text Types
- **Literary Nonfiction:** The most common type of informational text is literary nonfiction. It's also called creative nonfiction because the true story or event is told in an engaging, short story style. The reader may feel like they are reading a story, but all of the details are based on facts rather than fiction.

- **Expository:** Expository texts are most often used to provide detailed information about a person, thing, place, or event. This style of writing is most often seen in news articles and is usually presented in a literal, direct tone.

- **Argumentative:** Argumentative, or persuasive, texts generally present a problem or idea and work to convince the reader of a certain belief.

- **Procedural**: This kind of writing is called "how-to" writing, and it is typically in the context of a product. A list of instructions, features, or ingredients may be included in this type of text.

To teach the informational text types, teachers should present examples of each kind and have students read them and identify which type the text falls under.

Informational Text Structures
The following organizational structures are most common:

- **Problem/solution**—organized by an analysis/overview of a problem, followed by potential solution(s)

- **Cause/effect**—organized by the effects resulting from a cause or the cause(s) of a particular effect

- **Spatial order**—organized by points that suggest location or direction—e.g., top to bottom, right to left, outside to inside

- **Chronological/sequence order**—organized by points presented to indicate a passage of time or through purposeful steps/stages

- **Comparison/Contrast**—organized by points that indicate similarities and/or differences between two things or concepts

- **Order of importance**—organized by priority of points, often most significant to least significant or vice versa

The first step in identifying a text's structure is to determine the thesis or main idea. A **thesis statement** indicates the writer's purpose and may include the scope and direction of the text. It is usually presented at the beginning or end of a text, and it may be explicit or implicit.

Once a reader has a grasp of the thesis or main idea of the text, they can better determine its organizational structure. Test takers are advised to read informational text passages more than once in order to comprehend the material fully. It is also helpful to examine any text features present in the text including the table of contents, index, glossary, headings, footnotes, and visuals. The analysis of these features and the information presented within them, can offer additional clues about the central idea and structure of a text. The following questions should be asked when considering structure:

- How does the author assemble the parts to make an effective whole argument?

- Is the passage linear in nature and if so, what is the timeline or thread of logic?

- What is the presented order of events, facts, or arguments? Are these effective in contributing to the author's thesis?

- How can the passage be divided into sections? How are they related to each other and to the main idea or thesis?

- What key terms are used to indicate the organization?

Next, test takers should skim the passage, noting the first line or two of each body paragraph—the *topic sentences*—and the conclusion. Key **transitional terms**, such as *on the other hand, also, because, however, therefore, most importantly,* and *first,* within the text can also signal organizational structure. Based on these clues, readers should then be able to identify what type of organizational structure is being used.

Teachers can promote understanding of text structure by having students practice identifying the structure of each text they read. A good way to do this is by starting simple with paragraphs, and the teacher can provide a paragraph that exemplifies each type of text structure (cause/effect, comparison/contrast, spatial order, chronological order, problem/solution, and order of importance). After reading each paragraphs, students should match the paragraph to its' text structure.

Impact of Point of View on Overall Structure of Texts
Generally speaking, the majority of informational texts involves a third-person point of view. It is widely accepted in academic circles that the use of any other point of view for information purposes is likely to have a negative impact on the text's quality. Third-person point of view removes the author from associating the information with a personal bias and allows the reader to evaluate the content objectively. Third-person point of view strengthens informational texts with the use of validated research, facts, and statistics from a variety of

credible sources. The more factual evidence that is presented in informational texts along with the employment of third-person points of view, the more likely the work will be accepted as a reliable informational resource.

However, there are informational texts that use first-person points of view for specific reasons. For example, informational texts that are written with the intent to persuade a reader's feelings, opinions, actions, or reactions will often use first-person points of view. By giving the text a personal connection, authors can stress their expertise and experience with regard to the event or topic, which may carry weight on how readers relate to the information. Although this may prove to be advantageous to the author, the drawbacks to employing first-person point of view include the potential for readers to evaluate the work as too subjective and, therefore, unreliable.

In contrast, first-person point of view is the most frequently used in literary works. With the narrator playing an active role in the story's plot, readers are able to connect on an intimate level with the thoughts, emotions, and opinions being expressed.

It is important for authors to consider the main intent of their writing. The messages they wish to convey, the emotions they may wish to evoke, and the overall impressions they want to leave on their readers should ultimately guide authors toward the employment of a specific point of view.

Author's Purpose
In order for students to become independent readers and draw their own conclusions about what they read, it is critical that they learn to discern the **author's purpose**.

One obvious approach to teaching children how to reveal an author's purpose is to simply ask children why they think the author wrote this information. These types of open-ended class discussions allow children to express their ideas, explore theories, and consider what others have to say on the subject. Educators can record various answers and then ask the children to return to the text as detectives, looking for clues that support each theory.

Another approach to uncovering the author's purpose is for students to take a closer look at the written structure of the text and the vocabulary usage. For example, is the text's structure written in chronological order, simply listing events as they occurred? Does the text open up with a problem that is then resolved? Is the author using cause/effect or compare/contrast vocabulary? Learning about the structure of the text gives great insight into the author's purpose.

When children develop reading fluency, they are able to read a text with minimal to no errors, with consistent speed, and with appropriate expression, and they learn to connect with what they are reading on a personal level. As children read through an informational text, educators may ask how the students are feeling. Did they begin feeling one way and end up feeling another by the end of the text? When children examine their own personal feelings with regard to what they have read, they will be in a better position to explore the author's purpose.

Once children have had several opportunities to explore the author's purpose using a variety of informational texts, prompting them to write their own informational texts will help them to develop and strengthen a better understanding about writing with a purpose. Perhaps they can write a procedural text that lists the steps in how to ride a bike, or they can write a persuasive paper to try to convince their teacher that extra free time during the school day stimulates learning.

Learning to identify an author's purpose connects children with their reading on a deeper level. Instead of believing everything they read, they will begin to understand that there are many reasons why authors write, and they will further understand that they possess the ability to draw their own conclusions and make their own decisions on any given topic.

Major Idea

Some children struggle with identifying the main idea of an informational text. Identifying the **main idea** of a text requires that the reader understand the entire text and is able to zero in on one central, overarching idea amongst a sea of other information. The ability to sort through the entire text and arrive at the main idea takes a considerable amount of effort and practice for beginning readers.

Before prompting students to locate the main idea of a given text or passage, educators must first explain what the main idea actually is. Here are some guidelines, tips, and tricks to follow that will help children identify the main idea:

Identifying the Main Idea
The most important part of the text
Text title and pictures may reveal clues
Opening sentences and final sentences may reveal clues
Key vocabulary words that are repeatedly used may reveal clues

Providing students with simple lists of related vocabulary may be a logical starting point when teaching how to recognize a main idea. For instance, on a large chart, educators may list several fruits, vegetables, snacks, and meals, and then prompt the children to explain what they have in common. This also works well with a set of images, pictures, or photographs that all represent the same idea. After repeated practice, children will begin to strengthen their ability to center in on the main idea that connects all the elements on the list.

Once children begin to identify and demonstrate a clear understanding of the main idea in simple lists, educators may wish to introduce simple texts that gradually increase in complexity.

Features of Informational Text

Nearly every type of informational text contains features that make the text easier to navigate and comprehend. **Headings** include titles and subtitles that identify the topic of study. They also help a reader to arrive at a clearer understanding with regard to the text's main idea. Headings can help readers make connections between background knowledge and the information in the text, which helps them make predictions before reading begins. Headings also strategically organize a text into sections so that one section at a time can be studied.

Sidebars are found in the right or left margins of informational texts. Sidebars often provide the reader with helpful, additional information about a topic that appears on that particular page. By providing examples, interesting facts, definitions of key terms, and more, sidebars emphasize important information that the author wishes to convey.

Informational text features like table of contents, indexes, and glossaries can make navigation of the text easier and help readers find information faster. They can make it easier to find a certain chapter or concept that the student needs to know.

Text features like italics and bold print, help draw attention to certain words and phrases. They're often used to provide definitions or add emphasis to a certain word.

Hyperlinks are in-text links to specific website addresses that a reader may wish to visit to further their understanding of a specific topic. When authors insert hyperlinks into modern informational texts, they create a text that is more interactive, providing further resources for children to strengthen their comprehension of a given topic.

Supporting Details

Supporting details of texts are defined as those elements of a text that help readers make sense of the main idea. They either qualitatively and/or quantitatively describe the main idea, strengthening the reader's understanding.

Using simple sentences is an effective instructional approach when introducing children to supporting details. Educators may write out a simple sentence and ask the children to underline the main idea, as in the sentence that follows:

> The *apple* is hard, red, and juicy.

Once the main idea, the apple, is accurately identified, educators can now ask children to locate words that describe or support this main idea and highlight/circle each supporting word:

> The *apple* is hard, red, and juicy.

Simple sentence exercises will gradually become simple paragraphs and, eventually, full texts in which children are challenged with the task of locating the main idea and the supporting details. Children must learn to differentiate between trivial and supporting details by evaluating whether or not the detail in question further quantifies or qualifies the main idea. If the detail does neither, it is likely not important enough to be considered a supporting detail and can be left alone.

Graphic organizers can also be a helpful tool when working with main ideas and supporting details. There are many graphic organizers that help students to organize their analysis into clear and visible representations. The following are examples of graphic organizers that are commonly used when teaching the main idea and supporting details.

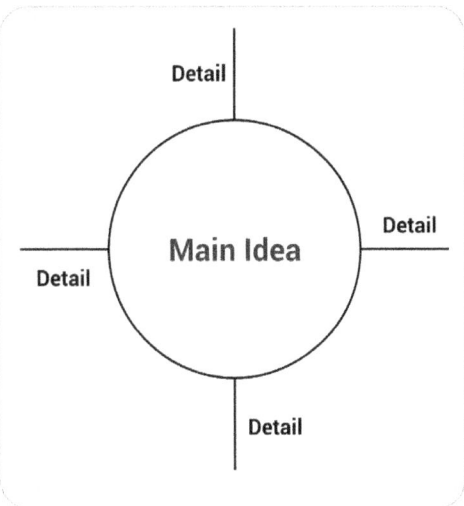

Children who demonstrate the ability to accurately identify a text's main idea and supporting details can further strengthen these skills by attempting to write their own texts with a main idea and supporting details. Likewise, graphic organizers can be used as tools that help children to organize their thoughts and ideas before they begin this writing process.

Visual or Graphic Aids
Visual features like diagrams, charts, graphs, and pictures help further comprehension through visual means. They add additional meaning and information to the text in another way.

Authors of informational texts will often employ the use of visual or graphic aids in strategic locations throughout the text in order to strengthen the reader's understanding of the topic at hand. **Visual aids** can provide an overview of key information, illustrate relationships among important text elements, and summarize the main idea. Visual aids are generally colorful and catch students' attention; they help to simplify what could be potentially complicated information. There are a multitude of visual aids that are frequently used in informational texts, including models, graphs, charts, tables, maps, drawings, photographs, and time lines. Some visual aids also involve a side bar, which defines key vocabulary necessary to understand the topic.

In most instances, children merely need to look at the visual aid to make an instant connection. The implementation of graphic aids in writing reduces instructional time and strengthens comprehension. During read alouds and guided reading sessions, educators may wish to model how to extract meaning from visual aids by connecting the graphic to specific elements in the text. Before reading begins, educators have students skim through the pages to find the visual aids and predict what the text may be about based on the text's graphics. Therefore, visual aids may often help students to identify the text's main idea.

The time it requires to read and process the written text is considerably longer than the time it takes to derive meaning from the graph. Helping students to identify and derive meaning from visual aids will help to strengthen their reading comprehension skills and overall literacy development.

Vocabulary
Vocabulary used throughout informational texts is generally quite different than vocabulary found in fictional print. For this reason, it is imperative that educators help children strengthen and increase their vocabulary inventory so that they can eventually become successful at reading and understanding informational text.

For instance, educators can point out **signal words** throughout texts to help children more readily and accurately identify the author's purpose. Authors employ specific vocabulary that spotlight their intent. For instance, if authors wish to list examples to support a main idea, they may use vocabulary such as *for example*, *such as*, or *as illustrated*. When displaying the chronological order of events, authors may use *first, lastly, before,* and *finally*. Some common compare and contrast vocabulary words include *but, same as, similar to, as opposed to,* and *however*. There are several key phrases that signal cause and effect relationships, including *because of, as a result of,* and *in order to*.

By using word walls and personal dictionaries, sorting vocabulary words according to theme, introducing text maps, and teaching children to become familiar with sidebars and glossaries in informational texts, educators will help expand their students' vocabularies and strengthen their abilities to read and comprehend informational texts successfully.

Using Technology to Support Students

<u>Critically Examine Online Resources and Foster Digital Literacy</u>
In order to have an education conducive to college and career readiness and success, students need online research and digital media writing skills.

With current digital technology, the writing process has become a much more collaborative experience. In higher education and in career settings, collaborative skills are essential. Publishing and presenting are now simplified such that completed work is often read by a wide variety of audiences. Writing can be instantly shared with parents, peers, educators, and the general public, including experts in the field. Students are more apt to take an interest in the writing process when they know that others are reading their writing. Feedback is also simplified because so many platforms allow comments from readers. Teachers can be interactive with the students throughout the process, allowing formative assessment and integration of personalized instruction.

Reference Materials and Media Resources
It is critical that educators teach students how to locate credible information and to reliably cite their sources using bibliographies. Platforms and apps for online learning are varied and plentiful. Here are some ideas for how to use technology for writing instruction in the classroom:

- Use a projector with a tablet to display notes and classwork for the group to see. This increases instructional time because notes are already available rather than having to be written in real-time. This also provides the ability to save, email, and post classwork and notes for students and parents to access on their own time. A student can work at their own pace and still keep up with instruction. Student screens can be displayed for peer-led teaching and sharing of class work.

- More technology in class means less paperwork. Digital drop-boxes can be used for students to turn in assignments. Teachers can save paper, keep track of student revisions of work, and give feedback electronically.

- Digital media can be used to differentiate instruction for multiple learning styles and multiple skill levels. Instead of using standardized textbook learning for everyone, teachers can create and collect resources for individualizing course content.

- Digital textbooks and e-readers can replace hardback versions of text that are prone to damage and loss. Students can instantly access definitions for new words, as well as annotate and highlight useful information without ruining a hardbound book.

- Library databases can be used to locate reliable research information and resources. There are digital tools for tracking citation information, allowing annotations for internet content, and for storing internet content.

- Mobile devices may be used in the classroom to encourage reading and writing when students use them to interact with classmates in digital spaces like Google Classroom.

- PowerPoint and other presentation software can be used to model writing for students and to provide a platform for presenting their work.

- Web quests can be used to help guide students on research projects. They can get relevant information on specific topics and decide what pieces to include in their writing.

- Students can write about technology as a topic. They can "teach" someone how to use various forms of technology, specific learning platforms, or apps.

- Students can learn to create webpages, usually through a central class website that offers the ability for each student to create an individual page on the site.

- Online feedback and grading systems can be used. There are many to choose from and the school district will often select one system like Gradebook or Skyward to use for every school, teacher, and classroom. Online grading systems allow parents, students, and teachers to view student grades in real time.

- Game show-style reviews can be created for units of study to use on computers or on an overhead projector.

- Students can make or use pre-created online flashcards to study concepts and prepare for tests.

- Publishing tools can be used to publish student work on the web or in class newspapers or social media sites.

Support Active Learning Across Content Areas
Using Technology Tools for Effective Communication

Different technological tools serve different functions. To function in the developing world, students need to learn and understand **digital literacy**—the knowledge, dexterity, and critical thinking skills involved in using technology to create, evaluate, and present information. The best techniques for instructing students on choosing and using technological tools involve educating them on the advantages and disadvantages of each, demonstrating how to use them, breaking down their different aspects, assigning students homework or projects in which they will utilize different technological resources, and instructing them on when it is appropriate to use each kind. The most common types of tools used for communication are as follows:

- Smartphones/apps
- Email
- Microsoft Office
- iMovie
- Skype
- Twitter
- Facebook
- Instagram
- Google Drive

- Various blogging websites
- Online bulletin boards
- Wikis

A good way to introduce students to varying technological tools is by using them in the classroom. It would be helpful to teach students how to use a PowerPoint presentation, for example, by giving a PowerPoint presentation. If a student asks a question to which the teacher does not know the answer, they can discover the answer together by using a reliable source on the Internet, projecting the process on the board, so that they can see exactly how it's done. Students can also receive homework and updates on school and classroom events through a personal blog or class bulletin board the teacher has designed so that they may become familiar with using online communication. Students can also be assigned to use personal blogs to practice and improve their writing skills.

The most effective method for learning new skills is a hands-on approach. Students can be educated on the pros and cons of each technological tool, but the best way for them to learn is to allow them to find out for themselves by assigning projects and asking them to give the reasoning behind choosing a specific tool. For example, they may be asked to do a project on some aspect of the Revolutionary War by choosing a media format. Ideas may include the following:

- Doing a presentation

- Filming and editing a video re-enactment of a great battle

- Writing a script in Microsoft Word or in a Google doc and having classmates act it out

- Creating Facebook statuses from the viewpoints of the forefathers in modern colloquial language

- Having a "Twitter war" between the British and the Colonials

- Asking various people to participate in a collaborative Wiki or Google Doc in which many people give their versions of aspects of the Revolutionary War

- Writing a blog narrating life as a soldier

- Posting photos of the signing of the Declaration of Independence

Students can then give their presentations to the classroom so that students can learn about the topic through different presentation styles.

Another way to engage students in using technology is to have them communicate with each other through the various methods of communication—e.g., starting a class Google Doc, creating a classroom Facebook group, or using a discussion board. This is also an excellent opportunity to encourage students to use Standard English through all methods of communication to enhance their writing skills and instill a sense of professionalism, which they will need throughout their lives.

For example, requiring that all students use complete sentences, proper spelling, and grammar through Facebook, Twitter, or blogs associated with homework or projects will encourage them to do so in their daily lives as well. Another example is requiring that students select tweets from their favorite celebrities or politicians, analyze their meaning and purpose, correct their grammar and spelling, and re-tweet them in the correct way. There are countless ways in which technology can be used in the classroom to enhance students' understanding of digital communication; all it requires is a little creativity.

Evaluating Technology-Based Strategies

It is hard to find a technological tool that will not be useful for students to explore. The more a student engages with the numerous different types of technology, the more digitally literate that student will become. Each type is effective and brings value to the table in its own way. When evaluating the effectiveness of a specific technology-based strategy, it's important to consider how this method is enhancing the student's digital literacy, as well as their critical thinking and communication skills. It is also necessary to evaluate the technology itself by asking relevant questions:

- Is it appropriate for the average age of the students in the classroom?
- Is it user friendly?
- Does it work consistently?
- Are there multiple ways to get help on learning how to use it?
- Are there trouble-shooting options?
- Does it have good reviews?
- Is it relevant to the content of the curriculum?
- Does it support and align to the learning objective?
- Is it more distracting than it is useful?
- Is it a tool that is/will be used often in the real world?
- Can it be used for more than one project or assignment?

One very effective teaching strategy is **collaborative learning**, in which two or more students work together to develop a project, work through an idea, or solve a problem. This method allows for students to play off each other's strengths and different experiences and learn how to communicate with their classmates to achieve goals. Technology can be used for collaborative learning in Google Drive, Skype, Google Hangouts, Nearpod, Padlet, and Periscope, in creating PowerPoint presentations together, or by conducting surveys with websites like Survey Monkey.

Another effective teaching method is **discussion**, in which students are given a topic or create a topic themselves and then use technology to engage in discourse. This can be done via discussion boards, such as ProBoards or Boardhost, or done live through programs such as Skype or Hangouts. Discussion strategies are extremely effective for enhancing communication skills and digital literacy.

A third method is **active learning**, in which the student engages in activities such as reading, writing, or teaching the subject to another student. Blogging is a great way to encourage active learning as it provides a medium through which students can reflect on what they've learned and respond to comments posted by the teacher or other students. Most of the suggestions made in the previous section—making presentations, creating video re-enactments, writing scripts, having mock Twitter or Facebook comment wars—are all forms of active learning. These types of activities solidify events, ideas, and skills in a student's mind in a way that memorization or flashcards do not as they utilize many different types of thinking and interaction.

One method that a teacher may employ depending on the class and circumstances is **distance learning**. Distance learning is any type of teaching method in which the student and teacher are not in the same place simultaneously. Many professors utilize distance learning through different kinds of technologies, including a live virtual lecture, computer simulations, interactive discussions, and virtual/audio learning environments. These strategies have their advantages in that one teacher can teach a large number of students and multiple locations, and students can communicate with fellow classmates across the globe.

Auditory learning is a strategy in which a student learns through listening. This typically happens via recorded lectures that can be downloaded as podcasts onto a classroom website, discussion board, or some other audio-simulated learning environment. **Visual learning** is learning through watching, in which ideas and concepts are illustrated through images, videos, or by observing a teacher complete a task, explain a concept, or solve a problem. This can be achieved through recorded videos, cartoons, virtual lectures, or by sitting in the classroom. Additionally, **kinesthetic learning** is active learning through physical interaction with an object or actively solving a problem, as opposed to passively listening or watching.

Every student has a different learning style which is unique to them—some learn better through listening while others learn better through doing. The best teaching methods employ all different learning strategies so that all the senses are engaged and every student has a chance at learning material based on their individual learning needs. Technology offers educators the tools do that.

Written, Visual, and Oral Information

Students in a modern classroom have access to a wide variety of instructional resources. From teacher-led instruction and classroom activities, traditional textbooks, encyclopedias, nonfiction magazines, and customized classroom libraries to desktop computers, iPads, tablets, laptops, online tutorials, and smart boards, there is a plethora of information waiting to be discovered. Learning how to integrate traditional written, visual, and oral information to other information provided on a multimedia platform can prove challenging, but it is well worth the effort. Since the vast majority of children from the primary school years and older are well equipped at using a variety of technology-based resources, educators who integrate technology in the classroom will likely succeed in helping children to progress both academically and socially. The classroom is as much a social setting as it is academic, and as society changes, so must the instructional approaches.

Time management is one of the initial tasks facing educators when setting up their academic year. Educators are responsible for teaching a wide range of subjects, specific domains within each subject, and numbers of skills within each domain. Designing long-range plans that take all of this into account and forming a framework for the academic year is the most logical starting point.

From this framework, educators can determine how to teach each discipline with an effective, time management approach. Taking the number of students, the possible varying academic and social levels, socioeconomic differences, and language barriers into account, teachers can begin to develop differentiated instructional approaches that cater to all the needs in the classroom. It is at this stage that both traditional resources and technology must find a way to complement each other in the classroom.

For instance, one effective approach is to instruct children to ensure that every research project involves a minimum of two textbook sources as well as a minimum of two technology-based sources. When introducing new topics or reinforcing a lesson, educators are still highly encouraged to use visual aids in the classroom, including word walls, personal dictionaries, and classroom labels. Modeling the effective use of hand-held books, reference guides, and magazines also provides children the opportunity to see how valuable written information continues to be in the world of education.

In order for children to experience a well-rounded, quality education, instructional days should be divided between effective, quality instruction, independent exploration and learning, and positive social interaction. Since the needs of children vary in each classroom, as well as their academic and social levels, each educator's decision on how to divide instructional time will also vary. However, having access to technology is paramount in every classroom and at every grade level.

Technology in the classroom helps children to become more actively engaged and encourages independent learning with the use of student-centered, project-based activities. From virtual math tools to collaborative class blogs, there are many ways for students to effectively engage in technology in the classroom.

Although technology plays an important role in the modern classroom, it is still important for educators to guide children, helping them use the technology in an effective, efficient, and responsible manner. Teaching children about cyber-bullying, copyright, plagiarism, and digital footprints will inevitably strengthen their ability to responsibly and safely conduct themselves online.

Educators also use technology for lesson planning, assessments, and evaluation. With a number of online programs available, educators are able to provide students, colleagues, administration, and parents with effective feedback and to develop and evaluate high-quality formative and summative assessments in an efficient manner.

By combining the use of technology along with teacher-centered instruction and traditional textbooks, educators will undoubtedly help to create a classroom with children who are actively engaged throughout the instructional day.

Visual and Oral Elements

Depending on home life and first language acquisition, children generally enter the primary years of school with a basic foundation of oral development as well as basic phonemic awareness. It is imperative to a young child's continued success in language development that educators provide students with language-rich lessons and activities throughout the instructional day.

Visual Instructional Techniques

Studies continue to show a strong correlation between language development and the use of visual aids. From the primary years of education through the post-secondary years, the use of visual aids as a way to enhance reading comprehension has proven to be very effective. In the primary grades, picture books provide students with visual cues that help them to decode unknown words and strengthen reading comprehension. Visual aids support and clarify meaning, helping to make the learning and reading process more enjoyable and more interactive. When educators engage the students in a **picture walk**, skimming through picture books prior to reading, children become more motivated to read. Even reluctant readers, struggling readers, and English language learners are more apt to pick up a picture book and attempt to read it from cover to cover, enjoying the graphics and using them as powerful clues to the text's overall meaning.

Graphic novels are also becoming a popular addition to classroom and school libraries. With a structural approach that is similar to comic books, graphic novels have a strong appeal to children in the middle school years, teen years, and beyond. The visual images within graphic novels help children to make immediate connections to a story's plot and help them to understand potentially more challenging information.

As a universal learning tool, visual aids help all learners to comprehend the meaning behind the words and strengthen their ability to retain information over a longer period of time.

Oral Instructional Techniques

When children are just learning to read, they benefit greatly from shared reading and oral reading experiences. Having a teacher or a classmate read a book aloud helps emergent readers connect their phonemic awareness skills to a growing understanding and application of print awareness. This will begin to form the foundation for more advanced reading skills in later years.

Oral reading also helps children strengthen their use of vocabulary and advances their vocabulary inventory. Educators and more advanced readers who model oral reading fluency—including rate, accuracy, and prosody—demonstrate to young readers that the process of reading is highly interactive and meaningful. Educators who spend significant time engaging in classroom discussions and asking and answering questions help children develop social interaction skills, listening comprehension skills, and oral communication skills.

When early and intensive instruction focuses on oral language development, educators set the groundwork for future reading success.

Oral and Visual Instructional Techniques

Multimedia presentations, such as PowerPoint or SlideShare, have been traditionally most effective at the higher education levels. However, as young children are more and more exposed to a world of technology, educators at the primary years are beginning to employ multimedia presentations in the classroom.

If carefully planned out, multimedia presentations can be used to enhance comprehension on virtually any subject. Using powerful graphic imagery that is directly relevant to the topic—coupled with effective textual language or audio—has been particularly effective in a growing number of classrooms.

Presenting students with the challenge of creating their own multimedia presentations can also be very rewarding for educators and students alike. Either independently, in pairs, or in groups, children take the learning process into their own hands with the opportunity to demonstrate the knowledge of a given subject by employing relevant written text and graphics.

Literary Text vs. Oral, Staged, or Filmed Version

Many of today's students are saturated with technology in their everyday lives. With the availability of iPads, iPods, personal computers, and smartphones, children as early as the primary grades are not only familiar with modern technology, but are becoming confident practitioners. Therefore, integrating technology in the classroom is a logical approach to helping children connect to the learning process and engage their interests.

With regard to English language arts instruction, technology can provide ample opportunities for educators to help strengthen students' critical thinking, oral communication, and reading comprehension skills. Since stories have always been used as a way of helping to explain the world and our place in it, they continue to be an integral part of any society's culture. The same story can be shared orally, in print, in film, or onstage, and each presentation provides similarities and differences with regard to the story's elements and to the audience's interpretation. By allowing children to compare and contrast various presentations of the same story, educators can increase students' motivation in English language arts.

Isolated scenes in films or documentaries can be used to begin a class discussion on a given topic. Children can openly discuss what version of the story they prefer and why. They can become detectives as they watch carefully for differences and similarities in the story's elements, such as setting, plot, and character traits. Educators who introduce a film or stage version of a literary work may wish to introduce the elements of lighting, dialogue, or special effects and begin a class discussion about how these elements, much like points of view, setting, and details in print, are critical to a film's structure.

If used strategically and with careful planning, the use of films, plays, and various technology-based story presentations can prove to be a very effective instructional strategy that strengthens students' understanding and appreciation of English language arts.

Multiple Literary Texts Addressing the Same Theme

Introducing children to similar themes in literature can increase motivation in even the most reluctant of readers. Consider the classic children's book, *Alice in Wonderland*, written in the 1800s. Children are introduced to a young girl who is bored with her life and discovers a secret rabbit hole that brings her on an exciting adventure in another world. The excitement quickly turns into danger, as she must work to escape the evil queen and find her way back to safety. Near the end of the book, readers discover that Alice was dreaming all along. In the novel, *Coraline*, written in 2002, the heroine, Coraline, feels neglected by her parents and discovers a secret door to a hidden world. Much like Alice, Coraline finds herself in peril and must try to outwit her evil "other" mother in order to return safely to her real parents.

Comparing two literary texts that address the same theme, whether it is human-versus-nature, human-versus-human, or rags-to-riches, can prove to be effective instructional techniques that prompt student engagement and strengthen interest in English language arts.

Multiple Informational Texts Addressing the Same Topic

When children begin to research topics for formal reports, presentations, or class discussions, it is important that they understand that information on a given topic comes in a variety of formats and is presented by many different points of view. Information is shared orally and is found in print and digital format, but not all information on a given topic will be the same. For instance, one text about the benefits of farming may completely contradict information found in another text. There are many reasons why contradictory information is found in two or more texts. Helping students consider the time period the text was written, the level of expertise of the author or authors, cultural points of view, and the author's purpose will help them strengthen their critical thinking skills, as well as allow them to develop their own interpretation and evaluation of the information.

It is critical that children begin to critique information found in print, online, or told orally and not just accept it at face value. These critical thinking skills will serve them well throughout their academic career and will play a fundamental role in their personal and professional lives.

Visual and Multimedia Elements in Texts

Graphic novels, comic books, fiction, folktales, myths, and poetry often include visual elements in the story. Whether in the form of drawings, photographs, sound, video, or animation, these visual elements work to strengthen the reader's understanding and interpretation of the author's message, help to set the story's tone, bring characters into perspective, and, possibly, provide the reader with alternative interpretations of the story's main idea.

Hyperlinks included in informational texts provide the reader with additional sources of information that strengthen the author's message. Informational texts also employ the use of graphs, charts, diagrams, and maps, which either work to compare and contrast information, demonstrate cause and effect, show a chronological timeline of events, or display trends and patterns.

Effective instructional approaches to literature incorporate how to interpret the various forms of visual and multimedia elements that exist within literary and informational texts. Modeling how to use visuals in various texts appropriately will undoubtedly strengthen students' reading comprehension and critical thinking skills.

Key Claims from Textual Evidence

The ability to identify significant claims made by the author and to support those claims with evidence found within the text is integral to the development of reading comprehension and critical thinking skills. Educators need to introduce key vocabulary words and phrases that authors use when stating and supporting claims. These vocabulary terms can be added to an ever-changing and expanding classroom word wall, incorporated into personal dictionaries, and captured on charts to further classroom discussions. Once children begin to identify key words and phrases as indicators of claims and claim evidence, they are ready to begin the more complex task of evaluating these claims.

When children can identify claims and show evidence that supports them, educators may wish to initiate a class discussion on whether or not these claims are valid. For instance, prompting a reader's background knowledge and personal experiences on the topic, examining the author's expertise on the subject, weighing any possible cultural or personal bias the author may have, and comparing/ contrasting the author's claims to claims made by other authors on the same subject will help children develop objectivity as they read.

Written Expression

Writing as a Recursive Process that Supports Self-Evaluation and Expression

Like with any complicated processes, writing development begins with the simplest form of indiscernible scribbles and progresses to fully formed words and, finally, to clearly written sentences and paragraphs. This is a complicated cognitive process that takes time and instruction to improve.

With very young students, emphasis can focus on simply making letters clear. After all, letters and word formation are the starting blocks of written language. The next phase in development can focus on actually creating words and making sure they are spelled correctly. When students are at the sentence development stage, grammar and linguistic rules become a priority. The foundations of the English language need to be firm for students to have good writing. When students have progressed to more advanced levels and are composing fully formed sentences with a specific purpose, it's time to incorporate content-related feedback.

Feedback at all levels of writing development is crucial; this is how students will learn to correct mistakes and strengthen growing skills. Instructor feedback must be clear while also being sensitive to the students' struggles or backgrounds. Differentiated instruction may be required to bolster students' writing skills. Feedback on the initial writing, or first draft, is key. The instructor should be able to assess any difficulties and then steer the student toward improving their writing in the revision stage. After revisions, instructors should examine how effective their feedback was in helping the writing improve overall.

Written expression refers to the ability of the writer to fluidly communicate meaning and purpose throughout the composition. Essentially, this refers not only to how clear the central focus of the piece is but how well the ideas surrounding the central focus are presented. If the writer can't successfully express the meaning and implications of the idea, the writing will not be strong.

Effective written expression utilizes detailed, clear communication. A writer doesn't need to unload elaborate diction throughout the paragraphs. Such an embellishment can be distracting to the reader, which actually defeats the principles behind effective writing. Sentences should be direct and emphasize language that, while engaging, remains simple enough for the audience to understand. This doesn't mean abstaining from using advanced words but rather keeping sentences direct and to the point. Students should avoid rambling line after line. Avoiding exaggerating language or overdramatic phrasing is also important. Not only can this confuse the reader, but it can also harm the writer's credibility.

A simple formula for effective writing is to introduce an idea, discuss it, and then make a conclusion. This applies for the written piece as a whole but must also be used within individual paragraphs. If a writer just introduces idea after idea with no substance, the reader is left with unsubstantiated claims. Without supporting evidence to understand the view, the reader is left with only opinion. With the implementation of facts and supporting details, this opinion is strengthened. Thus, the reasoning behind the central idea is clearly executed and can be considered seriously. This helps the writer achieve credibility.

Paragraph coherence is vital for effective written expression. Paragraph sequencing and information placement are essential to streamlining the entire piece. Evidence and supporting information should be used to transition from one section to another, up to the conclusion. This enables the information to be clearly expressed. The author should strive to write in a way that, as the piece progresses, the focus becomes clearer and more convincing. By the conclusion of the written piece, the author should also restate their thesis to solidify their views and reasoning.

Systematic, Explicit Methods to Teach the Steps of the Writing Process

An introduction to the writing process might begin with a discussion. Teachers can gauge students' knowledge about writing by asking them questions about the writing process, its steps, and its purpose. They may also ask about students' previous experiences with writing. It's important to emphasize that writing is a process, not something students complete once and move on from.

Before expecting students to write, teachers should model each step in the writing process. Based on a chosen topic, the teacher can brainstorm aloud, walking through their thought process and describing different methods for recording the results (for example, in a list, in an outline, or on a concept map). Students would then be given time to brainstorm about their own topics.

Next, the teacher may choose to share samples of drafts from previous students or ones they've completed themselves. Even better, they can model their thought process aloud in front of the class, writing a rough draft while the students watch.

Teachers can display anchor charts to remind students what to include (for example, beginning, middle, and end, and details) and what not to worry about in this step (for example, mistakes, neatness, structure).

The **revision step** includes changes like removing unnecessary information, adding helpful information, and moving text to improve flow. The teacher can point out the issues in the rough draft and make the appropriate edits, incorporating the use of a checklist or anchor chart if one is provided.

In the editing process, the teacher reviews the spelling, grammar, and punctuation of the students' writing. The **editing step** is a great time to catch any errors the students may have missed. This is a good time for a teacher-student conference to review the draft. Peer conferences are also an option. The teacher can act out a peer review conference with one student to show students what is expected from a peer review conference.

Before final submission, the teacher should share the final versions of the papers they've been working on as models, highlighting their strengths in how they meet the parameters of the assignment, especially compared to the rough drafts. Before publishing their final polished draft, students should read over their writing aloud and add necessary details (for example, a title and illustrations). Again, a checklist or anchor chart can be helpful.

Once all writing is complete, students can take turns sharing the final product in small groups or with the class. Peer feedback at this point can help guide future improvements in the next writing assignment.

The easiest way to guide the writing process is to give students time to work on it in class. This allows the teacher to check on students' progress and offer feedback as they go through the writing process. To promote improvement, teachers can make each part of the writing process (for example, rough draft, peer review conference) a part of the final grade for the assignment.

Strategies for Integrating Reading and Writing

Summarizing

Teaching students to summarize is another comprehension and analysis technique. They can complete rewriting exercises here as well. Students just need to do three things when they employ this technique. They should recall what they read, identify the main point of the texts, and exclude unnecessary information. Summarizing does not have to take place after students have finished reading texts; they can do it as they go along. Eventually, this type of summarizing will be second nature, and students will be able to assess the texts without stopping.

Teach students to summarize information. For example, you could ask students to take notes on the most important points in a text and then write a summary. Younger students do better with simple oral summaries, while older students can handle more complicated written work. Summarizing is a great way to improve comprehension. It also tests analysis skills, as students need to discern which points are important and which are just details.

<u>Annotation</u>
Teach your students to annotate texts by highlighting and making notes in the margins. For example, you might have students read a confusing passage, then annotate it by highlighting the most important pieces of information and defining difficult words. By annotating texts, students learn to recognize central points and research words or background information that they do not understand.

Teach your students to take notes. For students who are just learning to take notes, it may be helpful to practice reading a text as a class and making notes on the board. Teach your students useful skills like summarizing, picking out main points, and outlining arguments. For example, you could read a passage aloud and ask all the students to take notes. You could then have the class compare notes and write a collaborative summary of the text.

Have students apply metacognition to their comprehension by identifying the elements of a text that they cannot understand. For example, if a student says, "I don't understand this book," ask them to think about the specific aspects that confuse them and build a more detailed phrase like "I don't understand what happens in chapter four," or "I can't understand this word."

Digital Tools

Students and educators alike are living in a digital era. By incorporating technology into the classroom, educators can find ways to better connect with students, encourage students to become more actively engaged in the learning process, and embrace the many benefits of digital tools that enhance the learning and teaching experience.

Digital tools are an invaluable resource for the classroom. They can enhance the learning experience by providing new forms of engagement. This benefits both students and teachers. Apps, videos, websites, and games are just a few examples of digital tools that can provide unique educational content. These tools can help students work on collaboration and creativity. Digital tools can also improve accessibility in the classroom. Educational videos can aid visual learners, audiobooks can provide auditory learners with a new reading experience, and kinesthetic learners may learn new skills from building games. These are just a few examples of how digital tools may benefit different types of students.

When implementing digital tools, student engagement often sees great improvement. Maintaining student interest is a major key to effective learning. Teachers also benefit from digital tools in the learning space. They can record lectures for at-home learning, ease workloads by automating repetitive tasks such as grading, and streamline communication with students and their families. Overall, both students and teachers may benefit from the implementation of digital tools in the classroom. Technology is always advancing, and it is wise to take advantage of the benefits it offers.

Digital tools come in several forms, including images, video, animation, sound, and text, and they are used for a variety of functions. For the purpose of writing, digital tools can be used to further communicate a writer's point of view or even to publish a piece of writing. Digital tools in the classroom facilitate the learning process and prompt collaboration among students and teachers, as well as among the students themselves.

Communication

One of the most important elements of a successful classroom is communication. There are plenty of digital tools that can foster and encourage communication and help create an environment where students feel welcome and ready to learn. The Internet is a virtual highway of information that can be used to enhance both the learning and teaching experiences in the classroom. There are digital tools that allow children to interact and collaborate through strategic and critical thinking games, digital tools for messaging children, teachers, and parents, digital tools for creating visual effects, content sharing, feedback, grading, and so much more.

It is imperative, however, that educators thoroughly review sites before implementing their use in the classroom and that they further emphasize to children the importance of Internet safety, the impact of a digital footprint, and the concept of plagiarism. When used responsibly and effectively, digital tools actively work to engage children, teachers, and the parent community in the learning process both in and out of the classroom.

Websites like ClassDojo allow for instant and effective communication between teachers, students, and parents. It allows for a digital classroom points system, where teachers can click a button to give a student a point. Students can also take quizzes, participate in whole class online discussions, and keep track of their progress on their ClassDojo account.

Another great communication tool is Google Classroom. It's a comprehensive digital classroom where students can communicate with teachers instantly, view lessons and materials, and complete and submit assignments and assessments.

Remind is another communication tool that is commonly used in the classroom. It allows parents and students to sign up for classroom messages. Through Remind, the teacher can put out whole-class reminders and messages, message individual students or parents, and track assignments and upcoming tests.

The Seesaw app and website is also great for promoting communication between teachers, parents, and students. It allows for collaborative learning and showing off student work. It's a great way to encourage students to their best in hopes of having their work featured on Seesaw.

Writing

One of the fundamental parts of learning to write well is having your work reviewed. There are many online platforms where students can practice their writing skills and submit it for feedback. This includes both fiction and non-fiction writing. Hemingway Editor is a free website and app that will point out common errors in writing: spelling, grammar, run-on sentences, and confusing wording.

If a student is interested in getting feedback from other writers, Scribophile is an online workshop where students can submit their work for critique. This is useful for writers of all skill levels.

At the classroom level, resources like Microsoft Word and Google Drive make it easy for students to create, edit, and store their writing. They also spelling and grammar checks along with other writing tools that students can access as they revise their work.

Collaboration

There is a plethora of online platforms that encourage collaboration in the classroom. They allow students to share what they are learning with one another, work on group projects, and communicate virtually. Some platforms are utilitarian; others are designed for fun. A utilitarian option is Google Drive, which allows students to share documents, presentations, and more. A fun option is Kahoot, which students can use to create quiz games that an entire class can participate in. This kind of collaborative creation is one way to get students to practice their teamwork.

Reading

Publishing
In terms of publishing, students should use resources like Turnitin, Scribbr, and Grammarly to check for plagiarism or any major issues. While Turnitin only looks for plagiarism, other websites like Grammarly check for the overall tone, flow, and textual features (like grammar, spelling, etc).

Research Process
The following list depicts the steps relevant to the research process. Each step should be performed in chronological order, as they depend on each other for optimal work. For example, skipping the revise and edit step would result in a poorly written first draft.

- Step 1: Decide on a topic to research
- Step 2: Set the purpose of the research
- Step 3: Locate sources of information—print, digital, experts
- Step 4: Evaluate the sources
- Step 5: Summarize information and cite sources
- Step 6: Write draft
- Step 7: Revise and edit
- Step 8: Publish writing

Primary and Secondary Sources
Primary sources refer to first-hand accounts of events, a subject matter, an individual, or a time period. Primary sources also include original works of art. They can also be non-interpretive, factual pieces of information. Some examples include diaries, journals, letters, government records, maps, plays, novels, and songs.

Secondary sources refer to the analysis or interpretation of primary sources and are, therefore, usually considered more subjective than objective. In other words, researchers may discover contradictory information on the same subject from different secondary sources. Some examples include literary and film reviews, newspaper articles, and biographies.

Both primary and secondary sources of information are useful. They both offer invaluable insight that helps the writer learn more about the subject matter. However, researchers are cautioned to examine the information closely and to consider the time period as well as the cultural, political, and social climate in which accounts were given. Learning to distinguish between reliable sources of information and questionable accounts is paramount to a quality research report.

Reliable and Unreliable Sources
When conducting research, students must be able to distinguish between reliable and unreliable sources in order to develop a well-written research report. When choosing print sources, typically published works that have been edited and clearly identify the author or authors are considered credible sources. Peer-reviewed journals and research conducted by scholars are likewise considered to be credible sources of information.

When deciding on what Internet sources to use, it is also a sound practice for researchers to look closely at each website's universal resource locator, the *URL*. Generally speaking, websites with .edu, .gov, or .org as the Top Level Domain are considered reliable, but the researcher must still question any possible political or social bias. Personal blogs, tweets, personal websites, online forums, and any site that clearly demonstrates bias, strong opinions, or persuasive language are considered unreliable sources.

Paraphrasing and Plagiarizing

Paraphrasing: The restating of one's own words, text, passage, or any information that has already been heard, read, or researched

Plagiarizing: The copying of a text, passage, or any other information in print or digital format, and claiming the work as one's own

Credible Print and Digital Sources

Credible **print sources** are those that have been edited and published, reveal the author or authors, and clearly identify their expertise on the subject matter. Scholarly reviews are typically very reliable sources as they are written by experts in the field and, more often than not, have been evaluated by their respective peers. Credible **digital sources** may sometimes prove a little more difficult to discern, and researchers must employ due diligence to ensure the sources are reliable. Distinguishing between biased and unbiased websites, objective versus subjective information, as well as informative versus persuasive writing can prove confusing at times. By paying attention to a website's URL and carefully considering the language and tone applied to the writing, researchers should be able to evaluate the website's reliability.

Learning how to locate key information within sources requires a basic understanding of written structure. If the source of information is written well, there should be titles, subtitles, headings, and subheadings that researchers can use to zero in on key information. Additionally, informational texts often employ the use of an index and table of contents, which helps them locate specific information. Similarly, digital sources often employ titles, subtitles, headings, and subheadings, and they will generally offer a search box to look for specific information or key terms within the website.

Citing sources at the end of a research paper is critical to the overall quality of work. If sources are not cited or poorly cited, a researcher's work risks losing credibility. There are various accepted methods to use when citing information. The method used often depends on the preferences of the authority that has assigned the research. The most generally accepted methods for citing sources are MLA, APA, and Chicago style. Although each citation format is distinct in structure, order, and requirements, they all identify key information. Citation formats also ensure that published authors of given works receive full credit.

<u>Planning, Revising, and Editing</u>

Planning is the precursor to writing. This brainstorming stage is when writers consider their purpose and think of ideas that they can use in their writing. Graphic organizers are excellent tools to use during the planning stage. Graphic organizers can help students connect the writing purpose to supporting details, and they can help begin the process of structuring the writing piece. Brainstorming can be done independently, in partners, or as a whole-class activity.

As students begin writing their first draft of a writing piece, they need to continuously revise and edit their work. **Revisions** take place during and after the writing process. As students revise their writing, they are encouraged to frequently refer back to the planning stage. This helps ensure that they are staying focused and are remaining on topic. During the revising and editing stage, educators prompt students to reread their work several times and to focus on one aspect of their writing each time.

For example, the first review may be to examine the writing content, while the second review may focus on spelling, grammar, and punctuation. Another helpful strategy during this stage is to have students display the graphic organizers they used during the planning stage and read their work aloud to the class, in small groups, or with a partner to receive constructive feedback and to welcome other perspectives and ideas. Students are able to refer to the planning stage as the classmate reads and can make connections as to whether or not the writer has stayed on topic.

Developmental Stages of Writing	Description	Grade-Appropriate Continuum
Scribbling	Random marks, circles, and lines that may not resemble print, but represent ideas for the young writer	Praise the children's creativity and ask them to explain their work to you. Consider adding a sentence at the bottom of their work based on the children's ideas.
Letter-like symbols	Letter-like symbols start to randomly appear and may be mixed in with numbers and scribbles.	Praise the children's creativity and point to the letter-like symbols for discussion. Consider adding a sentence at the bottom of the work based on the children's ideas.
Strings of letters	Using strings of letters in a row, children are demonstrating the preliminary understanding of letter-to-sound relationships.	Praise the children's efforts in attempting to use letters to represent sounds. Ask the children to tell you the story or to read you the sentences and consider writing what they say at the bottom.
The emergence of beginning sounds	Children begin to use letters to represent actual words and may string the letters together in a row that can tell a story.	Praise the children's efforts in attempting to use letters to represent actual words. Help with spacing, building sound-letter correspondence, and expanding vocabulary.
Words represented by consonants	Children begin to leave spaces between words with a possible mixture of uppercase and lowercase letters.	Praise children's work as a prompt for further explanation of the story. Prompt children to use more details and to build more sentences.

Developmental Stages of Writing	Description	Grade-Appropriate Continuum
Initial, middle, final sounds	Children begin to write some basic sight words and familiar names, but all other words are spelled the way they sound.	Praise children's progress and continue to build vocabulary. Help children to organize writing with structure and sentence variety.
Transitional phase	Writing is beginning to approach conventional spelling.	Praise children's progress and model the use of effective wording by using specific vocabulary to expand ideas.
Standard spelling	Children begin to spell most words correctly, with a basic understanding that the spelling of many words is connected to the meaning.	Praise children's progress and challenge them to begin writing more complex sentences, expand ideas, and establish a clear purpose for writing.

Characteristics and Appropriate Instructional Methods for Teaching the Various Types of Writing

It is important to use appropriate instructional methods for teaching the various types of writing. Although general writing tips can be helpful, different writing types require different instructional methods. The types of writing include expository, persuasive, narrative, and descriptive.

Expository writing is meant to inform the reader about a concept. In this case, you would want to teach about the use of evidence in writing. Persuasive writing is meant to convince the reader of an argument. In this case, you could want to teach about how to present an opinion in writing. Narrative writing tells a story. In this case, you would want to teach about characters and plot. Descriptive writing presents the setting; it can also present imagery. In this case, you would want to teach about how to engage readers with metaphors and similes. These are just a few examples of how writing types differ and how instruction should vary accordingly.

Purpose, Key Components, and Subgenres of Writing
Effective writing, whether for the purpose of persuading, entertaining, or advancing a reader's knowledge, must be well planned and organized. In order to create a powerful piece of writing, authors must adhere to specific structural designs, apply a functional and logical order to their writing, and employ key elements.

The following chart outlines three types of writing and their respective purposes, the structural elements unique to each type of writing, and some examples of subgenres:

	Opinion/Persuasive	**Narrative**	**Informative**
Purpose	To persuade, influence, or prompt a call-to-action response	To entertain or to share a moral when writing fictional narratives To share factual information when writing nonfiction narratives	To convey information and advance a reader's knowledge of a given topic
Key components	Opening statement and point of view Well organized paragraphs with supportive evidence and/or examples Strong concluding statement that reinforces point of view	Fictional narratives: plot, characters, setting, point of view, tone Nonfictional Narratives: introductory paragraph Body: including details and descriptions of events and individuals Conclusion	Introduction Headings and Subheadings Body Conclusion Works Cited
Subgenres	Speeches, letters, reviews, advertisements, essays	Fictional narratives: folktales, fantasy, science-fiction, mystery, drama Nonfictional narratives: autobiographies, biographies, memoirs	How-to books, cookbooks, instructional manuals, textbooks

Informational/Expository

Expository or **informational writing** presents facts and information. Academic essays are one example of this type of writing. Due to its logical purpose, expository writing should be clear and linear. Writers should use strong evidence to back up their claims. Sources used should be scholarly and unbiased. However, just because expository writing is factual, it does not have to be boring. It is important to keep the writing engaging to capture readers' interest.

A proven way to teach informational and expository writing is by having students practice writing about a subject they choose. First, students should research and choose 2-3 sources about a subject they like. The teacher can set parameters on what categories students can choose from (animals, historical events, etc), provide a list of topics to choose from, or allow complete freedom of choice. After selections have been made and sources verified, the student should begin on the writing process, and the teacher may offer formative feedback as the student writes. At the time of writing, the teacher should display anchor charts on the format of informational essays (the first paragraph should be an introduction, followed by one or more body paragraphs, and finally a concluding paragraph).

Argument/Persuasive/Opinion

In the early elementary grades, students begin to write simple **opinion pieces**. Acting as a precursor to argumentative and persuasive writing, opinion pieces allow children to express how they feel on a certain subject based on preferences, express their likes and dislikes, and use personal knowledge, without relying too heavily on supporting evidence. Educators encourage children to write opinion pieces with the use of personal journals as well as reflective pieces, connecting personal experiences to various stories read.

Persuasive writing is used to convince readers of a particular opinion; writing should be informative and evidence based. However, unlike expository writing, it also aims to sway readers to believe in a particular position.

One example of persuasive writing would be an article on climate change that also presents a solution that the writer wants readers to support. This type of writing should have a strong thesis statement that lets readers know what the main idea is. It may also be important that the writing read as if it were speaking directly to the reader. This is one effective way to draw the reader in to what the author is saying. Students can practice persuasive writing by responding to a situation or question posed by the teacher. To encourage student participation, the teacher could make the assignment fun by asking students to write a persuasive essay on the next sport the class should play or next book the class should read.

Narrative

The goal of **narrative writing** is to tell a story, whether fictional or not. An example of fictional narrative writing would be a novel; autobiography is nonfictional narrative writing. Narrative writing is often the most personal and creative form of writing. There are multiple types of narrative writing, such as linear, non-linear, viewpoint, and descriptive. Narrative writing may include characters, plot, and setting. These elements help the writer to make the story imaginative and unique. Although narrative writing comes with a high degree of writer freedom, effective narrative writing requires just as much skill and practice as the other types of writing.

One way to have students practice narrative writing is to have them write an essay detailing the events of their summer or winter break. Display anchor charts reminding students of the necessary aspects of narrative writing (characters, plot, setting) and provide plenty of resources for independent spelling and grammar help (dictionaries, thesauruses, digital resources).

For fictional narrative writing, be sure to do a brief review on the structure of a story. First, the beginning sets the stage for the action, it's followed by a conflict or problem, then a sequence of events follow the initial conflict that bring rising tension or drama, the tension reaches a height at the climax of the story where readers should be "on the edge of their seats", and finally is followed by falling actions or events that happen after the climax that lead into the resolution and the ending of the story. Further enhance students' knowledge of stories by reading class novels and short stories regularly.

Spelling and Grammar

Methods to Connect the Teaching of Decoding and Encoding as Reciprocal Skills
Teaching of decoding and encoding should begin with linking sounds to letters and eventually combinations of letters. To decode a word, students must attribute sounds to letters and blend them together. To spell a word, they must break the word they've heard into individual sounds, remember the letter(s) and patterns that make those sounds, and write them down, which is much more challenging. Simultaneous explicit and systematic instruction in decoding and encoding positively affects students' abilities to read, write, and spell.

Teacher-led practice involves the teacher clearly articulating a sound (phoneme) before having students say the sound and then write the letter(s) that correspond with the sound. Once these skills have been solidified, students can begin segmenting the words they hear, identifying the phonemes, and writing the letter(s) that represent them. First, teachers teach explicitly through modeling, and then they walk students through active, guided practice before having students practice independently. Make practice engaging and multimodal (for example, by incorporating hand gestures and manipulable items).

Instruction should be systematic, starting with simple information and using lessons that sequentially build upon one another toward increasingly complex ideas. The curriculum should outline the progression of teaching letter combination patterns (phonemic awareness) and how they are used in reading and spelling rules. This incremental approach promotes mastery in one topic or skill before moving on to new topics and skills.

Approaches to Spelling Development

Spelling development systematically occurs in stages. Through each of these stages, multisensory strategies can be explicitly taught to help enhance a child's spelling development. Here are the spelling development stages as well as different strategies to help development in each of those stages:

Pre-phonetic stage: This stage begins an individual's spelling development, inclusive of key indicators such an incomplete understanding of the alphabetic principle and letter-sound correspondences. Students in this stage participate in **precommunicative writing**, characterized by the jumbling of abstract letter forms rather than a cohesive group of recognizable letters. These writing samples can be used as informal assessments to monitor students' understanding of the alphabetic principle and of letter-sound correspondences.

Pre-phonetic stage of spelling development

Semi phonetic stage: In this stage, students have an understanding that letters denote specific sounds. Though this understanding is there, the student may continue to struggle with letter recognition. In the students' writing, they may use individual letters in place of entire words (e.g., *U* for *you*). In other instances, they may omit multiple syllables within a word altogether. Writing in this stage is likely still incomprehensible. To aid in understanding the students' work, teachers can ask students to include drawings to supplement their writing samples.

Semiphonetic stage of writing

Phonetic stage: At this point, students will have mastered letter-sound correspondences and can spell most VC and CVC words. Although their physical representation of letters may be incorrect, phonetic spellers can write each letter of the alphabet. Due to their limited sight vocabulary, their spelling may be incorrect; however, these incorrectly spelled words are likely still phonetically accurate. Additionally, students are likely to use one letter to represent a digraph or letter blend (e.g., *f* for /ph/). Spelling instruction of common consonant patterns, short vowel sounds, and common affixes or rimes can begin during the phonetic stage. Word walls are beneficial during this stage as they provide visual groupings of words that share common consonant-vowel patterns or letter clusters. Students should be encouraged to contribute words to the wall. As a result, word walls promote strategic spelling, vocabulary development, common letter combinations, and common morphological units.

Phonetic stage of writing

Transitional stage: In this stage, the student is growing in their sight vocabulary and has a sustainable understanding of letter-sound correspondences. As a result, their spelling dependence on phonology decreases and instead, their dependence on visual representation and word structure increases. The student should be able to spell most conventionally spelled words but may still struggle with many irregular words. During this stage, instructors should differentiate spelling instruction. It is necessary that instruction be guided by data collected through informal observations and assessments so that lessons can be personalized, especially in the areas of sight word recognition, morphology, etymology, reading, and writing.

In this stage, students are also ready to begin learning about **homophones**; these are words that sound the same but have different spellings and meanings (e.g., *their* and *there*). Additionally, students should begin writing full sentences. Writing reinforces phonics, vocabulary, and correct spelling of words.

Transitional stage of spelling

Conventional/Correct stage: By this stage, students are comfortable with the basic rules of phonics and spell most words correctly. They can work with consonants, multiple vowel-consonant blends, homophones, digraphs, and irregular spellings. They should be able to recognize incorrectly spelled words. It is at the conventional stage that spelling instruction can begin to focus on content-specific vocabulary words and words with unusual spellings. Students should practice this content-specific language across a variety of activities and subjects when relevant. Students can keep track of words that they consistently spell incorrectly or find confusing in word banks so they can isolate and eventually eliminate their individualized errors.

Teaching the Structure of Written Language

When learning to speak, listen, read, or write in any language, students are tasked with multiple challenges. The study of the English language is no exception. The conventions of Standard English are complex and require comprehensive study and continual practice.

Rules of Grammar and Mechanics

Before educators teach reading or writing, they should themselves be masters of the language. They should know the conventions of grammar, punctuation, spelling, and structure of language to communicate clearly. They must also be able to interpret what students are saying to either affirm or revise it. Teachers are responsible for differentiating instruction so that students at all levels and aptitudes can succeed with language learning. Teachers need to be able to isolate gaps in skill sets and decide which skills need intervention in the classroom.

Syntax

Syntax is the way that words are ordered within a sentence and how the sentence flows grammatically. Syntax defines the grammatical rules necessary for sentence flow, like the fact that sentences need at least a subject and a verb.

A basic rule of syntax is that sentences usually follow the subject-verb-object order. For example, look at the sentence "Sally ate breakfast." Sally is the subject, ate is the verb, and breakfast is the object. The only way that this sentence makes sense is in the subject-verb-object order. Rewriting it like "Sally breakfast ate", or "Breakfast Sally ate", would make it not flow correctly or make sense.

Teachers need to have mastery of the conventions of English including:

- Nouns
- Collective Nouns
- Compound Subjects
- Pronouns
- Subjects, Objects, and Compounds
- Pronoun/Noun Agreement
- Indefinite Pronouns
- Choosing Pronouns
- Adjectives
- Compound Adjectives
- Verbs
- Infinitives
- Verb Tenses
- Participles
- Subject/Verb Agreement
- Active/Passive Voice
- Adverbs
- Double Negatives
- Comparisons
- Double Comparisons
- Prepositions
- Prepositional Phrases
- Conjunctions
- Interjections
- Articles
- Types of sentences
- Subjects and Predicates
- Clauses and Phrases
- Pronoun Reference Problems
- Misplaced Modifiers
- Dangling Participial Phrases
- Punctuation
- Periods
- Commas
- Semicolons and Colons
- Parentheses and Dashes
- Quotation Marks
- Apostrophes
- Hyphens
- Question Marks
- Exclamation Points
- Capitalization
- Spelling
- Noun Plurals
- Prefixes and Suffixes
- Spelling Hurdles
- Abbreviations
- Pronunciation
- Homonyms and other easy mix-ups

When teaching structure, grammar, and mechanics, it's important for teachers to remember a few key things. First, all the conventions of English (as listed above) should be taught explicitly through direct instruction. Teachers should not expect students to stumble upon the concepts through reading or other means.

One fun way to encourage student engagement is by turning the grammar skill or mechanic that students are learning about for the week into a scavenger hunt. For example, after a lesson on quotation marks, the teacher may have students bring written or photographic evidence of where they spot quotation marks in their daily activities. It's important to engage students in lessons in a variety of ways to increase their understanding and memorization of the concepts.

When it comes to writing, it's important to continually review and edit student work to display proper mechanics and grammar. For example, if a student continually begins sentences with a lowercase letter, it's important to correct their work with a capital letter instead and have a conversation with the student about the mechanic of capitalization and its use at the beginning of every sentence.

Parts of Speech

Words within the English language play very unique roles in the formation of coherent sentences. Each English word is categorized into a specific part of speech that carries a unique function. For instance, in order to create simple English language sentences, writers are required to incorporate a noun and a verb. However, when sentences become more complex, additional parts of speech are required.

The following chart outlines the parts of speech, along with a brief description of their function within an English sentence and concrete examples.

Part of Speech	Function	Examples
Noun	Identifies a person, place, or thing—can be concrete or abstract	Love, thought, man, woman, child, school, home, integrity, America
Pronoun	Replaces a noun	He, she, it, they
Verb	Depicts an action or state of being	Run, jump, fly, is, are
Adjective	Modifies nouns	Great idea, interesting thought, tall girl
Adverb	Modifies verbs, other adverbs, and adjectives	He has an *extremely* shy demeanor. She *quickly* ran away. They walked *very* clumsily together.
Preposition	Almost always combined with other key words in a sentence in order to indicate a time, location, or movement	*At* nine o'clock, *beside* the nightstand, *toward* the door
Conjunction	Connects words, clauses, or sentences, with related meaning	She *and* I have similar tastes in food. The teacher handed us the assignment, *but* we refused to accept it. The dogs ran and played, *while* the cats sat and stared.

Reading

Part of Speech	Function	Examples
Interjection	Brief exclamations that are added to sentences for emphasis or effect	*Wow!* I had no idea you could sing! "*Boo!*" she screamed, as she jumped out from behind the door.

Although an explicit approach to teaching the various parts of speech plays an integral role in the primary grades, it is equally as important that a child learns to recognize these parts of speech when reading and gradually learn to apply them to writing tasks. Being able to recognize and appropriately use various parts of speech demonstrates a growing command of the English language and its conventions.

Sentence Types

When children begin to connect letters to words and, gradually, words to sentences, those sentences are generally very simple, consisting of one subject and one verb. However, as children advance in their writing fluency, it is paramount to introduce more complex sentences.

Simple sentences are sentences that consist of one subject and one verb:

I run.

She eats.

They play.

At this stage, educators may prompt children to add some more detail to the simple sentences with adjectives or adverbs:

I run *quickly*.

She eats *very well*.

They play *together*.

Compound sentences contain two independent clauses connected by a conjunction:

I run, but she runs marathons.

I run is an **independent clause**. *She runs marathons* is another independent clause. Each clause could be a complete sentence that stands on its own. However, they are connected with the coordinating conjunction, *but*.

Complex sentences are structures in which two clauses exist, but one clause is **dependent** on the other—that is, it cannot form a sentence in its own right and requires the assistance of the independent clause in order for the sentence to be coherent. Here's an example:

Although he passed the exam, he remained very sad.

He remained very sad is an independent clause, but *although he passed the exam* is not, as it is dependent on the second part of the sentence in order for the sentence to be coherent.

Compound-complex sentences are structures that employ two or more independent clauses along with at least one dependent clause:

Though I preferred long distance running, I started speed walking, and I enjoyed it very much.

Though I preferred long-distance running is a dependent clause that relies on the independent clause *I started speed walking*. The second independent clause is *I enjoyed it very much*, making this sentence compound-complex.

Three Tiers of Vocabulary

Language is used for effective communication and can be thought of as a social tool. However, since communication is also used in educational and professional circles, language must be flexible enough to meet the challenges of each social structure.

Conversational language is the everyday language spoken at home, with family, and with friends. It is a relaxed form of communication that may carry regional dialects, slang, and even sayings that may only be known by those who are part of those intimate social circles.

Academic language refers to the understanding and application of key vocabulary terms in order to achieve academic success. From their introduction to formal education, students become acquainted with this language tier. It prompts higher-level thinking and challenges students to research, analyze, and push the boundaries of thought, belief, and imagination.

Domain-specific languages are now widely used to refer to computer-based languages—called DSLs—but they are also known as any language system that has been specifically designed to perform a task in a given domain. In domain-specific languages, people are able to communicate concepts unique to that particular domain, avoid redundancy, and stay focused and on target.

English Used in Stories, Dramas, or Poems

Register

Despite the fact that a standardized form of English is used in published academic and scientific language, several varieties of spoken and written English also exist. There are differences in how one speaks at home, with friends, to teachers, and to colleagues. In each social setting, a person's **register**—their level of formality—will likely change in order to appropriately address the audience. Written registers also vary, depending on a number of factors. For instance, when writing a research paper for professional purposes, formal language will be used, but when writing a letter to a friend, a person is more apt to employ a more casual register. The following statements indicate differences in register:

Call me back when you get this message.

I look forward to hearing back from you at your earliest convenience.

Although both statements express the writer's desire to further communicate with the receiver of the message, the degree of formality, the register, is strikingly different.

Dialect

A language also has several dialects, which are dependent on a great many factors. **Dialects** have specific grammatical rules and patterns that often differ from the standard rules of the language. For instance, within Britain, Canada, and the United States, there are several dialects of the English language. One need only travel from Newfoundland, in eastern Canada, to Louisiana, in the southern United States, to witness a striking difference in how the English language is spoken.

Written dialects and registers also exist. They vary, based on the type of written work, when it was created, where it was written, by whom it was written, for what purposes, and for what audience it was intended. Authors of dramas, stories, and poetry employ the use of dialect for a multitude of reasons. For instance, when authors wish to develop a clear picture of the setting and characters within a drama, dialect plays a significant role. Here are some examples of dialect:

"Bess, you is my woman now..."—from George Gershwin's opera, *Porgy and Bess*

"That ain't no matter."—from Mark Twain's novel, *Huckleberry Finn*

With the careful and skillful placement of written dialect, the author conveys the character's personality, situation, and social class.

Characteristics of Effective Writing

Writing Pieces for Specific Purposes

Aristotle's Rhetorical Triangle is perhaps the best visual representation to demonstrate the importance of effective writing. Three key areas require the writer's full attention and should be balanced accordingly throughout the writing process:

Ethos refers to the writer's credibility: What are the writer's qualifications regarding the subject of the writing? Is the author using an objective or subjective approach? Are the sources, evidence, and examples in the writing relevant and credible?

Pathos refers to the writer's ability to engage and connect with the intended audience: What details and imagery does the author use to ignite and excite the emotions, imagination, values, and beliefs of the audience?

Logos refers to the validity of the author's message: Is the author's message clearly discernible? Is it logical and well organized?

Each of these three areas are critical to the quality of the writing and require the author's full attention and consideration throughout the writing process, from the preliminary stages to the final published work. Writers are tasked with the responsibility of choosing appropriate language to connect with an audience and choosing a style that maintains interest, which helps the audience understand the writer's purpose and accept the writer's intent. Did the writer succeed, for instance, in entertaining, informing, or persuading the audience?

Evaluation of a Piece of Writing

Traditionally, evaluating a student's writing has been a one-sided affair performed by the educator at the end of the writing process. This is no longer the customary practice since research has clearly shown the importance of formative assessments, as well as the importance of including the students as welcomed and respected self-evaluators. However, no evaluation or assessment should take place unless the instructions given for a particular writing assignment have been made clear, and the students have received quality, comprehensive writing instruction, in general. Assuming these requirements have been met, assessment and evaluation can take on many forms.

Formative assessments help keep the students focused and on task, and they also help to drive instruction. For example, educators are able to determine a child's individual needs, as well as common errors made by many students in the class. During formative assessments, children receive constructive feedback, and educators focus on the individual needs of each student. Formative assessments may also require students to perform self-evaluation using a guided rubric, which helps advance writing skills and develop autonomy. Summative assessments are equally important and also come in many forms. Some summative assessments are curriculum-based to ensure the appropriate standards are being met. Others may be anecdotal, wherein educators write endnotes that highlight areas that require improvement, praise the student's effort and progress, and provide next-step instructions.

Regardless of the type of assessments used, it is critical to a student's continued success that each assessment be personal, meaningful, well understood, and constructive, providing a clear pathway for their continued advancement in the writing process.

Appropriate Revisions to Writing

Usage and mechanics are often mistakenly used as interchangeable terms in the educational field. In writing, **usage** refers to a student's ability to choose appropriate words that clearly express an idea, thought, or opinion, or accurately summarize information. Therefore, usage is a very important component of learning to be an effective writer. **Mechanics** involve the writer's ability to use capitalization, ending punctuation, apostrophes, and commas properly. For writing to be both coherent and fluent, mechanics play an important role. **Spelling** is a little less complicated to understand, as it refers to the student's ability to spell decodable and non-decodable words accurately. Learning how and when to correct errors in usage, mechanics, and spelling can be a source of frustration for educators, but it need not be. By creating a logical balance and manageable plan for correcting student writing, educators will help children to be more effective, lifelong writers. The key is balance.

Traditionally, English language educators have focused a great deal of evaluation and feedback on correcting mistakes in usage, mechanics, and spelling alone. Although it is widely accepted that these components are necessary in order to write fluent and coherent sentences, too much focus on correcting these areas—and not enough attention paid to the creative side of writing—may have a negative impact on the writing process.

Writing is a multi-step process in which a student must consider the message and the audience. Likewise, revisions should focus on specific areas. If revision requirements are too vague or all requirements are combined into one task, students can become confused and overwhelmed. Breaking up revisions into specific categories will help students to recognize, understand, and correct specific errors.

One revision task should focus solely on the conventions of the English language, including spelling, punctuation, and grammar. Another task should focus on language usage, wherein students consider the writing style chosen and evaluate whether or not this style is appropriate for delivering the intended message to the intended audience. The writing structure is another area of focus that allows the student to evaluate the introduction, body, and conclusion. Does the writing clearly introduce the topic, does the body gradually strengthen the writer's point of view with relevant and reliable sources and examples, and does the conclusion restate the writer's message in a concise and effective manner? Students should be actively involved in all revisions along with the educators in order for the revisions to make sense.

For example, instead of emphasizing or highlighting every spelling error, educators should ensure that their corrections reflect the task. In other words, if children are given a writing assignment that must incorporate their spelling words, they will undoubtedly expect the educator to correct and evaluate how well they spelled these key words. However, since the assignment also asked the children to use a creative approach to this writing assignment, educators would be doing students a disservice if they did not also offer praise and feedback on the children's writing creativity.

Developing a writing checklist with well-defined goals and sharing this checklist with the class helps educators keep the correction process clear and specific, and it provides children with the opportunity to self-correct and edit their work prior to submission. Using a standardized system of symbols that helps children focus on spelling, capitalization, or word choice is also an effective strategy. Displaying these symbols in a readily-accessible place in the classroom will allow them to self-correct and help their peers with the correction process.

For writing to be meaningful and for students to advance in their writing skills, educators should follow a balanced approach to correcting student work with frequent, timely, and appropriate feedback that reflects the task.

Clear and Coherent Writing

Coherent Writing

Coherent writing uses a logical order and consists of information that is both relevant to the topic and reliable. Coherent writing ensures that the language usage appropriately activates the audience's background knowledge and keeps the audience interested. For writing to be considered coherent, the author must also consider the structure and its relevance to the writing goal.

Writing Clarity

Although separate and distinct in definition, both coherent writing and writing clarity are interrelated and impact each other. For writing to be fully coherent, it must also be written clearly and for writing to be written clearly, it needs to be coherent. **Writing clarity** refers to the conventions of the English language. Has the author paid considerable attention to the spelling, grammar, and punctuation? For example, the misspelling of a word can confuse a reader and negatively impact writing clarity. The use of visual aids in the form of graphs, diagrams, maps, and charts can also greatly strengthen the writing clarity by allowing students to see examples of what they are reading.

Effectiveness of Writing Samples

The ultimate goal in every English language arts classroom is to advance students' ability to write coherently and effectively with relative ease. The process of writing begins in the very primary stages and continues throughout a student's academic career. With each passing year, students who receive effective writing instruction and constructive feedback will be able to practice and apply their writing skills to more complex writing assignments. To help students advance in their writing skills, evaluation and assessment of a student's writing should be ongoing and occur during and after instruction of each writing unit.

In order to evaluate the effectiveness of a student's writing, educators should continuously focus on formative and summative assessments that outline clear expectations for the student and the educator. **Formative assessments** allow both the student and the educator to monitor the student's writing progress with ongoing feedback, discussion, and guidance. For example, after formative assessments, educators may recognize that some students need further instruction on a given skill or would benefit from a modified writing assignment. **Summative assessments** should only be employed at the very end of an instructional unit and should be used to evaluate how well the student was able to apply specific writing skills to the assigned and completed task. Praising each student's writing progress and allowing time for one-to-one conferences are also valuable instructional techniques that build a student's confidence in the writing process.

The following are examples of assessment practices that help drive instruction and strengthen a student's understanding and application of writing skills for different types of writing.

Effective writing assessments:

- Rating scales and rubrics
- Student logs: student evaluation of writing exercises
- Small groups and peer evaluations
- POWER method: Plan, Organize, Write, Edit, Rewrite (self-assessment)
- Standardized and diagnostic assessments
- Formative assessments
- Summative assessments

Educators who give clear expectations at the beginning, throughout, and at the end of a writing task help students advance their writing skills and become more proficient writers across a number of disciplines and genres. Since there are different types of writing, and considering that writing occurs in all subjects and disciplines, all educators should plan and develop several opportunities for students to practice various types of writing. For example, depending on the students' age and grade level, short, creative, daily writing exercises at the beginning or end of class can be used as an effective opening or closing routine. One day, students can practice narrative writing and the next, persuasive. Teachers can offer an author's chair in which children can read excerpts of their informative, persuasive, or narrative writing, and answer questions from peers relevant to their writing.

Dedicating time to the writing process—with a variety of writing exercises and assignments that occur in every discipline—is paramount to a child's writing acquisition. Effective instructional and assessment practices help foster an appreciation of writing that will continue throughout a student's lifetime.

Practice Quiz

1. Which of these descriptions would give the most detailed and objective support for the claim that drinking and driving is unsafe?
    a. A dramatized television commercial reenacting a fatal drinking and driving accident, including heart-wrenching testimonials from loved ones
    b. The Department of Transportation's press release noting the additional drinking and driving special patrol units that will be on the road during the holiday season
    c. Congressional written testimony on the number of drinking and driving incidents across the country and their relationship to underage drinking statistics, according to experts
    d. A highway bulletin warning drivers of penalties associated with drinking and driving

2. What are the three interconnected indicators of reading fluency?
    a. Phonetics, word morphology, and listening comprehension
    b. Accuracy, rate, and prosody
    c. Syntax, semantics, and vocabulary
    d. Word exposure, phonetics, and decodable skills

3. A teacher needs to assess students' accuracy in reading grade-appropriate, high frequency, and irregular sight words. Which of the following strategies would be most appropriate for this purpose?
    a. The teacher gives students a list of words to study for a spelling test that will be administered the following week.
    b. The teacher allows students to bring their favorite books from home and has them read their selected text aloud independently.
    c. The teacher administers the Stanford structural analysis assessment to determine students' rote memory and application of morphemes contained within the words.
    d. The teacher records how many words each student reads correctly when reading aloud a list of a teacher-selected, grade-appropriate words.

4. Which of the following sentences correctly uses a hyphen?
    a. Last-year, many of the players felt unsure of the coach's methods.
    b. Some of the furniture she selected seemed a bit over - the - top for the space.
    c. Henry is a beagle-mix and is ready for adoption this weekend.
    d. Geena works to maintain a good relationship with her ex-husband to the benefit of their children.

5. How are typographic features useful when teaching reading comprehension?
    a. Typographic features are graphics used to illustrate the story and help students visualize the text.
    b. Typographic features give the answers in boldfaced print.
    c. Typographic features are not helpful when teaching reading comprehension and should not be used.
    d. Typographic features such as boldface, italics, and subheadings can be used to highlight important vocabulary or content or indicate changes in topics.

See answers on the next page.

Answer Explanations

1. C: The answer we seek has both the most detailed and objective information; thus, Choice C is the correct answer. The number of incidents and their relationship to a possible cause are both detailed and objective information. Choice A describing a television commercial with a dramatized reenactment is not particularly detailed. Choice B, a notice to the public informing them of additional drinking and driving units on patrol, is not detailed and objective information. Choice D, a highway bulletin, does not present the type of information required.

2. B: Key indicators of reading fluency include accuracy, rate, and prosody. Phonetics and decodable skills aid fluency. Syntax, semantics, word morphology, listening comprehension, and word exposure aid vocabulary development.

3. D: Accuracy is measured via the percentage of words that are read correctly with in a given text. Word-reading accuracy is often measured by counting the number of errors that occur per 100 words of oral reading. This information is used to select the appropriate level of text for an individual.

4. D: Choice D correctly places a hyphen after the prefix *ex* to join it to the word *husband*. Many words that begin with the prefixes *great*, *trans*, *ex*, *all*, and *self* require a hyphen. Choices A and C place hyphens in words where they are not needed. *Beagle mix* would only require a hyphen if coming before the word *Henry*, since it would be serving as a compound adjective in that instance. Choice B contains hyphens that are in the correct place but are formatted incorrectly since they include spaces between the hyphens and the surrounding words.

5. D: Typographic features that help students locate key ideas or understand the structure of a piece of text are important when teaching reading comprehension.

Mathematics

Numbers and Operations

Place Value System

Base-10 Numerals, Number Names, and Expanded Form

Numbers used in everyday life are constituted in a base-10 system. Each digit in a number, depending on its location, represents some multiple of 10, or quotient of 10 when dealing with decimals. Each digit to the left of the decimal point represents a higher multiple of 10. Each digit to the right of the decimal point represents a quotient of a higher multiple of 10 for the divisor. For example, consider the number 7,631.42. The digit one represents simply the number one. The digit 3 represents 3×10. The digit 6 represents $6 \times 10 \times 10$ (or 6×100). The digit 7 represents $7 \times 10 \times 10 \times 10$ (or 7×1000). The digit 4 represents $4 \div 10$. The digit 2 represents $(2 \div 10) \div 10$, or $2 \div (10 \times 10)$ or $2 \div 100$.

A number is written in **expanded form** by expressing it as the sum of the value of each of its digits. The expanded form in the example above, which is written with the highest value first down to the lowest value, is expressed as:

$$7{,}000 + 600 + 30 + 1 + 0.4 + .02$$

When verbally expressing a number, the **integer** part of the number (the numbers to the left of the decimal point) resembles the expanded form without the addition between values. In the above example, the numbers read "seven thousand six hundred thirty-one." When verbally expressing the decimal portion of a number, the number is read as a whole number, followed by the place value of the furthest digit (non-zero) to the right. In the above example, 0.42 is read "forty-two hundredths." Reading the number 7,631.42 in its entirety is expressed as "seven thousand six hundred thirty-one and forty-two hundredths." The word *and* is used between the integer and decimal parts of the number.

Composing and Decomposing Multi-Digit Numbers

Composing and decomposing numbers aids in conceptualizing what each digit of a multi-digit number represents. The standard, or typical, form in which numbers are written consists of a series of digits representing a given value based on their place value. Consider the number 592.7. This number is composed of 5 hundreds, 9 tens, 2 ones, and 7 tenths.

Composing a number requires adding the given numbers for each place value and writing the numbers in standard form. For example, composing 4 thousands, 5 hundreds, 2 tens, and 8 ones consists of adding as follows: $4{,}000 + 500 + 20 + 8$, to produce 4,528 (standard form).

Decomposing a number requires taking a number written in standard form and breaking it apart into the sum of each place value. For example, the number 83.17 is decomposed by breaking it into the sum of 4 values (for each of the 4 digits): 8 tens, 3 ones, 1 tenth, and 7 hundredths. The decomposed or "expanded" form of 83.17 is:

$$80 + 3 + 0.1 + 0.07$$

Place Value of a Given Digit

The decimal system consists of only ten different digits, 0 to 9, and is used to represent an infinite number of values. The place value system makes this infinite number of values possible. The position in which a digit is written corresponds to a given value. Starting from the decimal point (which is implied, if not physically present), each subsequent place value to the left represents a value greater than the one before it. Conversely, starting from the decimal point, each subsequent place value to the right represents a value less than the one before it.

The names for the place values to the left of the decimal point are as follows:

...	Billions	Hundred-Millions	Ten-Millions	Millions	Hundred-Thousands	Ten-Thousands	Thousands	Hundreds	Tens	Ones

*Note that this table can be extended infinitely further to the left.

The names for the place values to the right of the decimal point are as follows:

Decimal Point (.)	Tenths	Hundredths	Thousandths	Ten-Thousandths	...

*Note that this table can be extended infinitely further to the right.

When given a multi-digit number, the value of each digit depends on its place value. Consider the number 682,174.953. Referring to the chart above, it can be determined that the digit 8 is in the ten-thousands place. It is in the fifth place to the left of the decimal point. Its value is 8 ten-thousands or 80,000. The digit 5 is two places to the right of the decimal point. Therefore, the digit 5 is in the hundredths place. Its value is 5 hundredths or $\frac{5}{100}$ (equivalent to .05).

Value of Digits

In accordance with the base-10 system, the value of a digit increases by a factor of ten each place it moves to the left. For example, consider the number 7. Moving the digit one place to the left (70) increases its value by a factor of 10 ($7 \times 10 = 70$). Moving the digit two places to the left (700) increases its value by a factor of 10 twice ($7 \times 10 \times 10 = 700$). Moving the digit three places to the left (7,000) increases its value by a factor of 10 three times ($7 \times 10 \times 10 \times 10 = 7,000$), and so on.

Conversely, the value of a digit decreases by a factor of ten each place it moves to the right. (Note that multiplying by $\frac{1}{10}$ is equivalent to dividing by 10). For example, consider the number 40. Moving the digit one place to the right (4) decreases its value by a factor of 10 ($40 \div 10 = 4$). Moving the digit two places to the right (0.4), decreases its value by a factor of 10 twice ($40 \div 10 \div 10 = 0.4$) or ($40 \times \frac{1}{10} \times \frac{1}{10} = 0.4$). Moving the digit three places to the right (0.04) decreases its value by a factor of 10 three times ($40 \div 10 \div 10 \div 10 = 0.04$) or ($40 \times \frac{1}{10} \times \frac{1}{10} \times \frac{1}{10} = 0.04$), and so on.

Exponents to Denote Powers of 10

The value of a given digit of a number in the base-10 system can be expressed utilizing powers of 10. A **power of 10** refers to 10 raised to a given exponent such as 10^0, 10^1, 10^2, 10^3, etc. For the number 10^3, 10 is the base and 3 is the exponent. A base raised by an exponent represents how many times the base is multiplied by itself. Therefore, $10^1 = 10$, $10^2 = 10 \times 10 = 100$, $10^3 = 10 \times 10 \times 10 = 1,000$, $10^4 = 10 \times 10 \times 10 \times 10 = 10,000$, etc. Any base with a zero-exponent equals one.

Powers of 10 are utilized to decompose a multi-digit number without writing all the zeroes. Consider the number 872,349. This number is decomposed to $800,000 + 70,000 + 2,000 + 300 + 40 + 9$. When utilizing powers of 10, the number 872,349 is decomposed to:

$$(8 \times 10^5) + (7 \times 10^4) + (2 \times 10^3) + (3 \times 10^2) + (4 \times 10^1) + (9 \times 10^0)$$

The power of 10 by which the digit is multiplied corresponds to the number of zeroes following the digit when expressing its value in standard form. For example, 7×10^4 is equivalent to 70,000 or 7 followed by four zeros.

Rounding Multi-Digit Numbers

Rounding numbers changes the given number to a simpler and less accurate number than the exact given number. Rounding allows for easier calculations which estimate the results of using the exact given number. The accuracy of the estimate and ease of use depends on the place value to which the number is rounded. Rounding numbers consists of:

- Determining what place value the number is being rounded to
- Examining the digit to the right of the desired place value to decide whether to round up or keep the digit
- Replacing all digits to the right of the desired place value with zeros

To round 746,311 to the nearest ten thousand, the digit in the ten-thousands place should be located first. In this case, this digit is 4 (74<u>6</u>,311). Then, the digit to its right is examined. If this digit is 5 or greater, the number will be rounded up by increasing the digit in the desired place by one. If the digit to the right of the place value being rounded is 4 or less, the number will be kept the same. For the given example, the digit being examined is a 6, which means that the number will be rounded up by increasing the digit to the left by one. Therefore, the digit 4 is changed to a 5. Finally, to write the rounded number, any digits to the left of the place value being rounded remain the same and any to its right are replaced with zeros. For the given example, rounding 746,311 to the nearest ten thousand will produce 750,000.

To round 746,311 to the nearest hundred, the digit to the right of the three in the hundreds place is examined to determine whether to round up or keep the same number. In this case, that digit is a one, so the number will be kept the same and any digits to its right will be replaced with zeros. The resulting rounded number is 746,300.

Rounding place values to the right of the decimal follows the same procedure, but digits being replaced by zeros can simply be dropped. To round 3.752891 to the nearest thousandth, the desired place value is located (3.75<u>2</u>891) and the digit to the right is examined. In this case, the digit 8 indicates that the number will be rounded up, and the 2 in the thousandths place will increase to a 3. Rounding up and replacing the digits to the right of the thousandths place produces 3.753000 which is equivalent to 3.753. Therefore, the zeros are not necessary, and the rounded number should be written as 3.753.

When rounding up, if the digit to be increased is a 9, the digit to its left is increased by 1 and the digit in the desired place value is changed to a zero. For example, the number 1,598 rounded to the nearest ten is 1,600. Another example shows the number 43.72961 rounded to the nearest thousandth is 43.730 or 43.73.

Understanding Operations

Solving Multistep Mathematical and Real-World Problems
Problem Situations for Operations
Addition and subtraction are **inverse operations**. Adding a number and then subtracting the same number will cancel each other out, resulting in the original number, and vice versa. For example, $8 + 7 - 7 = 8$ and $137 - 100 + 100 = 137$. Similarly, multiplication and division are inverse operations. Therefore, multiplying by a number and then dividing by the same number results in the original number, and vice versa. For example, $8 \times 2 \div 2 = 8$ and $12 \div 4 \times 4 = 12$. Inverse operations are used to work backwards to solve problems. In the case that 7 and a number add to 18, the inverse operation of subtraction is used to find the unknown value ($18 - 7 = 11$). If a school's entire 4th grade was divided evenly into 3 classes each with 22 students, the inverse operation of multiplication is used to determine the total students in the grade ($22 \times 3 = 66$). Additional scenarios involving inverse operations are included in the tables below.

Mathematics

There are a variety of real-world situations in which one or more of the operators is used to solve a problem. The tables below display the most common scenarios.

Addition & Subtraction

	Unknown Result	Unknown Change	Unknown Start
Adding to	5 students were in class. 4 more students arrived. How many students are in class? $5 + 4 = ?$	8 students were in class. More students arrived late. There are now 18 students in class. How many students arrived late? $8 + ? = 18$ Solved by inverse operations $18 - 8 = ?$	Some students were in class early. 11 more students arrived. There are now 17 students in class. How many students were in class early? $? + 11 = 17$ Solved by inverse operations $17 - 11 = ?$
Taking from	15 students were in class. 5 students left class. How many students are in class now? $15 - 5 = ?$	12 students were in class. Some students left class. There are now 8 students in class. How many students left class? $12 - ? = 8$ Solved by inverse operations $8 + ? = 12 \rightarrow 12 - 8 = ?$	Some students were in class. 3 students left class. Then there were 13 students in class. How many students were in class before? $? - 3 = 13$ Solved by inverse operations $13 + 3 = ?$

	Unknown Total	Unknown Addends (Both)	Unknown Addends (One)
Putting together/ taking apart	The homework assignment is 10 addition problems and 8 subtraction problems. How many problems are in the homework assignment? $10 + 8 = ?$	Bobby has $9. How much can Bobby spend on candy and how much can Bobby spend on toys? $9 = ? + ?$	Bobby has 12 pairs of pants. 5 pairs of pants are shorts, and the rest are long. How many pairs of long pants does he have? $12 = 5 + ?$ Solved by inverse operations $12 - 5 = ?$

	Unknown Difference	Unknown Larger Value	Unknown Smaller Value
Comparing	Bobby has 5 toys. Tommy has 8 toys. How many more toys does Tommy have than Bobby? $5 + ? = 8$ Solved by inverse operations $8 - 5 = ?$ Bobby has $6. Tommy has $10. How many fewer dollars does Bobby have than Tommy? $10 - 6 = ?$	Tommy has 2 more toys than Bobby. Bobby has 4 toys. How many toys does Tommy have? $2 + 4 = ?$ Bobby has 3 fewer dollars than Tommy. Bobby has $8. How many dollars does Tommy have? $? - 3 = 8$ Solved by inverse operations $8 + 3 = ?$	Tommy has 6 more toys than Bobby. Tommy has 10 toys. How many toys does Bobby have? $? + 6 = 10$ Solved by inverse operations $10 - 6 = ?$ Bobby has $5 less than Tommy. Tommy has $9. How many dollars does Bobby have? $9 - 5 = ?$

Multiplication and Division

	Unknown Product	Unknown Group Size	Unknown Number of Groups
Equal groups	There are 5 students, and each student has 4 pieces of candy. How many pieces of candy are there in all? $5 \times 4 = ?$	14 pieces of candy are shared equally by 7 students. How many pieces of candy does each student have? $7 \times ? = 14$ Solved by inverse operations $14 \div 7 = ?$	If 18 pieces of candy are to be given out 3 to each student, how many students will get candy? $? \times 3 = 18$ Solved by inverse operations $18 \div 3 = ?$

	Unknown Product	Unknown Factor	Unknown Factor
Arrays	There are 5 rows of students with 3 students in each row. How many students are there? $5 \times 3 = ?$	If 16 students are arranged into 4 equal rows, how many students will be in each row? $4 \times ? = 16$ Solved by inverse operations $16 \div 4 = ?$	If 24 students are arranged into an array with 6 columns, how many rows are there? $? \times 6 = 24$ Solved by inverse operations $24 \div 6 = ?$

	Larger Unknown	Smaller Unknown	Multiplier Unknown
Comparing	A small popcorn costs $1.50. A large popcorn costs 3 times as much as a small popcorn. How much does a large popcorn cost? $1.50 \times 3 = ?$	A large soda costs $6 and that is 2 times as much as a small soda costs. How much does a small soda cost? $2 \times ? = 6$ Solved by inverse operations $6 \div 2 = ?$	A large pretzel costs $3 and a small pretzel costs $2. How many times as much does the large pretzel cost as the small pretzel? $? \times 2 = 3$ Solved by inverse operations $3 \div 2 = ?$

Mathematics

Remainders in Division Problems

If a given total cannot be divided evenly into a given number of groups, the amount left over is the **remainder**. Consider the following scenario: 32 textbooks must be packed into boxes for storage. Each box holds 6 textbooks. How many boxes are needed? To determine the answer, 32 is divided by 6, resulting in 5 with a remainder of 2. A remainder may be interpreted three ways:

- Add 1 to the quotient
  How many boxes will be needed? Six boxes will be needed because five will not be enough.

- Use only the quotient
  How many boxes will be full? Five boxes will be full.

- Use only the remainder
  If you only have 5 boxes, how many books will not fit? Two books will not fit.

Strategies and Algorithms to Perform Operations on Rational Numbers

A rational number is any number that can be written in the form of a ratio or fraction. Integers can be written as fractions with a denominator of 1 ($5 = \frac{5}{1}$; $-342 = \frac{-342}{1}$; etc.). Decimals that terminate and/or repeat can also be written as fractions ($47 = \frac{47}{100}$; $.\overline{33} = \frac{1}{3}$). For more on converting decimals to fractions, see the section *Converting Between Fractions, Decimals, and Percent*.

When adding or subtracting fractions, the numbers must have the same denominators. In these cases, numerators are added or subtracted, and denominators are kept the same. For example, $\frac{2}{7} + \frac{3}{7} = \frac{5}{7}$ and $\frac{4}{5} - \frac{3}{5} = \frac{1}{5}$. If the fractions to be added or subtracted do not have the same denominator, a common denominator must be found. This is accomplished by changing one or both fractions to a different but equivalent fraction. Consider the example $\frac{1}{6} + \frac{4}{9}$. First, a common denominator must be found. One method is to find the least common multiple (LCM) of the denominators 6 and 9. This is the lowest number that both 6 and 9 will divide into evenly. In this case the LCM is 18. Both fractions should be changed to equivalent fractions with a denominator of 18.

To obtain the numerator of the new fraction, the old numerator is multiplied by the same number by which the old denominator is multiplied. For the fraction $\frac{1}{6}$, 6 multiplied by 3 will produce a denominator of 18. Therefore, the numerator is multiplied by 3 to produce the new numerator $\left(\frac{1 \times 3}{6 \times 3} = \frac{3}{18}\right)$. For the fraction $\frac{4}{9}$, multiplying both the numerator and denominator by 2 produces $\frac{8}{18}$. Since the two new fractions have common denominators, they can be added:

$$\frac{3}{18} + \frac{8}{18} = \frac{11}{18}$$

When multiplying or dividing rational numbers, these numbers may be converted to fractions and multiplied or divided accordingly. When multiplying fractions, all numerators are multiplied by each other and all denominators are multiplied by each other. For example,

$$\frac{1}{3} \times \frac{6}{5} = \frac{1 \times 6}{3 \times 5} = \frac{6}{15}$$

and

$$\frac{-1}{2} \times \frac{3}{1} \times \frac{11}{100} = \frac{-1 \times 3 \times 11}{2 \times 1 \times 100} = \frac{-33}{200}$$

When dividing fractions, the problem is converted by multiplying by the reciprocal of the divisor. This is done by changing division to multiplication and "flipping" the second fraction, or divisor. For example, $\frac{1}{2} \div \frac{3}{5} \rightarrow \frac{1}{2} \times \frac{5}{3}$ and $\frac{5}{1} \div \frac{1}{3} \rightarrow \frac{5}{1} \times \frac{3}{1}$. To complete the problem, the rules for multiplying fractions should be followed.

Note that when adding, subtracting, multiplying, and dividing mixed numbers (ex. $4\frac{1}{2}$), it is easiest to convert these to improper fractions (larger numerator than denominator). To do so, the denominator is kept the same. To obtain the numerator, the whole number is multiplied by the denominator and added to the numerator. For example, $4\frac{1}{2} = \frac{9}{2}$ and $7\frac{2}{3} = \frac{23}{3}$. Also, note that answers involving fractions should be converted to the simplest form.

Rational Numbers and Their Operations
Irregular Products and Quotients
The following shows examples where multiplication does not result in a product greater than both factors, and where division does not result in a quotient smaller than the dividend.

If multiplying numbers where one or more has a value less than one, the product will not be greater than both factors. For example, $6 \times \frac{1}{2} = 3$ and $0.75 \times 0.2 = .15$. When dividing by a number less than one, the resulting quotient will be greater than the dividend. For example, $8 \div \frac{1}{2} = 16$, because division turns into a multiplication problem:

$$8 \div \frac{1}{2} \rightarrow 8 \times \frac{2}{1}$$

Another example is $0.5 \div 0.2$, which results in 2.5. The problem can be stated by asking how many times 0.2 will go into 0.5. The number being divided is larger than the number that goes into it, so the result will be a number larger than both factors.

Composing and Decomposing Fractions

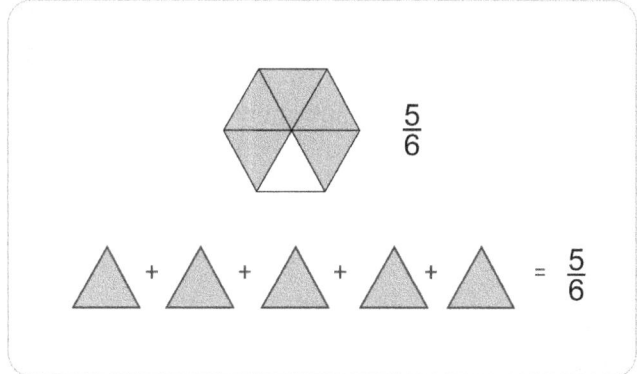

Fractions can be broken apart into sums of fractions with the same denominator. For example, the fraction $\frac{5}{6}$ can be decomposed into sums of fractions with all denominators equal to 6 and the numerators adding to 5. The fraction $\frac{5}{6}$ is decomposed as: $\frac{3}{6} + \frac{2}{6}$; or $\frac{2}{6} + \frac{2}{6} + \frac{1}{6}$; or $\frac{3}{6} + \frac{1}{6} + \frac{1}{6}$; or $\frac{1}{6} + \frac{1}{6} + \frac{1}{6} + \frac{2}{6}$; or:

$$\frac{1}{6} + \frac{1}{6} + \frac{1}{6} + \frac{1}{6} + \frac{1}{6}$$

A **unit fraction** is a fraction in which the numerator is 1. If decomposing a fraction into unit fractions, the sum will consist of a unit fraction added the number of times equal to the numerator. For example, $\frac{3}{4} = \frac{1}{4} + \frac{1}{4} + \frac{1}{4}$ (unit fractions $\frac{1}{4}$ added 3 times). **Composing fractions** is simply the opposite of decomposing. It is the process of adding fractions with the same denominators to produce a single fraction. For example,

$$\frac{3}{7} + \frac{2}{7} = \frac{5}{7}$$

and

$$\frac{1}{5} + \frac{1}{5} + \frac{1}{5} = \frac{3}{5}$$

Decrease in Value of a Unit Fraction

A unit fraction is one in which the numerator is 1 ($\frac{1}{2}, \frac{1}{3}, \frac{1}{8}, \frac{1}{20}$, etc.). The **denominator** indicates the number of *equal pieces* that the whole is divided into. The greater the number of pieces, the smaller each piece will be. Therefore, the greater the denominator of a unit fraction, the smaller it is in value. Unit fractions can also be compared by converting them to decimals. For example, $\frac{1}{2} = 0.5, \frac{1}{3} = 0.\overline{3}, \frac{1}{8} = 0.125, \frac{1}{20} = 0.05$, etc.

Use of the Same Whole When Comparing Fractions

Fractions all represent parts of the same whole. Fractions may have different denominators, but they represent parts of the same one whole, like a pizza. For example, the fractions $\frac{5}{7}$ and $\frac{2}{3}$ can be difficult to compare because they have different denominators. The first fraction may represent a whole divided into seven parts, where five parts are used. The second fraction represents the same whole divided into three parts, where two are used. It may be helpful to convert one or more of the fractions so that they have common denominators for converting to equivalent fractions by finding the LCM of the denominator. Comparing is much easier if fractions are converted to the equivalent fractions of $\frac{15}{21}$ and $\frac{14}{21}$. These fractions show a whole divided into 21 parts, where the numerators can be compared because the denominators are the same.

Order of Operations

When reviewing calculations consisting of more than one operation, the order in which the operations are performed affects the resulting answer. Consider 5 × 2 + 7. Performing multiplication then addition results in an answer of 17 (5 × 2 = 10; 10 + 7 = 17). However, if the problem is written 5 × (2 + 7), the order of operations dictates that the operation inside the parentheses must be performed first. The resulting answer is 45:

$$2 + 7 = 9, \text{ so } 5 \times 9 = 45$$

The order in which operations should be performed is remembered using the acronym **PEMDAS**. PEMDAS stands for parentheses, exponents, multiplication/division, and addition/subtraction. Multiplication and division are performed in the same step, working from left to right with whichever comes first. Addition and subtraction are performed in the same step, working from left to right with whichever comes first.

Consider the following example: 8 ÷ 4 + 8(7 − 7). Performing the operation inside the parentheses produces 8 ÷ 4 + 8(0) or 8 ÷ 4 + 8 × 0. There are no exponents, so multiplication and division are performed next from left to right resulting in: 2 + 8 × 0, then 2 + 0. Finally, addition and subtraction are performed to obtain an answer of 2. Now consider the following example: $6x3 + 3^2 − 6$. Parentheses are not applicable. Exponents are evaluated first, 6 × 3 + 9 − 6. Then multiplication/division forms 18 + 9 − 6. At last, addition/subtraction leads to the final answer of 21.

Properties of Operations

Properties of operations exist that make calculations easier and solve problems for missing values. The following table summarizes commonly used properties of real numbers.

Property	Addition	Multiplication
Commutative	$a + b = b + a$	$a \times b = b \times a$
Associative	$(a + b) + c = a + (b + c)$	$(a \times b) \times c = a \times (b \times c)$
Identity	$a + 0 = a; 0 + a = a$	$a \times 1 = a; 1 \times a = a$
Inverse	$a + (-a) = 0$	$a \times \frac{1}{a} = 1; a \neq 0$
Distributive	$a(b + c) = ab + ac$	

The **commutative property of addition** states that the order in which numbers are added does not change the sum. Similarly, the commutative property of multiplication states that the order in which numbers are multiplied does not change the product. The **associative property of addition and multiplication** state that the grouping of numbers being added or multiplied does not change the sum or product, respectively. The commutative and associative properties are useful for performing calculations. For example, (47 + 25) + 3 is equivalent to (47 + 3) + 25, which is easier to calculate.

The **identity property of addition** states that adding zero to any number does not change its value. The **identity property of multiplication** states that multiplying a number by one does not change its value. The **inverse property of addition** states that the sum of a number and its opposite equals zero. **Opposites** are numbers that are the same with different signs (ex. 5 and -5; $-\frac{1}{2}$ and $\frac{1}{2}$). The **inverse property of multiplication** states that the product of a number (other than zero) and its reciprocal equals one. **Reciprocal numbers** have numerators and denominators that are inverted (ex. $\frac{2}{5}$ and $\frac{5}{2}$). Inverse properties are useful for

Mathematics

canceling quantities to find missing values (see algebra content). For example, $a + 7 = 12$ is solved by adding the inverse of 7 (which is -7) to both sides in order to isolate a.

The **distributive property** states that multiplying a sum (or difference) by a number produces the same result as multiplying each value in the sum (or difference) by the number and adding (or subtracting) the products. Consider the following scenario: You are buying three tickets for a baseball game. Each ticket costs $18. You are also charged a fee of $2 per ticket for purchasing the tickets online. The cost is calculated: $3 \times 18 + 3 \times 2$. Using the distributive property, the cost can also be calculated $3(18 + 2)$.

Representing Rational Numbers and Their Operations
Concrete Models
Concrete objects are used to develop a tangible understanding of operations of rational numbers. Tools such as tiles, blocks, beads, and hundred charts are used to model problems. For example, a hundred chart (10×10) and beads can be used to model multiplication. If multiplying 5 by 4, beads are placed across 5 rows and down 4 columns producing a product of 20. Similarly, tiles can be used to model division by splitting the total into equal groups. If dividing 12 by 4, 12 tiles are placed one at a time into 4 groups. The result is 4 groups of 3. This is also an effective method for visualizing the concept of remainders.

Representations of objects can be used to expand on the concrete models of operations. Pictures, dots, and tallies can help model these concepts. Utilizing concrete models and representations creates a foundation upon which to build an abstract understanding of the operations.

Rational Numbers on a Number Line
A **number line** typically consists of integers (...3,2,1,0,-1,-2,-3...), and is used to visually represent the value of a rational number. Each rational number has a distinct position on the line determined by comparing its value with the displayed values on the line. For example, if plotting -1.5 on the number line below, it is necessary to recognize that the value of -1.5 is .5 less than -1 and .5 greater than -2. Therefore, -1.5 is plotted halfway between -1 and -2.

Number lines can also be useful for visualizing sums and differences of rational numbers. Adding a value indicates moving to the right (values increase to the right), and subtracting a value indicates moving to the left (numbers decrease to the left). For example, $5 - 7$ is displayed by starting at 5 and moving to the left 7 spaces, if the number line is in increments of 1. This will result in an answer of -2.

Multiplication and Division Problems

Multiplication and division are inverse operations that can be represented by using rectangular arrays, area models, and equations. Rectangular arrays include an arrangement of rows and columns that correspond to the factors and display product totals.

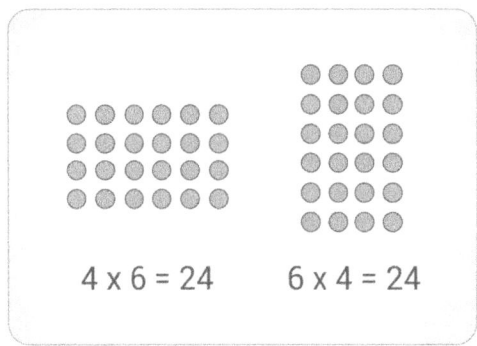

Another method of multiplication can be done with the use of an **area model**. An area model is a rectangle that is divided into rows and columns that match up to the number of place values within each number. Take the example 29 × 65. These two numbers can be split into simpler numbers: 29 = 25 + 4 and 65 = 60 + 5. The products of those 4 numbers are found within the rectangle and then summed up to get the answer. The entire process is:

$$(60 \times 25) + (5 \times 25) + (60 \times 4) + (5 \times 4) = 1{,}500 + 240 + 125 + 20 = 1{,}885$$

Here is the actual area model:

	25	4
60	60x25 1,500	60x4 240
5	5x25 125	5x4 20

```
   1,500
     240
     125
 +    20
   1,885
```

Dividing a number by a single digit or two digits can be turned into repeated subtraction problems. An area model can be used throughout the problem that represents multiples of the divisor. For example, the answer to 8580 ÷ 55 can be found by subtracting 55 from 8580 one at a time and counting the total number of subtractions necessary.

However, a simpler process involves using larger multiples of 55. First, $100 \times 55 = 5{,}500$ is subtracted from 8,580, and 3,080 is leftover. Next, $50 \times 55 = 2{,}750$ is subtracted from 3,080 to obtain 380. $5 \times 55 = 275$ is

Mathematics

subtracted from 330 to obtain 55, and finally, $1 \times 55 = 55$ is subtracted from 55 to obtain zero. Therefore, there is no remainder, and the answer is:

$$100 + 50 + 5 + 1 = 156$$

Here is a picture of the area model and the repeated subtraction process:

$$8580 \div 55$$

	55
100	5500
50	2750
5	275
1	55

```
    55 | 8580
        -5500   (100 x 55)
         3080
        -2750   (50 x 55)
          330
         -275   (5 x 55)
           55
          -55   (1 x 55)
            0
```

Comparing, Classifying, and Ordering Rational Numbers

A **rational number** is any number that can be written as a fraction or ratio. Within the set of rational numbers, several subsets exist that are referenced throughout the mathematics topics. Counting numbers are the first numbers learned as a child. Counting numbers consist of 1,2,3,4, and so on. **Whole numbers** include all counting numbers and zero (0,1,2,3,4...). **Integers** include counting numbers, their opposites, and zero (...-3,-2,-1,0,1,2,3,...). Rational numbers include integers, fractions, and decimals that terminate (1.7, 0.04213) or repeat ($0.13\overline{6}$).

When comparing or ordering numbers, the numbers should be written in the same format (decimal or fraction), if possible. For example, $\sqrt{49}$, 7.3, and $\frac{15}{2}$ are easier to order if each one is converted to a decimal: 7, 7.3, and 7.5 (converting fractions and decimals is covered in the following section). A number line is used to order and compare the numbers. Any number that is to the right of another number is greater than that number. Conversely, a number positioned to the left of a given number is less than that number.

Converting Between Fractions, Decimals, and Percent

To convert a fraction to a decimal, the numerator is divided by the denominator. For example, $\frac{3}{8}$ can be converted to a decimal by dividing 3 by 8 ($\frac{3}{8} = 0.375$). To convert a decimal to a fraction, the decimal point is dropped, and the value is written as the numerator. The denominator is the place value farthest to the right with a digit other than zero. For example, to convert .48 to a fraction, the numerator is 48, and the denominator is 100 (the digit 8 is in the hundredths place). Therefore,

$$0.48 = \frac{48}{100}$$

Fractions should be written in the simplest form, or reduced. To reduce a fraction, the numerator and denominator are divided by the largest common factor. In the previous example, 48 and 100 are both divisible by 4. Dividing the numerator and denominator by 4 results in a reduced fraction of $\frac{12}{25}$.

To convert a decimal to a percent, the number is multiplied by 100. To convert .13 to a percent, .13 is multiplied by 100 to get 13 percent. To convert a fraction to a percent, the fraction is converted to a decimal and then multiplied by 100. For example, $\frac{1}{5} = 0.20$ and 0.20 multiplied by 100 produces 20 percent.

To convert a percent to a decimal, the value is divided by 100. For example, 125 percent is equal to 1.25 ($\frac{125}{100}$). To convert a percent to a fraction, the percent sign is dropped, and the value is written as the numerator with a denominator of 100. For example, $80\% = \frac{80}{100}$. This fraction can be reduced ($\frac{80}{100} = \frac{4}{5}$).

Understanding Proportional Relationships and Percent

Applying Ratios and Unit Rates

A **ratio** is a comparison of two quantities that represent separate groups. For example, if a recipe calls for 2 eggs for every 3 cups of milk, this is expressed as a ratio. Ratios can be written three ways:

- With the word "to"
- Using a colon
- As a fraction

In the previous example, the ratio of eggs to cups of milk is written as 2 to 3, 2:3, or $\frac{2}{3}$. When writing ratios, the order is very important. The ratio of eggs to cups of milk is not the same as the ratio of cups of milk to eggs, 3:2.

In simplest form, both quantities of a ratio should be written as integers. These should also be reduced just as a fraction is reduced. For example, 5:10 is reduced to 1:2. Given a ratio where one or both quantities are expressed as a decimal or fraction, multiply both by the same number to produce integers. To write the ratio $\frac{1}{3}$ to 2 in simplest form, both quantities are multiplied by 3. The resulting ratio is 1 to 6.

A problem involving ratios may give a comparison between two groups. The problem may then provide a total and ask for a part, or provide a part and ask for a total. Consider the following: The ratio of boys to girls in the 11th grade class is 5:4. If there are a total of 270 11th grade students, how many are girls? The total number of **ratio pieces** should be determined first. The total number of 11th grade students is divided into 9 pieces. The ratio of boys to total students is 5:9, and the ratio of girls to total students is 4:9. Knowing the total number of students, the number of girls is determined by setting up a proportion:

$$\frac{4}{9} = \frac{x}{270}$$

A **rate** is a ratio comparing two quantities expressed in different units. A unit rate is a ratio in which the second quantity is one unit. Rates often include the word *per*. Examples include miles per hour, beats per minute, and price per pound. The word per is represented with a / symbol or abbreviated with the letter p and units abbreviated. For example, miles per hour is written as mi/h. When given a rate that is not in its simplest form (the second quantity is not one unit), both quantities are divided by the value of the second quantity. If 99 heartbeats were recorded in $1\frac{1}{2}$ minutes, both quantities are divided by $1\frac{1}{2}$ to determine the heart rate of 66 beats per minute.

Percent

The word **percent** means *per hundred*. Similar to a unit rate in which the second quantity is always one unit, a percent is a rate where the second quantity is always 100 units. If the results of a poll state that 47 percent of people support a given policy, this indicates that 47 out of every 100 individuals polled were in support. In other words, 47 per 100 support the policy. If an upgraded model of a car costs 110 percent of the cost of the base model, for every $100 that is spent for the base model, $110 must be spent to purchase the upgraded model. In other words, the upgraded model costs $110 per $100 for the cost of the base model.

When dealing with percentages, the numbers can be evaluated as a value in hundredths. For example, 15 percent is expressed as fifteen hundredths and is written as $\frac{15}{100}$ or 0.15.

Unit-Rate Problems

A rate is a ratio in which two terms are in different units. When rates are expressed as a quantity of one, they are considered **unit rates**. To determine a unit rate, the first quantity is divided by the second. Knowing a unit rate makes calculations easier than simply having a rate. For example, suppose a 3-pound bag of onions costs $1.77. To calculate the price of 5 pounds of onions, a proportion could show:

$$\frac{3}{1.77} = \frac{5}{x}$$

However, by knowing the unit rate, the value of pounds of onions is multiplied by the unit price. The unit price is calculated:

$$\frac{\$1.77}{3 \text{ lb}} = \$0.59/\text{lb}$$

Multiplying the weight of the onions by the unit price yields:

$$5 \text{ lb} \times \frac{\$0.59}{\text{lb}} = \$2.95$$

The *lb.* units cancel out.

Similar to unit-rate problems, unit conversions appear in real-world scenarios including cooking, measurement, construction, and currency. Given the conversion rate, unit conversions are written as a fraction (ratio) and multiplied by a quantity in one unit to convert it to the corresponding unit. To determine how many minutes are in $3\frac{1}{2}$ hours, the conversion rate of 60 minutes to 1 hour is written as $\frac{60 \text{ min}}{1 \text{ h}}$. Multiplying the quantity by the conversion rate results in:

$$3\frac{1}{2} \text{ h} \times \frac{60 \text{ min}}{1 \text{ h}} = 210 \text{ min}$$

(The *h* unit is canceled.)

To convert a quantity in minutes to hours, the fraction for the conversion rate is flipped to cancel the *min* unit. To convert 195 minutes to hours, $195 \text{ min} \times \frac{1 \text{ h}}{60 \text{ min}}$ is multiplied. The result is $\frac{195 \text{ h}}{60}$ which reduces to $3\frac{1}{4}$ h.

Converting units may require more than one multiplication. The key is to set up conversion rates so that units cancel each other out and the desired unit is left. To convert 3.25 yards to inches, given that 1 yd = 3 ft and 12 in = 1 ft, the calculation is performed by multiplying:

$$3.25 \text{ yd} \times \frac{3\text{ft}}{1\text{yd}} \times \frac{12\text{in}}{1\text{ft}}$$

The *yd* and *ft* units will cancel, resulting in 117 in.

Using Proportional Relationships

A **proportion** is a statement consisting of two equal ratios. Proportions will typically give three of four quantities and require solving for the missing value. The key to solving proportions is to set them up properly. Consider the following: 7 gallons of gas costs $14.70. How many gallons can you get for $20? The information is written as equal ratios with a variable representing the missing quantity:

$$\left(\frac{gallons}{cost} = \frac{gallons}{cost}\right) : \frac{7}{14.70} = \frac{x}{20}$$

To solve for *x*, the proportion is cross-multiplied. This means the numerator of the first ratio is multiplied by the denominator of the second, and vice versa. The resulting products are shown equal to each other. Cross-multiplying results in:

$$(7)(20) = (14.7)(x)$$

By solving the equation for *x* (see the algebra content), the answer is that 9.5 gallons of gas may be purchased for $20.

Percent problems can also be solved by setting up proportions. Examples of common percent problems are:

a. What is 15% of 25?
b. What percent of 45 is 3?
c. 5 is $\frac{1}{2}$% of what number?

Setting up the proper proportion is made easier by following the format: $\frac{is}{of} = \frac{percent}{100}$. A variable is used to represent the missing value. The proportions for each of the three examples are set up as follows:

a. $\frac{x}{25} = \frac{15}{100}$

b. $\frac{3}{45} = \frac{x}{100}$

c. $\frac{5}{x} = \frac{\left(\frac{1}{2}\right)}{100}$

By cross-multiplying and solving the resulting equation for the variable, the missing values are determined to be:

a. 3.75
b. $6.\overline{6}$%
c. 1,000

Mathematics

Basic Concepts of Number Theory

Prime and Composite Numbers

Whole numbers are classified as either prime or composite. A **prime number** can only be divided evenly by itself and one. For example, the number 11 can only be divided evenly by 11 and one; therefore, 11 is a prime number. A helpful way to visualize a prime number is to use concrete objects and try to divide them into equal piles. If dividing 11 coins, the only way to divide them into equal piles is to create 1 pile of 11 coins or to create 11 piles of 1 coin each. Other examples of prime numbers include 2, 3, 5, 7, 13, 17, and 19.

A **composite number** is any whole number that is not a prime number. A composite number is a number that can be divided evenly by one or more numbers other than itself and one. For example, the number 6 can be divided evenly by 2 and 3. Therefore, 6 is a composite number. If dividing 6 coins into equal piles, the possibilities are 1 pile of 6 coins, 2 piles of 3 coins, 3 piles of 2 coins, or 6 piles of 1 coin. Other examples of composite numbers include 4, 8, 9, 10, 12, 14, 15, 16, 18, and 20.

To determine if a number is a prime or composite number, the number is divided by every whole number greater than one and less than its own value. If it divides evenly by any of these numbers, then the number is composite. If it does not divide evenly by any of these numbers, then the number is prime. For example, when attempting to divide the number 5 by 2, 3, and 4, none of these numbers divide evenly. Therefore, 5 must be a prime number.

Factors and Multiples of Numbers

The **factors of a number** are all integers that can be multiplied by another integer to produce the given number. For example, 2 is multiplied by 3 to produce 6. Therefore, 2 and 3 are both factors of 6. Similarly, $1 \times 6 = 6$ and $2 \times 3 = 6$, so 1, 2, 3, and 6 are all factors of 6. Another way to explain a factor is to say that a given number divides evenly by each of its factors to produce an integer. For example, 6 does not divide evenly by 5. Therefore, 5 is not a factor of 6.

Multiples of a given number are found by taking that number and multiplying it by any other whole number. For example, 3 is a factor of 6, 9, and 12. Therefore, 6, 9, and 12 are multiples of 3. The multiples of any number are an infinite list. For example, the multiples of 5 are 5, 10, 15, 20, and so on. This list continues without end. A list of multiples is used in finding the least common multiple, or LCM, for fractions when a common denominator is needed. The denominators are written down and their multiples listed until a common number is found in both lists. This common number is the LCM.

Prime factorization breaks down each factor of a whole number until only prime numbers remain. All composite numbers can be factored into prime numbers. For example, the prime factors of 12 are 2, 2, and 3 ($2 \times 2 \times 3 = 12$). To produce the prime factors of a number, the number is factored, and any composite numbers are continuously factored until the result is the product of prime factors only. A factor tree, such as the one below, is helpful when exploring this concept.

Determining the Reasonableness of Results

Reasonableness of Results within a Context

When solving math word problems, the solution obtained should make sense within the given scenario. The step of checking the solution will reduce the possibility of a calculation error or a solution that may be *mathematically* correct but not applicable in the real world. Consider the following scenarios:

A problem states that Lisa got 24 out of 32 questions correct on a test and asks to find the percentage of correct answers. To solve the problem, a student divided 32 by 24 to get 1.33, and then multiplied by 100 to get 133 percent. By examining the solution within the context of the problem, the student should recognize that getting all 32 questions correct will produce a perfect score of 100 percent. Therefore, a score of 133 percent with 8 incorrect answers does not make sense, and the calculations should be checked.

A problem states that the maximum weight on a bridge cannot exceed 22,000 pounds. The problem asks to find the maximum number of cars that can be on the bridge at one time if each car weighs 4,000 pounds. To solve this problem, a student divided 22,000 by 4,000 to get an answer of 5.5. By examining the solution within the context of the problem, the student should recognize that although the calculations are mathematically correct, the solution does not make sense. Half of a car on a bridge is not possible, so the student should determine that a maximum of 5 cars can be on the bridge at the same time.

Mental Math Estimation

Once a result is determined to be logical within the context of a given problem, the result should be evaluated by its nearness to the expected answer. This is performed by approximating given values to perform mental math. Numbers should be rounded to the nearest value possible to check the initial results.

Consider the following example: A problem states that a customer is buying a new sound system for their home. The customer purchases a stereo for $435, 2 speakers for $67 each, and the necessary cables for $12. The customer chooses an option that allows him to spread the costs over equal payments for 4 months. How much will the monthly payments be?

After making calculations for the problem, a student determines that the monthly payment will be $145.25. To check the accuracy of the results, the student rounds each cost to the nearest ten (440 + 70 + 70 + 10) and determines that the total is approximately $590. Dividing by 4 months gives an approximate monthly payment of $147.50. Therefore, the student can conclude that the solution of $145.25 is very close to what should be expected.

When rounding, the place-value that is used in rounding can make a difference. Suppose the student had rounded to the nearest hundred for the estimation. The result (400 + 100 + 100 + 0 = 600; 600 ÷ 4 = 150) will show that the answer is reasonable but not as close to the actual value as rounding to the nearest ten.

Algebraic Thinking

Evaluating and Manipulating Algebraic Expressions and Equations

Differentiating Between Algebraic Expressions and Equations

An **algebraic expression** is a statement about an unknown quantity expressed in mathematical symbols. A **variable** is used to represent the unknown quantity, usually denoted by a letter. An **equation** is a statement in which two expressions (at least one containing a variable) are equal to each other. An algebraic expression can be thought of as a mathematical phrase and an equation can be thought of as a mathematical sentence.

Algebraic expressions and equations both contain numbers, variables, and mathematical operations. The following are examples of algebraic expressions: $5x + 3$, $7xy - 8(x^2 + y)$, and $\sqrt{a^2 + b^2}$. An expression can be simplified or evaluated for given values of variables. The following are examples of equations: $2x + 3 = 7$, $a^2 + b^2 = c^2$, and $2x + 5 = 3x - 2$. An equation contains two sides separated by an equal sign. Equations can be solved to determine the value(s) of the variable for which the statement is true.

Adding and Subtracting Linear Algebraic Expressions

An algebraic expression is simplified by combining like terms. A **term** is a number, variable, or product of a number and variables separated by addition and subtraction. For the algebraic expression $3x^2 - 4x + 5 - 5x^2 + x - 3$, the terms are $3x^2$, $-4x$, 5, $-5x^2$, x, and -3. **Like terms** have the same variables raised to the same powers (exponents). The like terms for this example are $3x^2$ and $-5x^2$, $-4x$ and x, 5 and -3. To combine like terms, the coefficients (numerical factor of the term including sign) are added, and the variables and their powers are kept the same. Note that if a coefficient is not written, it is an implied coefficient of 1 ($x = 1x$). The previous example will simplify to:

$$-2x^2 - 3x + 2$$

When adding or subtracting algebraic expressions, each expression is written in parentheses. The negative sign is distributed when necessary, and like terms are combined. Consider the following: add $2a + 5b - 2$ to $a - 2b + 8c - 4$. The sum is set as follows:

$$(a - 2b + 8c - 4) + (2a + 5b - 2)$$

In front of each set of parentheses is an implied positive one, which, when distributed, does not change any of the terms. Therefore, the parentheses are dropped and like terms are combined:

$$a - 2b + 8c - 4 + 2a + 5b - 2 = 3a + 3b + 8c - 6$$

Consider the following problem: Subtract $2a + 5b - 2$ from $a - 2b + 8c - 4$. The difference is set as follows:

$$(a - 2b + 8c - 4) - (2a + 5b - 2)$$

The implied one in front of the first set of parentheses will not change those four terms. However, distributing the implied -1 in front of the second set of parentheses will change the sign of each of those three terms:
$$a - 2b + 8c - 4 - 2a - 5b + 2$$

Combining like terms yields the simplified expression:

$$-a - 7b + 8c - 2$$

Distributive Property

The **distributive property** states that multiplying a sum (or difference) by a number produces the same result as multiplying each value in the sum (or difference) by the number and adding (or subtracting) the products. Using mathematical symbols, the distributive property states:

$$a(b + c) = ab + ac$$

The expression $4(3 + 2)$ is simplified using the order of operations. Simplifying inside the parentheses first produces 4×5, which equals 20. The expression $4(3 + 2)$ can also be simplified using the distributive property:

$$4(3 + 2) = 4 \times 3 + 4 \times 2 = 12 + 8 = 20$$

Mathematics

Consider the following example: $4(3x - 2)$. The expression cannot be simplified inside the parentheses because $3x$ and -2 are not like terms and therefore cannot be combined. However, the expression can be simplified by using the distributive property and multiplying each term inside of the parentheses by the term outside of the parentheses: $12x - 8$. The resulting equivalent expression contains no like terms, so it cannot be further simplified.

Consider the expression:

$$(3x + 2y + 1) - (5x - 3) + 2(3y + 4)$$

Again, there are no like terms, but the distributive property is used to simplify the expression. Note there is an implied one in front of the first set of parentheses and an implied -1 in front of the second set of parentheses. Distributing the 1, -1, and 2 produces:

$$1(3x) + 1(2y) + 1(1) - 1(5x) - 1(-3) + 2(3y) + 2(4)$$

$$3x + 2y + 1 - 5x + 3 + 6y + 8$$

This expression contains like terms that are combined to produce the simplified expression:

$$-2x + 8y + 12$$

Algebraic expressions are tested to be equivalent by choosing values for the variables and evaluating both expressions. For example, $4(3x - 2)$ and $12x - 8$ are tested by substituting 3 for the variable x and calculating to determine if equivalent values result.

Simple Expressions for Given Values

An **algebraic expression** is a statement written in mathematical symbols, typically including one or more unknown values represented by variables. For example, the expression $2x + 3$ states that an unknown number (x) is multiplied by 2 and added to 3. If given a value for the unknown number, or variable, the value of the expression is determined. For example, if the value of the variable x is 4, the value of the expression 4 is multiplied by 2, and 3 is added. This results in a value of 11 for the expression.

When given an algebraic expression and values for the variable(s), the expression is evaluated to determine its numerical value. To evaluate the expression, the given values for the variables are substituted (or replaced), and the expression is simplified using the order of operations. Parentheses should be used when substituting. Consider the following: Evaluate $a - 2b + ab$ for $a = 3$ and $b = -1$. To evaluate, any variable a is replaced with 3 and any variable b with -1, producing:

$$(3) - 2(-1) + (3)(-1)$$

Next, the order of operations is used to calculate the value of the expression, which is 2.

Parts of Expressions

Algebraic expressions consist of variables, numbers, and operations. A **term** of an expression is any combination of numbers and/or variables, and terms are separated by addition and subtraction. For example, the expression $5x^2 - 3xy + 4 - 2$ consists of 4 terms: $5x^2$, $-3xy$, $4y$, and -2. Note that each term includes its given sign (+ or −). The **variable** part of a term is a letter that represents an unknown quantity. The coefficient of a term is the number by which the variable is multiplied. For the term $4y$, the variable is y, and the coefficient is 4. Terms are identified by the power (or exponent) of its variable.

A number without a variable is referred to as a **constant**. If the variable is to the first power (x^1 or simply x), it is referred to as a **linear term**. A term with a variable to the second power (x^2) is quadratic, and a term to the third power (x^3) is cubic. Consider the expression $x^3 + 3x - 1$. The constant is -1. The linear term is $3x$. There is no quadratic term. The cubic term is x^3.

An algebraic expression can also be classified by how many terms exist in the expression. Any like terms should be combined before classifying. A **monomial** is an expression consisting of only one term. Examples of monomials are: 17, $2x$, and $-5ab^2$. A **binomial** is an expression consisting of two terms separated by addition or subtraction. Examples include $2x - 4$ and $-3y^2 + 2y$. A **trinomial** consists of 3 terms. For example, $5x^2 - 2x + 1$ is a trinomial.

Verbal Statements and Algebraic Expressions
An algebraic expression is a statement about unknown quantities expressed in mathematical symbols. The statement *five times a number added to forty* is expressed as $5x + 40$. An equation is a statement in which two expressions (with at least one containing a variable) are equal to one another. The statement *five times a number added to forty is equal to ten* is expressed as:

$$5x + 40 = 10$$

Real world scenarios can also be expressed mathematically. Suppose a job pays its employees \$300 per week and \$40 for each sale made. The weekly pay is represented by the expression $40x + 300$ where x is the number of sales made during the week.

Consider the following scenario: Bob had \$20 and Tom had \$4. After selling 4 ice cream cones to Bob, Tom has as much money as Bob. The cost of an ice cream cone is an unknown quantity and can be represented by a variable (x). The amount of money Bob has after his purchase is four times the cost of an ice cream cone subtracted from his original \$20 → $20 - 4x$. The amount of money Tom has after his sale is four times the cost of an ice cream cone added to his original \$4 → $4x + 4$. After the sale, the amount of money that Bob and Tom have is equal:

$$20 - 4x = 4x + 4$$

When expressing a verbal or written statement mathematically, it is vital to understand words or phrases that can be represented with symbols. The following are examples:

Symbol	Phrase
+	Added to; increased by; sum of; more than
−	Decreased by; difference between; less than; take away
×	Multiplied by; 3(4, 5...) times as large; product of
÷	Divided by; quotient of; half (third, etc.) of
=	Is; the same as; results in; as much as; equal to
x, t, n, etc.	A number; unknown quantity; value of; variable

Use of Formulas
Formulas are mathematical expressions that define the value of one quantity, given the value of one or more different quantities. Formulas look like equations because they contain variables, numbers, operators, and an equal sign. All formulas are equations, but not all equations are formulas. A formula must have more than one variable. For example, $2x + 7 = y$ is an equation and a formula (it relates the unknown quantities x and y). However, $2x + 7 = 3$ is an equation but not a formula (it only expresses the value of the unknown quantity x).

Formulas are typically written with one variable alone (or isolated) on one side of the equal sign. This variable can be thought of as the *subject* in that the formula is stating the value of the *subject* in terms of the relationship between the other variables. Consider the distance formula: $distance = rate \times time$ or $d = rt$. The value of the subject variable d (distance) is the product of the variable r and t (rate and time). Given the rate and time, the distance traveled can easily be determined by substituting the values into the formula and evaluating.

The formula $P = 2l + 2w$ expresses how to calculate the perimeter of a rectangle (P) given its length (l) and width (w). To find the perimeter of a rectangle with a length of 3 ft and a width of 2 ft, these values are substituted into the formula for l and w:

$$P = 2(3 \text{ ft}) + 2(2 \text{ ft})$$

Following the order of operations, the perimeter is determined to be 10 ft. When working with formulas such as these, including units is an important step.

Given a formula expressed in terms of one variable, the formula can be manipulated to express the relationship in terms of any other variable. In other words, the formula can be rearranged to change which variable is the *subject*. To solve for a variable of interest by manipulating a formula, the equation may be solved as if all other variables were numbers. The same steps for solving are followed, leaving operations in terms of the variables instead of calculating numerical values. For the formula $P = 2l + 2w$, the perimeter is the subject expressed in terms of the length and width. To write a formula to calculate the width of a rectangle, given its length and perimeter, the previous formula relating the three variables is solved for the variable w. If P and l were numerical values, this is a two-step linear equation solved by subtraction and division. To solve the equation $P = 2l + 2w$ for w, $2l$ is first subtracted from both sides:

$$P - 2l = 2w$$

Then both sides are divided by 2:

$$\frac{P - 2l}{2} = w$$

Dependent and Independent Variables

A variable represents an unknown quantity and, in the case of a formula, a specific relationship exists between the variables. Within a given scenario, variables are the quantities that are changing. If two variables exist, one is dependent and one is independent. The value of one variable depends on the other variable. If a scenario describes distance traveled and time traveled at a given speed, distance is dependent and time is independent. The distance traveled depends on the time spent traveling. If a scenario describes the cost of a cab ride and the distance traveled, the cost is dependent and the distance is independent. The cost of a cab ride depends on the distance traveled. Formulas often contain more than two variables and are typically written with the dependent variable alone on one side of the equation. This lone variable is the *subject* of the statement. If a formula contains three or more variables, one variable is dependent and the rest are independent. The values of all independent variables are needed to determine the value of the dependent variable.

The formula $P = 2l + 2w$ expresses the dependent variable P in terms of the independent variables, l and w. The perimeter of a rectangle depends on its length and width. The formula $d = rt$ ($distance = rate \times time$) expresses the dependent variable d in terms of the independent variables, r and t. The distance traveled depends on the rate (or speed) and the time traveled.

Solutions to Linear Equations and Inequalities

Multistep One-Variable Linear Equations and Inequalities

Linear equations and linear inequalities are both comparisons of two algebraic expressions. However, unlike equations in which the expressions are equal, linear inequalities compare expressions that may be unequal.

Mathematics

Linear equations typically have one value for the variable that makes the statement true. **Linear inequalities** generally have an infinite number of values that make the statement true.

When solving a linear equation, the desired result requires determining a numerical value for the unknown variable. If given a linear equation involving addition, subtraction, multiplication, or division, working backwards isolates the variable. Addition and subtraction are inverse operations, as are multiplication and division. Therefore, they can be used to cancel each other out.

The first steps to solving linear equations are distributing, if necessary, and combining any like terms on the same side of the equation. Sides of an equation are separated by an *equal* sign. Next, the equation is manipulated to show the variable on one side. Whatever is done to one side of the equation must be done to the other side of the equation to remain equal. Inverse operations are then used to isolate the variable and undo the order of operations backwards. Addition and subtraction are undone, then multiplication and division are undone.

For example, solve $4(t - 2) + 2t - 4 = 2(9 - 2t)$

Distributing:

$$4t - 8 + 2t - 4 = 18 - 4t$$

Combining like terms:

$$6t - 12 = 18 - 4t$$

Adding $4t$ to each side to move the variable:

$$10t - 12 = 18$$

Adding 12 to each side to isolate the variable:

$$10t = 30$$

Dividing each side by 10 to isolate the variable:

$$t = 3$$

The answer can be checked by substituting the value for the variable into the original equation, ensuring that both sides calculate to be equal.

Linear inequalities express the relationship between unequal values. More specifically, they describe in what way the values are unequal. A value can be greater than ($>$), less than ($<$), greater than or equal to ($\geq$), or less than or equal to ($\leq$) another value. $5x + 40 > 65$ is read as *five times a number added to forty is greater than sixty-five*.

When solving a linear inequality, the solution is the set of all numbers that make the statement true. The inequality $x + 2 \geq 6$ has a solution set of 4 and every number greater than 4 (4.01; 5; 12; 107; etc.). Adding 2 to 4 or any number greater than 4 results in a value that is greater than or equal to 6. Therefore, $x \geq 4$ is the solution set.

To algebraically solve a linear inequality, follow the same steps as those for solving a linear equation. The inequality symbol stays the same for all operations *except* when multiplying or dividing by a negative number. If multiplying or dividing by a negative number while solving an inequality, the relationship reverses (the sign flips). In other words, > switches to < and vice versa. Multiplying or dividing by a positive number does not change the relationship, so the sign stays the same. An example is shown below.

Solve $-2x - 8 \leq 22$ for the value of x.

Add 8 to both sides to isolate the variable:

$$-2x \leq 30$$

Divide both sides by -2 to solve for x:

$$x \geq -15$$

Solutions of a linear equation or a linear inequality are the values of the variable that make a statement true. In the case of a linear equation, the solution set (list of all possible solutions) typically consists of a single numerical value. To find the solution, the equation is solved by isolating the variable. For example, solving the equation $3x - 7 = -13$ produces the solution $x = -2$. The only value for x which produces a true statement is -2. This can be checked by substituting -2 into the original equation to check that both sides are equal. In this case, $3(-2) - 7 = -13 \rightarrow -13 = -13$; therefore, -2 is a solution.

Although linear equations generally have one solution, this is not always the case. If there is no value for the variable that makes the statement true, there is no solution to the equation. Consider the equation:

$$x + 3 = x - 1$$

There is no value for x in which adding 3 to the value produces the same result as subtracting one from the value. Conversely, if any value for the variable makes a true statement, the equation has an infinite number of solutions. Consider the equation:

$$3x + 6 = 3(x + 2)$$

Any number substituted for x will result in a true statement (both sides of the equation are equal).

By manipulating equations like the two above, the variable of the equation will cancel out completely. If the remaining constants express a true statement (ex. $6 = 6$), then all real numbers are solutions to the equation. If the constants left express a false statement (ex. $3 = -1$), then no solution exists for the equation.

Interpreting Solutions on a Number Line

Solving a linear inequality requires all values that make the statement true to be determined. For example, solving $3x - 7 \geq -13$ produces the solution $x \geq -2$. This means that -2 and any number greater than -2 produces a true statement. Solution sets for linear inequalities will often be displayed using a number line. If a value is included in the set ($\geq$ or $\leq$), a shaded dot is placed on that value and an arrow extending in the direction of the solutions. For a variable $>$ or $\geq$ a number, the arrow will point right on a number line, the direction where the numbers increase. If a variable is $<$ or $\leq$ a number, the arrow will point left on a number line, which is the direction where the numbers decrease. If the value is not included in the set ($>$ or $<$), an open (unshaded) circle on that value is used with an arrow in the appropriate direction.

Like this:

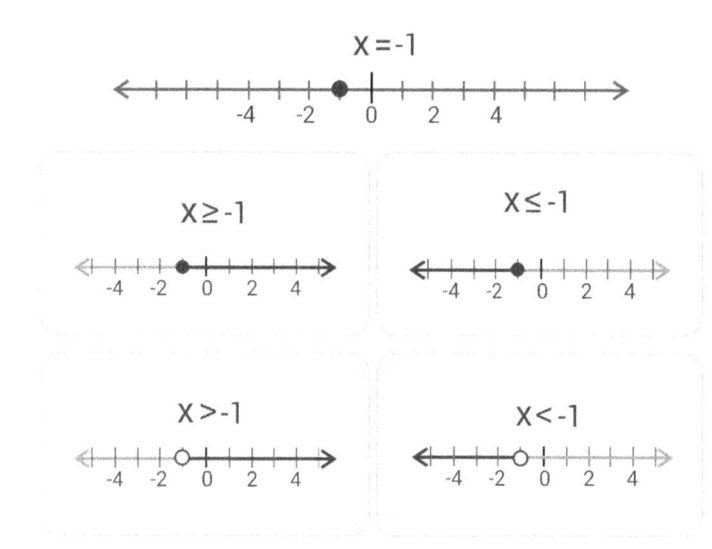

Similar to linear equations, a linear inequality may have a solution set consisting of all real numbers, or can contain no solution. When solved algebraically, a linear inequality in which the variable cancels out and results in a true statement (ex. $7 \geq 2$) has a solution set of all real numbers. A linear inequality in which the variable cancels out and results in a false statement (ex. $7 \leq 2$) has no solution.

Linear Relationships

Linear relationships describe the way two quantities change with respect to each other. The relationship is defined as linear because a line is produced if all the sets of corresponding values are graphed on a coordinate grid. When expressing the linear relationship as an equation, the equation is often written in the form $y = mx + b$ (slope-intercept form) where m and b are numerical values and x and y are variables (for example, $y = 5x + 10$). Given a linear equation and the value of either variable (x or y), the value of the other variable can be determined.

Suppose a teacher is grading a test containing 20 questions with 5 points given for each correct answer, adding a curve of 10 points to each test. This linear relationship can be expressed as the equation $y = 5x + 10$ where x represents the number of correct answers, and y represents the test score. To determine the score of a test with a given number of correct answers, the number of correct answers is substituted into the equation for x and evaluated. For example, for 10 correct answers, 10 is substituted for x:

$$y = 5(10) + 10 \rightarrow y = 60$$

Therefore, 10 correct answers will result in a score of 60. The number of correct answers needed to obtain a certain score can also be determined. To determine the number of correct answers needed to score a 90, 90 is substituted for y in the equation (y represents the test score) and solved:

$$90 = 5x + 10 \rightarrow 80 = 5x \rightarrow 16 = x$$

Therefore, 16 correct answers are needed to score a 90.

Linear relationships may be represented by a table of 2 corresponding values. Certain tables may determine the relationship between the values and predict other corresponding sets. Consider the table below, which displays the money in a checking account that charges a monthly fee:

Month	0	1	2	3	4
Balance	$210	$195	$180	$165	$150

An examination of the values reveals that the account loses $15 every month (the month increases by one and the balance decreases by 15). This information can be used to predict future values. To determine what the value will be in month 6, the pattern can be continued, and it can be concluded that the balance will be $120. To determine which month the balance will be $0, $210 is divided by $15 (since the balance decreases $15 every month), resulting in month 14.

Similar to a table, a graph can display corresponding values of a linear relationship.

The graph above represents the relationship between distance traveled and time. To find the distance traveled in 80 minutes, the mark for 80 minutes is located at the bottom of the graph. By following this mark directly up on the graph, the corresponding point for 80 minutes is directly across from the 150 kilometer mark. This information indicates that the distance travelled in 80 minutes is 160 kilometers. To predict information not displayed on the graph, the way in which the variables change with respect to one another is determined. In this case, distance increases by 40 kilometers as time increases by 20 minutes. This information can be used to continue the data in the graph or convert the values to a table.

Recognizing and Representing Patterns

Number and Shape Patterns
Patterns within a sequence can come in two distinct forms: the items (shapes, numbers, etc.) either repeat in a constant order, or the items change from one step to another in some consistent way. The **core** is the smallest unit, or number of items, that repeats in a repeating pattern. For example, the pattern ○○▲○○▲○... has a core that is ○○▲. Knowing only the core, the pattern can be extended. Knowing the number of steps in the core allows the identification of an item in each step without drawing/writing the entire pattern out. For example, suppose the tenth item in the previous pattern must be determined. Because the core consists of three items (○○▲), the core repeats in multiples of 3. In other words, steps 3, 6, 9, 12, etc. will be ▲ completing the core with the core starting over on the next step. For the above example, the 9th step will be ▲ and the 10th will be ○.

The most common patterns in which each item changes from one step to the next are arithmetic and geometric sequences. An **arithmetic sequence** is one in which the items increase or decrease by a constant difference. In other words, the same thing is added or subtracted to each item or step to produce the next. To determine if a sequence is arithmetic, determine what must be added or subtracted to step one to produce step two. Then, check if the same thing is added/subtracted to step two to produce step three. The same thing must be added/subtracted to step three to produce step four, and so on.

Consider the pattern 13, 10, 7, 4 . . . To get from step one (13) to step two (10) requires subtracting by 3. The next step is checking if subtracting 3 from step two (10) will produce step three (7), and subtracting 3 from step three (7) will produce step four (4). In this case, the pattern holds true. Therefore, this is an arithmetic sequence in which each step is produced by subtracting 3 from the previous step. To extend the sequence, 3 is subtracted from the last step to produce the next. The next three numbers in the sequence are 1, −2, −5.

A **geometric sequence** is one in which each step is produced by multiplying or dividing the previous step by the same number. To determine if a sequence is geometric, decide what step one must be multiplied or divided by to produce step two. Then check if multiplying or dividing step two by the same number produces step three, and so on. Consider the pattern 2, 8, 32, 128 . . . To get from step one (2) to step two (8) requires multiplication by 4. The next step determines if multiplying step two (8) by 4 produces step three (32), and multiplying step three (32) by 4 produces step four (128). In this case, the pattern holds true. Therefore, this is a geometric sequence in which each step is produced by multiplying the previous step by 4. To extend the sequence, the last step is multiplied by 4 and repeated. The next three numbers in the sequence are 512; 2,048; 8,192.

Although arithmetic and geometric sequences typically use numbers, these sequences can also be represented by shapes. For example, an arithmetic sequence could consist of shapes with three sides, four sides, and five sides (add one side to the previous step to produce the next). A geometric sequence could consist of eight blocks, four blocks, and two blocks (each step is produced by dividing the number of blocks in the previous step by 2).

Conjectures, Predictions, or Generalizations Based on Patterns

An arithmetic or geometric sequence can be written as a formula and used to determine unknown steps without writing out the entire sequence. (Note that a similar process for repeating patterns is covered in the previous section.) An arithmetic sequence progresses by a **common difference**. To determine the common difference, any step is subtracted by the step that precedes it. In the sequence 4, 9, 14, 19 . . . the common difference, or d, is 5. By expressing each step as a_1, a_2, a_3, etc., a formula can be written to represent the sequence. a_1 is the first step. To produce step two, step 1 (a_1) is added to the common difference (d):

$$a_2 = a_1 + d$$

To produce step three, the common difference (d) is added twice to a_1:

$$a_3 = a_1 + 2d$$

To produce step four, the common difference (d) is added three times to a_1:

$$a_4 = a_1 + 3d$$

Following this pattern allows a general rule for arithmetic sequences to be written. For any term of the sequence (a_n), the first step (a_1) is added to the product of the common difference (d) and one less than the step of the term ($n - 1$):

$$a_n = a_1 + (n - 1)d$$

Suppose the 8th term (a_8) is to be found in the previous sequence. By knowing the first step (a_1) is 4 and the common difference (d) is 5, the formula can be used:

$$a_n = a_1 + (n - 1)d \rightarrow a_8 = 4 + (7)5 \rightarrow a_8 = 39$$

In a geometric sequence, each step is produced by multiplying or dividing the previous step by the same number. The **common ratio**, or (r), can be determined by dividing any step by the previous step. In the sequence 1, 3, 9, 27 . . . the common ratio (r) is 3 ($\frac{3}{1} = 3$ or $\frac{9}{3} = 3$ or $\frac{27}{9} = 3$). Each successive step can be expressed as a product of the first step (a_1) and the common ratio (r) to some power. For example:

$$a_2 = a_1 \times r$$

$$a_3 = a_1 \times r \times r \text{ or } a_3 = a_1 \times r^2$$

$$a_4 = a_1 \times r \times r \times r \text{ or } a_4 = a_1 \times r^3$$

Following this pattern, a general rule for geometric sequences can be written. For any term of the sequence (a_n), the first step (a_1) is multiplied by the common ratio (r) raised to the power one less than the step of the term ($n - 1$):

$$a_n = a_1 \times r^{(n-1)}$$

Suppose for the previous sequence, the 7th term (a_7) is to be found. Knowing the first step (a_1) is one, and the common ratio (r) is 3, the formula can be used:

$$a_n = a_1 \times r^{(n-1)} \rightarrow a_7 = (1) \times 3^6 \rightarrow a_7 = 729$$

Corresponding Terms of Two Numerical Patterns

When given two numerical patterns, the corresponding terms should be examined to determine if a relationship exists between them. **Corresponding terms** between patterns are the pairs of numbers that appear in the same step of the two sequences. Consider the following patterns 1, 2, 3, 4 . . . and 3, 6, 9, 12 . . . The corresponding terms are: 1 and 3; 2 and 6; 3 and 9; and 4 and 12. To identify the relationship, each pair of corresponding terms is examined and the possibilities of performing an operation ($+$, $-$, $\times$, $\div$) to the term from the first sequence to produce the corresponding term in the second sequence are determined.

In this case:

$1 + 2 = 3$	or	$1 \times 3 = 3$
$2 + 4 = 6$	or	$2 \times 3 = 6$
$3 + 6 = 9$	or	$3 \times 3 = 9$
$4 + 8 = 12$	or	$4 \times 3 = 12$

The consistent pattern is that the number from the first sequence multiplied by 3 equals its corresponding term in the second sequence. By assigning each sequence a label (input and output) or variable (x and y), the

Mathematics

relationship can be written as an equation. If the first sequence represents the inputs, or x, and the second sequence represents the outputs, or y, the relationship can be expressed as: $y = 3x$.

Consider the following sets of numbers:

a	2	4	6	8
b	6	8	10	12

To write a rule for the relationship between the values for a and the values for b, the corresponding terms (2 and 6; 4 and 8; 6 and 10; 8 and 12) are examined. The possibilities for producing b from a are:

$2 + 4 = 6$ or $2 \times 3 = 6$

$4 + 4 = 8$ or $4 \times 2 = 8$

$6 + 4 = 10$

$8 + 4 = 12$ or $8 \times 1.5 = 12$

The consistent pattern is that adding 4 to the value of a produces the value of b. The relationship can be written as the equation $a + 4 = b$.

Geometry & Measurement, Data, Statistics, and Probability

Classifying One-, Two-, and Three-Dimensional Figures

Lines, Rays, and Line Segments

The basic unit of geometry is a **point**. A point represents an exact location on a plane, or flat surface. The position of a point is indicated with a dot and usually named with a single uppercase letter, such as point A or point T. A point is a place, not a thing, and therefore has no dimensions or size. A set of points that lies on the same line is called **collinear**.

A set of points that lies on the same plane is called **coplanar**.

The image above displays point A, point B, and point C.

A **line** is as series of points that extends in both directions without ending. It consists of an infinite number of points and is drawn with arrows on both ends to indicate it extends infinitely. Lines can be named by two points on the line or with a single, cursive, lower case letter. The two lines below could be named line *AB* or line *BA* or $\overleftrightarrow{AB}$ or $\overleftrightarrow{BA}$; and line *m*.

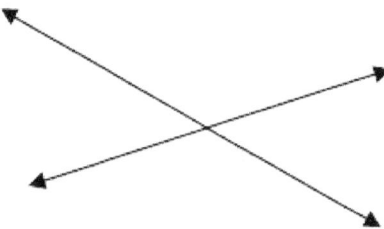

Two lines are considered parallel to each other if, while extending infinitely, they will never intersect (or meet). **Parallel lines** point in the same direction and are always the same distance apart. Two lines are considered perpendicular if they intersect to form right angles. Right angles are 90°. Typically, a small box is drawn at the intersection point to indicate the right angle.

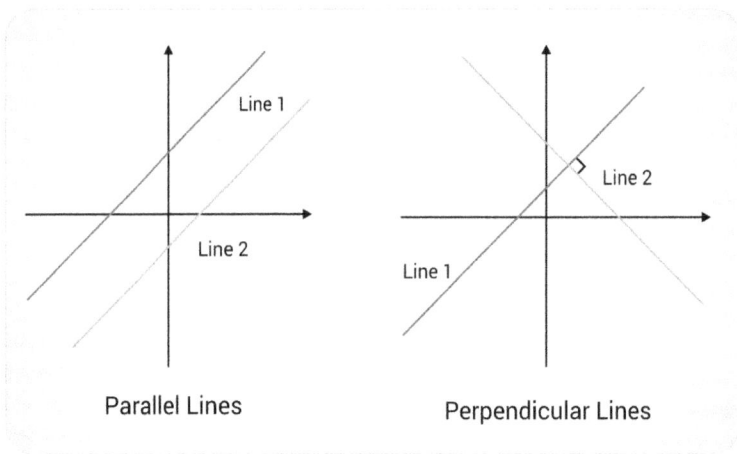

Parallel Lines   Perpendicular Lines

Line 1 is parallel to line 2 in the left image and is written as line 1 || line 2. Line 1 is perpendicular to line 2 in the right image and is written as line 1 ⊥ line 2.

A **ray** has a specific starting point and extends in one direction without ending. The endpoint of a ray is its starting point. Rays are named using the endpoint first, and any other point on the ray. The following ray can be named ray *AB* and written $\overrightarrow{AB}$.

Mathematics

A **line segment** has specific starting and ending points. A line segment consists of two endpoints and all the points in between. Line segments are named by the two endpoints. The example below is named segment KL or segment LK, written $\overline{KL}$ or $\overline{LK}$.

Classification of Angles

An **angle** consists of two rays that have a common endpoint. This common endpoint is called the **vertex of the angle**. The two rays can be called **sides of the angle**. The angle below has a vertex at point B and the sides consist of ray BA and ray BC. An angle can be named in three ways:

- 1. Using the vertex and a point from each side, with the vertex letter in the middle.
- 2. Using only the vertex. This can only be used if it is the only angle with that vertex.
- 3. Using a number that is written inside the angle.

The angle below can be written $\angle ABC$ (read angle ABC), $\angle CBA$, $\angle B$, or $\angle 1$.

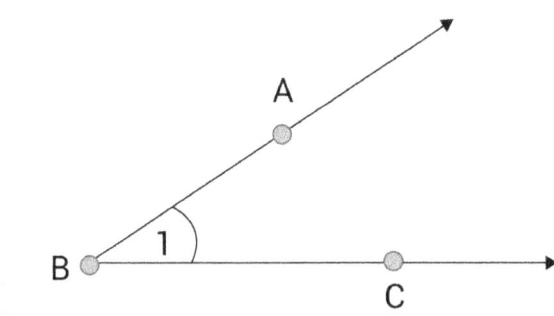

An angle divides a plane, or flat surface, into three parts: the angle itself, the interior (inside) of the angle, and the exterior (outside) of the angle. The figure below shows point M on the interior of the angle and point N on the exterior of the angle.

Mathematics

Angles can be measured in units called **degrees**, with the symbol °. The degree measure of an angle is between 0° and 180° and can be obtained by using a protractor.

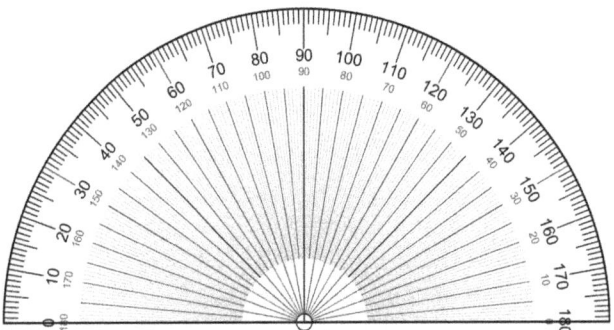

A **straight angle** (or simply a line) measures exactly 180°. A right angle's sides meet at the vertex to create a square corner. A **right angle** measures exactly 90° and is typically indicated by a box drawn in the interior of the angle. An **acute angle** has an interior that is narrower than a right angle. The measure of an acute angle is any value less than 90° and greater than 0°. For example, 89.9°, 47°, 12°, and 1°. An **obtuse angle** has an interior that is wider than a right angle. The measure of an obtuse angle is any value greater than 90° but less than 180°. For example, 90.1°, 110°, 150°, and 179.9°.

- Acute angles: Less than 90°
- Obtuse angles: Greater than 90°
- Right angles: 90°
- Straight angles: 180°

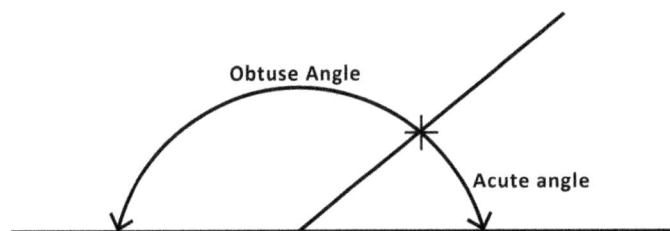

Two- and Three-Dimensional Shapes

A **polygon** is a closed geometric figure in a plane (flat surface) consisting of at least 3 sides formed by line segments. These are often defined as **two-dimensional shapes**. Common two-dimensional shapes include

Mathematics

circles, triangles, squares, rectangles, pentagons, and hexagons. Note that a circle is a two-dimensional shape without sides.

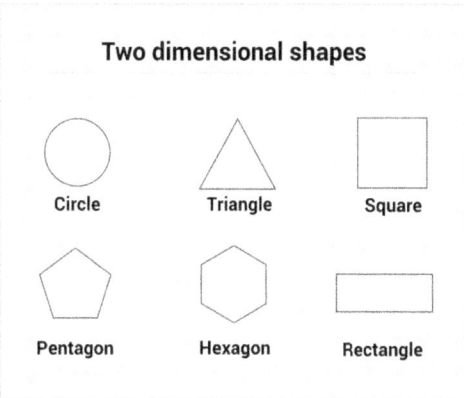

A solid figure, or simply solid, is a figure that encloses a part of space. Some solids consist of flat surfaces only while others include curved surfaces. Solid figures are often defined as **three-dimensional shapes**. Common three-dimensional shapes include spheres, prisms, cubes, pyramids, cylinders, and cones.

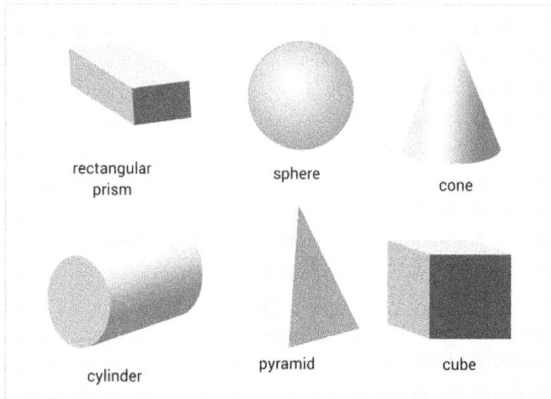

Composing two- or three-dimensional shapes involves putting together two or more shapes to create a new larger figure. For example, a semi-circle (half circle), rectangle, and two triangles can be used to compose the figure of the sailboat shown below.

Similarly, solid figures can be placed together to compose an endless number of three-dimensional objects.

Decomposing two- and three-dimensional figures involves breaking the shapes apart into smaller, simpler shapes. Consider the following two-dimensional representations of a house:

This complex figure can be decomposed into the following basic two-dimensional shapes: large rectangle (body of house); large triangle (roof); small rectangle and small triangle (chimney). Decomposing figures is often done more than one way. To illustrate, the figure of the house could also be decomposed into: two large triangles (body); two medium triangles (roof); two smaller triangles of unequal size (chimney).

Mathematics

Polygons and Solids

A **polygon** is a closed two-dimensional figure consisting of three or more sides. Polygons can be either convex or concave. A polygon that has interior angles all measuring less than 180° is **convex**. A **concave** polygon has one or more interior angles measuring greater than 180°. Examples are shown below.

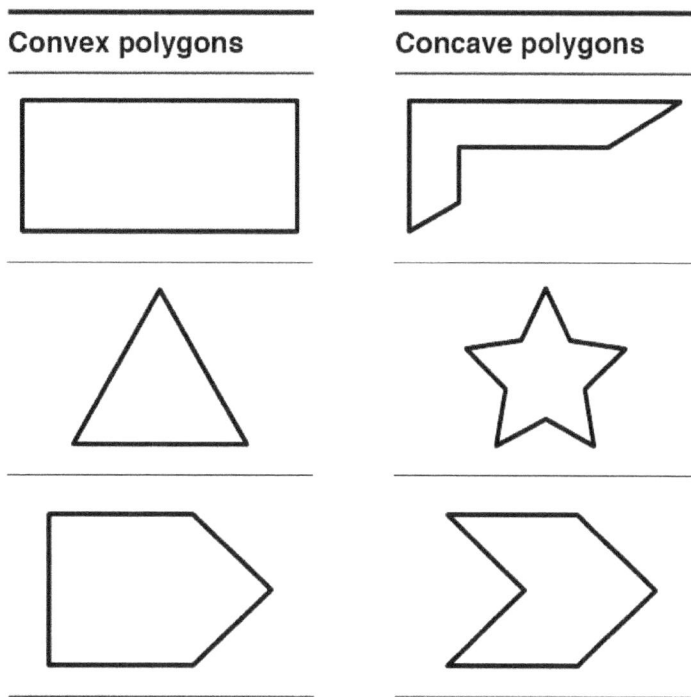

Polygons can be classified by the number of sides (also equal to the number of angles) they have. The following are the names of polygons with a given number of sides or angles:

# of sides	3	4	5	6	7	8	9	10
Name of polygon	Triangle	Quadrilateral	Pentagon	Hexagon	Septagon (or heptagon)	Octagon	Nonagon	Decagon

Equiangular polygons are polygons in which the measure of every interior angle is the same. The sides of **equilateral polygons** are always the same length. If a polygon is both equiangular and equilateral, the polygon is defined as a **regular polygon**. Examples are shown below.

133

Triangles can be further classified by their sides and angles. A triangle with its largest angle measuring 90° is a **right triangle**. A triangle with the largest angle less than 90° is an **acute triangle**. A triangle with the largest angle greater than 90° is an **obtuse triangle**. Below is an example of a right triangle.

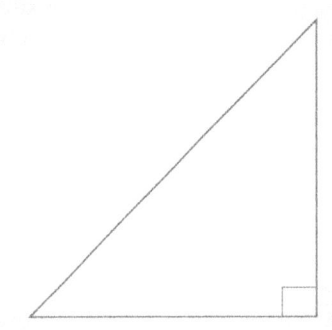

A triangle consisting of two equal sides and two equal angles is an **isosceles triangle**. A triangle with three equal sides and three equal angles is an **equilateral triangle**. A triangle with no equal sides or angles is a **scalene triangle**.

Isosceles triangle:

Equilateral triangle:

Mathematics

Scalene triangle:

Quadrilaterals can be further classified according to their sides and angles. A quadrilateral with exactly one pair of parallel sides is called a **trapezoid**. A quadrilateral that shows both pairs of opposite sides parallel is a **parallelogram**. Parallelograms include rhombuses, rectangles, and squares. A **rhombus** has four equal sides. A **rectangle** has four equal angles (90° each). A **square** has four 90° angles and four equal sides. Therefore, a square is both a rhombus and a rectangle.

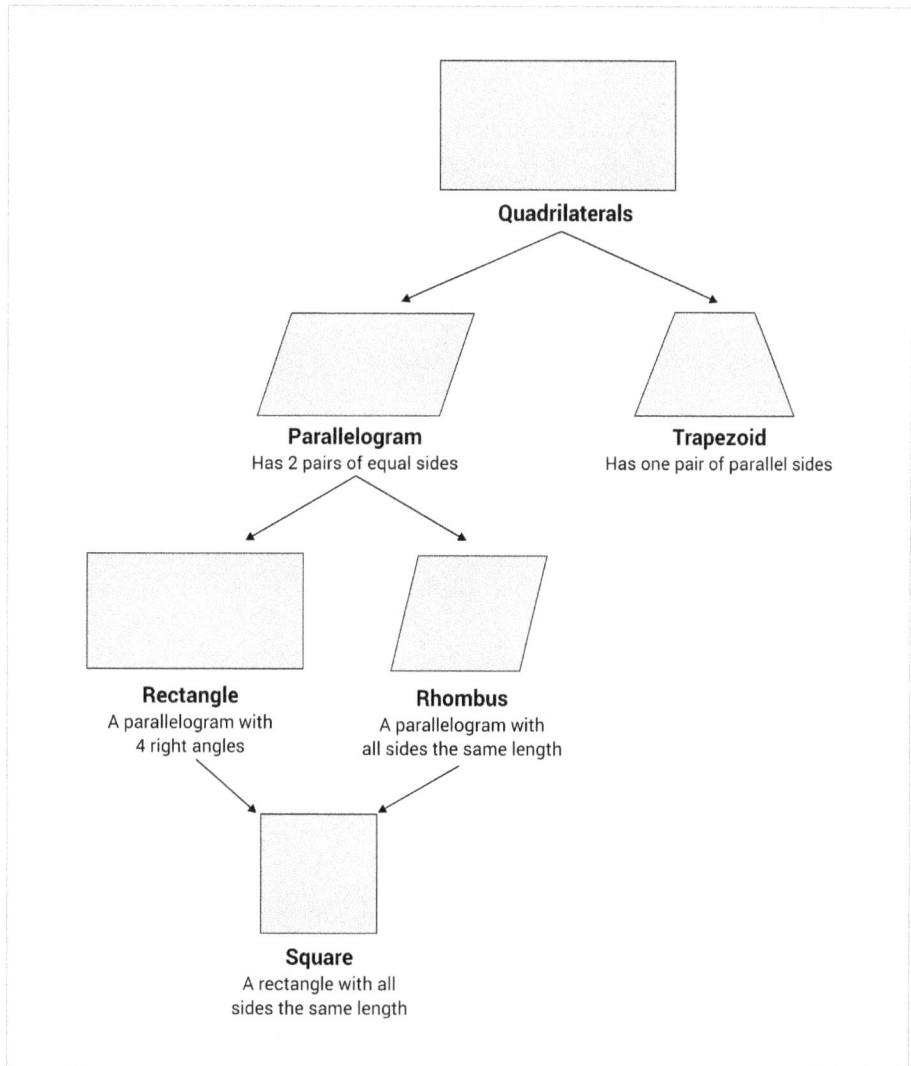

A **solid** is a three-dimensional figure that encloses a part of space. Solids consisting of all flat surfaces that are polygons are called **polyhedrons**. The two-dimensional surfaces that make up a polyhedron are called **faces**. Types of polyhedrons include prisms and pyramids. A **prism** consists of two parallel faces that are congruent (or the same shape and same size) and lateral faces going around (which are parallelograms).

A **prism** is further classified by the shape of its base, as shown below:

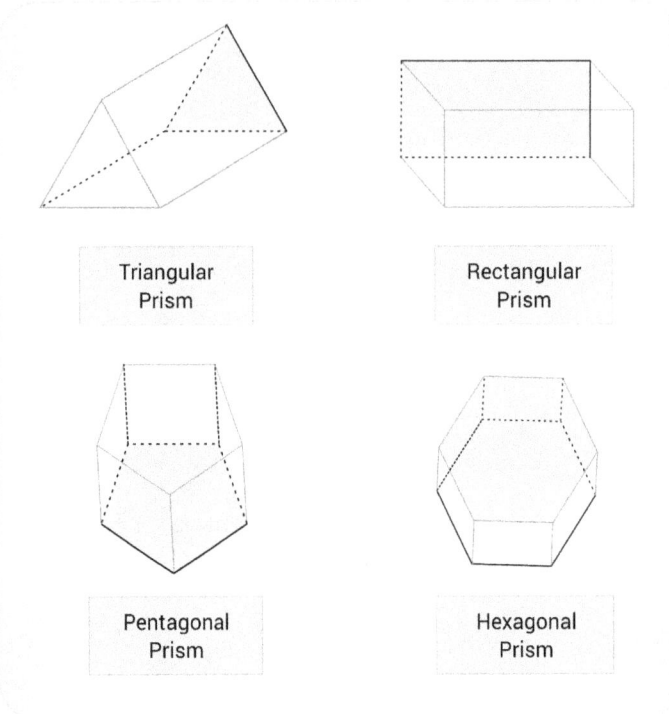

A **pyramid** consists of lateral faces (triangles) that meet at a common point called the **vertex** and one other face that is a polygon, called the **base**. A pyramid can be further classified by the shape of its base, as shown below.

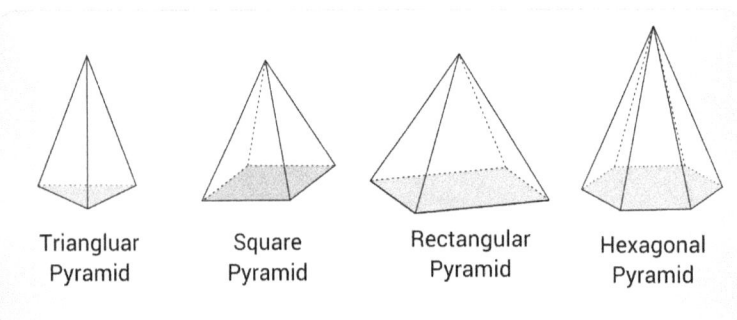

A **tetrahedron** is another name for a triangular pyramid. All the faces of a tetrahedron are triangles.

Solids that are not polyhedrons include spheres, cylinders, and cones. A **sphere** is the set of all points a given distance from a given center point. A sphere is commonly thought of as a three-dimensional circle. A **cylinder**

Mathematics

consists of two parallel, **congruent** (same size) circles and a lateral curved surface. A **cone** consists of a circle as its base and a lateral curved surface that narrows to a point called the vertex.

Similar polygons are the same shape but different sizes. More specifically, their corresponding angle measures are congruent (or equal) and the length of their sides is proportional. For example, all sides of one polygon may be double the length of the sides of another. Likewise, similar solids are the same shape but different sizes. Any corresponding faces or bases of similar solids are the same polygons that are proportional by a consistent value.

Perimeter, Area, Surface Area, and Volume

Three-Dimensional Figures with Nets

A **net** is a construction of two-dimensional figures that can be folded to form a given three-dimensional figure. More than one net may exist to fold and produce the same solid, or three-dimensional figure. The bases and faces of the solid figure are analyzed to determine the polygons (two-dimensional figures) needed to form the net.

Consider the following triangular prism:

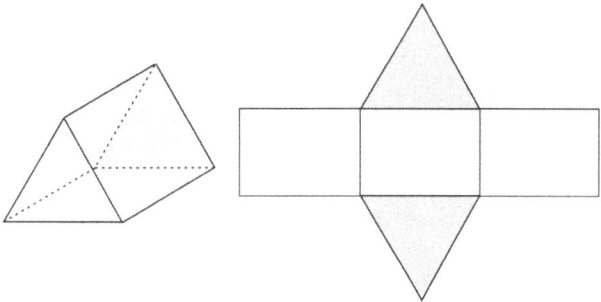

The surface of the prism consists of two triangular bases and three rectangular faces. The net beside it can be used to construct the triangular prism by first folding the triangles up to be parallel to each other, and then folding the two outside rectangles up and to the center with the outer edges touching.

Consider the following cylinder:

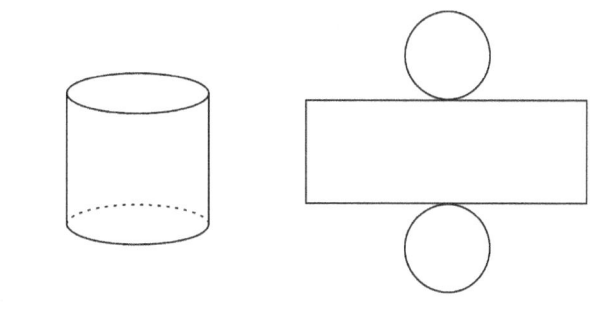

The surface consists of two circular bases and a curved lateral surface that can be opened and flattened into a rectangle. The net beside the cylinder can be used to construct the cylinder by first folding the circles up to be parallel to each other, and then curving the sides of the rectangle up to touch each other. The top and bottom of the folded rectangle should be touching the outside of both circles.

Consider the following square pyramid below on the left. The surface consists of one square base and four triangular faces. The net below on the right can be used to construct the square pyramid by folding each triangle towards the center of the square. The top points of the triangle meet at the vertex.

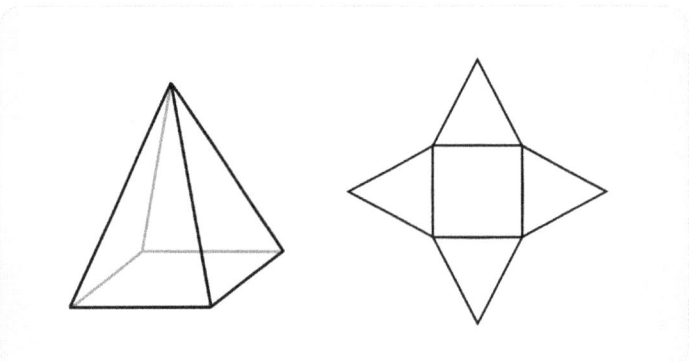

Surface Area of Three-Dimensional Figures

The **area of a two-dimensional figure** refers to the number of square units needed to cover the interior region of the figure. This concept is similar to wallpaper covering the flat surface of a wall. For example, if a rectangle has an area of 10 square centimeters (written 10 cm^2), it will take 10 squares, each with sides one centimeter in length, to cover the interior region of the rectangle. Note that area is measured in square units such as: square centimeters or cm^2; square feet or ft^2; square yards or yd^2; square miles or mi^2.

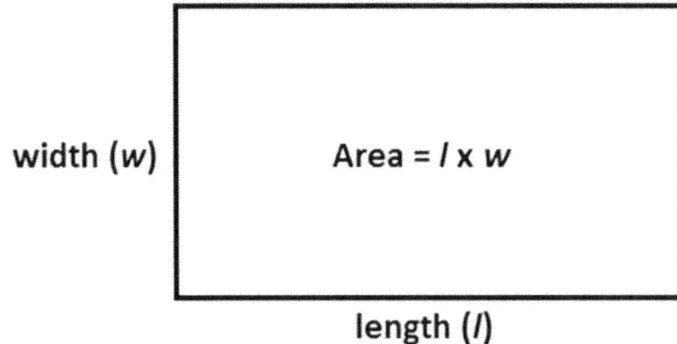

The **surface area of a three-dimensional figure** refers to the number of square units needed to cover the entire surface of the figure. This concept is similar to using wrapping paper to completely cover the outside of a box. For example, if a triangular pyramid has a surface area of 17 square inches (written 17 in^2), it will take 17 squares, each with sides one inch in length, to cover the entire surface of the pyramid. Surface area is also measured in square units.

Many three-dimensional figures (solid figures) can be represented by nets consisting of rectangles and triangles. The surface area of such solids can be determined by adding the areas of each of its faces and bases. Finding the surface area using this method requires calculating the areas of rectangles and triangles. To find the area (A) of a rectangle, the length (l) is multiplied by the width:

$$(w) \rightarrow A = l \times w$$

Mathematics

The area of a rectangle with a length of 8 cm and a width of 4 cm is calculated:

$$A = (8 \text{ cm}) \times (4 \text{ cm}) \rightarrow A = 32 \text{ cm}^2$$

To calculate the area (A) of a triangle, the product of $\frac{1}{2}$, the base (b), and the height (h) is found:

$$A = \frac{1}{2} \times b \times h$$

Note that the height of a triangle is measured from the base to the vertex opposite of it forming a right angle with the base. The area of a triangle with a base of 11 cm and a height of 6 cm is calculated:

$$A = \frac{1}{2} \times (11 \text{ cm}) \times (6 \text{ cm}) \rightarrow A = 33 \text{ cm}^2$$

Consider the following triangular prism, which is represented by a net consisting of two triangles and three rectangles.

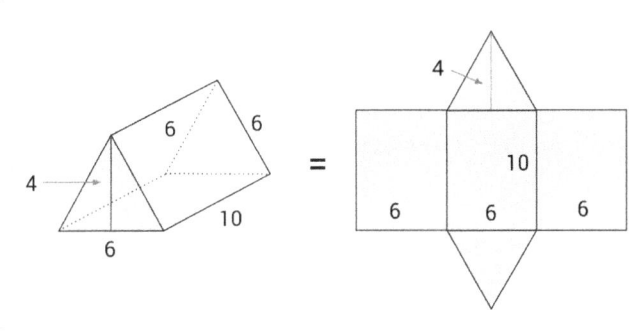

The **surface area of the prism** can be determined by adding the areas of each of its faces and bases. The surface area:

$$SA = area\ of\ triangle + area\ of\ triangle + area\ of\ rectangle \\ + area\ of\ rectangle + area\ of\ rectangle$$

$$SA = \left(\frac{1}{2} \times b \times h\right) + \left(\frac{1}{2} \times b \times h\right) + (l \times w) + (l \times w) + (l \times w)$$

$$SA = \left(\frac{1}{2} \times 6 \times 4\right) + \left(\frac{1}{2} \times 6 \times 4\right) + (6 \times 10) + (6 \times 10) + (6 \times 10)$$

$$SA = (12) + (12) + (60) + (60) + (60)$$

$$SA = 204 \text{ square units}$$

Area and Perimeter of Polygons

Perimeter is the measurement of a distance around something or the sum of all sides of a polygon. Think of perimeter as the length of the boundary, like a fence. In contrast, **area** is the space occupied by a defined enclosure, like a field enclosed by a fence.

When thinking about perimeter, think about walking around the outside of something. When thinking about area, think about the amount of space or **surface area** something takes up.

Squares

The **perimeter of a square** is measured by adding together all of the sides. Since a square has four equal sides, its perimeter can be calculated by multiplying the length of one side by 4. Thus, the formula is $P = 4 \times s$, where s equals one side. For example, the following square has side lengths of 5 meters:

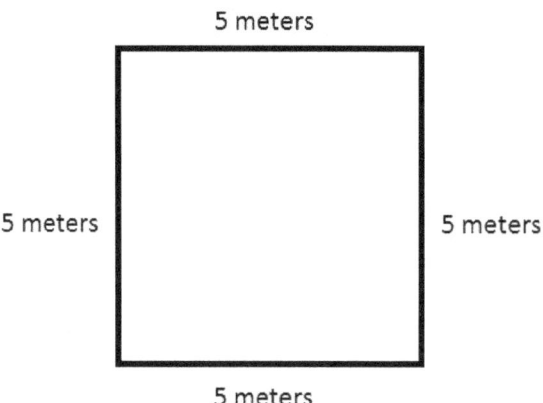

The perimeter is 20 meters because 4 times 5 is 20.

The **area of a square** is the length of a side squared. For example, if a side of a square is 7 centimeters, then the area is 49 square centimeters. The formula for this example is $A = s^2 = 7^2 = 49$ square centimeters.

Rectangle

Like a square, a **rectangle's perimeter** is measured by adding together all of the sides. But as the sides are unequal, the formula is different. A rectangle has equal values for its lengths (long sides) and equal values for its widths (short sides), so the perimeter formula for a rectangle is:

$$P = l + l + w + w = 2l + 2w$$

l equals length
w equals width

For example, if the length of a rectangle is 10 inches and the width 8 inches, then the perimeter is 36 inches because:

$$P = 2l + 2w = 2(10) + 2(8) = 20 + 16 = 36 \text{ inches}$$

The area is found by multiplying the length by the width, so the formula is $A = l \times w$.

An example is if the rectangle has a length of 6 inches and a width of 7 inches, then the area is 42 square inches:

$$A = lw = 6(7) = 42 \text{ square inches}$$

Triangles

A **triangle's perimeter** is measured by adding together the three sides, so the formula is $P = a + b + c$, where a, b, and c are the values of the three sides. The area is the product of one-half the base and height so the formula is:

$$A = \frac{1}{2} \times b \times h$$

Mathematics

It can be simplified to:

$$A = \frac{bh}{2}$$

The base is the bottom of the triangle, and the height is the distance from the base to the peak. If a problem asks to calculate the area of a triangle, it will provide the base and height.

For example, if the base of the triangle is 2 feet and the height 4 feet, then the area is 4 square feet. The following equation shows the formula used to calculate the area of the triangle:

$A = \frac{1}{2}bh = \frac{1}{2}(2)(4) = 4$ square feet

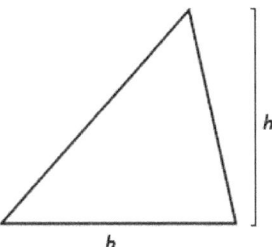

Circles

A circle's perimeter—also known as its **circumference**—is measured by multiplying the diameter by π.

Diameter is the straight line measured from a point on one side of the circle to a point directly across on the opposite side of the circle.

π is referred to as **pi** and is equal to 3.14 (with rounding).

So, the formula is $\pi \times d$.

This is sometimes expressed by the formula $C = 2 \times \pi \times r$, where r is the radius of the circle. These formulas are equivalent, as the radius equals half of the diameter.

The area of a circle is calculated through the formula:

$$A = \pi \times r^2$$

The test will indicate either to leave the answer with π attached or to calculate to the nearest decimal place, which means multiplying by 3.14 for π.

Arc

The **arc of a circle** is the distance between two points on the circle. The length of the arc of a circle in terms of **degrees** is easily determined if the value of the central angle is known. The length of the arc is simply the value of the central angle. In this example, the length of the arc of the circle in degrees is 75°.

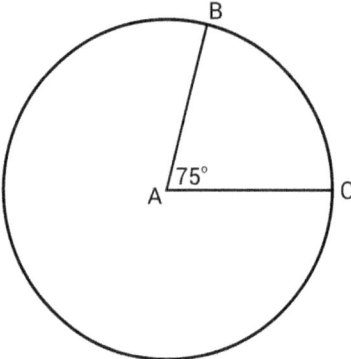

To determine the length of the arc of a circle in distance, the values for both the central angle and the radius must be known. This formula is:

$$\frac{central\ angle}{360°} = \frac{arc\ length}{2\pi r}$$

The equation is simplified by cross-multiplying to solve for the arc length. In the following example, to solve for arc length, substitute the values of the central angle (75°) and the radius (10 inches) into the equation above.

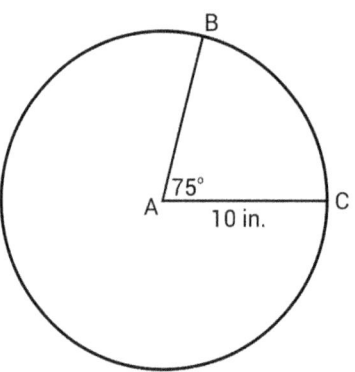

$$\frac{75°}{360°} = \frac{arc\ length}{2(3.14)(10\ in)}$$

To solve the equation, first cross-multiply: $4{,}710 = 360(arc\ length)$. Next, divide each side of the equation by 360. The result of the formula is that the arc length is 13.1 (rounded).

Mathematics

Parallelograms

Similar to triangles, the height of the parallelogram is measured from one base to the other at a 90° angle (or perpendicular).

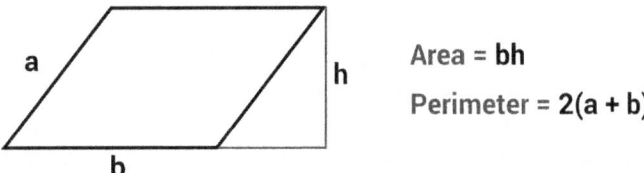

Trapezoid

The **area of a trapezoid** can be calculated using the formula: $A = \frac{1}{2} \times h(b_1 + b_2)$, where h is the height and b_1 and b_2 are the parallel bases of the trapezoid:

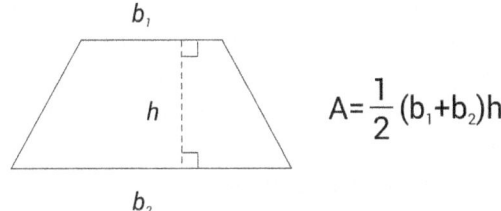

Regular Polygon

The area of a regular polygon can be determined by using its perimeter and the length of the apothem. The **apothem** is a line from the center of the regular polygon to any of its sides at a right angle. (Note that the perimeter of a regular polygon can be determined given the length of only one side.) The formula for the area (A) of a regular polygon is $A = \frac{1}{2} \times a \times P$, where a is the length of the apothem, and P is the perimeter of the figure. Consider the following regular pentagon:

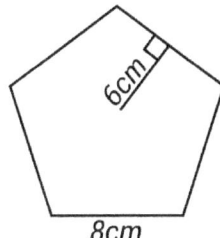

To find the area, the perimeter (P) is calculated first: 8 cm × 5 → P = 40 cm. Then the perimeter and the apothem are used to find the area (A):

$$A = \frac{1}{2} \times a \times P \to A = \frac{1}{2} \times (6 \text{ cm}) \times (40 \text{ cm}) \to A = 120 \text{ cm}^2$$

Note that the unit is:

$$\text{cm}^2 \to \text{cm} \times \text{cm} = \text{cm}^2$$

Irregular Shapes

The perimeter of an irregular polygon is found by adding the lengths of all of the sides. In cases where all of the sides are given, this will be very straightforward, as it will simply involve finding the sum of the provided lengths. Other times, a side length may be missing and must be determined before the perimeter can be calculated.

Consider the example below:

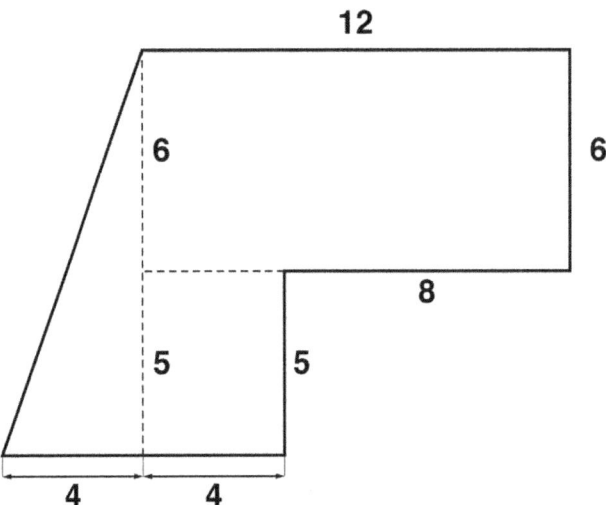

All of the side lengths are provided except for the angled side on the left. Test takers should notice that this is the hypotenuse of a right triangle. The other two sides of the triangle are provided (the base is 4 and the height is $6 + 5 = 11$). The Pythagorean Theorem can be used to find the length of the hypotenuse, remembering that:

$$a^2 + b^2 = c^2$$

Substituting the side values provided yields:

$$(4)^2 + (11)^2 = c^2$$

Therefore,

$$c = \sqrt{16 + 121} = 11.7$$

Finally, the perimeter can be found by adding this new side length with the other provided lengths to get the total length around the figure:

$$4 + 4 + 5 + 8 + 6 + 12 + 11.7 = 50.7$$

144

Although units are not provided in this figure, remember that reporting units with a measurement is important.

The area of irregular polygons is found by decomposing, or breaking apart, the figure into smaller shapes. When the area of the smaller shapes is determined, the area of the smaller shapes will produce the area of the original figure when added together. Consider the earlier example:

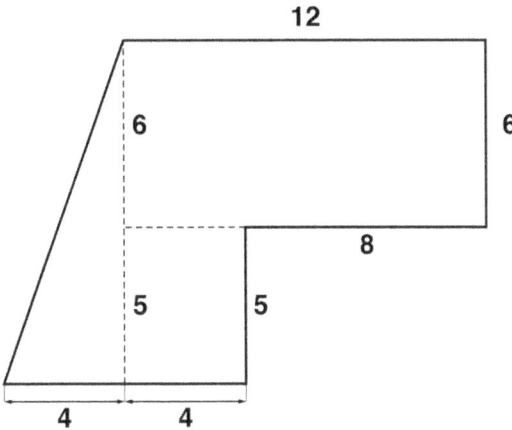

The irregular polygon is decomposed into two rectangles and a triangle. The area of the large rectangle ($A = l \times w \rightarrow A = 12 \times 6$) is 72 square units. The area of the small rectangle is 20 square units ($A = 4 \times 5$). The area of the triangle ($A = \frac{1}{2} \times b \times h \rightarrow A = \frac{1}{2} \times 4 \times 11$) is 22 square units. The sum of the areas of these figures produces the total area of the original polygon:

$A = 72 + 20 + 22 \rightarrow A = 114$ square units

Here's another example:

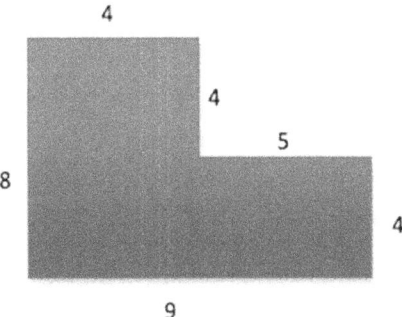

This irregular polygon is decomposed into two rectangles. The area of the large rectangle ($A = l \times w \rightarrow A = 8 \times 4$) is 32 square units. The area of the small rectangle is 20 square units ($A = 4 \times 5$). The sum of the areas of these figures produces the total area of the original polygon:

$A = 32 + 20 \rightarrow A = 52$ square units

Right Rectangular Prisms
A **right rectangular prism** consists of:

- Two congruent (same size and shape) rectangles as the parallel *bases* (top and bottom).
- Two congruent rectangles as the *side* faces.

Mathematics

- Two congruent rectangles as the *front and back* faces.

It is called a right prism because the base and sides meet at right angles.

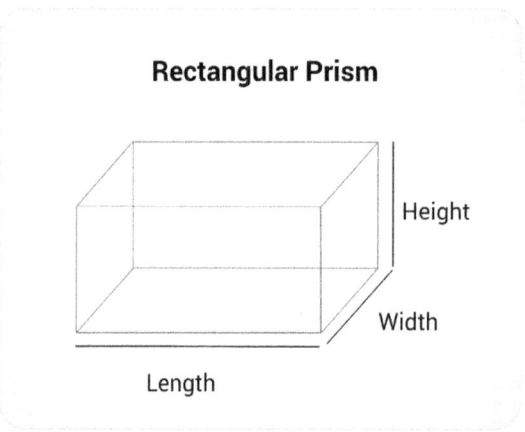

Rectangular Prism

The length and width of the prism is the length and width of the rectangular base. The height of the prism is the measure from one base to the other.

The surface area of three-dimensional figures can be found by adding the areas of each of its bases and faces. The areas of a right rectangular prism are found as follows: two bases → $A = l \times w$; front and back faces → $A = l \times h$; two side faces → $A = w \times h$. The sum of these six areas will equal the surface area of the prism.

$$Surface\ area = area\ of\ 2\ bases + area\ of\ front\ and\ back + area\ of\ 2\ sides$$

This is true for all right rectangular prisms leading to the formula for surface area:

$$SA = 2 \times l \times w + 2 \times l \times h + 2 \times w \times h$$

$$SA = 2(l \times w + l \times h + w \times h)$$

Given the right rectangular prism below, the surface area is calculated as follows:

$$SA = 2\left(3\tfrac{1}{2}\text{ft}\right)\left(2\tfrac{1}{2}\text{ft}\right) + 2\left(3\tfrac{1}{2}\text{ft}\right)\left(1\tfrac{1}{2}\text{ft}\right) + 2\left(2\tfrac{1}{2}\text{ft}\right)\left(1\tfrac{1}{2}\text{ft}\right) \rightarrow SA = 35.5\text{ ft}^2$$

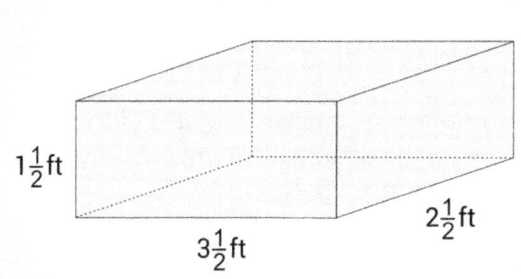

The **volume of a solid** (three-dimensional figure) is the number of cubic units needed to fill the space that the figure occupies. This concept is similar to filling a box with blocks. Volume is a three-dimensional measurement. Therefore, volume is expressed in cubic units such as cubic centimeters (cm³), cubic feet (ft³), and cubic yards (yd³). If a rectangular prism has a volume of 30 cubic meters (30 m³), it will take 30 cubes, each with sides one meter in length, to fill the space occupied by the prism. A simple formula can be used to determine the volume of a right rectangular prism. The area of the base of the prism ($l \times w$) will indicate how many "blocks" are needed to cover the base. The height (h) of the prism will indicate how many "levels" of blocks are needed to construct the prism.

Therefore, to find the volume (V) of a right rectangular prism, the area of the base ($l \times w$) is multiplied by the height (h):

$$V = l \times w \times h$$

The volume of the prism shown above is calculated:

$$V = \left(3\frac{1}{2} \text{ft}\right) \times \left(2\frac{1}{2} \text{ft}\right) \times \left(1\frac{1}{2} \text{ft}\right) \rightarrow V = 13.125 \text{ ft}^3$$

Effects of Changes to Dimensions on Area and Volume

Similar polygons are figures that are the same shape but different sizes. Likewise, similar solids are different sizes but are the same shape. In both cases, corresponding angles in the same positions for both figures are congruent (equal), and corresponding sides are proportional in length. For example, the triangles below are similar. The following pairs of corresponding angles are congruent: ∠A and ∠D; ∠B and ∠E; ∠C and ∠F. The corresponding sides are proportional:

$$\frac{AB}{DE} = \frac{6}{3} = 2$$

$$\frac{BC}{EF} = \frac{9}{4.5} = 2$$

$$\frac{CA}{FD} = \frac{10}{5} = 2$$

In other words, triangle ABC is the same shape but twice as large as triangle DEF.

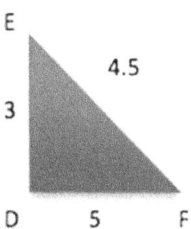

An example of similar triangular pyramids is shown below.

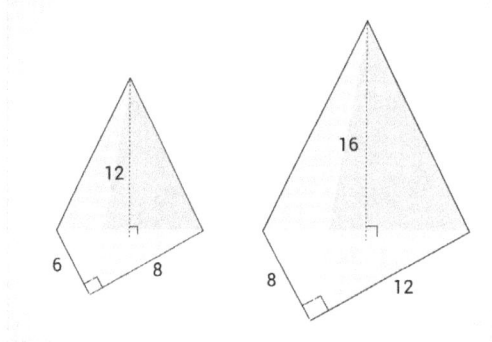

Given the nature of two- and three-dimensional measurements, changing dimensions by a given scale (multiplier) does not change the area of volume by the same scale. Consider a rectangle with a length of 5 centimeters and a width of 4 centimeters. The area of the rectangle is 20 cm². Doubling the dimensions of the rectangle (multiplying by a scale factor of 2) to 10 centimeters and 8 centimeters *does not* double the area to 40 cm². Area is a two-dimensional measurement (measured in square units). Therefore, the dimensions are multiplied by a scale that is squared (raised to the second power) to determine the scale of the corresponding areas. For the previous example, the length and width are multiplied by 2. Therefore, the area is multiplied by 2^2, or 4. The area of a 5 cm × 4 cm rectangle is 20 cm². The area of a 10 cm × 8 cm rectangle is 80 cm².

Volume is a three-dimensional measurement, which is measured in cubic units. Therefore, the scale between dimensions of similar solids is cubed (raised to the third power) to determine the scale between their volumes. Consider similar right rectangular prisms: one with a length of 8 inches, a width of 24 inches, and a height of 16 inches; the second with a length of 4 inches, a width of 12 inches, and a height of 8 inches. The first prism, multiplied by a scalar of $\frac{1}{2}$, produces the measurement of the second prism. The volume of the first prism, multiplied by $(\frac{1}{2})^3$, which equals $\frac{1}{8}$, produces the volume of the second prism. The volume of the first prism is 8 in × 24 in × 16 in which equals 3,072 in³. The volume of the second prism is 4 in × 12 in × 8 in which equals 384 in³:

$$3{,}072 \text{ in}^3 \times \frac{1}{8} = 384 \text{ in}^3$$

The rules for squaring the scalar for area and cubing the scalar for volume only hold true for similar figures. In other words, if only one dimension is changed (changing the width of a rectangle but not the length) or dimensions are changed at different rates (the length of a prism is doubled and its height is tripled) the figures are not similar (same shape). Therefore, the rules above do not apply.

Components of the Coordinate Plane

X-Axis, Y-Axis, Origin, and Four Quadrants

The **coordinate plane**, sometimes referred to as the **Cartesian plane**, is a two-dimensional surface consisting of a horizontal and a vertical number line. The horizontal number line is referred to as the *x*-**axis**, and the vertical number line is referred to as the *y*-**axis**. The *x*-axis and *y*-axis intersect (or cross) at a point called the **origin**. At the origin, the value of the *x*-axis is zero, and the value of the *y*-axis is zero. The coordinate plane identifies the exact location of a point that is plotted on the two-dimensional surface. Like a map, the location of all points on the plane are in relation to the origin. Along the *x*-axis (horizontal line), numbers to the right of the origin are positive and increasing in value (1, 2, 3,...) and to the left of the origin numbers are negative and decreasing in value $(-1, -2, -3,...)$. Along the y-axis (vertical line), numbers above the origin are positive and increasing in value and numbers below the origin are negative and decreasing in value.

The x- and y-axis divide the coordinate plane into four sections. These sections are referred to as quadrant one, quadrant two, quadrant three, and quadrant four, and are often written with Roman numerals I, II, III, and IV.

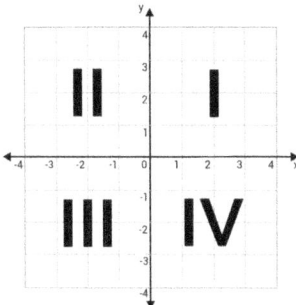

The upper right section is **Quadrant I** and consists of points with positive x-values and positive y-values. The upper left section is **Quadrant II** and consists of points with negative x-values and positive y-values. The bottom left section is **Quadrant III** and consists of points with negative x-values and negative y-values. The bottom right section is **Quadrant IV** and consists of points with positive x-values and negative y-values.

Solving Problems in the Coordinate Plane

The location of a point on a coordinate grid is identified by writing it as an ordered pair. An **ordered pair** is a set of numbers indicating the x-and y-coordinates of the point. Ordered pairs are written in the form (x, y) where x and y are values which indicate their respective coordinates. For example, the point $(3, -2)$ has an x-coordinate of 3 and a y-coordinate of -2.

Mathematics

Plotting a point on the coordinate plane with a given coordinate means starting from the origin $(0, 0)$. To determine the value of the x-coordinate, move right (positive number) or left (negative number) along the x-axis. Next, move up (positive number) or down (negative number) to the value of the y-coordinate. Finally, plot and label the point. For example, plotting the point $(1, -2)$ requires starting from the origin and moving right along the x-axis to positive one, then moving down until straight across from negative 2 on the y-axis. The point is plotted and labeled. This point, along with three other points, are plotted and labeled on the graph below.

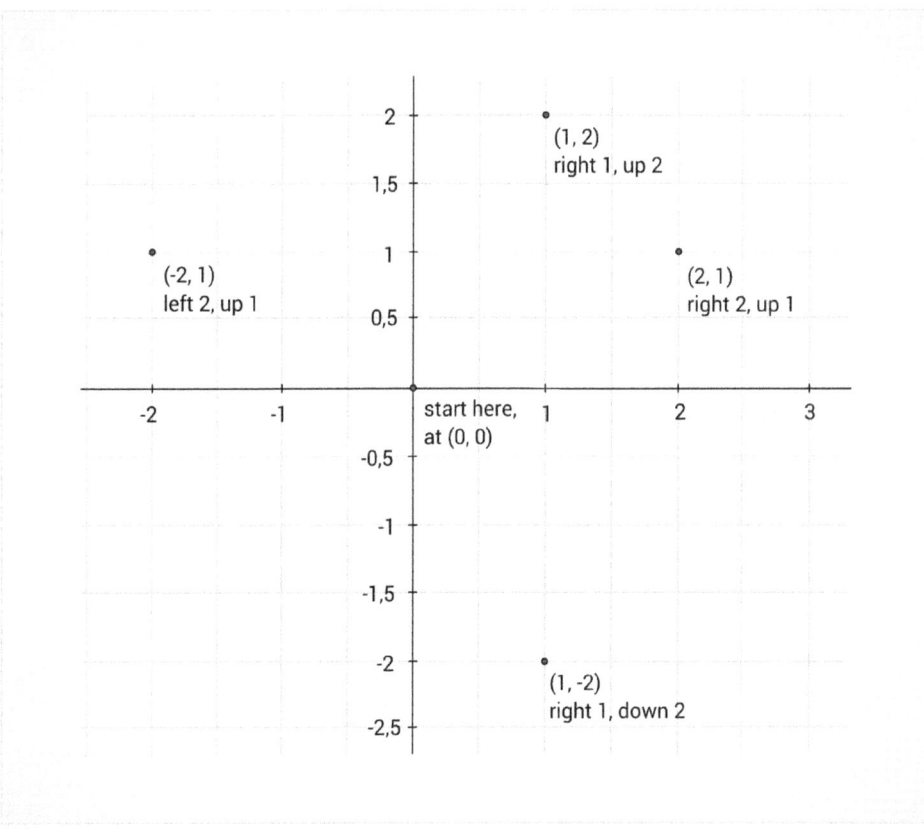

To write the coordinates of a point on the coordinate grid, a line should be traced directly above or below the point until reaching the x-axis (noting the value on the x-axis). Then, returning to the point, a line should be traced directly to the right or left of the point until reaching the y-axis (noting the value on the y-axis). The ordered pair (x, y) should be written with the values determined for the x- and y-coordinates.

Polygons can be drawn in the coordinate plane given the coordinates of their vertices. These coordinates can be used to determine the perimeter and area of the figure. Suppose triangle RQP has vertices located at the points:

$R(-2,0)$, $Q(2,2)$, and $P(2,0)$. By plotting the points for the three vertices, the triangle can be constructed as follows:

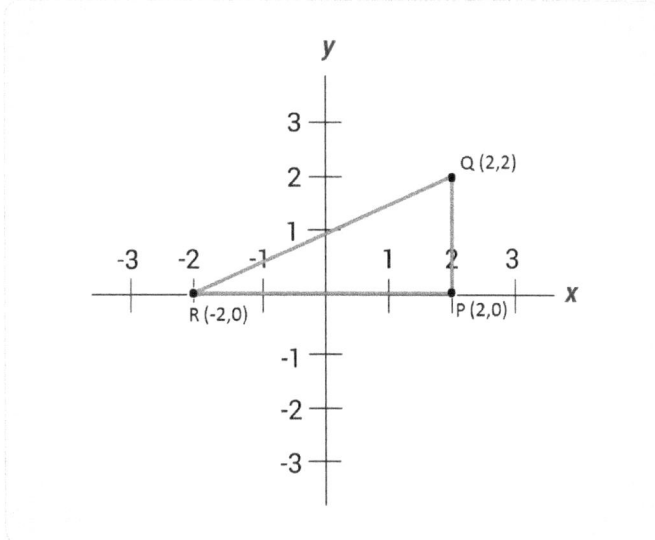

Because points R and P have the same y-coordinates (they are directly across from each other), the distance between them is determined by subtracting their x-coordinates (or simply counting units from one point to the other): $2 - (-2) = 4$. Therefore, the length of side RP is 4 units. Because points Q and P have the same x-coordinate (they are directly above and below each other), the distance between them is determined by subtracting their y-coordinates (or counting units between them): $2 - 0 = 2$. Therefore, the length of side PQ is 2 units. Knowing the length of side RP, which is the base of the triangle, and the length of side PQ, which is the height of the triangle, the area of the figure can be determined by using the formula $A = \frac{1}{2}bh$.

To determine the perimeter of the triangle, the lengths of all three sides are needed. Points R and Q are neither directly across nor directly above and below each other. Therefore, the distance formula must be used to find the length of side RQ.

The distance formula is as follows:

$$d = \sqrt{(x_2 - x_1)^2 + (y_2 - y_1)^2}$$

$$d = \sqrt{(2 - (-2))^2 + (2 - 0)^2}$$

$$d = \sqrt{(4)^2 + (2)^2}$$

$$d = \sqrt{16 + 4}$$

$$d = \sqrt{20}$$

The perimeter is determined by adding the lengths of the three sides of the triangle.

Mathematics

Solving Problems Involving Measurement

Elapsed Time, Money, Length, Volume, and Mass

Word problems involving elapsed time, money, length, volume, and mass require determining which operations (addition, subtraction, multiplication, and division) should be performed, and using and/or converting the proper unit for the scenario.

The following table lists key words that can be used to indicate the proper operation:

Addition	Sum, total, in all, combined, increase of, more than, added to
Subtraction	Difference, change, remaining, less than, decreased by
Multiplication	Product, times, twice, triple, each
Division	Quotient, goes into, per, evenly, divided by half, divided by third, split

Identifying and utilizing the proper units for the scenario requires knowing how to apply the conversion rates for money, length, volume, and mass. For example, given a scenario that requires subtracting 8 inches from $2\frac{1}{2}$ feet, both values should first be expressed in the same unit (they could be expressed $\frac{2}{3}$ ft & $2\frac{1}{2}$ ft, or 8 in and 30 in). The desired unit for the answer may also require converting back to another unit.

Consider the following scenario: A parking area along the river is only wide enough to fit one row of cars and is $\frac{1}{2}$ kilometers long. The average space needed per car is 5 meters. How many cars can be parked along the river? First, all measurements should be converted to similar units: $\frac{1}{2}$ km = 500 m. The operation(s) needed should be identified. Because the problem asks for the number of cars, the total space should be divided by the space per car. 500 meters divided by 5 meters per car yields a total of 100 cars. Written as an expression, the meters unit cancels and the cars unit is left: $\frac{500 \text{ m}}{5 \text{ m/car}}$ the same as $500 \text{ m} \times \frac{1 \text{ car}}{5 \text{ m}}$ yields 100 cars.

When dealing with problems involving elapsed time, breaking the problem down into workable parts is helpful. For example, suppose the length of time between 1:15pm and 3:45pm must be determined. From 1:15pm to 2:00pm is 45 minutes (knowing there are 60 minutes in an hour). From 2:00pm to 3:00pm is 1 hour. From 3:00pm to 3:45pm is 45 minutes. The total elapsed time is 45 minutes plus 1 hour plus 45 minutes. This sum produces 1 hour and 90 minutes. 90 minutes is over an hour, so this is converted to 1 hour (60 minutes) and 30 minutes. The total elapsed time can now be expressed as 2 hours and 30 minutes.

Measuring Lengths of Objects

The length of an object can be measured using standard tools such as rulers, yard sticks, meter sticks, and measuring tapes. The following image depicts a yardstick:

Choosing the right tool to perform the measurement requires determining whether United States customary units or metric units are desired, and having a grasp of the approximate length of each unit and the approximate

Mathematics

length of each tool. The measurement can still be performed by trial and error without the knowledge of the approximate size of the tool.

For example, to determine the length of a room in feet, a United States customary unit, various tools can be used. These include a ruler (typically 12 inches/1 foot long), a yardstick (3 feet/1 yard long), or a tape measure displaying feet (typically either 25 feet or 50 feet). Because the length of a room is much larger than the length of a ruler or a yardstick, a tape measure should be used to perform the measurement.

When the correct measuring tool is selected, the measurement is performed by first placing the tool directly above or below the object (if making a horizontal measurement) or directly next to the object (if making a vertical measurement). The next step is aligning the tool so that one end of the object is at the mark for zero units, then recording the unit of the mark at the other end of the object. To give the length of a paperclip in metric units, a ruler displaying centimeters is aligned with one end of the paper clip to the mark for zero centimeters.

Directly down from the other end of the paperclip is the mark that measures its length. In this case, that mark is three small dashes past the 3-centimeter mark. Each small dash is 1 millimeter (or .1 centimeters). Therefore, the length of the paper clip is 3.3 centimeters.

To compare the lengths of objects, each length must be expressed in the same unit. If possible, the objects should be measured with the same tool or with tools utilizing the same units. For example, a ruler and a yardstick can both measure length in inches. If the lengths of the objects are expressed in different units, these different units must be converted to the same unit before comparing them. If two lengths are expressed in the same unit, the lengths may be compared by subtracting the smaller value from the larger value. For example, suppose the lengths of two gardens are to be compared. Garden A has a length of 4 feet, and garden B has a length of 2 yards. 2 yards is converted to 6 feet so that the measurements have similar units. Then, the smaller length (4 feet) is subtracted from the larger length (6 ft): 6 ft − 4 ft = 2 ft. Therefore, garden B is 2 feet larger than garden A.

Mathematics

Relative Sizes of United States Customary Units and Metric Units

The United States customary system and the metric system each consist of distinct units to measure lengths and volume of liquids. The U.S. customary units for length, from smallest to largest, are: inch (in), foot (ft), yard (yd), and mile (mi). The metric units for length, from smallest to largest, are: millimeter (mm), centimeter (cm), decimeter (dm), meter (m), and kilometer (km). The relative size of each unit of length is shown below.

U.S. Customary	Metric	Conversion
12 in = 1 ft	10 mm = 1 cm	1 in = 2.54 cm
36 in = 3 ft = 1 yd	10 cm = 1 dm(decimeter)	1m ≈ 3.28 ft ≈ 1.09 yd
5,280 ft = 1,760 yd = 1 mi	100 cm = 10 dm = 1 m	1 mi ≈ 1.6 km
	1,000 m = 1 km	

The U.S. customary units for volume of liquids, from smallest to largest, are: fluid ounces (fl oz), cup (c), pint (pt), quart (qt), and gallon (gal). The metric units for volume of liquids, from smallest to largest, are: milliliter (mL), centiliter (cL), deciliter (dL), liter (L), and kiloliter (kL). The relative size of each unit of liquid volume is shown below.

U.S. Customary	Metric	Conversion
8 fl oz = 1 c	10 mL = 1 cL	1 pt ≈ 0.473 L
2 c = 1 pt	10 cL = 1 dL	1 L ≈ 1.057 qt
4 c = 2 pt = 1 qt	1,000 mL = 100 cL = 10 dL = 1 L	1 gal ≈ 3.785 L
4 qt = 1 gal	1,000 L = 1 kL	

The U.S. customary system measures weight (how strongly Earth is pulling on an object) in the following units, from least to greatest: ounce (oz), pound (lb), and ton. The metric system measures mass (the quantity of matter within an object) in the following units, from least to greatest: milligram (mg), centigram (cg), gram (g), kilogram (kg), and metric ton (MT). The relative sizes of each unit of weight and mass are shown below.

U.S. Measures of Weight	Metric Measures of Mass
16 oz = 1 lb	10 mg = 1 cg
2,000 lbs = 1 ton	100 cg = 1 g
	1,000 g = 1 kg
	1,000 kg = 1 MT

Note that weight and mass DO NOT measure the same thing.

Time is measured in the following units, from shortest to longest: second (sec), minute (min), hour (h), day (d), week (wk), month (mo), year (yr), decade, century, millennium. The relative sizes of each unit of time is shown below.

- 60 sec = 1 min
- 60 min = 1 h
- 24 hr = 1 d
- 7 d = 1 wk
- 52 wk = 1 yr
- 12 mo = 1 yr
- 10 yr = 1 decade
- 100 yrs = 1 century
- 1,000 yrs = 1 millennium

Conversion of Units

When working with different systems of measurement, conversion from one unit to another may be necessary. The conversion rate must be known to convert units. One method for converting units is to write and solve a proportion. The arrangement of values in a proportion is extremely important. Suppose that a problem requires converting 20 fluid ounces to cups. To do so, a proportion can be written using the conversion rate of 8 fl oz = 1 c with x representing the missing value. The proportion can be written in any of the following ways:

$$\frac{1}{8} = \frac{x}{20} \left(\frac{c\ for\ conversion}{fl\ oz\ for\ conversion} = \frac{unknown\ c}{fl\ oz\ given} \right)$$

$$\frac{8}{1} = \frac{20}{x} \left(\frac{fl\ oz\ for\ conversion}{c\ for\ conversion} = \frac{fl\ oz\ given}{unknown\ c} \right)$$

$$\frac{1}{x} = \frac{8}{20} \left(\frac{c\ for\ conversion}{unknown\ c} = \frac{fl\ oz\ for\ conversion}{fl\ oz\ given} \right)$$

$$\frac{x}{1} = \frac{20}{8} \left(\frac{unknown\ c}{c\ for\ conversion} = \frac{fl\ oz\ given}{fl\ oz\ for\ conversion} \right)$$

To solve a proportion, the ratios are cross-multiplied and the resulting equation is solved. When cross-multiplying, all four proportions above will produce the same equation:

$$(8)(x) = (20)(1) \rightarrow 8x = 20$$

Divide by 8 to isolate the variable x, the result is $x = 2.5$. The variable x represented the unknown number of cups. Therefore, the conclusion is that 20 fluid ounces converts (is equal) to 2.5 cups.

Sometimes converting units requires writing and solving more than one proportion. Suppose an exam question asks to determine how many hours are in 2 weeks. Without knowing the conversion rate between hours and weeks, this can be determined knowing the conversion rates between weeks and days, and between days and hours. First, weeks are converted to days, then days are converted to hours. To convert from weeks to days, the following proportion can be written:

$$\frac{7}{1} = \frac{x}{2} \left(\frac{days\ conversion}{weeks\ conversion} = \frac{days\ unknown}{weeks\ given} \right)$$

Cross-multiplying produces: $(7)(2) = (x)(1) \rightarrow 14 = x$. Therefore, 2 weeks is equal to 14 days. Next, a proportion is written to convert 14 days to hours:

$$\frac{24}{1} = \frac{x}{14} \left(\frac{conversion\ hours}{conversion\ days} = \frac{unknown\ hours}{given\ days} \right)$$

Cross-multiplying produces:

$$(24)(14) = (x)(1) \rightarrow 336 = x$$

Therefore, the answer is that there are 336 hours in 2 weeks.

Mathematics

Statistical Concepts

Identifying Statistical Questions

The field of **statistics** describes relationships between quantities that are related, but not necessarily in a deterministic manner. For example, a graduating student's salary will often be higher when the student graduates with a higher GPA, but this is not always the case. Likewise, people who smoke tobacco are more likely to develop lung cancer, but, in fact, it is possible for non-smokers to develop the disease as well. Statistics describes these kinds of situations, where the likelihood of some outcome depends on the starting data.

Descriptive statistics involves analyzing a collection of data to describe its broad properties such average (or mean), what percent of the data falls within a given range, and other such properties. An example of this would be taking all of the test scores from a given class and calculating the average test score. **Inferential statistics** attempts to use data about a subset of some population to make inferences about the rest of the population. An example of this would be taking a collection of students who received tutoring and comparing their results to a collection of students who did not receive tutoring, then using that comparison to try to predict whether the tutoring program in question is beneficial.

Measures of Center and Range

The center of a set of data (statistical values) can be represented by its mean, median, or mode. These are sometimes referred to as **measures of central tendency**.

Mean

The first property that can be defined for this set of data is the **mean**. This is the same as the average. To find the mean, add up all the data points, then divide by the total number of data points. For example, suppose that in a class of 10 students, the scores on a test were 50, 60, 65, 65, 75, 80, 85, 85, 90, 100. Therefore, the average test score will be:

$$\frac{50 + 60 + 65 + 65 + 75 + 80 + 85 + 85 + 90 + 100}{10} = 75.5$$

The mean is a useful number if the distribution of data is normal (more on this later), which roughly means that the frequency of different outcomes has a single peak and is roughly equally distributed on both sides of that peak. However, it is less useful in some cases where the data might be split or where there are some outliers. **Outliers** are data points that are far from the rest of the data. For example, suppose there are 10 executives and 90 employees at a company. The executives make $1000 per hour, and the employees make $10 per hour. Therefore, the average pay rate will be:

$$\frac{\$1000 \times 10 + \$10 \times 90}{100} = \$109 \text{ per hour}$$

In this case, this average is not very descriptive since it's not close to the actual pay of the executives or the employees.

Median

Another useful measurement is the **median**. In a data set, the median is the point in the middle. The **middle** refers to the point where half the data comes before it and half comes after, when the data is recorded in numerical order. For instance, these are the speeds of the fastball of a pitcher during the last inning that he pitched (in order from least to greatest):

90, 92, 93, 93, 95, 96, 97, 97, 97

There are nine total numbers, so the middle or *median* number is the 5th one, which is 95.

In cases where the number of data points is an even number, then the average of the two middle points is taken. In the previous example of test scores, the two middle points are 75 and 80. Since there is no single point, the average of these two scores needs to be found.

The average is:

$$\frac{75 + 80}{2} = 77.5$$

The median is generally a good value to use if there are a few outliers in the data. It prevents those outliers from affecting the "middle" value as much as when using the mean.

Since an outlier is a data point that is far from most of the other data points in a data set, this means an outlier also is any point that is far from the median of the data set. The outliers can have a substantial effect on the mean of a data set, but they usually do not change the median or mode, or do not change them by a large quantity. For example, consider the data set (3, 5, 6, 6, 6, 8). This has a median of 6 and a mode of 6, with a mean of $\frac{34}{6} \approx 5.67$. Now, suppose a new data point of 1000 is added so that the data set is now (3, 5, 6, 6, 6, 8, 1000). The median and mode, which are both still 6, remain unchanged. However, the average is now $\frac{1034}{7}$, which is approximately 147.7. In this case, the median and mode will be better descriptions for most of the data points.

Outliers in a given data set are sometimes the result of an error by the experimenter, but oftentimes, they are perfectly valid data points that must be taken into consideration.

Mode

One additional measure to define for *X* is the **mode**. This is the data point that appears most frequently. If two or more data points all tie for the most frequent appearance, then each of them is considered a mode. In the case of the test scores, where the numbers were 50, 60, 65, 65, 75, 80, 85, 85, 90, 100, there are two modes: 65 and 85.

Range

The **range** of a data set is the difference between the highest and the lowest values in the set. The range can be considered the span of the data set. To determine the range, the smallest value in the set is subtracted from the largest value.

Best Description of a Set of Data

Measures of central tendency, namely mean, median, and mode, describe characteristics of a set of data. Specifically, they are intended to represent a *typical* value in the set by identifying a central position of the set. Depending on the characteristics of a specific set of data, different measures of central tendency are more indicative of a typical value in the set.

When a data set is grouped closely together with a relatively small range and the data is spread out somewhat evenly, the mean is an effective indicator of a typical value in the set. Consider the following data set representing the height of sixth grade boys in inches: 61 inches, 54 inches, 58 inches, 63 inches, 58 inches. The mean of the set is 58.8 inches. The data set is grouped closely (the range is only 9 inches) and the values are spread relatively evenly (three values below the mean and two values above the mean). Therefore, the mean value of 58.8 inches is an effective measure of central tendency in this case.

When a data set contains a small number of values either extremely large or extremely small when compared to the other values, the mean is not an effective measure of central tendency. Consider the following data set representing annual incomes of homeowners on a given street: $71,000; $74,000; $75,000; $77,000; $340,000. The mean of this set is $127,400. This figure does not indicate a typical value in the set, which contains four out of five values between $71,000 and $77,000. The median is a much more effective measure of central tendency for data sets such as these. Finding the middle value diminishes the influence of outliers, or numbers that may appear out of place, like the $340,000 annual income. The median for this set is $75,000 which is much more typical of a value in the set.

The **mode of a data set** is a useful measure of central tendency for categorical data when each piece of data is an option from a category. Consider a survey of 31 commuters asking how they get to work with results summarized below.

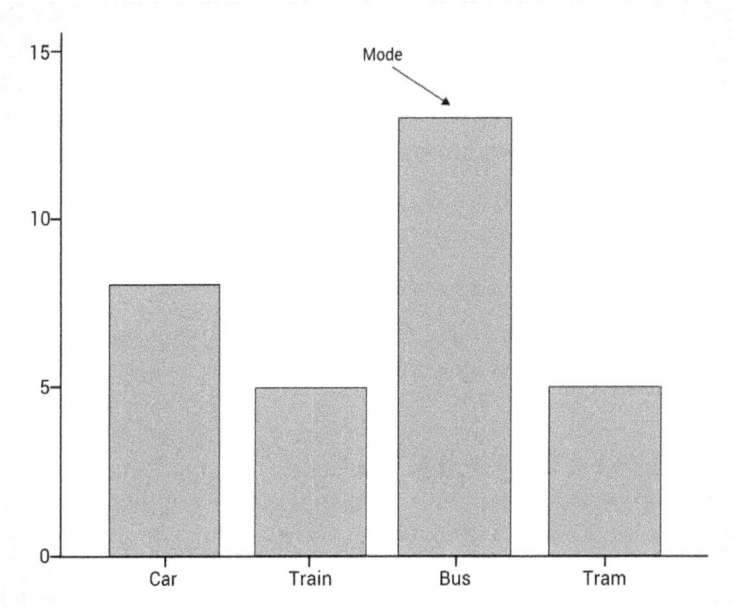

The mode for this set represents the value, or option, of the data that repeats most often. This indicates that the bus is the most popular method of transportation for the commuters.

Effects of Changes in Data
Changing all values of a data set in a consistent way produces predictable changes in the measures of the center and range of the set. A linear transformation changes the original value into the new value by either adding a given number to each value, multiplying each value by a given number, or both. Adding (or subtracting) a given value to each data point will increase (or decrease) the mean, median, and any modes by the same value. However, the range will remain the same due to the way that range is calculated. Multiplying (or dividing) a given value by each data point will increase (or decrease) the mean, median, and any modes, and the range by the same factor.

Consider the following data set, call it set P, representing the price of different cases of soda at a grocery store: $4.25, $4.40, $4.75, $4.95, $4.95, $5.15. The mean of set P is $4.74. The median is $4.85. The mode of the set is $4.95. The range is $0.90. Suppose the state passes a new tax of $0.25 on every case of soda sold. The new data set, set T, is calculated by adding $0.25 to each data point from set P. Therefore, set T consists of the following values: $4.50, $4.65, $5.00, $5.20, $5.20, $5.40. The mean of set T is $4.99. The median is $5.10. The mode of the set is $5.20. The range is $.90. The mean, median and mode of set T is equal to $0.25 added to the mean, median, and mode of set P. The range stays the same.

Now suppose, due to inflation, the store raises the cost of every item by 10 percent. Raising costs by 10 percent is calculated by multiplying each value by 1.1. The new data set, set I, is calculated by multiplying each data point from set T by 1.1. Therefore, set I consists of the following values: $4.95, $5.12, $5.50, $5.72, $5.72, $5.94. The mean of set I is $5.49. The median is $5.61. The mode of the set is $5.72. The range is $0.99. The mean, median, mode, and range of set I is equal to 1.1 multiplied by the mean, median, mode, and range of set T because each increased by a factor of 10 percent.

Describing a Set of Data

A set of data can be described in terms of its center, spread, shape and any unusual features. The **center of a data** set can be measured by its mean, median, or mode. Measures of central tendency are covered in the *Measures of Center and Range* section. The **spread of a data set** refers to how far the data points are from the center (mean or median). The spread can be measured by the range or by the quartiles and interquartile range. A data set with all its data points clustered around the center will have a small spread. A data set covering a wide range of values will have a large spread.

When a data set is displayed as a histogram or frequency distribution plot, the shape indicates if a sample is normally distributed, symmetrical, or has measures of skewness or kurtosis. When graphed, a data set with a normal distribution will resemble a bell curve.

If the data set is symmetrical, each half of the graph when divided at the center is a mirror image of the other. If the graph has fewer data points to the right, the data is skewed right. If it has fewer data points to the left, the data is skewed left.

Kurtosis is a measure of whether the data is heavy-tailed with a high number of outliers, or light-tailed with a low number of outliers.

A description of a data set should include any unusual features such as gaps or outliers. A **gap** is a span within the range of the data set containing no data points. An outlier is a data point with a value either extremely large or extremely small when compared to the other values in the set.

Representing and Interpreting Data

Interpreting Displays of Data

A set of data can be visually displayed in various forms allowing for quick identification of characteristics of the set. **Histograms**, such as the one shown below, display the number of data points (vertical axis) that fall into given intervals (horizontal axis) across the range of the set. The histogram below displays the heights of black cherry trees in a certain city park. Each rectangle represents the number of trees with heights between a given five-point span. For example, the furthest bar to the right indicates that two trees are between 85 and 90 feet. Histograms can describe the center, spread, shape, and any unusual characteristics of a data set.

A **box plot**, also called a **box-and-whisker plot**, divides the data points into four groups and displays the five-number summary for the set as well as any outliers. The five-number summary consists of:

- The lower extreme: the lowest value that is not an outlier
- The higher extreme: the highest value that is not an outlier
- The median of the set: also referred to as the second quartile or Q_2
- The first quartile or Q_1: the median of values below Q_2
- The third quartile or Q_3: the median of values above Q_2

Calculating each of these values is covered in the next section, *Graphical Representation of Data*.

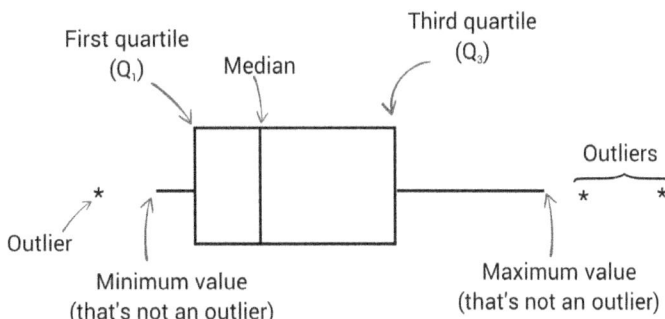

Suppose the box plot displays IQ scores for 12th grade students at a given school. The five number summary of the data consists of: lower extreme (67); upper extreme (127); Q_2 or median (100); Q_1 (91); Q_3 (108); and outliers (135 and 140). Although all data points are not known from the plot, the points are divided into four quartiles each, including 25% of the data points. Therefore, 25% of students scored between 67 and 91, 25% scored between 91 and 100, 25% scored between 100 and 108, and 25% scored between 108 and 127. These percentages include the normal values for the set and exclude the outliers. This information is useful when comparing a given score with the rest of the scores in the set.

A **scatter plot** is a mathematical diagram that visually displays the relationship or connection between two variables. The independent variable is placed on the *x*-axis, or horizontal axis, and the dependent variable is placed on the *y*-axis, or vertical axis. When visually examining the points on the graph, if the points model a linear relationship, or if a line of best-fit can be drawn through the points with the points relatively close on either side, then a correlation exists. If the line of best-fit has a positive slope (rises from left to right), then the variables have a positive correlation. If the line of best-fit has a negative slope (falls from left to right), then the variables have a negative correlation. If a line of best-fit cannot be drawn, then no correlation exists. A positive or negative correlation can be categorized as strong or weak, depending on how closely the points are graphed around the line of best-fit.

Graphical Representation of Data

Various graphs can be used to visually represent a given set of data. Each type of graph requires a different method of arranging data points and different calculations of the data. Examples of histograms, box plots, and scatter plots are discussed in the previous section *Interpreting Displays of Data*. To construct a histogram, the range of the data points is divided into equal intervals. The frequency for each interval is then determined, which reveals how many points fall into each interval. A graph is constructed with the vertical axis representing the frequency and the horizontal axis representing the intervals. The lower value of each interval should be labeled along the horizontal axis. Finally, for each interval, a bar is drawn from the lower value of each interval to the lower value of the next interval with a height equal to the frequency of the interval. Because of the intervals, histograms do not have any gaps between bars along the horizontal axis.

A scatter plot displays the relationship between two variables. Values for the independent variable, typically denoted by x, are paired with values for the dependent variable, typically denoted by y. Each set of corresponding values are written as an ordered pair (x, y). To construct the graph, a coordinate grid is labeled with the x-axis representing the independent variable and the y-axis representing the dependent variable.

Each ordered pair is graphed.

Like a scatter plot, a **line graph** compares variables that change continuously, typically over time. Paired data values (ordered pairs) are plotted on a coordinate grid with the x- and y-axis representing the variables. A line is drawn from each point to the next, going from left to right. The line graph below displays cell phone use for given years (two variables) for men, women, and both sexes (three data sets).

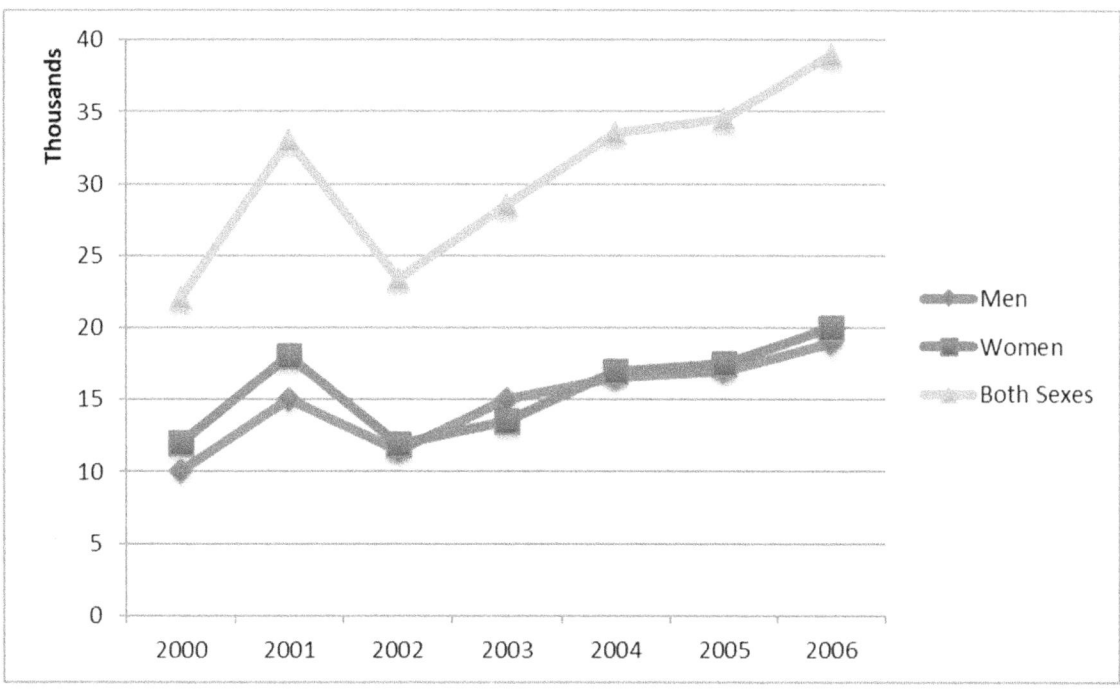

A **line plot**, also called **dot plot**, displays the frequency of data (numerical values) on a number line. To construct a line plot, a number line is used that includes all unique data values. It is marked with x's or dots above the value the number of times that the value occurs in the data set.

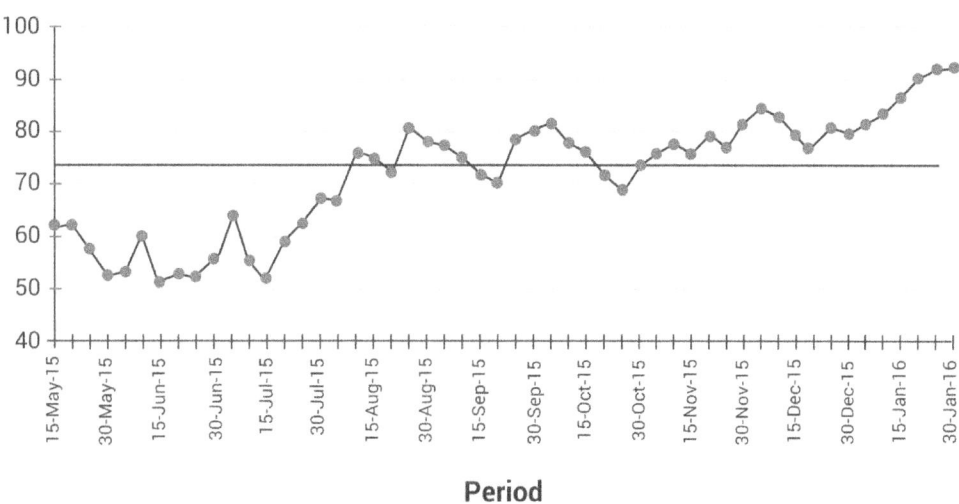

A **bar graph** looks similar to a histogram but displays categorical data. The horizontal axis represents each category and the vertical axis represents the frequency for the category. A bar is drawn for each category (often different colors) with a height extending to the frequency for that category within the data set. A **double bar graph** displays two sets of data that contain data points consisting of the same categories. The double bar graph below indicates that two girls and four boys like Pad Thai the most out of all the foods, two boys and five girls like pizza, and so on.

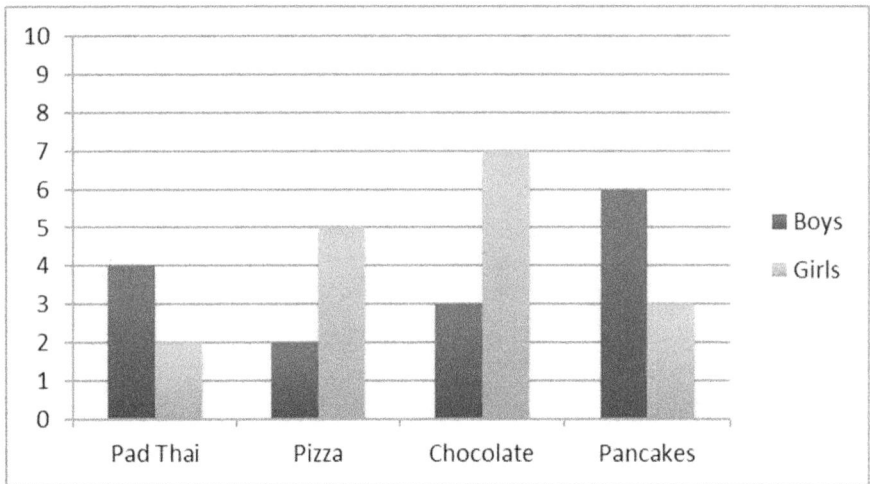

A circle graph, also called a **pie chart**, displays categorical data with each category representing a percentage of the whole data set. To construct a circle graph, the percent of the data set for each category must be determined. To do so, the frequency of the category is divided by the total number of data points and converted to a percent. For example, if 80 people were asked their favorite pizza topping and 20 responded cheese, then cheese constitutes 25% of the data ($\frac{20}{80} = 0.25 = 25\%$). Each category in a data set is represented by a *slice* of the circle proportionate to its percentage of the whole.

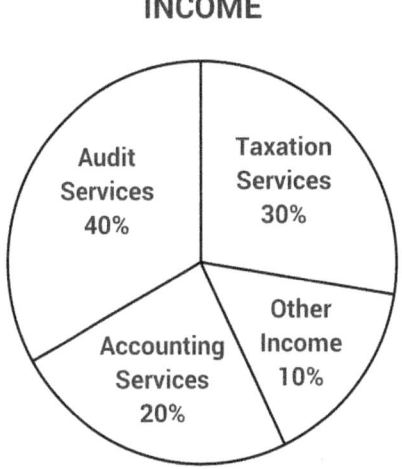

Choice of Graphs to Display Data

Choosing the appropriate graph to display a data set depends on what type of data is included in the set and what information must be displayed. Histograms and box plots can be used for data sets consisting of individual values across a wide range. Examples include test scores and incomes. Histograms and box plots will indicate the center, spread, range, and outliers of a data set. A histogram will show the shape of the data set, while a box

Mathematics

plot will divide the set into quartiles (25% increments), allowing for comparison between a given value and the entire set.

Scatter plots and line graphs can be used to display data consisting of two variables. Examples include height and weight, or distance and time. A correlation between the variables is determined by examining the points on the graph. Line graphs are used if each value for one variable pairs with a distinct value for the other variable. Line graphs show relationships between variables.

Line plots, bar graphs, and circle graphs are all used to display categorical data, such as surveys. Line plots and bar graphs both indicate the frequency of each category within the data set. A line plot is used when the categories consist of numerical values. For example, the number of hours of TV watched by individuals is displayed on a line plot. A bar graph is used when the categories consist of words. For example, the favorite ice cream of individuals is displayed with a bar graph. A circle graph can be used to display either type of categorical data. However, unlike line plots and bar graphs, a circle graph does not indicate the frequency of each category. Instead, the circle graph represents each category as its percentage of the whole data set.

Interpreting the Probability of Events

Probabilities Relative to Likelihood of Occurrence

Probability is a measure of how likely an event is to occur. Probability is written as a fraction between zero and one. If an event has a probability of zero, the event will never occur. If an event has a probability of one, the event will definitely occur. If the probability of an event is closer to zero, the event is unlikely to occur. If the probability of an event is closer to one, the event is more likely to occur. For example, a probability of $\frac{1}{2}$ means that the event is equally as likely to occur as it is not to occur. An example of this is tossing a coin. To calculate the probability of an event, the number of favorable outcomes is divided by the number of total outcomes. For example, suppose you have 2 raffle tickets out of 20 total tickets sold. The probability that you win the raffle is calculated:

$$\frac{number\ of\ favorable\ outcomes}{total\ number\ of\ outcomes} = \frac{2}{20} = \frac{1}{10}$$

Therefore, the probability of winning the raffle is $\frac{1}{10}$ or 0.1.

Chance is the measure of how likely an event is to occur, written as a percent. If an event will never occur, the event has a 0% chance. If an event will certainly occur, the event has a 100% chance. If an event will sometimes occur, the event has a chance somewhere between 0% and 100%. To calculate chance, probability is calculated, and the fraction is converted to a percent.

The probability of multiple events occurring can be determined by multiplying the probability of each event. For example, suppose you flip a coin with heads and tails, and roll a six-sided die numbered one through six. To find the probability that you will flip heads AND roll a two, the probability of each event is determined, and those fractions are multiplied. The probability of flipping heads is $\frac{1}{2}\left(\frac{1\ side\ with\ heads}{2\ sides\ total}\right)$, and the probability of rolling a two is $\frac{1}{6}\left(\frac{1\ side\ with\ a\ 2}{6\ total\ sides}\right)$. The probability of flipping heads AND rolling a 2 is:

$$\frac{1}{2} \times \frac{1}{6} = \frac{1}{12}$$

The above scenario with flipping a coin and rolling a die is an example of independent events. Independent events are circumstances in which the outcome of one event does not affect the outcome of the other event. Conversely, dependent events are ones in which the outcome of one event affects the outcome of the second event. Consider the following scenario: a bag contains 5 black marbles and 5 white marbles. What is the probability of picking 2 black marbles without replacing the marble after the first pick?

The probability of picking a black marble on the first pick is $\frac{5}{10}\left(\frac{5 \text{ black marbles}}{10 \text{ total marbles}}\right)$. Assuming that a black marble was picked, there are now 4 black marbles and 5 white marbles for the second pick. Therefore, the probability of picking a black marble on the second pick is $\frac{4}{9}\left(\frac{4 \text{ black marbles}}{9 \text{ total marbles}}\right)$. To find the probability of picking two black marbles, the probability of each is multiplied:

$$\frac{5}{10} \times \frac{4}{9} = \frac{20}{90} = \frac{2}{9}$$

Practice Quiz

1. If $-3(x+4) \geq x+8$, what is the value of x?
    a. $x = 4$
    b. $x \geq 2$
    c. $x \geq -5$
    d. $x \leq -5$

2. Which inequality represents the values displayed on the number line?

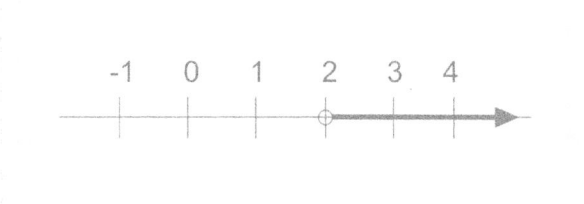

    a. $x < 2$
    b. $x \leq 2$
    c. $x > 2$
    d. $x \geq 2$

3. What is the 42nd item in the pattern: ▲○○□▲○○□▲...?
    a. ○
    b. ▲
    c. □
    d. None of the above

4. If a car can travel 300 miles in four hours, how far can it go in an hour and a half?
    a. 100 miles
    b. 112.5 miles
    c. 135.5 miles
    d. 150 miles

5. Greg buys a $10 lunch with 5% sales tax. He leaves a $2 tip after paying his bill. How much money does he spend?
    a. $12.50
    b. $12
    c. $13
    d. $13.25

See answers on the next page.

Answer Explanations

1. D: Solve a linear inequality in a similar way to solving a linear equation. First, start by distributing the −3 on the left side of the inequality.

$$-3x - 12 \geq x + 8$$

Then, add 12 to both sides.

$$-3x \geq x + 20$$

Next, subtract x from both sides.

$$-4x \geq 20$$

Finally, divide both sides of the inequality by −4. Don't forget to flip the inequality sign because you are dividing by a negative.

$$x \leq -5$$

2. C: $x > 2$. The open dot indicates that the value is not included in the set. The arrow pointing right indicates that numbers greater than two (numbers get larger to the right) are included in the set. Therefore, the set includes numbers greater than two, which can be written as $x > 2$.

3. A: The core of the pattern consists of 4 items: ▲○○□. Therefore, the core repeats in multiples of 4, with the pattern starting over on the next step. The highest multiple of 4 that's below 42 is 40. Step 40 is the end of the core (□), so step 41 will start the core over (▲) and step 42 is ○.

4. B: 300 miles in four hours is $\frac{300}{4} = 75$ miles per hour. In 1.5 hours, the car will go 1.5×75 miles, or 112.5 miles.

5. A: The tip is not taxed, so he pays 5% tax only on the $10. To find 5% of $10, calculate $0.05 \times \$10 = \$0.50$. Add up $10 + $0.50 + $2 to get $12.50.

Social Studies

United States History, Government, and Citizenship

Colonization and Expansion in U.S. History

When examining how Europeans explored what would become the United States of America, one must first examine why Europeans came to explore the New World as a whole. In the fifteenth century, tensions increased between the Eastern and Mediterranean nations of Europe and the expanding Ottoman Empire to the east. As war and piracy spread across the Mediterranean, the once-prosperous trade routes across Asia's Silk Road began to decline, and nations across Europe began to explore alternative routes for trade.

Italian explorer **Christopher Columbus** proposed a westward route. Contrary to popular lore, the main challenge that Columbus faced in finding backers was not proving that the world was round. In fact, much of Europe's educated elite knew that the world was round; the real issue was that they rightly believed that a westward route to Asia, even assuming a lack of obstacles, would be too long to be practical. Nevertheless, Columbus set sail in 1492 after obtaining support from Spain and arrived in the West Indies three months later.

Spain launched further expeditions to the new continents and established **New Spain**. The colony consisted not only of Central America and Mexico, but also the American Southwest and Florida. France claimed much of what would become Canada, along with the Mississippi River region and the Midwest. In addition, the Dutch established colonies that covered New Jersey, New York, and Connecticut. Each nation managed its colonies differently, and thus influenced how they would assimilate into the United States. For instance, Spain strove to establish a system of Christian missions throughout its territory, while France focused on trading networks and had limited infrastructure in regions such as the Midwest.

Even in cases of limited colonial growth, the land of America was hardly vacant, because a diverse array of Native American nations and groups were already present. Throughout much of colonial history, European settlers commonly misperceived native peoples as a singular, static entity. In reality, Native Americans had a variety of traditions depending on their history and environment. Additionally, their culture continued to change through the course of interactions with European settlers; for instance, tribes such as the Cheyenne and Comanche used horses, which were introduced by white settlers, to become powerful warrior nations. However, a few generalizations can be made: many, but not all, tribes were matrilineal, which gave women a fair degree of power, and land was commonly seen as belonging to everyone. These differences, particularly European settlers' continual focus on land ownership, contributed to increasing prejudice and violence.

Situated on the Atlantic Coast, the Thirteen Colonies that would become the United States of America constituted only a small portion of North America. Even those colonies had significant differences that stemmed from their different origins. For instance, the Virginia colony under John Smith in 1607 started with male bachelors seeking gold, whereas families of Puritans settled Massachusetts. As a result, the Thirteen Colonies—Virginia, Massachusetts, Connecticut, Maryland, New York, New Jersey, Pennsylvania, Delaware, Rhode Island, New Hampshire, Georgia, North Carolina, and South Carolina—had different structures and customs that would each influence the United States.

Competition among several imperial powers in eastern areas of North America led to conflicts that would later bring about the independence of the United States. The French and Indian War from 1754 to 1763, which was a subsidiary war of the Seven Years' War, ended with Great Britain claiming France's Canadian territories as well as the Ohio Valley. The war was costly for all the powers involved, which led to increased taxes on the Thirteen Colonies. In addition, the new lands to the west of the colonies attracted new settlers, and they came into conflict with Native Americans and British troops that were trying to maintain the boundaries laid out by treaties between Great Britain and the Native American tribes. These growing tensions with Great Britain, as well as other issues, eventually led to the American Revolution, which ended with Britain relinquishing its control of the colonies.

Britain continued to hold onto its other colonies, such as Canada and the West Indies, which reflects the continued power of multiple nations across North America, even as the United States began to expand across the continent. Many Americans advocated expansion regardless of the land's current inhabitants, but the results were often mixed. Still, events both abroad and within North America contributed to the growth of the United States. For instance, the French Revolution and rise of Napoleon led to the Louisiana Purchase in 1803, when France sold a large chunk of land consisting of Louisiana and much of the Midwest to the United States. Meanwhile, as Spanish power declined, Mexico claimed independence in 1821, but the new nation became increasingly vulnerable to foreign pressure. In the Mexican-American War (1846-1848), Mexico surrendered territory to the United States that became California, Nevada, Utah, and New Mexico, as well as parts of Arizona, Colorado, and Wyoming.

Even as the United States sought new inland territory, American interests were also expanding overseas via trade. As early as 1784, the ship ***Empress of China*** traveled to China to establish trading connections. American interests had international dimensions throughout the nation's history. For instance, during the presidency of Andrew Jackson, the ship ***Potomac*** was dispatched to Sumatra in 1832 to avenge the deaths of American sailors. This incident exemplifies how U.S. foreign trade connected with imperial expansion.

This combination of continental and seaward growth adds a deeper layer to American development, because it was not purely focused on western expansion. For example, take the 1849 Gold Rush; a large number of Americans and other immigrants traveled to California by ship and settled western territories before more eastern areas, such as Nevada and Idaho. Therefore, the United States' early history of colonization and expansion is a complex network of diverse cultures.

American Revolution and the Founding of the Nation

The **American Revolution** largely occurred as a result of changing values in the Thirteen Colonies that broke from their traditional relationship with England. Early in the colonization of North America, the colonial social structure tried to mirror the stratified order of Great Britain. In England, the landed elites were seen as intellectually and morally superior to the common man, which led to a paternalistic relationship. This style of governance was similarly applied to the colonial system; government was left to the property-owning upper class, and the colonies as a whole could be seen as a child dutifully serving "Mother England."

However, the colonies' distance from England meant that actual hereditary aristocrats from Britain only formed a small percentage of the overall population that did not fill all the positions of power. By the mid-eighteenth century, much of the American upper class consisted of local families who acquired status through business rather than lineage. Despite this, representatives from Britain were appointed to govern the colonies. As a result, a rift began to form between the colonists and British officials.

Tensions began to rise in the aftermath of the French and Indian War of 1754 to 1763. To recover the financial costs of the long conflict, Great Britain drew upon its colonies to provide the desired resources. Since the American colonists did not fully subscribe to the paternal connection, taxation to increase British revenue, such as the **Stamp Act of 1765**, was met with increasing resistance. Britain sent soldiers to the colonies and enacted the **1765 Quartering Act** to require colonists to house the troops. In 1773, the **Tea Act**, which legitimized Britain's taxing of the colonies, led disgruntled colonists to raid ships importing tea and destroy their contents in an act known as the **Boston Tea Party**.

Uncertain about whether they should remain loyal to Britain, representatives from twelve colonies formed the First Continental Congress in 1774 to discuss what they should do next. When Patriot militiamen at Lexington and Concord fought British soldiers in April 1775, the **Revolutionary War** began. While the rebel forces worked to present the struggle as a united, patriotic effort, the colonies remained divided throughout the war. Thousands of colonists, known as **Loyalists** or **Tories**, supported Britain. Even the revolutionaries proved to be significantly fragmented, and many militias only served in their home states. The Continental Congress was also divided over whether to reconcile with Britain or push for full separation. These issues hindered the ability of the revolutionary armies to resist the British, who had superior training and resources at their disposal.

Even so, the **Continental Army**, under **General George Washington**, gradually built up a force that utilized Prussian military training and backwoods guerrilla tactics to make up for their limited resources. Although the British forces continued to win significant battles, the Continental Army gradually reduced Britain's will to fight as the years passed. Furthermore, Americans appealed to the rivalry that other European nations had with the British Empire. The support was initially limited to indirect assistance, but aid gradually increased. After the American victory at the Battle of Saratoga in 1777, France and other nations began to actively support the American cause by providing much-needed troops and equipment.

In 1781, the primary British army under **General Cornwallis** was defeated by an American and French coalition at Yorktown, Virginia, which paved the way for peace negotiations. The **Treaty of Paris in 1783** ended the war, recognized the former colonies' independence from Great Britain, and gave America control over territory between the Appalachian Mountains and Mississippi River. However, the state of the new nation was still uncertain. The new nation's government initially stemmed from the state-based structure of the Continental Congress and was incorporated into the Articles of Confederation in 1777.

The **Articles of Confederation** emphasized the ideals of the American Revolution, particularly the concept of freedom from unjust government. Unfortunately, the resulting limitations on the national government left most policies—even ones with national ramifications—up to individual states. For instance, states sometimes simply decided to not pay taxes. Many representatives did not see much value in the National Congress and simply did not attend the meetings. Some progress was still made during the period, such as the **Northwest Ordinance of 1787**, which organized the western territories into new states; nevertheless, the disjointed links in the state-oriented government inhibited significant progress.

Although many citizens felt satisfied with this decentralized system of government, key intellectuals and leaders in America became increasingly disturbed by the lack of unity. An especially potent fear among them was the potential that, despite achieving official independence, other powers could threaten America's autonomy. In 1786, poor farmers in Massachusetts launched an insurrection, known as **Shays' Rebellion**, which sparked fears of additional uprisings and led to the creation of the **Constitutional Convention in 1787**.

While the convention initially intended to correct issues within the Articles of Confederation, speakers, such as **James Madison**, compellingly argued for the delegates to devise a new system of government that was more centralized than its predecessor. The Constitution was not fully supported by all citizens, and there was much debate about whether or not to support the new government. Even so, in 1788, the Constitution was ratified. Later additions, such as the **Bill of Rights**, would help protect individual liberty by giving specific rights to citizens. In 1789, **George Washington** became the first president of the newly created executive branch of the government, and America entered a new stage of history.

U.S. History from Founding to Present

One early development was the growth of political parties—something that Washington tried and failed to stop from forming. Federalists, such as **Alexander Hamilton**, wanted to expand the national government's power, while Democratic-Republicans, such as **Thomas Jefferson**, favored states' rights. The United States suffered multiple defeats by Britain in the War of 1812, but individual American victories, such as the **Battle of New Orleans**, still strengthened nationalistic pride.

In the aftermath of the war, the Federalists were absorbed into the Democratic-Republicans, which began the **Era of Good Feelings**. However, two new parties eventually emerged. The Democrats, whose leader **Andrew Jackson** became president in 1828, favored "Jacksonian" democracy, which emphasized mass participation in elections. However, Jackson's policies largely favored white male landowners and suppressed opposing views. The Whigs supported Federalist policies but also drew on democratic principles, particularly with marginalized groups such as African Americans and women.

At the same time, settlers continued to expand west in search of new land and fortune. The Louisiana Purchase of 1803 opened up large amounts of land west of the Mississippi River, and adventurers pushed past even those boundaries toward the western coast. The vision of westward growth into the frontier is a key part of American popular culture, but the expansion was often erratic and depended on a combination of incentives and assurances of relative security. Hence, some areas, such as California and Oregon, were settled more quickly than other areas to the east. Some historians have pointed to the growth of the frontier as a means through which American democracy expanded.

However, the matter of western lands became an increasingly volatile issue as the controversy over slavery heightened. Not all northerners supported abolition, but many saw the practice as outdated and did not want it to expand. Abolitionists formed the Republican Party, and their candidate, **Abraham Lincoln**, was elected as president in 1860. In response, Southern states seceded and formed the **Confederate States of America**. The ensuing **Civil War** lasted from 1861 to 1865 and had significant consequences. Slavery was abolished in the United States, and the power of individual states was drastically curtailed. After being reunified, Southern states worked to retain control over freed slaves, and the Reconstruction period was followed by **Jim Crow** segregation. As a result, Black people were barred from public education, unable to vote, and forced to accept their status as second-class citizens.

After the Civil War, the United States increasingly industrialized and became part of the larger Industrial Revolution, which took place throughout the western world. Steps toward industrialization had already begun as early as Jackson's presidency, but the full development of American industry took place in the second half of the nineteenth century. Railroads helped link cities like Chicago to locations across the West, which allowed for rapid transfer of materials. New technologies, such as electricity, allowed leisure time for those with enough wealth. Even so, the **Gilded Age** was also a period of disparities, and wealthy entrepreneurs rose while impoverished workers struggled to make their voices heard.

The late nineteenth and early twentieth centuries not only marked U.S. expansion within North America but also internationally. For instance, after the **Spanish-American War in 1898**, the United States claimed control over Guam, Puerto Rico, and the Philippines. Rivalries in Europe culminated in World War I, in which great powers ranging from France to Russia vied for control in a bloody struggle. America did not enter the war until 1917, but had a critical role in the final phase of the war. During the peace treaty process, **President Woodrow Wilson** sought to establish a **League of Nations** in order to promote global harmony, but his efforts only achieved limited success.

After World War I, the United States largely stayed out of international politics for the next two decades. Still, American businesses continued overseas ventures and strengthened the economy in the 1920s. However, massive speculation in the stock market in 1929 triggered the **Great Depression**—a financial crisis that spread worldwide as nations withdrew from the global economy. The crisis shepherded in the presidency of **Franklin D. Roosevelt**, who reformed the Democratic Party and implemented new federal programs known as the **New Deal**.

Social Studies

The Great Depression had ramifications worldwide and encouraged the rise of fascist governments in Italy and Germany. Highly dictatorial, fascism emphasized nationalism and militarism. World War II began when the Axis powers of Germany, Italy, and Japan built up their military forces and launched invasions against neighboring nations in 1939. As part of the Allied powers—which included Britain, France, and the Soviet Union–America defeated the Axis powers in 1945 and asserted itself as a global force.

The **Union of Soviet Socialist Republics** had emerged through the **Bolshevik Revolution in 1917** in Russia and militantly supported **Communism**—a socialist system of government that called for the overthrow of capitalism. Although the Soviet Union formed an alliance with the United States during World War II, relations chilled, and the Cold War began in 1947. Although no true war was declared between the two nations, both the Union of Soviet Socialist Republics (USSR) and the United States engaged in indirect conflict by supporting and overthrowing foreign governments.

Meanwhile, the **Civil Rights Movement** began to grow as marginalized groups objected to racial segregation and abuse by whites across the nation. Civil rights leaders such as **Martin Luther King Jr**. argued for nonviolent resistance, but others, such as **Malcolm X**, advocated more radical approaches. Civil rights groups became increasingly discontented during the Vietnam War because they felt they were being drafted for a foreign war that ignored domestic problems. Even so, significant reforms, such as the **Voting Rights Act of 1965**, opened up new opportunities for freedom and equality in America.

In 1991, the Soviet Union collapsed, leaving the United States as the dominant global power. However, as the United States struggled to fill the void left by the Soviet Union, questions arose about America's role in the world. Terrorist acts, such as the 9/11 attack on the World Trade Center in 2001, have shed doubt on the United States' ability to enforce its authority on an international scale.

Twentieth-Century Developments in the United States

American technology continued to develop in new directions throughout the course of the twentieth century. A key example is the invention of the modern assembly line. Assembly lines and conveyor belts had already become a prominent part of industrial work, but **Henry Ford** combined conveyor belts with the system of assembly workers in 1913 in order to produce Model T automobiles. This streamlined production system, in which multiple parts were assembled by different teams along the conveyors, allowed industries in the United States to grow ever larger.

Ford's assembly lines also promoted the growth of the automobile as a means of transportation. Early cars were an expensive and impractical novelty and were primarily the toys of the rich. The Model T, on the other hand, was relatively affordable, which made the car available to a wider array of consumers. Many of the automobiles' early issues, such as radiator leaks and fragile tires, were gradually corrected, and this made the car more appealing than horses. With the support of **President Eisenhower**, the **Federal Aid Highway Act of 1956** paved the way for a network of interstates and highways across the nation.

At the same time, a revolutionary approach to transportation was emerging: flight. Blimps and balloons were already gaining popularity by the turn of the twentieth century, but aviators struggled to create an airplane. The first critical success was by the **Wright Brothers** in 1903, and they demonstrated that aircrafts did not need to be lighter than air. In time, airplanes surpassed the popularity of balloons and blimps, which tended to be more volatile. Aircraft also added a new dimension to warfare, and aircraft carriers became an integral piece of the American Navy during World War II.

Furthermore, by demonstrating that heavier-than-air vehicles could carry passengers upward, the stage was set for the space race in the second half of the twentieth century. In 1958, the U.S. government created the **National Aeronautics and Space Administration (NASA)** to head the budding initiative to extend American

Social Studies

power into space. After the Soviet Union successfully launched the **Sputnik satellite** into Earth's orbit in 1957 and sent the first human in space in 1961, the United States intensified its own space program through the **Apollo missions**. **Apollo 11** successfully landed on the Moon in 1969 with **Buzz Aldrin** and **Neil Armstrong**. Later ventures into space would focus on space shuttles and satellites, and the latter significantly enhanced communications worldwide.

The twentieth century also made considerable advancements in communications and media. Inventions such as the radio greatly boosted communication across the nation and world, such that news could be reported immediately rather than take days. Furthermore, motion pictures evolved from black-and-white movies at theaters to full-color television sets in households. From animation to live films, television matured into a compelling art form in popular culture. Live-action footage gave a new layer to news broadcasts and proved instrumental in the public's reaction to events, such as the Civil Rights Movement and the Vietnam War. With the success of the space program, satellites became a fundamental piece of Earth's communications network by transmitting signals across the planet instantaneously.

Further communications advancements resulted from the development of computer technology. The early computers were enormous behemoths that were too bulky and expensive for anything but government institutions. However, computers gradually became smaller while still storing large amounts of data. A turning point came with the 1976 release of the Apple computer by entrepreneurs **Steve Wozniak** and **Steve Jobs**. The computer had a simplistic design that made it marketable for a mass consumer audience, and computers eventually became household items. Similarly, the networks that would become the Internet originated as government systems, but in time they were extended to commercial avenues that became a vibrant element of modern communications.

However, other advancements in American science during the twentieth century were aimed toward more lethal purposes. In response to the multiple wars throughout the century, the United States built up a powerful military force, and new technologies were devised for that purpose. One of the deadliest creations was the **atomic bomb**, which split molecular atoms to produce powerful explosions; in addition to the sheer force of the bombs, the aftereffects included toxic radiation and electronic shutdowns. Developed and used in the last days of World War II, the nuclear bomb was the United States' most powerful weapon during the Cold War.

On the other hand, the twentieth century also marked new approaches to the natural environments in America. In reaction to the depletion of natural habitats by industrialization and overhunting, **President Theodore Roosevelt** helped preserve areas for what would become the National Parks in 1916. Laws, such as the **Clean Water Act of 1972**, helped improve the health of ecosystems, which benefitted not only wildlife but people across the nation. This also led to the development of alternative energy sources such as wind and solar power.

America continues to change and grow into the twenty-first century by building on preexisting ideas but also pioneering new concepts. As globalization becomes an increasingly prominent phenomenon, American businesses strive to adapt their products to consumers worldwide while also funneling in new ideas from other nations. Yet many of the current developments in American enterprises stem in part from earlier events in American history. For instance, the environmental movement has expanded to address new issues such as global warming. NASA continues its space exploration endeavors, but entrepreneurs hope one day to travel to Mars. Therefore, the history of technology within the United States remains an engaging and relevant subject in the present.

Connections between Causes and Effects

When examining the historical narratives of events, it is important to understand the relationship between causes and effects. A **cause** can be defined as something—an event, social change, or other factor—that contributes to the occurrence of certain events; the results of causes are called **effects**. Those terms may seem simple enough, but they have drastic implications on how one explores history. Events such as the American Revolution or the Civil Rights Movement may appear to occur spontaneously, but a closer examination will reveal that these events depended on earlier phenomena and patterns that influenced the course of history.

For example, although the battles at Concord and Lexington may seem to be instantaneous eruptions of violence during the American Revolution, they stemmed from a variety of factors. The most obvious influences behind those two battles were the assortment of taxes and policies imposed on the Thirteen Colonies following the French and Indian War from 1754 to 1763. Taxation without direct representation, combined with the deployment of British soldiers to enforce these policies, greatly increased American resistance. Earlier events, such as the Boston Massacre and the Boston Tea Party, similarly stemmed from conflicts between British soldiers and local colonists over perceived tyranny and rebelliousness. Therefore, the start of the American Revolution progressed from preceding developments.

Furthermore, there can be multiple causes and effects for any situation. The existence of multiple causes can be seen through the settling of the American West. Many historians have emphasized the role of Manifest Destiny—the national vision of expanding across the continent—as a driving force behind the growth of the United States. Yet there were many different influences behind the expansion westward. Northern abolitionists and Southern planters saw the frontier as a way to either extend or limit slavery. Economic opportunities in the West also encouraged travel westward, as did the gradual pacification of Native American tribes.

Even an individual cause can be subdivided into smaller factors or stretched out in a gradual process. Although there were numerous issues that led to the Civil War, slavery was the primary cause. However, that topic stretched back to the very founding of the nation, and the existence of slavery was a controversial topic during the creation of the Declaration of Independence and the Constitution. The abolition movement as a whole did not start until the 1830s, but nevertheless, slavery was a cause that gradually grew more important over the following decades. In addition, opponents of slavery were divided by different motivations—some believed that it stifled the economy, while others focused on moral issues.

On the other end of the spectrum, a single event can have numerous results. The rise of the telegraph, for example, had several effects on American history. The telegraph allowed news to travel much quicker and turned events into immediate national news, such as the sinking of the USS Maine, which sparked the Spanish-American War. In addition, the telegraph helped make railroads run more efficiently by improving the links between stations. The faster speed of both travel and communications led to a shift in time itself, and localized times were replaced by standardized time zones across the nation.

The importance of grasping cause-and-effect relationships is critical in interpreting the growth and development of the Civil Rights Movement. Historical narratives of the movement often focus on charismatic individuals, such as Martin Luther King Jr., and they certainly played a key leadership role. Even so, elements of the movement had already emerged in previous decades through the growth of the **National Association for the Advancement of Colored People (NAACP)** and other organizations. Several factors proved critical to the formation of civil rights organizations during the 1950s. African American veterans returning from World War II, as well as those continuing to serve in the military, called for equal rights. Furthermore, the United States' role as a key member of the United Nations, which included African countries, required the federal government to take racial discrimination seriously.

A specific example in the Civil Rights Movement are the sit-ins during the 1960s, in which black and white students defied segregation policies in restaurants and other establishments. The wave is often thought to originate from spontaneous activism by students in Greensboro, North Carolina. However, there had already been other sit-ins, such as at **Royal Ice Cream Parlor** in Durham, North Carolina, in 1957. In fact, the sit-ins would not have spread as quickly without a preexisting network of activists across the nation, which in part stemmed from the growth of organizations through various local and national movements. By looking at such cases closely, it becomes clear that no event occurs without one—if not multiple—causes behind it, and that each historical event can have a variety of direct and indirect consequences.

One of the most critical elements of cause-and-effect relationships is how they are relevant not only in studying history but also in contemporary events. Much of the current political debate about social security and health care stems from FDR's New Deal in the 1930s, and at the time some people criticized the programs for being too extensive, while others argued that he did not go far enough with his vision. Current environmental concerns have their origins in long-term issues that reach back centuries. The United States' mixed history of global isolation and foreign intervention continues to influence foreign policy approaches today. Most of all, people must realize that events and developments today will likely have a number of consequences later on. Therefore, the study of cause and effect remains vital in understanding the past, the present, and the future.

Nature, Purpose, and Forms of Government

The United States of America's government, as outlined by the **Constitution**, is designed to serve as a compromise between democracy and preceding monarchical systems. The American Revolution brought independence from Britain and freedom from its aristocratic system of governance. On the other hand, the short-lived Articles of Confederation revealed the significant weaknesses of state-based governance with limited national control. By dividing power between local, state, and federal governments, the United States can uphold its value of individual liberties while also providing a sense of order to the country.

The **federal government**, which is in charge of laws that affect the entire nation, is split into three main branches: executive, judicial, and legislative. It is important to realize that the three segments of the federal government are intended to stand as equal counterparts to the others, and that none of them have absolute power. The **executive branch** centers on the president, the vice president, and the Cabinet. The president and vice president are elected every four years. Also known as the **commander-in-chief**, the **president** is the official head of state and serves as the nation's head diplomat and military leader. The **vice president** acts as the president of the Senate in the legislative branch, while the president appoints members of the Cabinet to lead agencies, including the Treasury and Department of Defense. However, the president can only sign and veto laws and cannot initiate them himself.

Instead, the **legislative branch**, specifically Congress, proposes and debates laws. **Congress** is bicameral because it is divided into two separate legislative houses. Each state's representation in the **House of Representatives** is determined proportionally by population, with the total number of voting seats limited to 435. The **Senate**, in contrast, has only two members per state and a total of one hundred senators. Members of both houses are intended to represent the interests of the constituents in their home states and to bring their concerns to a national level while also being consistent with the interests of the nation as a whole. Drafts of laws, called **bills**, are proposed in one chamber and then are voted upon according to that chamber's rules; should the bill pass the vote in the first house of Congress, the other legislative chamber must approve it before it can be sent to the president. Congress also has a variety of other powers, such as the rights to declare war, collect taxes, and impeach the president.

The **judicial branch**, though it cannot pass laws itself, serves to interpret the laws. At the federal level, this is done through several tiers of judicial bodies. At the top, the **Supreme Court** consists of judges appointed by the president; these judges serve for life, unless they resign from their position or are removed by Congress for improper behavior. The Supreme Court's decisions in trials and other judgments rest on the justices' interpretations of the Constitution and enacted laws. As the Constitution remains fundamental to the American legal system, the Supreme Court's rulings on how laws follow or fail to uphold the Constitution have powerful implications on future rulings. Beneath the Supreme Court, there are a number of other federal judicial bodies—courts of appeals, district courts, and courts of special jurisdiction.

While the federal government manages the nation, state governments address issues pertaining to their specific territory. In the past, states claimed the right, known as **nullification**, to refuse to enforce federal laws that they considered unconstitutional. However, conflicts between state and federal authority have led to increased federal power, and states cannot defy federal laws. Even so, the **Tenth Amendment** limits federal power to those specifically granted in the Constitution, and the rest of the powers are retained by the states and citizens. Therefore, individual state governments are left in charge of decisions with immediate effects on their citizens, such as state laws and taxes. Like the federal government, state governments consist of executive, judicial, and legislative branches, but the exact configuration of those branches varies between states. For instance, while most states follow the bicameral structure of Congress, Nebraska has only a single legislative chamber. **State governments** have considerable authority within their states, but they cannot impose their power on other states, nor can they secede from the United States.

Local governments, which include town governments, county boards, library districts, and other agencies, are especially variable in their composition. They often reflect the overall views of their state governments but also have their own values, rules, and structures. Generally, local governments function in a democratic fashion, although the exact form of government depends on its role. Depending on the location within the state, local government may have considerable or minimal authority based on the population and prosperity of the area; some counties may have strong influence in the state, while others may have a limited impact.

Native American tribes are treated as dependent nations that answer to the federal government but may be immune to state jurisdiction. As with local governments, the exact form of governance is left up to the tribes, which ranges from small councils to complex systems of government. Other U.S. territories, including the District of Columbia (site of Washington, D.C.) and acquired islands, such as Guam and Puerto Rico, have representation within Congress, but their legislators cannot vote on bills.

As members of a democracy, U.S. citizens are empowered to elect most government leaders, but the process varies between branch and level of government. Presidential elections at the national scale use the **Electoral College system**. Rather than electing the president directly, citizens cast their ballots to select electors, who generally vote for a specific candidate, that represent each state in the college. Legislative branches at the federal and state level are also determined by elections, albeit without an Electoral College. In some areas, judges are elected, but in other states judges are appointed by elected officials. It should also be noted that the two-party system was not built into the Constitution but gradually emerged over time.

Key Documents and Speeches in U.S. History

With more than two hundred years of history, American leaders have produced several important documents and speeches. One of the most essential is the **Declaration of Independence**, which the **Second Continental Congress** ratified on **July 4, 1776**. Although many historians and politicians have drawn upon the words of the Declaration to demonstrate the American ideal of freedom, most of them focus on the **preamble**, which focuses on the necessity of fair government and the right to overthrow tyrants. The main body of the document consists of a set of grievances against **King George III**. Still, this document was instrumental in American history because it asserted American independence from Great Britain. Even so, it is important to note that the Declaration did not immediately lead to the United States; the document does not outline the government of the soon-to-be independent colonies, and independence would not become reality until Britain agreed.

The colonies' first blueprint for government was the **Articles of Confederation**, which was ratified in 1777. The document declared that the confederacy would be called the United States of America and that the individual states would have "a firm league of friendship" with each other. The emphasis on friendship and cooperation highlights how the confederation was a voluntary effort that states could follow or ignore as they saw fit. Still, the document also revealed the importance of obeying decisions made by Congress as a whole; while this was not very effective during the confederation period, the framework would live on to a degree in the following Constitution.

Much like the Declaration of Independence, the **1787 Constitution of the United States** is most remembered for the preamble, which takes a more philosophical approach. However, the body of the Constitution is highly complex, and it covers the framework and responsibilities of the different branches of the federal government and the limits to state power. These details are very important and help to define the key institutions within the government. To resolve later issues not addressed in the Constitution, the fifth article in the document establishes a process to modify the government, and the first ten amendments are known as the **Bill of Rights**. Under the Tenth Amendment, powers not specifically allotted to Congress by the Constitution are reserved for the people and to individual states.

George Washington was the first president of the United States. His administration and **Farewell Address** set many precedents for the nation. In his address, he noted the rise of regional feelings, and he urged citizens to uphold their duty to the nation above sectionalism because he felt that America was strongest when united. The issue of regional conflicts and national identity would become increasingly important in years to come, especially during the Civil War. Washington also argued against intervention in European affairs, and this warning would become the cornerstone for advocates of American isolation. On the other hand, his advice that political parties are detrimental to democracy failed to halt the development of the party system.

Washington's fears about sectional conflict were confirmed at the start of the Civil War, when the southern states seceded from the Union. As the president during that tumultuous time, Abraham Lincoln was seen by many to embody the Union as a whole. This was demonstrated through his **Gettysburg Address** in November of 1863. After the difficult and bloody **Battle of Gettysburg** ended in a Union victory, crowds gathered for the dedication of the Soldiers' National Cemetery. Although he was not the main speaker of the event, Lincoln's short yet eloquent speech proved to be the most significant. Drawing upon the Declaration of Independence's assertion that "all men are created equal," he argued that the current war was a test of that ideal. He emphasized the importance of the United States as a whole and argued that it must endure as a Union for the sake of the world.

In January 1863, Lincoln indicated his opposition to slavery through the **Emancipation Proclamation**. Although it was an executive order instead of a law passed by Congress, this document was not challenged by the courts and helped determine the objectives of the Civil War. The proclamation asserted that all slaves in Confederate territories were free. One must note that some southern states remained in the Union, and therefore, were not affected by this proclamation. Even so, the order helped establish a basis for later laws and amendments that would end slavery in the United States.

Another presidential attempt to set a new precedent for American policy was **Woodrow Wilson's Fourteen Points**, which were outlined in a speech he gave to Congress in 1918 after the United States had entered World War I. Wilson saw the United States as a protector of democracy in the world and said that we could reform world policy by fighting in the war. Wilson called for an end to private negotiations, which had contributed to the secret alliances behind the war. He argued for nations to come together in an international body to determine world policies. The negotiations after the war only partially fulfilled Wilson's ambitions by creating a weak League of Nations, but his vision of U.S. involvement in global affairs would become a key aspect of American foreign policy.

Even as the United States began playing a more active role on the international stage of politics, internal issues such as civil rights remained important, as shown in **Martin Luther King Jr.**'s "I Have a Dream" speech. A leader in the Civil Rights Movement, King gave his speech as part of the 1963 March on Washington. Drawing on Lincoln's past speech at Gettysburg, King argued that America's journey to true equality was not over. His references to biblical passages gave the speech a spiritual tone, but he also mentioned specific locations across the nation to emphasize that local struggles were tied with national consequences. Through its optimistic tone, Dr. King's speech reflects not only civil rights activism but also the American dream of freedom and progress.

Rights and Responsibilities of Citizenship in a Democracy

Citizens living in a democracy have several rights and responsibilities to uphold. The first duty is to uphold the established laws of the government. In a democracy, a system of nationwide laws is necessary to ensure that there is some degree of order. Therefore, citizens must try to obey the laws and help enforce them because a law that is inadequately enforced is almost useless. Optimally, a democratic society's laws will be accepted and followed by the community as a whole.

However, conflict can occur when an unjust law is passed. For instance, much of the Civil Rights Movement centered around **Jim Crow laws** in the South that supported segregation between Black and White people. Yet these practices were encoded in state laws, which created a dilemma for African Americans who wanted equality but also wanted to respect the law. Fortunately, a democracy offers a degree of protection from such laws by creating a system in which government leaders and policies are constantly open to change in accordance with the will of citizens. Citizens can influence the laws that are passed by voting for and electing members of the legislative and executive branches to represent them at the local, state, and national levels.

This, however, requires citizens to be especially vigilant in protecting their liberties because they cannot depend solely on the existing government to meet their needs. To assert their role in a democracy, citizens should be active voters and speak out on issues that concern them. Even with these safeguards, it is possible for systems to be implemented that inhibit active participation. For instance, many southern states had laws that prevented Black people from voting. Under such circumstances, civil rights leaders felt that they had no choice but to resist the laws in order to defend their personal rights. Once voting became possible, civil rights groups strove to ensure that their votes counted by changing state and national policy.

An extension of citizens' voting rights is their ability to run as elected officials. By becoming leaders in the government, citizens can demonstrate their engagement and help determine government policy. The involvement of citizens in the selection of leaders is vital to democracy because it helps to prevent the formation of an elite group that does not answer to the public. Without the engagement of citizens who run for office, voters are limited in their ability to select candidates that appeal to them. In this case, voting options would become stagnant, which inhibits the ability of the nation to grow and change over time. As long as citizens are willing to take a stand for their vision of America, America's government will remain dynamic and diverse.

These features of a democracy give it the potential to reshape itself continually in response to new developments in society. For a democracy to function, it is of the utmost importance that citizens care about the course of politics and be aware of current issues. Apathy among citizens is a constant problem that threatens the endurance of democracies. Citizens should have a desire to take part in the political process, or else they simply accept the status quo and fail to fulfill their role as citizens.

Moreover, they must have acute knowledge of the political processes and the issues that they can address as citizens. A fear among the Founding Fathers was the prevalence of mob rule, in which the common people did not take interest in politics except to vote for their patrons; this was the usual course of politics in the colonial era, as the common people left the decisions to the established elites. Without understanding the world around them, citizens may not fully grasp the significance of political actions and thereby fail to make wise decisions in that regard. Therefore, citizens must stay informed about current affairs, ranging from local to national or global matters, so that they can properly address them as voters or elected leaders.

Furthermore, knowledge of the nation's history is essential for healthy citizenship. History continues to have an influence on present political decisions. For instance, Supreme Court rulings often take into account previous legal precedents and verdicts, so it is important to know about those past events and how they affect the current processes. It is especially critical that citizens are aware of the context in which laws were established because it helps clarify the purpose of those laws. An understanding of the problems with the Articles of Confederation allows people to comprehend some of the reasons behind the framework of the Constitution. In addition, history shapes the course of societies and the world; therefore, citizens should draw on this knowledge of the past to realize the full consequences of current actions. Issues such as climate change, conflict in the Middle East, and civil rights struggles are rooted in events and cultural developments that reach back centuries and should be addressed.

Therefore, education is a high priority in democracies because it has the potential to instill generations of citizens with the right mindset and knowledge required to do their part in shaping the nation. Education should cover a variety of different subjects, ranging from mathematics to biology, so that individuals can explore whatever paths they wish to take in life. Even so, social studies are especially important because students should understand how democracies function and understand the history of the nation and world. Historical studies should cover national and local events as well because they help provide the basis for the understanding of contemporary politics. Social studies courses should also address the histories of foreign nations because contemporary politics increasingly has global consequences. In addition, history lessons should remain open to multiple perspectives, even those that might criticize a nation's past actions, because citizens should be exposed to diverse perspectives that they can apply as voters and leaders.

Geography, Anthropology, and Sociology

World and Regional Geography

Geography is essential in understanding the world as a whole. This requires a study of spatial distribution, which examines how various locations and physical features are arranged in the world. The most common element in geography is the **region**, which refers to a specific area that is separate from surrounding ones. Regions can be defined based on a variety of factors, including environmental, economic, or political features, and these different kinds of regions can overlap with each other.

It is also important to know the difference between location and place. A **location**, defined either through its physical position or through its relation to other locations, determines where something is, and this characteristic is static. A **place**, on the other hand, describes a combination of physical and human elements in relation to each other; the determination of place is therefore changeable depending on the movement of individuals and groups.

Social Studies

Geography is visually conveyed using maps, and a collection of maps is called an **atlas**. To illustrate some key points about geography, please refer to the map below.

This is a traditional map of the world that displays all of the countries and six of the seven continents. **Countries**, the most common approach to political regions, can be identified by their labels. The **continents** are not identified on this map, with the exception of Australia, but they are larger landmasses that encompass most of the countries in their respective areas; the other five visible continents are North America, South America, Europe, Africa, and Asia. The seventh continent, Antarctica, is found at the South Pole and has been omitted from the map.

The absence of Antarctica leads into the issues of distortion, in which geographical features are altered on a map. Some degree of distortion is to be expected with a two-dimensional flat map of the world because the Earth is a sphere. A map projection transforms a spherical map of the world into a flattened perspective, but the process generally alters the spatial appearance of landmasses. For instance, Greenland often appears, such as in the map above, larger than it really is.

Furthermore, Antarctica's exclusion from the map is, in fact, a different sort of distortion—that of the mapmakers' biases. Mapmakers determine which features are included on the map and which ones are not. Antarctica, for example, is often missing from maps because, unlike the other continents, it has a limited human population. Moreover, a study of the world reveals that many of the distinctions on maps are human constructions.

Even so, maps can still reveal key features about the world. For instance, the map above has areas that seem almost three-dimensional and jut out. They represent mountains and are an example of **topography**, which is a method used to display the differing elevations of the terrain. A more detailed topographical map can be viewed below.

On some colored maps, the oceans, represented in blue between the continents, vary in coloration depending on depth. The differences demonstrate **bathymetry**, which is the study of the ocean floor's depth. Paler areas represent less depth, while darker spots reflect greater depth.

Please also note the many lines running horizontally and vertically along the map. The horizontal lines, known as **parallels**, mark the calculated **latitude** of those locations and reveal how far north or south these areas are from the equator, which bisects the map horizontally. Generally, with exceptions depending on specific environments, climates closer to the equator are warmer because this region receives the most direct sunlight. The **equator** also serves to split the globe between the Northern and Southern hemispheres.

Longitude, as signified by the vertical lines, determines how far east or west different regions are from each other. The lines of longitude, known as **meridians**, are also the basis for time zones, which allocate different times to regions depending on their position eastward and westward of the prime meridian. As one travels west between time zones, the given time moves backward accordingly. Conversely, if one travels east, the time moves forward.

There are two particularly significant longitude-associated dividers in this regard. The **prime [Greenwich] meridian**, as displayed below, is defined as zero degrees in longitude, and thus determines the other lines. The line circles the globe north and south, and therefore divides the world into the Eastern and Western hemispheres. It is important to not confuse the Greenwich meridian with the **International Date Line**, which is an invisible line in the Pacific Ocean that was created to represent the change between calendar days. By traveling westward across the International Date Line, a traveler would essentially leap forward a day. For example, a person departing from the United States on Sunday would arrive in Japan on Monday. By traveling eastward across the line, a traveler would go backward a day. For example, a person departing from China on Monday would arrive in Canada on Sunday.

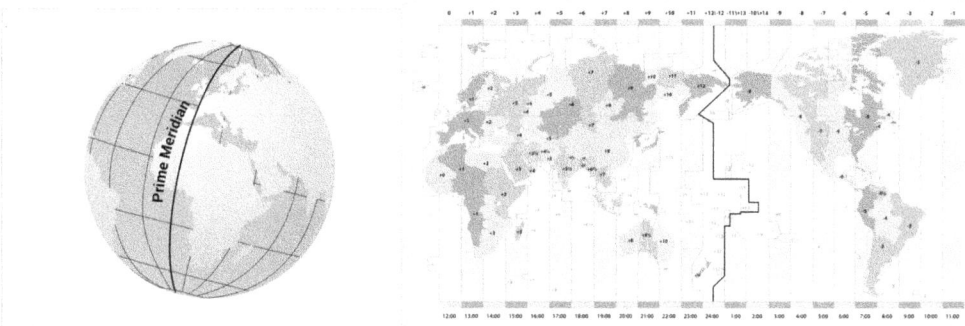

Although world maps are useful in showing the overall arrangement of continents and nations, it is also important at times to look more closely at individual countries because they have unique features that are only visible on more detailed maps.

For example, take the following map of the United States of America. It should be noted that the country is split into multiple states that have their own culture and localized governments. Other countries are often split into various divisions, such as provinces, and while these features are ignored for the sake of clarity on larger maps, they are important when studying specific nations. Individual states can be further subdivided into counties and townships, and they may have their own maps that can be examined for closer analysis.

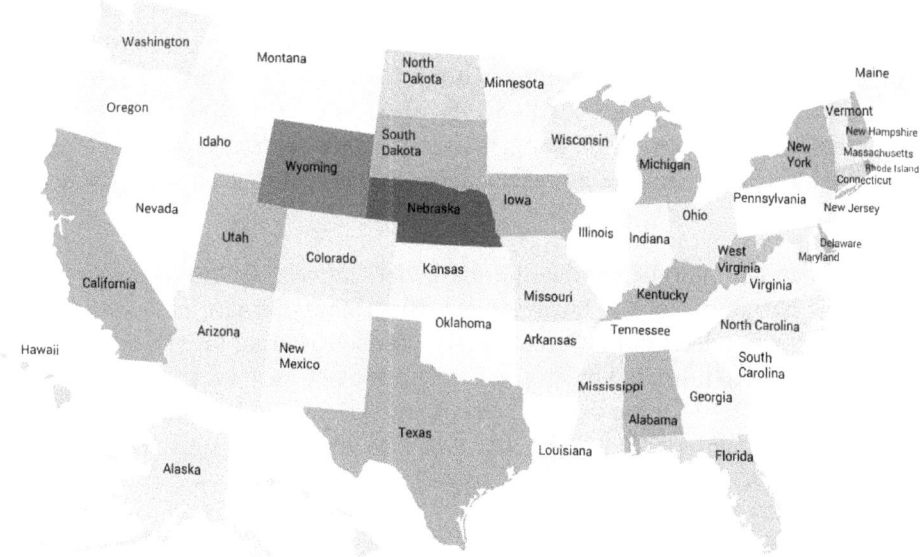

Finally, one of the first steps in examining any map should be to locate the map's key or legend, which will explain what features different symbols represent on the map. As these symbols can be arbitrary depending on the maker, a key will help to clarify the different meanings.

Interaction of Physical and Human Systems

Humans have always interacted with nature, and humanity has been shaped by, and in turn reshaped environments. Using tools to accomplish things they cannot do on their own, humans have proven highly adaptable to different environments. However, the specific ecosystems have helped to shape human development as individuals and as groups. The Earth is highly diverse and has many different ecosystems, each with its own flora and fauna. The specific resources available in different places have, therefore, influenced how humans develop.

Water has proved vital in determining the course of human civilizations. As humans require water daily to survive, proximity to water has always been of utmost necessity. Many human settlements originated adjacent to sources, and only in time expanded to other areas. Water is also essential for the growth of plants, which form a considerable portion of the human diet. In the wild, edible plants grow in places where they can thrive but may not be conveniently located for harvesting by humans. Therefore, humans gradually learned to grow plants themselves in places of their own choice. Humans also diverted water sources to new areas for themselves and to irrigate crops, thus transforming ecosystems.

Another important factor in the relationships between humans and nature has been the role of other animals. From small pests, such as weevils and rodents, to predators, including crocodiles and bears, many species of animals have often posed threats to humans, and conflict increased as humans expanded into environments inhabited by other creatures. On the other hand, animals are invaluable to humans because they can provide sustenance and clothing. This led to hunting and domestication of animal species. Domestication of both plants and animals involves humans breeding species to fit their own needs, which leads to new qualities that would normally not appear in the wild.

However, despite the considerable role that humans can play in altering environments, these changes have remained limited to local levels for much of human history. This does not mean that humans did not affect their ecosystems; some Native American tribes, for instance, used regular fires or hunting methods to maintain environments suitable for their needs. Even so, for much of human existence, nature was seen not simply as an obstacle but rather a power of its own right that was above human interference. **Natural phenomena** such as severe weather, diseases, and famine all kept human populations in check. Many pantheons of deities center on the gods' roles as arbitrary powers in the natural world, which reflects the lack of influence that humans had in the larger course of environmental changes.

Therefore, **natural resources** such as water and food were often seen as forces to be respected. Natural environments were recognized as vital regions, and alterations to fully exploit the resources were limited so that the resources could remain adequately sustainable. **Riparian customs** meant that water was the right of those with immediate access to it, and ownership changed accordingly with who lived nearby. However, increasing **industrialization** meant that natural resources such as water and lumber became resources that could be commoditized. In addition, appropriation gave water rights to those individuals or businesses that had first used the resource instead of being based on physical proximity.

Another instrumental change in the relationship between humans and nature is the increasing global connections worldwide. In many cases, earlier changes to environments occurred at local levels, with travel between different regions requiring considerable time and effort. The ability to travel around the world quickly has sharply altered that dynamic. Many local ecosystems, and the human cultures that developed accordingly, originated in separate circumstances that created unique plants and animals. Now products from one part of the world can be transported to entirely different environments and create new exchanges of goods. In some cases, the transferred species escape into the wild, and they often have traits for which the local environments are not prepared. This can result in invasive species that quickly grow and overpower native species.

A key symbol of artificial environments created by humans since early civilization has been the city, which is a human center of habitation that exists separate from the countryside around it. The creation of cities usually requires significant changes to the environment in which it is located, and the city must provide for the needs of residents without being compromised by nature. Yet the city has always remained connected to the rest of the world and to nature. Because a city generally lacks the capacity for agriculture and few natural resources are located within its confines, urban populations rely on resources from outlying areas for nourishment. The city, in turn, acts as a processing center for nearby settlements and offers rural workers and farmers the opportunity to sell their goods to a larger market.

Furthermore, the city, while an artificial construct, is still an environment in its own right. Although many species of animals have perished with the creation of cities, others, such as coyotes and pigeons, have adapted to urban life, thereby creating new ecosystems within cities. Natural connections within cities used to be stronger and more common because people would raise livestock within the city and regularly reuse garbage for livestock feed. While less hygienic, this helped stimulate natural cycles within the city. Recent efforts in many cities to create natural pockets, such as parks and community gardens, have also strengthened the ties between cities and the natural world. In a sense, the city reflects humanity's mixed relationship with nature as a whole: while humans continue to reshape the environment, they also remain linked to nature.

Uses of Geography

Geography helps people better understand the role that location plays in the past, present, and future. Historians make frequent use of maps in their studies to get a clearer picture of how history unfolded. Since the beginning of history, many different groups have fought conflicts that originated from struggles for land or other resources; therefore, knowing the location and borders of different empires and kingdoms helps reveal how they interacted with each other. In addition, environmental factors, such as access to water and the proximity of mountains, often help to shape the course of civilizations. Even single events and battles make more sense with maps that show how the warring sides met and maneuvered.

Furthermore, determining the geography of historical events, in particular geographical change over time, is essential due to the role that physical settings play in the present. Many important geographic landmarks continue to exist in the world, and they are often commemorated for their roles in history. Yet the physical geography has sometimes changed significantly. For instance, the **Aswan Dam** significantly reshaped the flow of the **Nile River**, which was the heart of ancient Egyptian society; without knowledge of the past geography, it is difficult to fully understand the civilization's context and how it differs from the present reality.

History also depends on archaeology, the study of human artifacts, for the evidence necessary to make conclusions about cultures. These items are generally buried, which helps preserve the artifacts yet makes it difficult to locate them. Historical geography helps in that regard by ascertaining key sites of human activity that could potentially retain artifacts. These insights help archaeologists discover new aspects of ancient cultures, which in turn strengthen historical arguments. Maps themselves sometimes serve as artifacts in their own right because they help reveal how humans of earlier periods viewed the world.

Along with the historical implications, knowledge of the world's geography remains important for people in the present day. The most immediate use of geography is in navigation. Tools such as Global Positioning Systems have helped improve navigation, but they too represent an approach to geography that demonstrates how it continues to have a fundamental role in human society. Humans have even begun mapping the trajectories of planets and even their individual terrains.

However, beyond the direct uses for navigation, geography is invaluable in comprehending modern cultures and events. Whether through their proximity to other nations or their relation to environmental features, such as forests and deserts, societies remain deeply connected to their geographical settings. Therefore, to fully understand current affairs, such as wars and poverty, people must have a firm grasp on geographic settings. For instance, a study of nations in Africa, many of which continue to suffer from poverty, would require a close examination of geographic factors. The borders of many African countries were arbitrarily determined during the colonial period, and the conflicts of ethnic groups divided by these borders have influenced current struggles. On the environmental end, some nations have been significantly affected by desertification and deforestation, which makes studies of their ecological geography important as well.

Two recent key developments have made geography more important than ever before. The first change is the globalization of culture, economics, and politics. For much of human history, geography was most important at localized scales. Many people spent their entire lives in isolated communities, with intermittent trade between different centers. Geography was still important, but many people did not need to be familiar with anything other than their immediate locations. Today, on the other hand, places around the world are intricately connected to each other. Travel is relatively easy and quick and enables people to venture between different regions like never before. Areas that used to be geographically isolated from each other can now exchange ideas and products on an unprecedented scale.

In addition, due to the multinational relationship of politics, conflicts that would have been geographically isolated in the past can have international ramifications. Latin American revolutions, such as in Nicaragua during the Cold War, were seen as having larger implications in the struggle between American democracy and Soviet communism, which led to foreign interventions and wars that affected multiple countries. Therefore, geography is critical to not only addressing the current effects of globalization but also understanding how global interactions may influence international politics and economics in the future.

The second major factor in geography's role in modern events is the rising importance of environmental policies and climate change. Scientific developments have increasingly revealed how the planet as a whole can be considered a large ecosystem in its own right, with its own strengths and frailties. A change in one part of the environment, such as industrialization in India and China, can have larger consequences for neighboring regions and for the world as a whole. Geographical insights help to show how the world functions and how humans can work to improve their relationship with the natural world.

Moreover, as climate changes become more evident in the world, geography helps illustrate the effects of new environmental phenomena. For instance, scientists have studied the topography of nations to determine how rising sea levels will alter the land via flooding, and local and national governments are using these findings to prepare for the coming changes. Furthermore, the continued scrutiny of the state of the Earth's geography reveals how climate change is transforming the planet at this very moment, as regional climates shift and islands vanish under the sea. As a result, geography will continue to have a role in future developments.

Different Cultural Backgrounds

When studying different cultures, it is important to realize that cultures are always changing in response to individuals and groups within it. Therefore, one must avoid stereotyping members of a certain culture or overgeneralizing. For example, American culture is highly diverse with multiple ethnic groups. Many ethnic communities have resided in the United States for generations, so it is incorrect to label them as a foreign culture, yet each group must be closely examined to understand American culture as a whole.

This diversity within larger classifications of cultures can be seen with Native Americans. There are many different tribes of Native Americans, and each has its own unique history and characteristics. Nevertheless, a few general qualities describe most Native American groups. First of all, Native Americans continue to struggle to escape the poverty that they were historically forced into during white settlement of the United States. Many, but not all, tribes have been traditionally matrilineal—with ancestry defined through female lineage—and emphasized communal sharing and a sustainable relationship with nature, but the American government often suppressed these customs. This has led many Native Americans to begin protecting their surviving heritage, including their rights to traditional religious practices and access to historical artifacts.

South of the United States, Mexico has a vibrant yet troubled culture. Mexico was one of the principal colonies of Spain, and the culture is therefore a diverse blend of Spanish and native customs. One enduring legacy of Spain's rule is the prominence of Roman Catholicism, albeit mixed with pre-Spanish concepts; for instance, the traditional Day of the Dead embodies both pre-Columbian and Christian ideals. On the other hand, the Spanish system of large estates created significant class disparities. Furthermore, Mexico's war for independence and conflicts with other nations drastically destabilized its government, and the nation continues to struggle with corruption and violence. Still, Mexico retains a rich culture that celebrates its complex history. Mexican families are generally large and cooperate to help each other.

French national identity is relatively new because regional ties were prevalent until the French Revolution in the 1790s. A rising sense of nationalism unites French culture today, but various regions maintain their own local traditions. Much of France has been traditionally agricultural, but the globalization of the food trade has disrupted local markets and led to mass migration to cities. Reflecting Catholic values, most of France's families follow a nuclear model of a two-parent household with children.

South Africa is culturally and ethnically diverse, but historically white settlers used apartheid to oppress and isolate other groups. However, previously marginalized ethnic groups are now actively working to assert their own identity within South Africa. Rural communities tend to be more traditional, while people within cities have adopted new values. South Africa is largely patriarchal with defined gender roles that give men dominance over women. Efforts to strengthen South Africa's industries have depleted many of its natural resources and created a growing environmental crisis that is particularly devastating to rural populations.

Laying claim to the legacies of ancient Persia, Iran's culture was at the crossroads of trade routes between multiple continents for centuries, which gave it a long and diverse background. Iran is primarily Islamic, with the majority of Muslims belonging to the Shi'a faith. They believe that their religious leaders, imams, are divinely appointed as the religious successors, known as **caliphs**, to the prophet Muhammad; even so, other religions such as Judaism and Zoroastrianism are also practiced in the country. Iran's patriarchal culture generally restricts the role of women, but women have nevertheless become more involved in the civil service, sciences, and other fields.

Russia's culture is built on a rich history but has been especially influenced by the dominance of communism until the Soviet Union's dissolution in 1991. The use of state police and other agents to enforce government policies led to a sense of paranoia and distrust of anyone outside the family. On the other hand, this situation created strong support networks within families that led to strong relationships with relatives. The Soviet Union's drive to industrialize also led to numerous current environmental issues across Russia.

As with Russia, the People's Republic of China's modern culture is deeply influenced by decades of Communist rule. Under the leadership of Mao, China enacted massive efforts to strengthen Chinese industry and agriculture at the cost of environmental damage; China continues to undergo intense industrial operations in the present, which has caused pollution in the cities. On the other hand, China takes great pride in its long traditions and history that date back thousands of years. China has been traditionally patriarchal, and children have been expected to respect and care for their elders. Chinese culture is not monolithic, and there are many different ethnic groups within the country, including the Han, Manchu, and Uyghur. However, the one-child policy from 1978 to 2015 has destabilized long-term family dynamics by putting considerable pressure on single children to look after their parents.

Japan's family structure has also been disrupted in the modern era. Japanese culture is built on a sense of interdependence within families and the community, but a low birthrate has led to a rising number of elderly relatives and few children, which has unsettled the traditional foundation. Even so, Japan embraces a blend of modern advancements and traditional customs. Japanese culture is built on multiple layers of social status, and people use different forms of language depending on their relationship with others. As a result, traditional Japanese society is highly formal, but recent generations have become more open to new ideas. As Japan's islands have limited space and resources, it has been at the forefront of many natural conservation efforts, although some controversial traditions, such as whaling, still persist.

World History and Economics

Major Contributions of Classical Civilizations

There were a number of powerful civilizations during the classical period. **Mesopotamia** was home to one of the earliest civilizations between the Euphrates and the Tigris rivers in the Near East. The rivers provided water and vegetation for early humans, but they were surrounded by desert. This led to the beginning of irrigation efforts to expand water and agriculture across the region, which resulted in the area being known as the **Fertile Crescent**.

The organization necessary to initiate canals and other projects led to the formation of cities and hierarchies, which would have considerable influence on the structure of later civilizations. For instance, the new hierarchies established different classes within the societies, such as kings, priests, artisans, and workers. Over time, these city-states expanded to encompass outside territories, and the city of Akkad became the world's first empire in 2350 B.C. In addition, Mesopotamian scribes developed systemized drawings called **pictograms**, which were the first system of writing in the world; furthermore, the creation of wedge-shaped **cuneiform tablets** preserved written records for multiple generations.

Later, Mesopotamian kingdoms made further advancements. For instance, **Babylon** established a sophisticated mathematical system based on numbers from one to sixty; this not only influenced modern concepts, such as the number of minutes in each hour, but also created the framework for math equations and theories. In addition, the Babylonian king Hammurabi established a complex set of laws, known as the **Code of Hammurabi**, which would set a precedent for future legal systems.

Meanwhile, another major civilization began to form around the Nile River in Africa. The Nile's relatively predictable nature allowed farmers to use the river's water and the silt from floods to grow many crops along its banks, which led to further advancements in irrigation. Egyptian rulers mobilized the kingdom's population for incredible construction projects, including the famous pyramids. Egyptians also improved pictographic writing with their more complex system of **hieroglyphs**, which allowed for more diverse styles of writing. The advancements in writing can be seen through the Egyptians' complex system of religion, with documents such as the **Book of the Dead** outlining not only systems of worship and pantheons of deities but also a deeper, more philosophical concept of the afterlife.

While civilizations in Egypt and Mesopotamia helped to establish class systems and empires, other forms of government emerged in Greece. Despite common ties between different cities, such as the Olympic Games, each settlement, known as a **polis**, had its own unique culture. Many of the cities were oligarchies, in which a council of distinguished leaders monopolized the government; others were dictatorships ruled by tyrants. Athens was a notable exception by practicing an early form of democracy in which free, landholding men could participate, but it offered more freedom of thought than other systems.

Taking advantage of their proximity to the Mediterranean Sea, Greek cities sent expeditions to establish colonies abroad that developed their own local traditions. In the process, Greek merchants interacted with Phoenician traders, who had developed an alphabetic writing system built on sounds instead of pictures. This diverse network of exchanges made Greece a vibrant center of art, science, and philosophy. For example, the Greek doctor Hippocrates established a system of ethics for doctors called the **Hippocratic Oath**, which continues to guide the modern medical profession. Complex forms of literature were created, including the epic poem *The Iliad*, and theatrical productions were also developed. Athens in particular sought to spread its vision of democratic freedom throughout the world, which led to the devastating Peloponnesian War between allies of Athens and those of oligarchic Sparta from 431 to 404 B.C.

Alexander the Great helped disseminate Greek culture to new regions. Alexander was in fact an heir to the throne of Macedon, which was a warrior kingdom to the north of Greece. After finishing his father's work of unifying Greece under Macedonian control, Alexander successfully conquered Mesopotamia, which had been part of the Persian Empire. The spread of Greek institutions throughout the Mediterranean and Near East led to a period of Hellenization, during which various civilizations assimilated Greek culture; this allowed Greek traditions, such as architecture and philosophy, to endure into the present day.

Greek ideas were later assimilated, along with many other concepts, into the **Roman Empire**. Located west of Greece on the Italian peninsula, Rome greatly expanded its territories and grew to be a powerful empire through the conquering of its neighboring civilizations; by 44 B.C., Rome had conquered much of Western Europe, northern Africa, and the Near East. Romans were very creative, and they adapted new ideas and innovated new technologies to strengthen their power. For instance, Romans built on the engineering knowledge of Greeks to create arched pathways, known as **aqueducts**, to transport water for long distances and devise advanced plumbing systems.

One of Rome's greatest legacies was its system of government. Early Rome was a republic, a democratic system in which leaders are elected by the people. Although the process still heavily favored wealthy elites, the republican system was a key inspiration for later institutions such as the United States. Octavian "Augustus" Caesar later made Rome into an empire, and the senate had only a symbolic role in the government. The new imperial system built on the examples of earlier empires to establish a vibrant dynasty that used a sophisticated legal code and a well-trained military to enforce order across vast regions. Even after Rome itself fell to barbarian invaders in fifth century A.D., the eastern half of the empire survived as the Byzantine Empire until 1453 A.D. Furthermore, the Roman Empire's institutions continued to influence and inspire later medieval kingdoms, including the Holy Roman Empire; even rulers in the twentieth century called themselves Kaiser and Tsar, titles which stem from the word "Caesar."

In addition, the Roman Empire was host to the spread of new religious ideas. In the region of Israel, the religion of **Judaism** presented a new approach to worship via **monotheism**, which is the belief in the existence of a single deity. An offshoot of Judaism called **Christianity** spread across the Roman Empire and gained popularity. While Rome initially suppressed the religion, it later backed Christianity and allowed the religious system to endure as a powerful force in medieval times.

Twentieth-Century Development in World History

At the turn of the twentieth century, imperialism had led to powers, such as France, the United States, and Japan, to establish spheres of influence throughout the world. The combination of imperial competition and military rivalries led to the outbreak of World War I when **Archduke Ferdinand of Austria** was assassinated in 1914. The war pitted **the Allies**, including England, France, and Russia, against the Central Powers of Austria-Hungary, Germany, and the **Ottoman Empire**—a large Islamic realm that encompassed Turkey, Palestine, Saudi Arabia, and Iraq. The rapid advances in military technology turned the war into a prolonged bloodbath that took its toll on all sides. By the end of the war in 1918, the Ottoman Empire had collapsed, the Austrian-Hungarian Empire was split into multiple countries, and Russia had descended into a civil war that would lead to the rise of the Soviet Union and Communism.

The **Treaty of Versailles** ended the war, but the triumphant Allies also levied heavy fines on Germany, which led to resentment that would be accentuated by the Great Depression of the 1930s. The **Great Depression** destabilized the global economy and led to the rise of fascism, a militarized and dictatorial system of government, in nations such as Germany and Italy. The rapid expansion of the Axis Powers of Germany, Italy, and Japan led to the outbreak of World War II. The war was even more global than the previous conflicts, with battles occurring in Europe, Africa, and Asia. World War II encouraged the development of new technologies, such as advanced radar and nuclear weapons, that would continue to influence the course of future wars.

In the aftermath of World War II, the **United Nations** was formed as a step toward promoting international cooperation. Based on the preceding League of Nations, the United Nations included countries from around the world and gave them a voice in world policies. The formation of the United Nations coincided with the independence of formerly colonized states in Africa and Asia, and those countries joined the world body. A primary goal of the United Nations was to limit the extent of future wars and prevent a third world war. While the United Nations could not prevent the outbreak of wars, it nevertheless tried to peacefully resolve them. In addition to promoting world peace, the United Nations also helped protect human rights.

Even so, the primary leadership in the early United Nations was held by the United States and its allies, which contributed to tensions with the Soviet Union. The United States and the Soviet Union, while never declaring war on each other, fueled a number of proxy wars and coups across the world in what would be known as the **Cold War**. Cold War divisions were especially noticeable in Europe, where communist regimes ruled the eastern region and democratic governments controlled the western portion. These indirect struggles often involved interference with foreign politics, and sometimes local people began to resent Soviet or American attempts to influence their countries. For instance, American and Soviet interventions in Iran and Afghanistan contributed to fundamentalist Islamic movements. The Cold War ended when the Soviet Union collapsed in 1991, but the conflict affected nations across the globe and continues to influence current issues.

Another key development during the twentieth century, as noted earlier with the United Nations, was that most colonized nations broke free from imperial control and asserted their independence. Although these nations achieved autonomy and recognition in the United Nations, they still suffered from the legacies of imperialism. The borders of many countries in Africa and Asia were arbitrarily determined by colonists with little regard to the arrangement of native populations. Therefore, many former colonies have suffered conflicts between different ethnic groups; this was also the case with the British colony in India, which became independent in 1947. Violence occurred when it split into India and Pakistan because the borders were largely based on religious differences. In addition, former colonial powers continue to assert economic control that inhibits the growth of native economies. On the other hand, the end of direct imperialism has helped a number of nations, such as India and Iran, rise as world powers that have significant influence on the world as a whole.

Additionally, there were considerable environmental reforms worldwide during the twentieth century. In reaction to the growing effects of industrialization, organizations around the world protested policies that damaged the environment. Many of these movements were locally based, but others expanded to address various environmental threats across the globe. The United Nations helped carry these environmental reforms forward by making them part of international policies. For instance, in 1997, many members of the United Nations signed a treaty, known as the **Kyoto Protocol**, that tried to reduce global carbon dioxide emissions.

Most significantly, the twentieth century marked increasing globalization. The process had already been under way in the nineteenth century as technological improvements and imperial expansions connected different parts of the world, but the late twentieth century brought globalization to a new level. Trade became international, and local customs from different lands also gained prominence worldwide. Cultural exchanges occur on a frequent basis, and many people have begun to ponder the consequences of such rapid exchanges. One example of globalization was the 1993 establishment of the European Union—an economic and political alliance between several European nations.

Cross-Cultural Comparisons in World History Instruction

Cross-cultural interactions are the very heart of world history and must be closely examined to understand the world's historical patterns. One of the main reasons why cross-cultural studies are so important is because cultures are not necessarily synonymous with political entities, such as states. Many countries, ranging from China to Greece, historically have many subcultures that should be considered individually. For example, a study of culture in the United States would need to consider multiple ethnic and regional groups. Even individual states and cities have their own traditions. On the other hand, these multiple cultures often coalesce into a larger, national culture that defines the overall society and politics of the nation. Therefore, cross-cultural studies of different subgroups in a larger body allow people to understand how the different parts of a culture interact and connect with each other.

Furthermore, cultures are not always restricted by the borders of nations, and cultural phenomena may extend through multiple countries. This can be seen in the spread of the Spanish language across Central and South America as well as other regions. The Spanish language and other various traditions tie the different countries together with a common culture. Even so, each nation changes the culture and gives it a unique style. A study of the culture in a single nation may be very insightful, but it would be incomplete if it failed to account for aspects of the culture beyond that country. In addition, this means that different cultures can overlap with each other and that the cultures of different countries may intersect in ways that their borders do not. By examining multiple cultures and how they are linked with each other, larger cultural patterns become apparent, which makes these studies critical in world history.

Throughout history, cultures have not existed in isolation but rather have been affected by other traditions. A key influence in how different cultures develop is not only their setting and history but how they interact with neighboring cultures. For instance, the conflict from 499 to 449 B.C. between the Persian Empire and the Greek city-states helped to influence the course of Greek culture by creating a national sense of dichotomy between the Greek ideal of freedom and Persian autocracy. Aside from direct impacts such as wars, cultures can influence each other through interactions that spread some concepts while also adopting new ideas from their neighbors. Pasta became a phenomenon in Italy in part because the Silk Road linked Italy with China, which already had similar foods.

The pervasiveness of globalization in the present day has increased the importance of cross-cultural comparison and made it a topic of immediate relevance. The world now has a truly global market in which travel, communications, and trade function on an international scale. This means that people of different cultures can now interact with each other much more easily than in earlier centuries, which allows for a rapid exchange of ideas and goods between cultures. Furthermore, despite the international scope of modern trade, many globalized markets strive to build on the appeal of local cultures. Doing so gives the products a genuine and unique quality that resonates with consumers. Yet it is critical to realize how local cultures are transformed and combined with concepts from other cultures in the global market. For example, sushi is a traditional food in Japan, but its export to other nations has led chefs to create new culinary fusions, such as sushi tacos.

Cross-cultural comparisons also help to reveal common patterns in human society. Sometimes different cultures develop similar concepts without directly interacting with each other. For instance, both the Mayan culture in Central America and the ancient Egyptians independently developed pyramid structures. Although the similarities have sparked rumors that these civilizations were connected, it is most likely that each version originated independently. Close examination of the two types of pyramids and their respective cultures reveals significant differences amidst the similarities. These comparisons are important because they show how human cultures converge and diverge in their patterns of growth. A key function of historical study is to gain a better understanding and appreciation of how humanity develops. By examining the commonalities and differences between cultures, people can begin to theorize what factors influence the course of civilizations. However, such studies must account for the complex manners through which cultures interact with each other.

Terms and Concepts of Economics

Economics form a key component of human society. Studies of economies can be divided between **macroeconomics**, which considers the larger economy as a whole, and **microeconomics**, which focuses on the actions of smaller groups, households, and individuals. However, the most basic principle of economics comes down to resources. A **resource** can be defined as an object or material that can be used for some purpose. **Natural resources** come directly from the environment, whereas items altered through human activity are considered manufactured goods. Resources can be further divided into **renewable resources**, which are gradually replenished given enough time and proper circumstances, and **nonrenewable resources**, which regenerate slowly or not at all. In addition, there are four main types of economic resources: **land**, which includes most natural resources; **labor**, the services provided by individuals to create products; **capital**, which encompasses human-manufactured resources; and **entrepreneurship**, the process in which individuals utilize available resources for business ventures that generate new products.

Early on, human civilizations functioned using a **barter system**, where people would trade certain goods for other items. It remains common in some parts of the world today. However, the difficulty of storing and transporting products, such as livestock and minerals, for exchange, led to the development of monetary systems. **Money** is an object, such as a coin or a paper bill, which can be exchanged for any commercial product. It is important to note that money on its own often has no worth; **paper money**, for example, is a rather flimsy material with little actual use outside of its monetary worth. It only has value when members of a society agree that it can be used to make purchases.

Due to the artificial nature of money within societies, prices fluctuate depending on the supply and demand of products. **Supply** refers to the available quantity of a specific good or resource. In contrast, demand accounts for the quantity that buyers wish to obtain. These two factors influence several economic patterns. The **law of supply** states that the quantity available for purchase is directly related to the price, while the **law of demand** states that the price of an item is inversely related to the demand for the item. Thus, raising prices increases supply and reduces demand.

Furthermore, the value of money in part depends on the amount that is circulated in the market. A surplus of money has the potential to devalue the currency, which lowers the worth of each unit of money. This process, called **inflation**, has a detrimental effect on the economy as prices generally increase. However, the opposite trend, **deflation**, can also be detrimental; thus, political leaders usually strive to find a stable balance between the two ends of the spectrum. By finding equilibrium between supply and demand, an economy's prices remain relatively stable.

Economies, by nature, have limited access to certain resources, which creates a conflict between supply and demand. **Scarcity** occurs when the demand for a product exceeds its availability. Scarcity in part depends on the choices of individuals as they determine which products they want more than others. **Choices**, in turn, are influenced by the perceived costs of pursuing certain options over others. The costs and benefits of specific choices often differ depending on the individuals' perceptions of the options. When people believe that a certain service's or product's benefits outweigh its necessary costs, they may choose to pay more for the desired benefits. It is important to realize that the laws of supply and demand are not absolute, and they may fluctuate depending on the situation.

Supply and demand can be further affected by **monopolies**, in which an individual or group holds sole or primary access to a given product or service. The individuals controlling a monopoly can limit the supply in a manner that best suits themselves but not necessarily the consumers. Monopolies are often asserted through the creation of barriers that limit access to the resources or services. For instance, patents give exclusive rights for inventions and discoveries to their respective creators or the firms that sponsored them. Without restraints, a monopoly can significantly limit economic development and prosperity of a society.

Effects of Economics on Population, Resources, and Technology

Economics are closely linked with the flow of resources, technology, and population in societies. The use of natural resources, such as water and fossil fuels, has always depended in part on the pressures of the economy. A supply of a specific good may be limited in the market, but with sufficient demand the sellers are incentivized to increase the available quantity. Unfortunately, the demand for certain objects can often be unlimited, and a high price or limited supply may prevent consumers from obtaining the product or service. If the sellers succumb to the consumers' demand and continue to exploit a scarce resource, supply could potentially be exhausted.

The resources for most products, both renewable and nonrenewable, are finite. This is a particularly difficult issue with nonrenewable resources, but even renewable resources often have limits: **organic products** such as trees and animals require stable populations and sufficient habitats to support those populations. Furthermore, the costs of certain decisions can have detrimental effects on other resources. For example, industrialization provides economic benefits in many countries but also has had the negative effect of polluting surrounding environments; the pollution, in turn, often eliminates or harms fish, plants, and other potential resources.

The control of resources within an economy is particularly important in determining how resources are used. While the demand may change with the choices of consumers, the range of supply depends on the objectives of the people producing the goods. They determine how much of their supply they allot for sale, and in the case of monopolies, they might have sole access to the resource. They might choose to limit their use of the resources or instead gather more to meet the demand. As they pay for the products, consumers can choose which sellers they rely on for the supply. In the case of a monopoly, though, consumers have little influence over the company's decision because there is no alternative supplier. Therefore, the function of supply within an economy can drastically influence how the resources are exploited.

The availability of resources, in turn, affects the human population. Humans require basic resources such as food and water for survival, as well as additional resources for healthy lifestyles. Therefore, access to these resources helps determine the survival rate of humans. For much of human existence, economies have had limited ability to extract resources from the natural world, which restricted the growth rate of populations. However, the development of new technologies, combined with increasing demand for certain products, has pushed resource use to a new level. On the one hand, this led to higher living standards that ensured that fewer people would die. However, this has also brought mass population growth. Admittedly, countries with higher standards of living often have lower birthrates. Even so, the increasing exploitation of resources has sharply increased the world's population as a whole to unsustainable levels. The rising population leads, in turn, to more demand for resources that cannot be met. This creates poverty, reduced living conditions, and higher death rates. As a result, economics can significantly influence local and world population levels.

Technology is also intricately related to population, resources, and economics. The role of demand within economies has incentivized people to innovate new technologies that enable societies to have a higher quality of life and greater access to resources. Entrepreneurs expand technologies by finding ways to create new products for the market. The **Industrial Revolution**, in particular, illustrates the relationship between economics and technology because the ambitions of businessmen led to new infrastructure that enabled more efficient and sophisticated use of resources. Many of these inventions reduced the amount of work necessary for individuals and allowed the development of leisure activities, which in turn created new economic markets. However, economic systems can also limit the growth of technology. In the case of monopolies, the lack of alternative suppliers reduces the incentive to meet and exceed consumer expectations. Moreover, as demonstrated by the effects of economics on resources, technology's increasing ability to extract resources can lead to their depletion and create significant issues that need to be addressed.

Government's Role in Economics and the Impact of Economics on Government

Governments have considerable influence over the flow of economies, which makes it important to understand the relationships between them. When a government has full control over the economic decisions of a nation, it is called a **command system**. This was the case in many absolute monarchies such as eighteenth-century France; **King Louis XIV** built his economy on the concept of **mercantilism**, which believed that the state should manage all resources, particularly by accumulating gold and silver. This system of economics discouraged exports and thereby limited trade.

In contrast, the **market system** is guided by the concept of capitalism, in which individuals and businesses have the freedom to manage their economic decisions. This allows for private property and increases the opportunities for entrepreneurship and trade. Early proponents of capitalism emphasized **laissez-faire** policies, which means "let it be," and argued that the government should not be involved with the economy at all. They believe the market is guided by the concept of self-interest and that individuals will optimally work for their personal success. However, individuals' interests do not necessarily correlate with the needs of the overall economy. For instance, during a financial recession, consumers may decide to save up their money rather than make purchases; doing so helps them in the short run but further reduces demand in a slumping economy. Therefore, most capitalist governments still assert a degree of control over their economies while still allowing for private business.

Likewise, many command system economies, such as monarchical France, still relied heavily on private businesses maintained by wealthy businessmen. With the end of most absolute monarchies, communism has been the primary form of command system economies in the modern era. **Communism** is a form of socialism that emphasizes communal ownership of property and government control over production. The high degree of government control gives more stability to the economy, but it also creates considerable flaws. The monopolization of the economy by the government limits its ability to respond to local economic conditions because certain regions often have unique resources and needs. With the collapse of the Soviet Union and other communist states, command systems have been largely replaced with market systems.

The U.S. government helps to manage the nation's economy through a market system in several ways. First and foremost, the federal government is responsible for the production of money for use within the economy; depending on how the government manages the monetary flow, it may lead to a stable economy, deflation, or inflation. Second, state and federal governments impose taxes on individuals, corporations, and goods. For instance, a tariff might be imposed on imports in order to stimulate demand for local goods in the economy. Third, the government can pass laws that require additional regulation or inspections. In addition, the government has passed antitrust laws to inhibit the growth of private monopolies, which could limit free growth in the market system. Debates continue over whether the government should take further action to manage private industries or reduce its control over the private sector.

Just as governments can affect the direction of the economy, the state of the economy can have significant implications on government policies. Financial stability is critical in maintaining a prosperous state. A healthy economy will allow for new developments that contribute to the nation's growth and create jobs. On the other hand, an economic crisis, such as a recession or depression, can gravely damage a government's stability. Without a stable economy, business opportunities plummet, and people begin to lose income and employment. This, in turn, leads to frustration and discontent in the population, which can lead to criticism of the government. This could very well lead to demands for new leadership to resolve the economic crisis.

The dangers of a destabilized economy can be seen with the downfall of the French monarchy. The mercantilist approach to economics stifled French trade. Furthermore, regional aristocracies remained exempt from government taxes, which limited the government's revenues. This was compounded by expensive wars and poor harvests that led to criticism of King Louis XIV's government. The problems persisted for decades, and Louis XIV was forced to convene the **Estates-General**, a legislative body of representatives from across France, to address the crisis. The economic crises at the end of the eighteenth century were critical in the beginning of the French Revolution. Those financial issues, in turn, at least partially stemmed from both the government's control of the economy through mercantilism and its inability to impose economic authority over local regions.

Practice Quiz

1. Which of the following civilizations developed the first democratic form of government?
    a. Roman Empire
    b. Ancient Greece
    c. Achaemenid Empire
    d. Zhou Dynasty

2. What is the difference between a primary source and a secondary source?
    a. Secondary sources are usually fictional, while primary sources are always true.
    b. Primary sources are context-specific, first-hand accounts, and secondary sources usually synthesize primary sources with some historical distance.
    c. Secondary sources are almost always first-hand accounts, while primary sources are second-hand fictional testimonies.
    d. There are no major differences between primary sources and secondary sources.

3. Which of the following was NOT a movement that was going on in the 1960s?
    a. Civil Rights Movement
    b. End the War Movement
    c. Women's Rights Movement
    d. LGBTQ Rights Movement

4. Which of the following is NOT part of the US government's system of checks and balances?
    a. The president may veto a bill passed by Congress.
    b. The Supreme Court can try the president for high crimes and misdemeanors committed in office.
    c. Congress must approve all of the president's appointments to the Supreme Court.
    d. Congress can pass a budget that limits what the president can spend on defense.

5. What was the Triple Entente?
    a. The Triple Entente was a free trade agreement between the United States, Britain, and France.
    b. The Triple Entente was a free trade agreement between Britain, France, and Germany.
    c. The Triple Entente was a military alliance between Austria-Hungary, Germany, and the Ottoman Empire.
    d. The Triple Entente was a military alliance between Britain, France, and Russia.

See answers on the next page.

Answer Explanations

1. B: Ancient Greeks created many of the cultural and political institutions that form the basis of modern western civilization. Athens was an important Greek democracy, and all adult men could participate in politics after they had completed their military service. The Roman Empire, Choice *A*, evolved from the Roman Republic, but it was not democratic. The Achaemenid Empire and Zhou Dynasty, Choices *C* and *D*, were imperial monarchies that did not allow citizens to have much, if any, political voice.

2. B: Primary sources are context-specific, first-hand accounts, and secondary sources usually synthesize primary sources with some historical distance. Choice *A* is incorrect because both primary and secondary sources can be fictional or realistic. Choice *C* is wrong for two reasons. First, it confuses the fact that primary sources are first-hand accounts and secondary sources can be second-hand testimonies. Second, secondary sources aren't always fictional. Choice *D* is incorrect because primary sources and secondary sources are drastically different in scope and context.

3. B: End the War Movement. The 1960s were a time of growth for the United States. Everyone was pushing for rights and for changes to the system, and people were beginning to challenge the government. End the War was still a decade off, however, with Vietnam still around the corner. Choice *A* is incorrect because the Civil Rights Movement, led by leaders like Martin Luther King Jr., dominated the 1960s leading up to the Civil Rights Act. Choices *C* and *D* are incorrect because women's rights were also key throughout the decade, as well as the movement for LGBTQ rights.

4. B: Congress may try the president for high crimes and misdemeanors; the chief justice of the Supreme Court, however, does preside over the hearings. The president has the power to veto any law passed by Congress, and Congress can override the president's veto. Congress approves or rejects the president's picks for the Supreme Court and federal courts. Congress also controls the federal budget, which can limit what the president can spend on the military.

5. D: During the early twentieth century, Britain sought military alliances with France and Russia after Germany militarized and expanded its colonies. The military alliance between Britain, France, and Russia was known as the **Triple Entente**, and it was one of the complex alliance systems that contributed to the start of World War I. Thus, Choice *D* is the correct answer. The Triple Entente was not a free trade agreement, so Choices *A* and *B* are both incorrect. The military alliance between Austria-Hungary, Germany, and the Ottoman Empire fought the Triple Entente as Central Powers during World War I. So, Choice *C* is incorrect.

Science

Earth Science

Structure of Earth System

Earth is a complex system of the **atmosphere** (air), **hydrosphere** (water), as well as continental land (land). All work together to support the **biosphere** (life).

The atmosphere is divided into several layers: the troposphere, stratosphere, mesosphere, and thermosphere. The **troposphere** is at the bottom and is about seven and a half miles thick. Above the troposphere is the 30-mile-thick **stratosphere**. Above the stratosphere is the **mesosphere**, a 20-mile layer, followed by the **thermosphere**, which is more than 300 miles thick.

The troposphere is closest to Earth and has the greatest pressure due to the pull of gravity on its gas particles as well as pressure from the layers above. 78 percent of the atmosphere is made of nitrogen. Surprisingly, the oxygen that we breathe only makes up 21 percent of the gases, and the carbon dioxide critical to insulating Earth makes up less than 1 percent of the atmosphere. There are other trace gases present in the atmosphere, including water vapor.

Although the stratosphere has minimal wind activity, it is critical for supporting the biosphere because it contains the ozone layer, which absorbs the sun's damaging ultra-violet rays and protects living organisms. Due to its low level of air movement, airplanes travel in the stratosphere. The mesosphere contains few gas particles, and the gas levels are so insignificant in the thermosphere that it is considered space.

Visible light is colors reflecting off particles. If all colors reflect, we see white; if no colors reflect, we see black. This means a colored object is reflecting only that color—a red ball reflects red light and absorbs other colors.

Because the thermosphere has so few particles to reflect light rays (photons), it appears black. The troposphere appears blue in the day, and various shades of yellow and orange at sunset due to the angle of the Sun hitting particles that refract, or bend, the light. In certain instances, the entire visible spectrum can be seen in the form of rainbows. Rainbows occur when sunlight passes through water droplets and is refracted in many different directions by the water particles.

The **hydrosphere**, or water-containing portion of the Earth's surface, plays a major role in supporting the biosphere. In the picture below, a single water molecule (molecular formula H_2O) looks like a mouse head. The small ears of the mouse are the two hydrogen atoms connected to the larger oxygen atom in the middle.

Each hydrogen atom has one **proton** (positively charged, like the plus end of a magnet) in its **nucleus** (center), while oxygen has eight protons in its center. Hydrogen also has only one electron (negatively charged, like the minus end of a magnet) orbiting around the nucleus. Because hydrogen has only one proton, its electron is pulled more toward the oxygen nucleus (more powerful magnet). This makes hydrogen exist without an electron most of the time, so it is positively charged. On the other hand, oxygen often has two extra electrons (one from each hydrogen), so it is negatively charged. These bonds between the oxygen and hydrogen are called **covalent bonds**.

This charged situation is what makes water such a versatile substance; it also causes different molecules of water to interact with each other.

In a solid form (ice), water lines up in a crystal structure because the positive hydrogen atoms prefer to be next to the negative oxygen atoms that belong to other water molecules. These attractions are represented by the blue lines in the molecular picture of ice above. As heat is added and the ice melts, the water molecules have more kinetic energy and move faster; therefore, they are unable to perfectly arrange in the lattice structure of ice and turn into liquid. If enough heat is added, the water molecules will have so much kinetic energy they vaporize into gas. At this point, there are no bonds holding the water together because the molecules aren't close enough.

Notice how ice in its intricate arrangement has more space between the particles than liquid water, which shows that the ice is less dense than water. This contradicts the scientific fact that solids are denser than liquids. In water's case only, the solid will float due to a lower density! This is significant for the hydrosphere, because if temperatures drop to lower than freezing, frozen water will float to the surface of lakes or oceans and insulate the water underneath so that life can continue in liquid water. If ice was not less dense than liquid water, bodies of water would freeze from the bottom up and aquatic ecosystems would be trapped in a block of ice.

The hydrosphere has two components: **seawater** and **freshwater** (less than 5 percent of the hydrosphere). Water covers more than 70 percent of the Earth's surface.

The final piece of the biosphere is the **lithosphere**, the rocky portion of Earth. **Geology** is the study of solid earth. Earth's surface is composed of elemental chunks called **minerals**, which are simply crystallized groups of bonded atoms. Minerals that have the same composition but different arrangements are called **polymorphs**, like graphite and diamonds. All minerals contain physical properties such as **luster** (shine), color, hardness, density, and boiling point. Their **chemical properties**, or how they react with other compounds, are also different. Minerals combine to form the rocks that make up Earth.

Earth has distinct layers—a thin, solid outer surface, a dense, solid core, and the majority of its matter between them. It is kind of like an egg: the thin crust is the shell, the inner core is the yolk, and the mantle and outer core that compose the space in between are like the egg white.

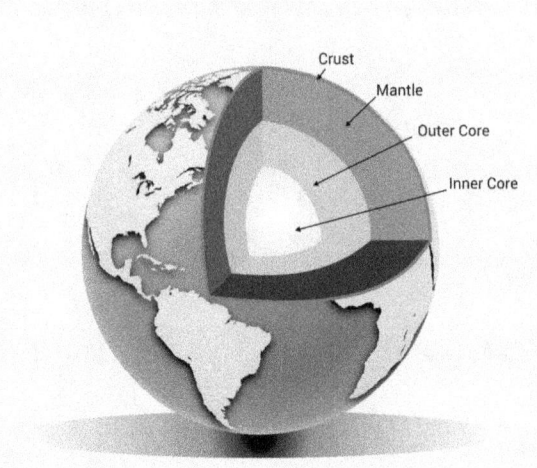

The outer crust of Earth consists of igneous or sedimentary rocks over metamorphic rocks (dense compacted rock underneath). The crust, combined with the upper portion of the mantle, forms the lithosphere, which is broken into several different plates, like puzzle pieces.

Major plates of the lithosphere

<u>Major Plates of the Lithosphere</u>
The **mantle** is divided in three zones. The thin zone adjacent to the crust is solid rock (the lower part of the lithosphere). Below that is the **asthenosphere**, which contains liquid magma (molten rock). The lower mantle

is completely solid rock. Underneath the mantle is the outer core, a molten layer rich with iron and nickel, followed by the compact, solid, inner core.

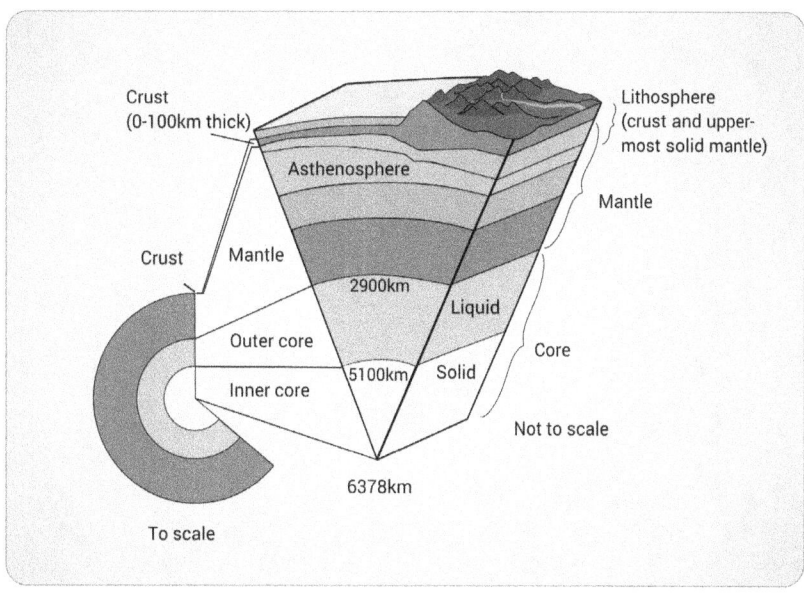

The inner and outer cores contain the densest elements (mostly iron with some nickel), which explains why they are at the center of Earth: dense elements sink. Moving from outside in, Earth gets hotter and hotter, with inner core temperatures as hot as the surface of the sun. One source of this immense heat is **nuclear fission**, which occurs when a heavy element's nucleus breaks into smaller and smaller pieces and in the process produces huge amounts of energy. Some power plants that run on fission energy are used to produce electricity. The problem with fission is that it releases huge amounts of radiation. In Chernobyl, Ukraine in 1986, a power plant explosion killed thirty-one people and exposed hundreds to radiation, a known source of mutation and cancer.

Nuclear fusion is the opposite reaction, combining small elements into a larger atom. This process produces three to four times as much energy as fission. Nuclear fusion releases energy hotter than the sun, so some believe that finding a way to use it as an energy source may be a meaningful endeavor. Scientists haven't been able to construct a facility that can harness such high temperatures, but research is currently underway.

Even though the inner and outer cores contain the same elements, the inner core is solid while the outer core is liquid, indicating that they have different melting points. How can this be? This is because tremendous pressure (the weight of the world, literally) on the inner core is so forceful that the particles remain close together and stay in their solid form, making it harder to melt.

Processes of Earth

The **water cycle** is the cycling of water between its three physical states: solid, liquid, and gas. The Sun is a critical component of the water cycle because its thermal energy heats up surface liquid water so much that parts of it evaporate. **Transpiration** is a similar process that occurs when the Sun evaporates water from plant pores called **stomata**. As water vapor rises into the atmosphere through **evaporation** and transpiration, it eventually condenses and forms clouds heavy with liquid water droplets. The liquid (or solid ice or snow) will precipitate back to Earth, collect on land, and either be absorbed by soil or run-off to the oceans and lakes where it will accumulate, circulate, and evaporate once again.

Clouds are condensed water vapor, which is water that has cooled from a gas to liquid, like the droplets on the outside of a glass of lemonade on a hot summer day. That water on the glass is water vapor that cooled enough to slow down the moving particles so that they become denser, forming a liquid. In the sky, water vapor combines in different ways so clouds appear in different forms. Cloud height, shape, and behavior results in a variety of different types:

- High-Clouds
    - Cirrus: wispy and thread-like
    - Cirrostratus: like cirrus clouds, but wider and thicker sheets. They have a halo effect where sunlight and moonlight refract through.
    - Cirrocumulus: a cross between cirrus and cirrostratus clouds. These have rows of round puffs like a cotton-ball stretched out.
    - Contrails: clouds made by jets
- Mid-Clouds
    - Altostratus: thick, stretched clouds that block sunlight and are blue-grayish in color
    - Nimbostratus: a thick altostratus cloud accompanied by rain
    - Altocumulus: layered rolls of clouds

Science

- Low-Clouds
    - Cumulus: white, round, puffy clouds
    - Stratus: wide, thick, stretched-out, gray clouds that may cause drizzle
    - Fog: lazy stratus clouds that have drooped so low that they reach Earth's surface
    - Cumulonimbus: the angry cloud that brings thunderstorms, hail, and tornadoes. It looks like a thick mountain.
    - Stratocumulus: stretched-out, grayish, puffy, cumulus clouds

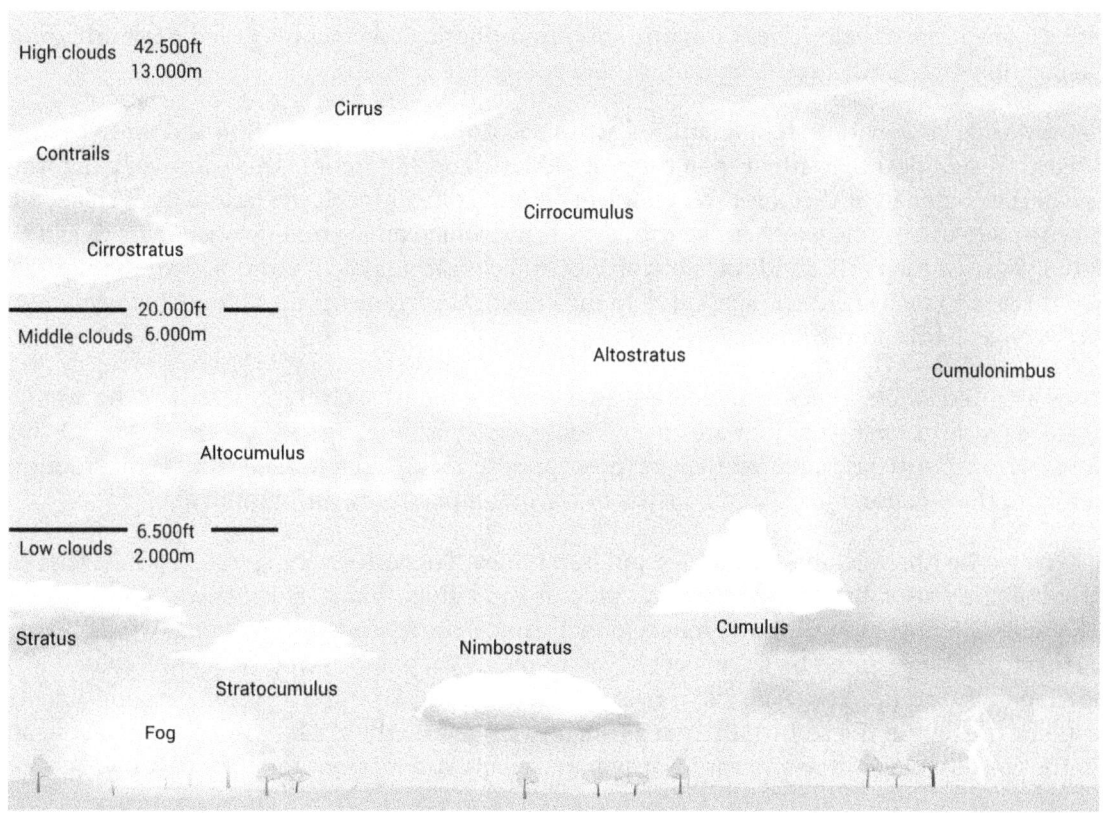

Precipitation comes in many different forms:

- **Rain** occurs due to water vapor condensing on dust particles in the troposphere. As more and more water condenses, the drops will eventually enlarge and accumulate mass, becoming so heavy that they fall to Earth.

- If the temperature is above the freezing point, the water falls as rain. Rain can freeze on the ground if the temperature on Earth's surface is colder than that of the troposphere. Freezing rain causes extremely dangerous driving conditions due to the slickness of the ice.

- **Sleet** freezes on its way down as opposed to freezing upon impact. Sleet starts as ice that melts as it falls through the atmosphere due to hitting spots of warmer temperature, and then it freezes again before hitting the ground.

- **Hail** is precipitation of balls of ice. Hail begins as ice at very cold temperatures in the atmosphere. Instead of precipitating sheets of ice like sleet storms, hailstorms precipitate ice that looks like rocks because hail is formed during thunderstorms. The massive winds throw hail up and down so more and more water vapor condenses and freezes on the original ice. Layer upon layer of ice combine, creating hail sometimes as large as golf balls.

- **Snow** forms as loosely packed ice crystals. Snow is less dangerous than the other frozen forms of precipitation and can produce beautiful snowflakes.

Even though seasons have predictable temperatures, there can be significant differences day to day. In the troposphere, the Sun's heat is trapped by the blanket of greenhouse gases and creates warm, low-pressure air. Because warm gas particles move faster and have less space between them, they are less dense than colder air, and they rise. Cool air moves below the warm air. This atmospheric movement is called **general circulation** and is the source of wind. Earth's spinning motion also causes wind.

Weather depends in a large part on temperature. Earth's equator is closest to the Sun and receives more heat, so this area of Earth is significantly warmer than the poles (Arctic and Antarctic). This warm air can form huge bubbles, as can the colder air at the poles. When warm air and cold air meet, the boundary is called a **front**. Fronts can be the site of extreme weather like thunderstorms, which are caused by water particles in clouds quickly rubbing against each other and transferring electrons, creating positive and negative regions. Lightning occurs when there is a massive electric spark due to the electrical current within a cloud, between two clouds, and even between a cloud and the ground.

While seasons are predictable trends in temperatures over a few months, **climate** describes the average weather and temperature patterns for a particular area over a long period of time, upwards of thirty years. While **fall** describes a season and **rain** describes weather, **rainforest** describes a climate. The climate of a rainforest, due to its proximity to the equator and oceans, consists of warm temperatures with humid air.

Even more extreme weather includes tornadoes and hurricanes. **Tornadoes** are spinning winds that can exceed 300 miles per hour and are caused by changing air pressure and quick winds. Hurricanes, typhoons, and tropical cyclones (the same phenomenon with different regional names) are storms with spinning winds that form over the ocean. **Hurricanes** are caused by warm ocean water quickly evaporating and rising to a colder, lower-pressure portion of the atmosphere. The fast movement of the warm air starts a cyclone around a central origination point (the eye of the storm). **Blizzards** are also caused by the clash of warm air and cold air. They occur when the cold Arctic air moves toward warmer air and involve massive amounts of snow.

Precipitation and run-off are constantly affecting the surface of Earth, as the run-off weathers rocks or breaks them down from the original bedrock into pieces called regolith. Regolith sizes range from microscopic to large and quickly form either soil or sediment. **Weathering** is the process of breaking rock while **erosion** is the process of moving rock. Weathering can be caused by both physical and chemical changes. Mechanical forces such as roots growing, animal contact, wind, and extreme weather cause weathering. Another cause is the water cycle, which includes flowing water, moving glaciers, and liquid ice seeping into rocks and cracking them as water freezes and expands. Chemical weathering actually transforms the regolith into clay and soft minerals. One consequence of chemical weathering is corrosive acid rain.

Rocks cover the surface of Earth. Igneous rock comes from the molten, hot, liquid magma circulating beneath Earth's surface in the upper mantle. Through vents called **volcanoes**, magma explodes or seeps onto the Earth's surface. Magma is not uniform; it varies in its elemental composition, gas composition, and thickness or viscosity. There are three main types of volcanoes: shield, cinder, and composite.

Shield volcanoes are the widest because their thin magma flows out of a central crater calmly and quietly, like a gentle fountain. This flowing magma results in layers of solid lava. The slow flow results in a convex hill that spans a wide area.

Like shield volcanoes, **cinder volcanoes** typically have a central crater and thin lava. In contrast to shield volcanoes, they are small, cone-shaped hills with steep sides. They are made of volcanic debris, or cinders. They are often found as secondary volcanoes near shield and composite volcanoes. In cinder volcanoes, the central vent spews lava that shatters into rock and debris and settles around it, resulting in its characteristic cone shape. Cinder volcanoes are surrounded by ashy, loose, magma dust.

Composite volcanoes (also called stratovolcanoes) are the most common and the tallest type of volcano. Their thick magma gets stuck at the vent, and as more and more builds up, the volcano eventually explodes and removes the clog. These eruptions generate loose debris, and once the plug has been violently expelled, the thick lava oozes out like a fountain. These volcanoes are the most dangerous with their extremely violent behavior and huge height. Most volcanoes are located around cracks in Earth's lithosphere.

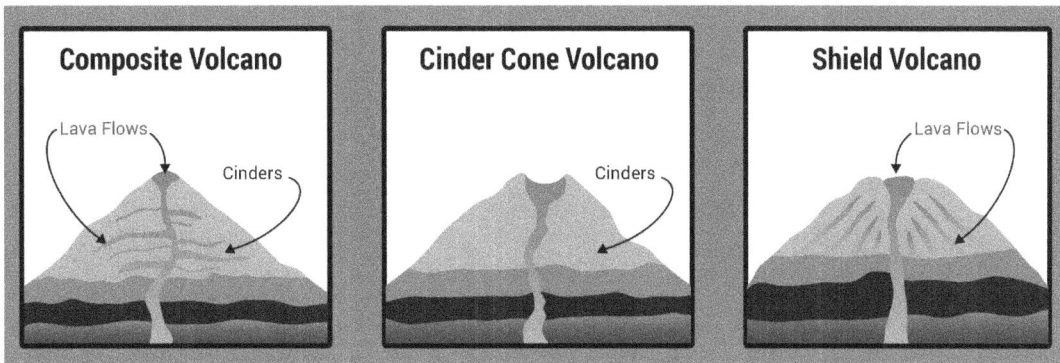

Once magma makes it to the surface, it is called **lava**. Once it cools, it solidifies into igneous rock. Common examples of igneous rock are obsidian, pumice, and granite. Weathering and erosion result in these rocks becoming soil or sediment and accumulating in layers mostly found in the ocean. These loose sediments settle over time and compress to become a uniform rock in a process called **lithification**. Examples of sedimentary rock include shale, limestone, and sandstone. As layers are piled atop each other, the bottom rock experiences an intense amount of pressure and transforms into metamorphic rock. Examples of metamorphic rocks are marble and slate. After long periods of time, the metamorphic rock moves closer to the asthenosphere and becomes liquid hot magma.

Magma's eventual fate is lava and igneous rock, and the cycle starts anew:

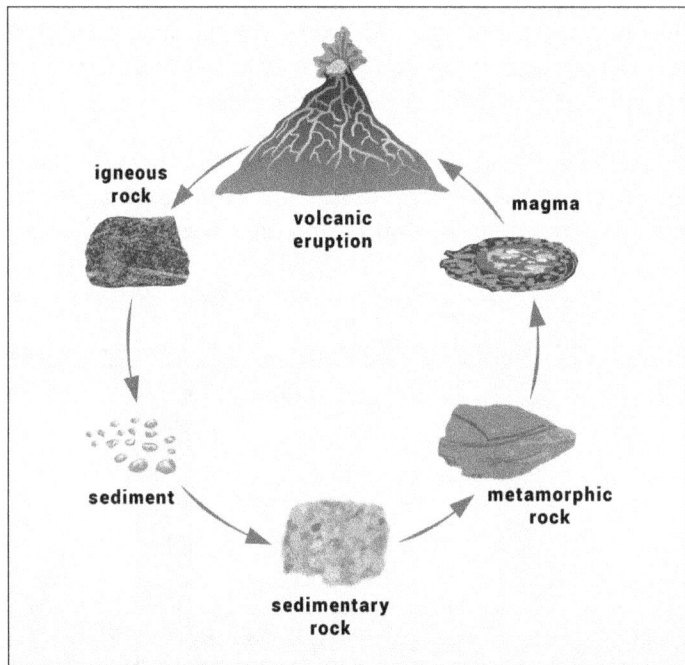

How does magma return to the surface if the lithosphere presses it down? Intense heat from the Earth's core travels to the upper mantle via **convection**. Convection involves thermal energy (heat) that converts into kinetic energy (movement), resulting in rapidly circulating molecules. Convection moves heat energy through fluids. In a pot of boiling water, the water closest to the burner becomes hot, causing its particles to move faster. Faster-moving molecules have more space between them and become less dense, so they rise. Some will vaporize, and some hit the cool air and slow down, becoming dense and sinking. Likewise, Earth's interior particles undergo convection (the heat source being the nuclear fission from the core), and the rock in the upper mantle will acquire so much kinetic energy that magma will be expelled from underneath Earth to the surface.

There are seven or eight major plates in the lithosphere and several minor plates. These tectonic plates explain the changing topography, or shape, of Earth.

There are three types of boundaries between plates: divergent, convergent, and transform. All boundaries can be sites of volcanic activity. A **divergent boundary** occurs when plates separate. Lava fills in the space the plates create and hardens into rock, which creates oceanic crust. In a **convergent boundary**, if one of the plates is in the ocean, that plate is denser due to the weight of water. The dense ocean plate will slip under the land plate, causing a subduction zone where the plate moves underneath. Where plates converge on land, the continental crusts are both lighter with a similar density, and as a result they will buckle together and create mountains.

In **transform boundaries**, adjacent plates sliding past each other create friction and pressure that destroy the edges of the boundary and cause earthquakes. Transform boundaries don't produce magma, as they involve lateral movement.

Just as plates pushing together cause mountains, **canyons** are deep trenches caused by plates moving apart. Weather and erosion from rivers and precipitation run-off also create canyons. **Deltas** form when rivers dump their sediments and water into oceans. They are triangular flat stretches of land that are kind of like a triangular spatula; the handle represents the river and the triangle represents the mouth of a delta.

Sand dunes are another landform caused by wind or waves in combination with the absence of plants to hold sand in place. These are found in sandy areas like the desert or the ocean.

Earth History

A popular theory about the beginning of the universe is called the **Big Bang Theory**. It proposes that about fourteen billion years ago, a dense ball of matter exploded, releasing particles and energy.

From there, many scientists propose:

- Earth formed 4.6 billion years ago, and life didn't appear until approximately 3.5 billion years ago.

- At Earth's birth, it was an inhospitable place of active volcanoes, intense heat, lightning, and constant bombardment with space debris (rocks and dust). Heat vaporized all liquid water, and the anaerobic atmosphere (without oxygen) was composed of poisonous gases.

- Over time, the landscape changed, and once organic molecules (proteins, fats, carbohydrates, and DNA) and organisms came on the scene, water and oxygen became available, and the biosphere began.

- The last 542 million years have been divided into three eras: Paleozoic, Mesozoic, and Cenozoic. The **Paleozoic era** started with the **Cambrian Explosion**, when the animal kingdom expanded and diversified from invertebrates (simple animals without backbones) in the Pre-Cambrian Era. The era ended with the Permian mass extinction, where most animal species disappeared, probably due to volcanic eruptions.

- After the Permian extinction, the **Mesozoic era** began the reign of the dinosaurs. **Angiosperm** (flowering plants) life also exploded in the Mesozoic Era. The Cretaceous mass extinction ended the era, when nearly half of marine life and large portions of terrestrial species were decimated.

- Our most recent era is the **Cenozoic era**, and life continues to proliferate.

Our insight into the development of Earth has been fueled by fossil evidence. **Paleontology** is the study of fossils, which requires the study of rock layers. Sedimentary rocks exist as layers called **strata** and contain remains of once-living organisms. The depth at which a fossil is found within a layer of rock indicates the fossil's age. The lower the layer, the older the fossil.

Fossils are remnants of organisms, such as teeth and bones. These structures, like petrified wood, have been preserved so well due to minerals seeping into the bone and acting as preservatives. Fossils can also be completely intact organisms found in glaciers or sap. Trace fossils are not actual parts of an organism but evidence that the organism was there, like a footprint or an imprint of a leaf.

Calculating the age of organisms in rock layers is based on the amounts of two different forms of radioactive elements like carbon. **Carbon-12** is the non-radioactive form, and **Carbon-14** is the radioactive form. In fossils, Carbon-12 won't decrease over time, but Carbon-14 will. Scientists can compare the amounts of Carbon-12 and Carbon-14 to estimate the age of fossils. The smaller the amount of Carbon-14, the older the fossil.

Earth and the Universe

Earth is part of a solar system that rotates around a star. Our solar system is a miniscule portion of the universe, with our Sun being just one of trillions upon trillions of stars. Almost every existing star belongs to a galaxy, clusters of stars, rocks, ice, and space dust. Between galaxies there is nothing, just darkness. There could be as many as a hundred billion galaxies. There are three main types of galaxies: spiral, elliptical, and irregular.

The majority of galaxies are spiral galaxies, with a large, central galactic bulge, which is a cluster of older stars. They look like a disk with arms circulating stars and gas. Elliptical galaxies have no particular rotation pattern. They can be spherical or extremely elongated and do not have circulating arms.

Irregular galaxies have no pattern and can vary significantly in size and shape:

Earth's galaxy, the **Milky Way**, is a spiral galaxy and contains hundreds of billions of stars.

Pre-stars form from nebulas, clouds of gas and dust that can combine to form two types of small stars: brown and red dwarfs. **Stars** produce enormous amounts energy by combining hydrogen atoms to form helium via nuclear fusion. **Brown dwarfs** don't have enough hydrogen to undergo much fusion and fizzle out. **Red dwarfs** have plenty of gas (hydrogen) to undergo nuclear fusion and mature into white dwarfs. When they use all of their fuel (hydrogen), a burst of energy expands the star into a **red giant**. Red giants eventually condense into a **white dwarf**, which is a star approaching the end of its life.

Stars that undergo nuclear fusion will run out of gas quickly and burst in violent explosions called **supernovas**. This burst releases as much energy in a few seconds as the Sun will release in its entire lifetime. The particles from the explosion will condense into the smallest type of star, a **neutron star**; this will eventually condense into a **black hole**, which has such a high amount of gravity that not even light energy can escape.

Earth's Sun is currently a red dwarf; it is early in its life cycle. As the center of Earth's solar system, the Sun has planets and space debris (rocks and ice) orbiting around it. The various forms of space debris include:

- **Comet**: made of rock and ice with a tail due to the melting ice

- **Asteroid**: a large rock orbiting a star. The asteroid belt lies between Mars and Jupiter and separates the smaller rocky planets (Mercury, Venus, Earth, and Mars) from the larger, gassy planets (Jupiter, Saturn, Uranus, and Neptune). Pluto is not considered a planet anymore due to its small size and distance from the Sun.

- **Meteoroid**: a mini-asteroid with no specific orbiting pattern

- **Meteor**: a meteoroid that has entered Earth's atmosphere and starts melting due to the warmth provided by our insulating greenhouse gases. These are commonly known as "falling stars."

- **Meteorite**: a meteor that hasn't completely burned away and lands on Earth. One is believed to have caused the Cretaceous mass extinction.

Each planet travels around the Sun in an **elliptic orbit**. The time it takes for one complete orbit is considered a year. The gravity of the massive Sun keeps the planets rotating, and the farther the planets are from the Sun, the slower they move and the longer their orbits. Earth's journey is little bit over 365 days a year. Because Mercury is so close to the Sun, one year for Mercury is actually only 88 Earth days. The farthest planet, Neptune, has a year that is about 60,255 Earth days long. Planets not only rotate around the Sun, but they also spin like a top. The time it takes for a planet to complete one spin is considered one day. On Earth, one day is about 24 hours. On Jupiter, one day is about nine Earth hours, while a day on Venus is 241 Earth days.

Planets may have natural satellites that rotate around them called **moons**. Some planets have no moons and some have dozens. In 1969, astronaut Neil Armstrong became the first man to set foot on Earth's only moon.

Science

Earth Patterns

The temperature on the Sun varies from its core to its atmosphere. Its atmospheric temperature is predicted at over one million degrees Fahrenheit. The Sun accounts for two types of energy reaching Earth: light energy and thermal (heat) energy.

Plants absorb the light energy and they use it to perform photosynthesis.

$$6\,CO_2 + 6\,H_2O \longrightarrow C_6H_{12}O_6 + 6\,O_2$$

The thermal energy is transferred to Earth's atmosphere through radiation. Unlike the transfer of heat through convection, radiation is a direct transfer—there are no particles in space to transfer the sun's heat. Once thermal energy reaches Earth, the carbon dioxide in the atmosphere acts as a blanket to trap the heat.

The heat from the Sun as well as the orbit and position of Earth cause seasons. As discussed, Earth rotates around the Sun and spins on an axis. Earth is slightly tilted on its side. An imaginary line around the middle called the **equator** splits the Earth into the northern and southern hemispheres.

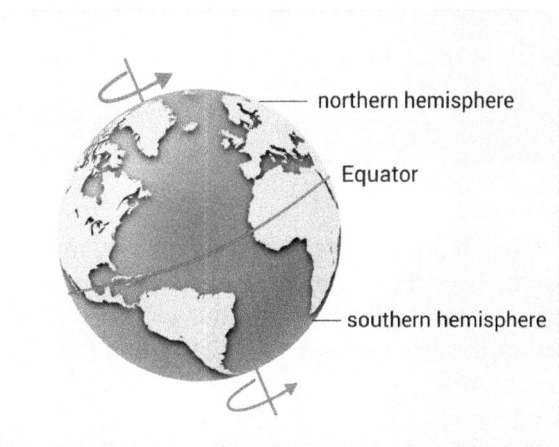

To understand seasons and the heating of the planet, refer to this picture:

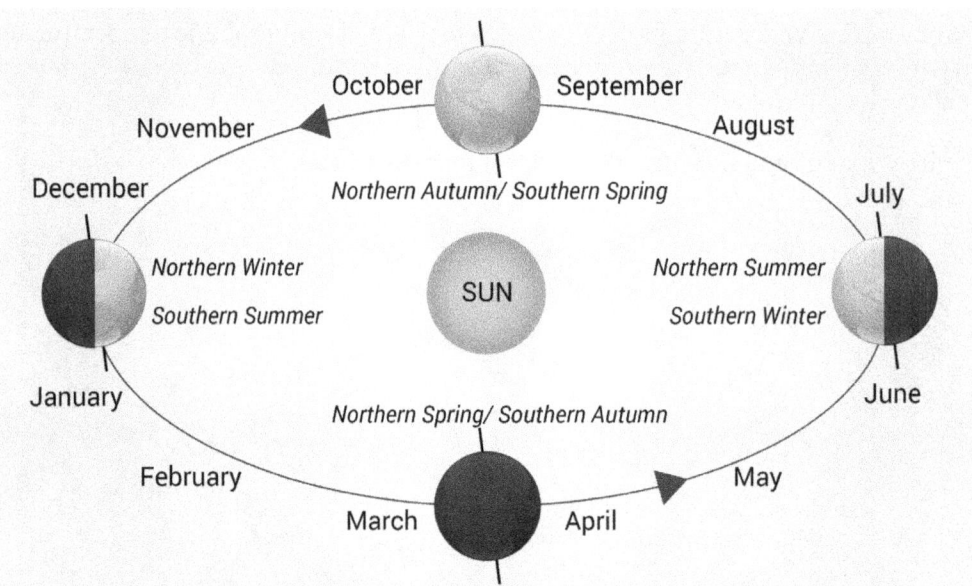

Observing July, these facts are apparent:

- Earth is tilted so that the northern hemisphere is pointing towards the sun. The southern hemisphere is pointed away.

- Because the north is tilted toward the sun, it gets more daylight in July than the southern hemisphere.

These observations explain why in July, the northern hemisphere experiences summer while the southern hemisphere experiences winter.

Notice in December that the opposite is true: the southern hemisphere gets more daylight compared to the northern hemisphere.

In spring and fall, both the north and the south get around the same sun exposure; therefore, those seasons have milder temperatures.

As the Earth rotates, the distribution of light slowly changes, which explains why seasons gradually change. In June, the northern hemisphere experiences the summer solstice, the day with the most daylight. As the Earth continues to orbit, its days will get shorter and shorter until the winter solstice, the shortest day of the year. Equinoxes occur in the fall and the spring and represent the days when the amount of daylight and darkness are relatively equal.

Just as the Earth orbits the Sun, the Moon orbits the earth. The Moon is much closer to Earth than the Sun. And even though the Moon is so close to the Earth, the Moon contains no life because it lacks water and an atmosphere. Without greenhouse gases to blanket the sun's heat, temperatures on the Moon are very low at night.

The Moon is visible from Earth because it reflects sunlight at certain points in its orbit. The Moon's orbit has a predictable pattern. It has two main phases, waxing and waning. When the Moon is waxing, it goes from a new moon to a full moon. Notice that only the left side of the Moon is dark during the waxing phase. The waning phase goes from full moon to new moon. Only the right side of the moon is dark when it is waning.

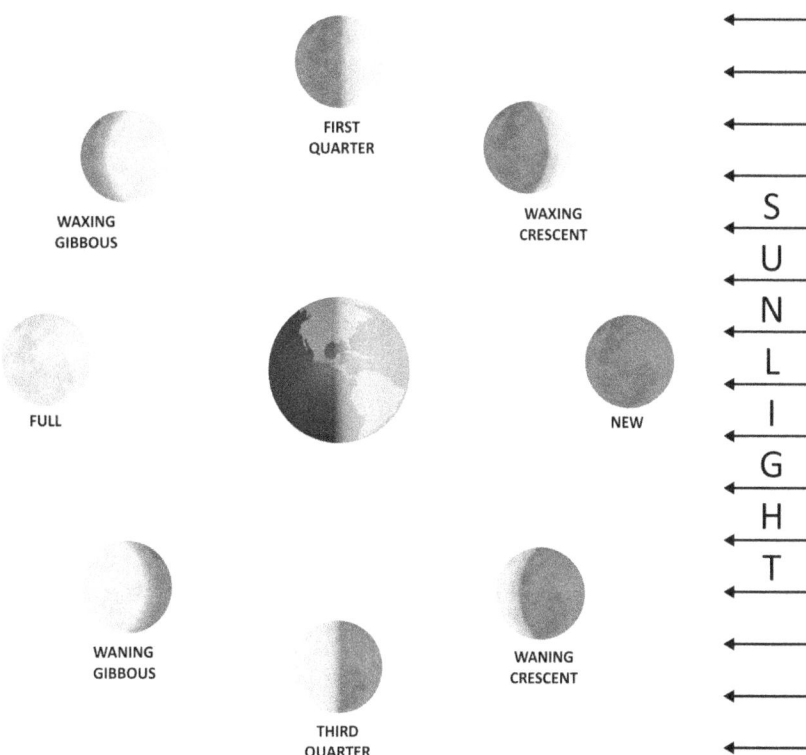

This picture shows that when the Moon is behind the Earth, then the Moon's entire surface is reflected and we see a full moon. When the Moon is between the Earth and the Sun, it is invisible at night, which is called a **new moon**.

Half-moons are visible when the Moon and the Earth are in a line that is perpendicular to the direction of sunlight. Only half of the Moon reflects light to the Earth at night, as seen in the figure above.

A moon that looks larger than a half-moon is called a **gibbous moon**, and a moon that looks smaller is called a **crescent moon**.

Eclipses occur when the Earth, the Sun, and the Moon are all aligned—the Earth blocks the others from seeing each other. If they are perfectly lined up, a total eclipse happens, and if they are only a little lined up, there is a partial eclipse.

There are two types of eclipses: lunar and solar. A **lunar eclipse** occurs when the Earth interrupts the Sun's light reflecting off of the full moon. Earth will then cast a shadow on the Moon, and particles in earth's atmosphere refract the light so some reaches the surface of the Moon, causing the Moon to look yellow, brown, or red.

During a new moon, when the Moon is between the Earth and the Sun, the Moon will interrupt the sunlight, casting a shadow on Earth. This is called a **solar eclipse**.

The Moon also affects ocean tide due to gravity. Earth is much larger than the Moon and has a very significant gravitational force that keeps us on the ground even though it is spinning very quickly. The Moon is much smaller than Earth, but because it is so close, it has a pulling effect on Earth's oceans. When it is closest to Earth, it pulls the water more, resulting in high tide. When the Moon is farthest from Earth, it pulls the ocean less and is called **low tide**.

Science as a Human Endeavor

Two of the worst earthquakes in history occurred in 1556 and 1976, causing 830,000 and 255,000 deaths, respectively. Earthquakes near the ocean cause massive tidal waves called tsunamis. In Indonesia in 2004, a tsunami resulted in 230,000 deaths. **Seismology** is the study of earthquakes. Understanding earthquakes can help predict them and possibly even prevent them.

Earthquakes have an initial source of plate movement called the **focus**. At the focus, there is a significant amount of tension, like the force of resistance generated by bending a wooden stick. Eventually, with enough pressure, there is so much tension that the stick breaks. The separate pieces that were once in a curved formation due to the strain will slip back into their original shape. This is called **elastic rebound** when it occurs at plate boundaries. After elastic rebound, the movement spreads outwards from the focus and causes waves of kinetic energy. These rolling vibrations are called **seismic waves**. Slipping back into place takes several adjustments called **aftershocks**, which are less severe than the initial movement but can still cause a significant amount of destruction. A logarithmic scale called the **Richter scale** measures the amplitude of seismic waves. An earthquake magnitude of 10 has the largest amplitude, and a magnitude of 1 has the smallest.

Science as an Inquiry

Science begins with questions—it is difficult to have an answer when there are no questions. A great source of inquiry for scientists has been weather. The study of weather is called **meteorology**. **Meteorologists** measure temperature, air pressure, wind speed, wind direction, and humidity, all in hopes of predicting how and where air and water vapor will move and behave. These questions inspire meteorologists to use weather balloons and satellites to study weather and make educated guesses. As knowledge grows, technologies also improve and facilitate better weather forecasting. The impressive **Doppler radar** has provided scientists with meaningful data since the 1980s, allowing them to better predict the weather with more certainty.

Research

Another aspect of science is **research**, which is the search for answers for a scientific inquiry. One of the largest areas of scientific research is space exploration. Of course, people have always wondered about the universe, but the United States didn't make space research a priority until the 1940s and 1950s "space race" with the Soviet Union. In 1957, Russia launched a satellite called **Sputnik**, which fueled the intense competition between the two countries. In space research, the question that accelerated space exploration was "How can man travel into space safely?" This question fueled the creation of NASA (the National Aeronautics and Space Administration) on October 1, 1958.

NASA research continues today. They observe the sky, launch satellites and telescopes into space, and study the data collected. Currently, there are a multitude of satellites and land vehicles or "rovers" on Mars collecting data with the hope of one day finding a way for humans to live there. In fact, the target date for human occupation on Mars is somewhere in the 2030s.

Process of Science

Theories are well-supported ideas that evolve from hypotheses and experimentation. A **hypothesis** is an educated guess about a scientific process or object. Once every angle of investigation has been examined and all evidence supports a hypothesis, only then can it be called a **theory**. It is important to know that theory development is a process. As technology advances and more aspects of science can be explored, evidence might no longer support a theory. With non-supportive data, either the theory can be modified or completely thrown out while new investigations are developed to examine other explanations.

For example, plate tectonic theory didn't appear until the early 20th century. People thought the Earth was static and immobile. Only after many years of investigation and evidence did skeptics finally concede that the Earth's surface was broken into plates. This theory wasn't universally accepted until the late 1960s and was considered revolutionary.

Early evidence that supported plate tectonics was publicized in the 1910s by Alfred Wegener, who observed that the South American and African borders to the Atlantic Ocean seemed like they could fit together like puzzle pieces. He proposed the idea of Pangaea, a massive supercontinent that existed long ago and must have broken into pieces due to a process called **continental drift**. Other evidence supporting plate tectonics were similar fossils found in Africa and South America, suggesting that they were once connected. But skeptics continued to scoff at the theory. Then, in the 1960s it was discovered, with the help of early computers, that a continental shelf (an underwater boundary between plates) between the two continents had a remarkable fit that was very unlikely to be due to chance.

Life Science

Structure and Function of Living Systems

Living Characteristics and Cells

Every living organism is made up of **cells**, and these cells come in various shapes and sizes, depending on the organism. There are two types of cells: **prokaryotes** and **eukaryotes**. The big difference between them is that eukaryotes have a nucleus and prokaryotes do not. The structures that will be covered in this section will be bacteria, protist, fungus, plant, and animal cells:

Bacteria	Protist, Fungus, Plant, Animal
DNA Ribosomes Cytoplasm Cell Membrane Cell Wall	DNA Ribosomes Cytoplasm Cell Membrane Cell Wall (except animal cells) Unique structures Nucleus Mitochondria Chloroplasts (only autotrophs, or organisms that can produce their own food. Only protists and plants are producers).

Below is an example of a plant cell:

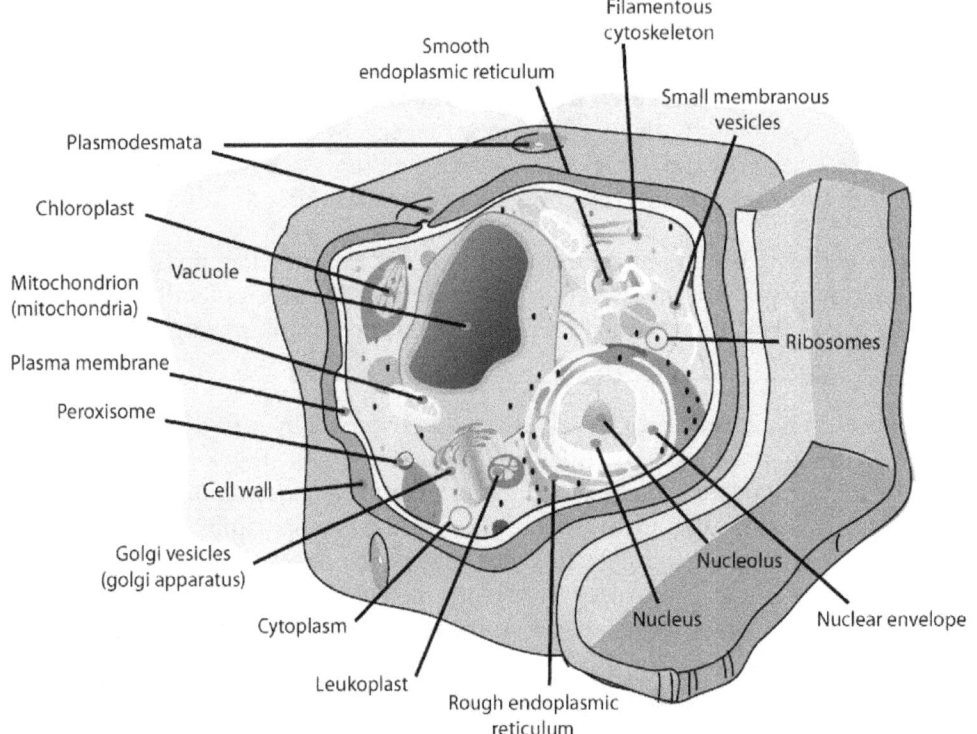

Science

Below is an example of an animal cell:

Below is an example of a bacteria cell:

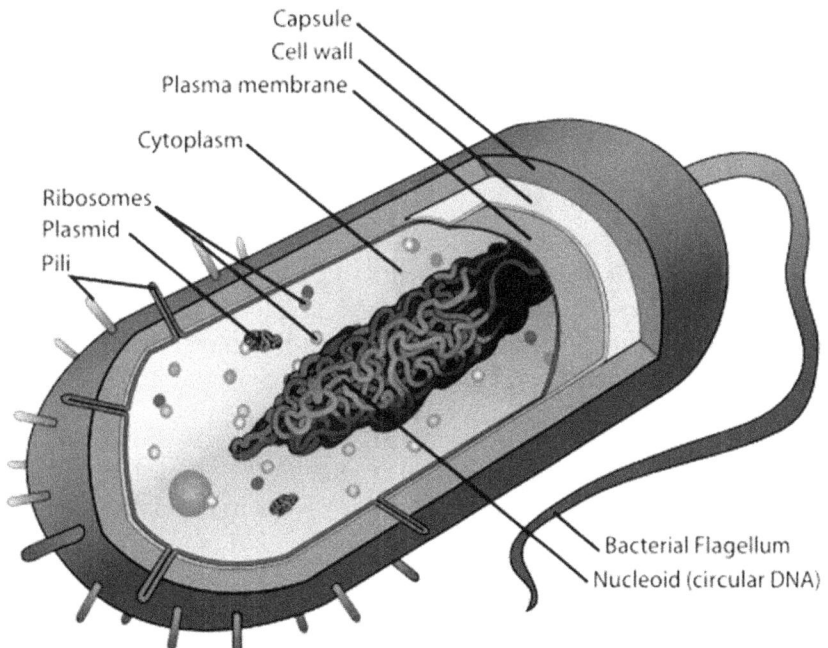

Like all cells, bacterial cells contain **DNA**, the genetic material that gives instructions for every single structure and process that the cell undergoes. DNA is a code made up of four letters: A (adenine), T (thymine), G (guanine), and C (cytosine). There are billions of these letters in DNA, and the order of these letters tells a cell exactly what to do and how to do it (just like reading a book of instructions).

Because DNA doesn't do anything on its own, all cells must have a means of decoding DNA and turning it into the structure, which is the function of **ribosomes**—they are protein-makers. If DNA is like a recipe, then the ribosomes are like the chef.

DNA and ribosomes sit in a fluid called **cytoplasm**, which contains a **cytoskeleton** (a network of proteins) that holds them in place. All cells need a covering to contain everything inside—these are called **cell membranes** in animals or cell walls for plant cells.

Bacteria can also have a capsule and a flagellum, which are all external structures. A **capsule** is sticky and causes bacteria to cluster with other cells or on food. Only about 50 percent of bacteria can move, and those that do often have a **flagellum**, which is a whip-like structure like a tadpole's tail.

Viruses are commonly thought of as living organisms, but many scientists argue they aren't for two reasons: (1) they are not cells, and (2) they cannot reproduce by themselves. Both qualities are required for an organism to be considered alive. Viruses are unique in that they require a host in order to make proteins and reproduce, because viruses don't have all of the complex tools of a living cell. When a virus has infected a host, it acts like a living organism—it moves and reproduces—but outside of a host, it does nothing. A virus can survive outside of a host, but it cannot reproduce. Scientists are still trying to properly define a virus, so we can currently say that viruses are not like bacteria or any other living thing.

Eukaryotic cells are more complex than prokaryotic cells. They make up all the organisms in the kingdoms protist, fungus, plant, and animal. Eukaryotic cells are also larger than prokaryotes and contain a nucleus and other organelles.

Eukaryotic cells hold their DNA inside a nucleus in pieces called chromosomes. **Chromosomes** are a cell's way of organizing long strands of DNA in twisted-up bundles. Imagine a room filled with rolls of toilet paper compared to a room that has all of those rolls unraveled and thrown everywhere; it would be a mess!

Other important organelles include chloroplasts and mitochondria. **Chloroplasts** can be found in cells called autotrophs, which can convert sunlight into energy. Plants are autotrophs. **Mitochondria** are little energy factories found in almost every type of cell. They use chemical reactions to make little packets of energy that can be used by other parts of the cell.

Cellular Organization

Prokaryotes contain ribosomes, DNA, cytoplasm, a cell membrane, a cytoskeleton, and a cell wall. Eukaryotes vary between kingdoms but contain all of these structures except a cell wall because animal cells require so much mobility. Large, land-dwelling animals typically compensate with an exoskeleton (like insects) or an endoskeleton (like humans and other mammals, reptiles, and birds) for structure.

All bacterial cells are **unicellular** (existing as just one cell). Almost all types of protist and some species in fungi kingdom are unicellular, but they still have the complicated organelles of eukaryotes. A few protists, almost all fungi, and all plants and animals are multicellular. Multicellularity leads to development of structures that are perfectly designed for their function.

Cells combine to form **tissue**. Tissue combines to form **organs**. Organs combine to form **organ systems**, and organ systems combine to form one **organism**. The structures of all of these combinations allow for the maximum functionality of an organism, as demonstrated by the nervous system.

A **neuron** is a cell in the nervous system designed to send and receive electrical impulses. Neurons have dendrites, which are sensors waiting to receive a message. Neurons also have an **axon**, a long arm that sends the message to the neighboring neuron. The axon also has insulation known as **myelin** that speeds the message along. Many neurons combine to form a **nerve**, the tissue of the nervous system, which is like a long wire. The structure of this nerve is perfect—it is a long cable whose function is to send signals to the brain so the brain can process the information and respond. Nerve tissue combines with other tissue to form the **brain**, a complex structure of many parts.

The brain also has glands (epithelial tissue) that release hormones to control processes in our body. The brain and spinal cord together form the central nervous system that controls the stimulus/response signaling in our body. The nervous system coordinates with the circulatory system to make our heart beat, the digestive system to control food digestion, the muscular system to move an arm, the respiratory system to facilitate breathing, and all other body systems to make the entire organism functional. Cells are the basic building block in our bodies, and their structure is critical for their function and the function of the tissues, organs, and systems that they comprise.

In the graphic below, the left depicts a neuron, and the right depicts the nervous system. A neuron is a nerve cell, and it is the basic building block of the nervous system. Cell, tissue, organ, and organ system structure are critical for function.

The following table lists organ systems in the human body:

Name	Function	Main organs
Nervous	Detect stimuli and direct response	Brain and spinal cord
Circulatory	Pump blood to deliver oxygen to cells so they can perform cellular respiration	Heart
Respiratory	Breathe in oxygen (reactant for cellular respiration) and release carbon dioxide waste	Lungs
Muscular	Movement	Heart and muscles
Digestive	Break down food so that glucose can be delivered to cells for energy	Stomach, small intestine, lots of others
Skeletal	Support and organ protection	All sorts of joints, skull, ribcage

Life Processes

When we eat a hamburger, we're eating more than carbohydrates; we're also eating proteins and fats. Plants provide more than just carbohydrates when we eat them; they also are able to use the light energy to make proteins, fats, and, of course, their DNA, because if they didn't have DNA, they'd have no instructions to grow.

The following organic compounds and their atoms don't magically appear in organisms—life has to either grab the nutrients from soil or seeds or eat them.

- Carbohydrates, proteins, fats, and DNA/RNA have carbon, hydrogen, and oxygen
- DNA, proteins, and fats also have phosphorus
- DNA and proteins also have nitrogen
- Proteins also can have sulfur

Plants need all of these elements to make food. Where do they get them? Remember that Earth's atmosphere is a conglomerate of different gases, including nitrogen. Bacteria in the soil are able to convert that nitrogen into a usable form, and the roots of plants absorb the critical nitrogen. Carbon and oxygen get into the plant via photosynthesis (carbon dioxide), as does the element hydrogen, because plants take in water, which contains hydrogen. Phosphorus and sulfur are absorbed in plants through soil. Since heterotrophs cannot make their own food, they have to eat an autotroph (or eat something that ate an autotroph) in order to obtain these critical elements.

Cycles are a recurring pattern in science, and making food is no exception. When living things die, fungi and bacteria act as decomposers and break down the material. That's actually why dead things and rotten meat smell bad; the decomposers have broken them down so much that gases containing carbon, oxygen, phosphorus, nitrogen, and even smelly sulfur are released. Remember that sulfur is heavy in protein, and eggs are protein-rich. It makes sense that rotten eggs have an unpleasant smell as they release sulfur because they're mostly protein. Once living things decompose, all the elements eventually recycle back to the atmosphere or to the soil, and the atoms are available to construct molecules once again.

Energy

Energy is everywhere and is one of the few things in the universe believed to be constant. That means that in the whole universe, if all the energy could be measured (energy in all the stars, atoms, etc.), the amount of energy that was present at the beginning of time is exactly the same as it is now. The only difference is that energy has been converted into different forms. For example, a plant gets its energy from the Sun, using it to grow bigger and stronger; therefore, the Sun's energy is converted and stored inside the plant. Then a person eats the plant, using its stored energy. In this example, energy exists in the form of light, growth, and movement (picking the plant and chewing it).

Only with the energy food provides can organisms exist. Think of a construction team and a pile of bricks and mortar. The bricks are not going to just arrange themselves into a building. However, if a construction team uses their muscles and energy, the complex building can be built. If the construction team runs out of food, though, they will become exhausted and will be unable to construct the building.

The human body is the same way. Organs (heart, brain, stomach, etc.) are like the bricks. The chemical reactions in the body are like the workers. Energy is the food that the workers need to build the organism. The food of life is sugar, specifically glucose. A candy bar, soda, or a slice of birthday cake can provide a boost of energy because of all the sugar they contain. There are many bonds between the molecules of sugar, holding them in place (like the mortar holding the bricks in a building). When the bonds are broken in digestion, all that energy is released so that living things can invest that energy into chemical reactions.

Two chemical reactions are critical for living things: **photosynthesis** and **respiration**.

Any producer must have a chloroplast in order to convert light energy into food, usually in the form of a carbohydrate. **Chloroplasts** are organelles that look like little green beans because they contain the pigment **chlorophyll**, which is able to absorb the sunlight's energy in the form of photons, or light rays. Some prokaryotes are also photosynthetic, and although they don't have a chloroplast because they're too simple and don't contain organelles, they have a pigment in order to make their own food.

Plants need water and sunlight to live. Plants suck up water from their roots. The sunlight they need is absorbed by the chlorophyll in chloroplasts, which are clustered and concentrated in their leaves. Interestingly, the chlorophyll actually is able to absorb every color of light except for green, which is why leaves look green: they reflect green light. If the roots take in water and the leaves take in carbon dioxide and sunlight energy, why are stems important? The stems in plants are an example of how structure helps function. The stem is like a skeleton for plants; it holds the leaves high so they can be closer to the sun.

Plants are critical for life on Earth because they absorb the energy from the Sun and invest it in the bonds that make sugar. Sugar passes through the food chain to provide energy for all living organisms. Plants and other **autotrophs** can make their own energy, while **heterotrophs** (which cannot make their own energy) consume the sugar, break it down, and convert it into usable energy with their mitochondria.

Cellular Respiration in the Mitochondria

The **glucose** that provides energy does nothing by itself; it is the bonds between atoms holding these complex glucose molecules together that hold the energy. When the molecule is intact, the bonds between them hold energy in the form of potential energy. When the bonds are broken, that potential energy is released and becomes available to the workers in the cell to perform chemical reactions.

The process of cellular respiration breaks the bonds in an organelle called the **mitochondria** in eukaryotes (protists, fungi, plants, animals).

Note that the equation for cellular respiration is the almost exact opposite of photosynthesis:

$$C_6H_{12}O_6 + 6O_2 \rightarrow 6CO_2 + 6H_2O + 36ATP$$

The only difference between the above equation and photosynthesis is the new product: ATP. **ATP** is a conversion of light energy into usable pockets of energy that provide energy to all the workers in cells that do the chemical reactions. While glucose is like a $100 bill with lots of energy in its bonds, ATP is like one hundred $1 bills that can be invested here and there as needed.

Bacteria do not have mitochondria, so they perform different reactions in their cytoplasm that produce much less energy (2ATP).

Reproduction and Heredity

Growth and Development

Unlike viruses, all living organisms can independently reproduce, but reproduction occurs differently between bacteria and the more complex kingdoms. Bacteria reproduce via **binary fission**, which is a simpler process than eukaryotic division because it doesn't involve splitting a nucleus and doesn't have a web of proteins to pull chromosomes apart. Prokaryotes have simpler DNA compared to cells that have a much larger number of individual chromosomes (humans have two sets of 23 chromosomes—one set from mom and one set from dad, for a total of 46 chromosomes). Think of going from class to class with two identical binders (like bacteria) versus going from class to class with 23 identical pairs of binders (humans); it would be much more difficult to organize the large set of binders than the smaller one.

Binary fission in bacteria is therefore relatively easy. Bacteria copy their DNA in a process called **DNA replication**, grow, and then the replicated DNA moves to either side, and two new cells are made.

Eukaryotic cell division is part of a well-defined cycle with the following phases:

- **G1 phase**: The cell is growing and working.

- **S phase**: The cell is getting too large, so it copies its DNA because it wants to make sure the two new cells have the full instruction manual that is DNA.

- **G2 phase**: The cell uses its workers to get ready for cell division.

- **M phase**: Chromosomes condense and line up in the middle of the cell. The copies are sent to either side.

- **Cytokinesis**: The moment when the cytoplasm is officially split in two, and then two identical daughter cells are produced and enter G1 phase.

The M phase has subdivisions because it quickly goes through a series of events. Each sub-phase of events is described and illustrated below.

PHASE	PHASE EVENTS	ANIMAL CELL DIAGRAM	PLANT CELL DIAGRAM
Interphase (G1, S, and G2)	DNA is loose and spread out and contained in nucleus. This is important because it is actively growing and needs access to its instructions to do chemical reactions correctly. Chromosomes are replicated (copied) in S phase so that they look like an X. Each side of the X has identical DNA.		
Prophase	Nucleus disappears and DNA condenses into chromosomes		
Metaphase	Chromosomes line up in center and proteins from either side of cell attach to them		
Anaphase	Proteins shorten and pull chromosomes apart so that one half (either left side of X or right side of X) of DNA goes to each new cell		
Telophase and Cytokinesis	Nuclei reform and chromosomes start to spread out
Animal cells: cytoplasm to split in half
Plant cells: cell plate (new cell wall) forms between daughter cells and extends (animal cells don't have a cell wall)		

Organism Reproduction

For bacteria, cell reproduction is the same as organism reproduction; **binary fission** is an asexual process that produces two new cells that are clones of each other because they have identical DNA.

Eukaryotes are more complex than prokaryotes and can go through **sexual reproduction**. They produce **gametes** (sex cells). Females make eggs and males make sperm. The process of making gametes is called **meiosis**, which is similar to mitosis except for the following differences:

- There are two cellular divisions instead of one.

- Four genetically different haploid daughter cells (one set of chromosomes instead of two) are produced instead of two genetically identical diploid daughter cells.

- A process called crossing over (**recombination**) occurs, which makes the daughter cells genetically different. If chromosomes didn't cross over and rearrange genes, siblings could be identical clones. There would be no genetic variation, which is a critical factor in the theory of evolution of organisms.

In sexual reproduction, a sperm fertilizes an egg and creates the first cell of a new organism, called the **zygote**. The zygote will go through countless mitotic divisions over time to create the adult organism.

Heredity: Patterns of Inheritance

All living things are a product of their DNA, specifically portions of their DNA called genes that code for different characteristics.

Learned behavior is not affected by DNA and is not hereditable. Changes in appearance like a woman painting her toenails, a bird whose feathers accidentally fall out due to a tornado, or a person getting a scar are also not heritable. Heritable characteristics are those coded by DNA like eye color, hair color, and height.

A man named **Gregor Mendel** is considered the father of genetics. He was a monk and a botanist, and through extensive experiments with pea plants, he figured out a great deal about heredity.

Our genetic code comes in pairs. Each chromosome contains many genes, and since we have one chromosome from our mom and one chromosome from our dad, we have two copies of each gene. Genes come in different forms called **alleles**, which determine the organism's **traits**, the way an organism looks or behaves. For some traits, there are only two alleles: a **dominant allele** and a **recessive allele**. Even though eye color is a bit more complicated, pretend that brown eyes are dominant over blue eyes, and there are the only two alleles:

- B = Brown eyes
- b = blue eyes

A child inherits these alleles from his parents. There are three possible combinations a child can inherit, dependent on his parents' alleles:

- BB (homozygous dominant)
- Bb (heterozygous)
- bb (homozygous recessive)

The combination of genes above will determine the trait in the offspring. If the child gets any combination with a B, the more powerful allele, his eyes will be brown. Only the bb combination will give the child blue eyes. In this example, the combination of alleles is called a **genotype**, and the actual eye color the child has is called a **phenotype**.

Change Over Time

The **theory of natural selection** is one of the fundamental tenets of evolution. It affects the **phenotype**, or visible characteristics, of individuals in a species, which ultimately affects the genotype, or genetic makeup, of those same individuals. **Charles Darwin** was the first to explain the theory of natural selection, and it is described by **Herbert Spencer** as favoring survival of the fittest.

Natural selection encompasses three assumptions:

- A species has heritable traits: All traits have some likelihood of being propagated to offspring.

- The traits of a species vary: Some traits are more advantageous than others.

- Individuals of a species are subject to differing rates of reproduction: Some individuals of a species may not get the opportunity to reproduce while others reproduce frequently.

Over time, certain variations in traits may increase both the survival and reproduction of certain individuals within a species. The desirable heritable traits are passed on from generation to generation. Eventually, the desirable traits will become more common and permeate the entire species.

Adaptation

The **theory of adaptation** is defined as an alteration in a species that causes it to become more well-suited to its environment. It increases the probability of survival, thus increasing the rate of successful reproduction. As a result, an adaptation becomes more common within the population of that species.

For examples, bats use reflected sound waves (echolocation) to prey on insects, and chameleons change colors to blend in with their surroundings to evade detection by its prey and predators. These adaptations are believed to be brought about by natural selection.

Adaptive radiation refers to the idea of rapid diversification within a species into an array of unique forms. It's thought to happen as a result of changes in a habitat creating new challenges, ecological niches, or natural resources.

Darwin's finches are often thought of as an example of the theory of adaptive radiation. Charles Darwin documented 13 varieties of finches on the Galapagos Islands. Each island in the chain presented a unique and changing environment, which was believed to cause rapid adaptive radiation among the finches. There was also diversity among finches inhabiting the same island. Darwin believed that as a result of natural selection, each variety of finch developed adaptations to fit into its native environment.

A major difference in Darwin's finches had to do with the size and shapes of beaks. The variation in beaks allowed the finches to access different foods and natural resources, which decreased competition and preserved resources. As a result, various finches of the same species were allowed to coexist, thrive, and diversify. Finches had:

- Short beaks, which were suited for foraging for seeds
- Thin, sharp beaks, which were suited for preying on insects
- Long beaks, which were suited for probing for food inside plants

Darwin believed that the finches on the Galapagos Islands resulted from chance mutations in genes transmitted from generation to generation.

Life Cycle

The life cycle of an organism refers to every stage of that organism's life, starting with a zygote and developing until the organism becomes an adult who can reproduce themself. Here's a look at the life cycles of many animals.

Chicken	Hens are female chickens, and they lay about one egg per day. If there is no rooster (male chicken) around to fertilize the egg, the egg never turns into a chick and instead becomes an egg that we can eat. If a rooster is around, he mates with the female chicken and fertilizes the egg. Once the egg is fertilized, the tiny little embryo (future chicken) will start as a white dot adjacent to the yolk and albumen (egg white) and will develop for 21 days. The mother hen sits on her clutch of eggs (several fertilized eggs) to incubate them and keep them warm. She will turn the eggs to make sure the embryo doesn't stick to one side of the shell. The embryo continues to develop, using the egg white and yolk nutrients, and eventually develops an "egg tooth" on its beak that it uses to crack open the egg and hatch. Before it hatches, it even chirps to let the mom know of its imminent arrival!
Frog	Frogs mate similar to the way chickens do, and then lay eggs in a very wet area. Sometimes, the parents abandon the eggs and let them develop on their own. The eggs, like chickens', will hatch around 21 days later. Just like chickens, a frog develops from a yolk, but when it hatches, it continues to use the yolk for nutrients. A chicken hatches and looks like a cute little chick, but a baby frog is actually a tadpole that is barely developed. It can't even swim around right away, although eventually it will develop gills, a mouth, and a tail. After more time, it will develop teeth and tiny legs and continue to change into a fully grown frog! This type of development is called **metamorphosis**.
Fish	Most fish also lay eggs in the water, but unlike frogs, their swimming sperm externally fertilize the eggs. Like frogs, when fish hatch, they feed on a yolk sac and are called **larvae**. Once the larvae no longer feed on their yolk and can find their own nutrients, they are called fry, which are basically baby fish that grow into adulthood.
Butterfly	Like frogs, butterflies go through a process called **metamorphosis**, where they completely change into a different looking organism. After the process of mating and internal fertilization, the female finds the perfect spot to lay her eggs, usually a spot with lots of leaves. When the babies hatch from the eggs, they are in the larva form, which for butterflies is called a **caterpillar**. The larvae eat and eat and then go through a process like hibernation and form into a **chrysalis**, or a **chrysalis**. When they hatch from the cocoon, the butterflies are in their adult form.
Bugs	After fertilization, other bugs go through incomplete metamorphosis, which involves three states: eggs that hatch, nymphs that look like little adults without wings and molt their exoskeleton over time, and adults.

All of these organisms depend on a proper environment for development, and that environment depends on their form. Frogs need water, caterpillars need leaves, and baby chicks need warmth in order to be born.

Regulation and Behavior

DNA is the instruction manual for every organism, including humans. It is identical in our cells (except for minor mutations); so why are neurons and heart muscles so different in function and appearance? The key is that in different cells, different parts of the DNA are read. Our DNA is an encyclopedia set with 46 volumes (chromosomes). The instructions for heart cells are different from instructions for neurons. And these instructions are scattered throughout the 46 volumes. It is still not completely understood how a cell chooses what parts of the encyclopedia to read, but it is known that different cells read different portions of our DNA.

Protein enzymes facilitate chemical reactions; they are the workers in the cell. Some unwind the DNA so that RNA can copy the genes in a process called **transcription**. **RNA** is similar to DNA except that it is single-stranded and has the base U, which stands for **uracil**, instead of the T in DNA. Another similarity between DNA and RNA is that they are both made of a base, a phosphate, and a sugar, though DNA is made of deoxyribose sugar and RNA is made of ribose sugar.

The final protein can have many destinations; it can become part of the cytoskeleton that holds the organelles in place, act as an enzyme, go to the cell membrane and act as a marker protein (a tag to identify the cell), act as a **transport protein** (allows materials to pass in and out of the cell), or as a **receptor protein** (can receive chemical messages like hormones and initiate reactions in the cell to respond), or leave the cell and become something else, like a person's hair and fingernails!

In the cell, processes are regulated at the DNA level because transcription and translation are tightly regulated. At the organism level, the entire nervous system controls activity. In humans, a stimulus is received by the sensory neuron, travels up the nerve to the brain, and a response travels down to whatever motor neuron is necessary for movement.

Sensory neurons detect environmental stimulus involving sight, sound, touch, taste, and smell.

Diversity of Life

Due to the speciation that has occurred over the last 3.5 billion years since life first appeared, the variety of organisms is astronomical. Scientists have identified about 2 million species, and they suspect that there are at least 8 million others out there.

A man named **Carolus Linnaeus** developed a naming system to try to create some order in classifying all species. For example, the classification of humans through the seven levels, from all-inclusive to the most specific, looks like this:

One benefit of this universal naming system is that because some organisms have different common names, like the roly-poly and doodlebug, or the cougar and panther, it allows scientists to have a common language. Due to the sheer magnitude of species, scientists need the seven levels, but when referring to organisms, their official names are just the last two: **genus** and **species**. Humans are simply referred to as **Homo sapiens**. This two-name system is called **binomial nomenclature**.

There are currently six kingdoms, although the prokaryotes (simpler cells) used to be lumped together into one kingdom called **Monera**. Currently, there are two prokaryotic kingdoms, **Archaebacteria** and **Eubacteria**.

Archaebacteria
Prokaryotes that have a cell membrane made of fats. They live in harsh places including extremely hot areas (volcanic vents or hot springs) and extremely salty locations (Utah's Salt Lake). These are the rarest prokaryotes.

Eubacteria
Common bacteria that have a cell membrane made of a protein-carbohydrate blend. They make up the vast majority of existing prokaryotes. An example is staphylococcus.

Protista
This kingdom consists of eukaryotes. Most are unicellular. This kingdom is the most diverse and can be divided into three types: fungus-like (including slime-molds), plant-like (including algae), and animal-like (including amoeba). Some scientists believe that there is so much diversity within the kingdom that they should be split into separate kingdoms, but so far they remain in one group.

Animal-like protists are **heterotrophs** (they do not make their own food), and plant-like protists are **autotrophs** (they make their own food). Fungus-like protists are heterotrophs. Like actual fungi, these organisms externally digest their food by acting as parasites and decomposers. Animal-like protists ingest their food via phagocytosis (cell eating) or by absorbing it.

Depending on the particular protists, some produce asexually via mitosis and others reproduce sexually.

Science

Fungi

Fungi are eukaryotic heterotrophs that digest their food externally. Many of them, including common mushrooms and toadstools, act as decomposers by breaking down dead organisms then absorbing the broken down nutrients. Other fungi accomplish ingestion as parasites feeding off of living organisms, as in the case of a yeast infection. All fungi are multicellular with one exception—**yeast**. Fungi have cell walls made of a complex carbohydrate called **chitin**. Most fungi reproduce sexually and asexually.

Plantae

Plants are multicellular autotrophs like daisies, roses, and pine trees. They are closely related to the aquatic producer, algae, but different in that algae don't contain true roots, stems, or leaves. Plants are **photosynthesizers**, and their cells have surrounding cell walls made of the starch cellulose.

Animalia

Animals are multicellular heterotrophs, like fungi, except that animals move and internally ingest their food by consuming it. Animals are the only kingdom to not have cells with cell walls due to their flexibility and ability to move. The animal kingdom is very diverse and includes humans, jellyfish, and spiders, as well as all sorts of other organisms.

Interdependence of Organisms

The biosphere has layers and layers of complexity:

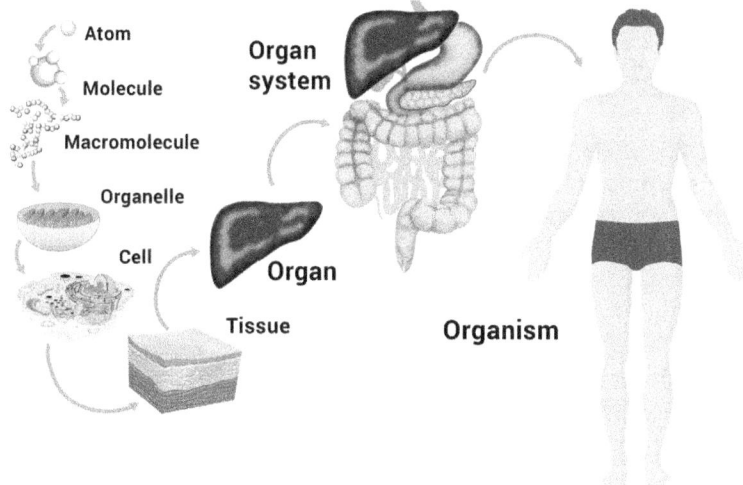

All organisms work together so that life can exist. An organism represents one of a species, like the fish below, and all organisms serve a particular function. The fish's niche is to eat aquatic producers and excrete waste that acts as fertilizer.

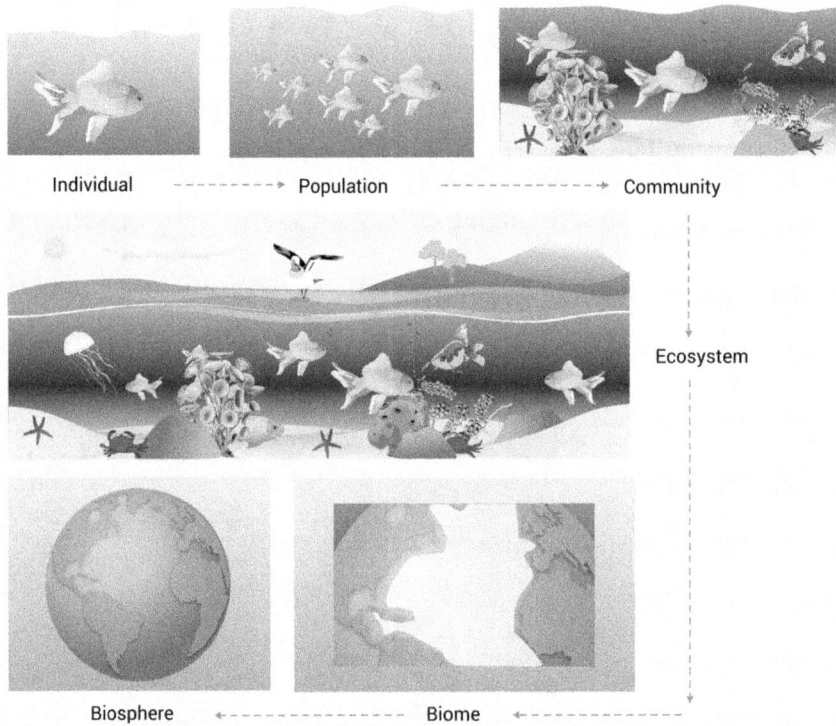

This fish is just one organism within a population. A **population** represents multiple individuals living in the same habitat. The community includes every biotic factor (living organism) within an ecosystem, in this case, the fish, jellyfish, algae, crab, bacteria, etc. An ecosystem includes all the biotic factors as well as the **abiotic**, which includes anything non-living—for the fish, that's a rock, a shipwreck, and a nearby glacier. For biomes, add weather and climate into the mix. The biosphere is all of Earth, which is the combination of all biomes.

We already discussed that producers (plants, protists, and even some bacteria) photosynthesize and make the food that provides energy required for all chemical reactions to occur and therefore all life to exist. A non-photosynthesizer must find and eat food, and this feeding relationship can be visualized in food chains. Consider this food chain:

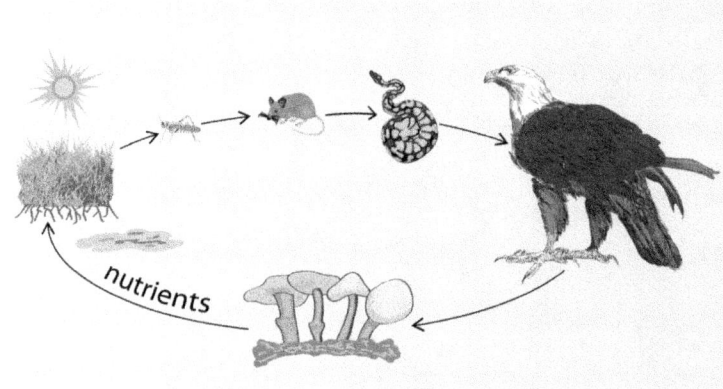

Science

The true source of the energy for every living organism is the Sun. Plants absorb the Sun's energy to make glucose and are on the **first trophic level** (feeding level). The grasshopper on the **second trophic level** is an example of an herbivore and is a primary consumer, as he is the first eater in the food chain. Unfortunately, he receives only 10 percent of the energy that the plant absorbed (this is known as the 10 percent rule) because the other 90 percent of energy was either used by the plant to grow or will be lost as heat.

The mouse on the **third trophic level** is the secondary consumer, or second eater. Food chains are not as inclusive as **food webs**, which show all feeding relationships in an ecosystem. Looking at this food chain suggests that mice are carnivores (eaters of animals), but mice also eat berries and plants, so they are actually considered omnivores (eaters of both plants and animals). The mouse only gets 10 percent of the energy from the grasshopper, which is actually only 1 percent of the original energy provided by the Sun. The snake on the fourth trophic level is a carnivore, as is the hawk on the highest trophic level.

The arrows in the food chain show the transfer of energy, and fungi as well as bacteria act as decomposers, which break down organic material. Decomposers act at every trophic level because they feed on all organisms; they are non-discriminating omnivores. Decomposers are critical for life, as they recycle the atoms and building blocks of organisms.

Feeding relationships and **predator-prey relationships** (hunter-hunted, like the hawk and the rabbit in the food web above) are not the only relationships in an ecosystem. There also can be competition within and between species. For example, in the food chain above, the rabbit and snail both eat grass, showing a relationship called **competition**, when two organisms want the same thing. Other relationships include symbiotic relationships, which represent two species living together. Symbiosis comes in three varieties:

- **Mutualism**: an arrangement where both organisms help each other. An example is the relationship between birds and flowers. When birds consume the nectar that the flower produces, pollen rubs on the bird's body so that when it travels to a neighboring plant, it helps with fertilization. The plant helps the bird by providing food, and the bird helps the plant by helping it reproduce. This is a win-win.

- **Parasitism**: when one organism is hurt while the other is helped. Fleas and dogs are a prime example. Fleas suck the dog's blood, and dogs are itchy and lose blood. This is a win-lose.

- **Commensalism**: when one organism is helped and the other is neither harmed nor helped. For example, barnacles are crusty little creatures that attach themselves to whales. They don't feed on the whale like a parasite. Instead, they use the whale to give them a free ride so they have access to food. The whales don't care about the barnacles. This is a win-do not care.

Personal Health

Early childhood educators can introduce young children to a wide variety of healthy behaviors that will help improve overall health. An important concept to begin teaching students is that optimal health is brought about through routine practice of daily healthy behaviors and an overall commitment to a healthy lifestyle. For example, educators can discuss the importance of establishing regular physical activity and daily healthy eating habits and that, through these habits, students can control their body weight and help avoid obesity. Obesity is a modifiable risk factor for many diseases including insulin-resistant Type 2 diabetes mellitus and cardiovascular disease. It is important and empowering for children to start to understand their roles and responsibilities in healthy habits and disease prevention. By giving them the necessary knowledge and tools to put the information into practice in their lives, educators can increase the self-efficacy and behaviors of even young children. In this way, early childhood educators can be instrumental in bringing about a healthier generation of young children who have an awareness of their health and an understanding of their own influence on risk factors for certain diseases. The following are healthy behaviors that can lead to a healthy body and mind:

Nutrition

Children should be taught how to identify foods and the importance of consuming a daily variety of food within each healthy food group. The benefits of trying new foods, especially those from other cultures, can help students understand diversity and challenge their preconceived notions about different cultures and flavors. Older children can learn how to prepare simple foods, recognize the USDA recommended daily allowances of each food group in order to keep the body healthy, and classify foods based on their group and health benefits. Older students can also learn about the role of various nutrients in the body such as fat, fiber, and protein, and how to select nutrient-dense foods from a given list. Children benefit from understanding what makes a food healthy and knowing options for healthy meals and snacks. By the third grade, students can start learning how to read nutrition labels, how to compare foods based on nutrition labels, and how to modify food choices to improve healthfulness, such as replacing low-fiber foods with higher fiber choices, like opting for apples instead of applesauce. When students are in the fourth grade, educators can start talking about portion sizes and the relationship between food consumption and physical activity on energy balance and weight control. In the context of introducing the basics about calories, prevention of obesity and the ramifications of an unhealthy diet can also be discussed. Children in the fifth and sixth grades can learn about the differences in types of fats, examples of common vitamins and minerals and food sources of these nutrients, the disadvantages of "empty-calories," and how to recognize misleading nutrition information.

Physical Activity

In childhood, regular physical activity improves strength and endurance, helps build healthy bones and muscles, controls weight, reduces anxiety and stress, increases self-esteem, and may improve blood pressure and cholesterol. Children should get at least sixty minutes of physical activity daily. Typically, young children are less concerned about their physical fitness and more concerned about having fun; therefore, physical education should center on fun and play as a means to engage the body in activity. Play-centered physical education programs are an effective means to promote children's movement development and meet their requisite activity needs for health. Early childhood educators should develop physical education programs that focus on the enjoyment of movement rather than sport-specific skill mastery for two reasons. Firstly, play-centered activity will help the child be more engaged and likely to adopt a positive attitude towards exercise; and secondly, in early childhood, basic general fitness and movement skills are more important than mastery of highly specialized skills unique to certain sports. Young children also tend to lack the gross and fine motor skills and perceptual abilities needed for such highly specialized skills, which can lead to frustration or simply an inability to perform the activity.

For optimal results, it is best for early childhood educators to establish an environment of student-centered learning in regards to physical education. Because young children at any given age can have vastly different motor and physical abilities from each other, it is imperative that the educator simply set standards of enjoyment, movement, and physical discovery rather than specific mastery of skills. This prevents boredom in more physically advanced children and bewilderment and demotivation in less skilled children. It is prudent for educators to provide a variety of options within every activity and game so that children can figure out what appeals and works for them at their own developmental level. This also starts children on the path to understanding themselves and evaluating choices at a young age within a fun, playful environment and begins to get their minds processing not just what to do but how to do it as well.

Educators should use simple instructions that are age-appropriate in terms of the steps and level of complexity, visual demonstrations of movements, and drills that help reinforce the skill. During practice and exploration of the new skill, educators should focus on positive feedback and evaluation to guide the children in learning. When teaching new skills, especially to toddlers and young children, instructions lasting longer than twenty seconds or that contain more than just a couple of steps will cause students to lose interest or get overwhelmed. It is typically advantageous to have very short instructional periods interspersed between longer breaks to play and try out the skills. To help manage a large group of small, active children, simple rules and expectations should be laid out with consequences for improper behavior.

Children should learn about the methods and benefits of a proper warm-up and cool-down, how to set goals to make exercise part of their daily routine, and the benefits of physical activity. Older children can learn about the effects of exercise on the heart and how to locate their pulse during and after exercise, how to stay physically active through more than just sports, and how to create a personal fitness plan.

Sleep

Early childhood educators should talk about the importance of sleep and why parents set a "bedtime," as well as healthy sleep hygiene and establishing a sleep schedule. Children can learn about how much sleep they need and ways to improve the quality of sleep, such as physical activity and avoiding screen time before bed. Young children who may experience nightmares can benefit from learning relaxation techniques as well as talking about their fears and feelings to trusted adults.

Stress Management

Students should be educated about stress management and exposed to techniques such as mental imagery, relaxation, deep breathing, aerobic exercise, and meditation. Children can be guided through progressive muscle relaxation and should be taught signs of excessive nervousness and stress, how to manage test and performance anxiety, and when and how to get help with excessive stress.

Healthy Relationships

Healthy family and social relationships are important to overall health and happiness. Studies have pointed to a negative impact of parental fighting on a child's wellbeing, including sleep and exercise habits, nutrition choices, stress, and social adjustment. Early childhood educators should talk about aspects of healthy relationships such as communication, emotional support, sharing, and respect. Younger children should learn skills that are helpful in making friends, cultivating relationships, and resolving conflict, especially as they relate to peers and siblings. Cooperation, taking turns, using words rather than physical means to communicate feelings, and exploring feelings are helpful concepts to instill. Older children should begin to be exposed to dating etiquette and forming healthy romantic relationships. Educators should work to create a classroom environment of inclusion where students have an awareness of peers who may feel left out and work to include everyone. Within discussions of healthy relationships, educators should talk about accepting and appreciating diversity, including differences in cultures, religions, families, physical appearance and abilities, interests, intellect, emotions, lifestyle, and, in older children, sexual orientations. Life skills – such as having self-esteem, making decisions, calming oneself when angry or upset, and using listening skills – should be addressed.

Hydration

Early childhood educators should teach students about the importance of hydration and signs of dehydration as well as healthy choices for fluids, with a special emphasis on water. Children and their parents should be encouraged to send kids to school with a water bottle, and classrooms or hallways should be equipped with water fountains that children can access and use with limited supervision or assistance.

Safety Behaviors

Children should learn basic safety behaviors and the importance of following rules to prevent common injuries. Basic safety behaviors include wearing sunscreen and sunglasses when going outdoors; wearing protective gear in sports such as bicycle helmets, reflective vests, appropriate pads and cups, etc.; and using a car seat and/or always wearing a seat belt. Young children should learn about household safety such as not touching burners and not putting their fingers in electrical sockets nor opening the door to strangers. Educators should have children practice the "no, go, and tell" procedure for unsafe situations. For example, if a stranger offers the child an unknown substance, the child should know how to firmly refuse, carefully leave the situation, and tell a trusted adult. In this lesson, educators should also help children to identify trusted adults in their families and communities.

Educators can also discuss community safety measures such as using sidewalks, contacting city services (police, fire, and ambulance) in emergencies, and crossing the street safely by using crosswalks, holding hands, and looking both ways before crossing. Children should also learn about the health consequences of smoking, how to avoid secondhand smoke, and how to identify and avoid poisonous household substances. Fire safety such as "stop, drop, and roll" and emergency evacuation procedures should be rehearsed. Older children can learn about safety rules for various types of weather and how weather affects their personal safety, what different traffic signs mean, water/swim safety rules, and the importance of weighing consequences before taking risks.

Hygiene

Young children should learn about germs and the spread of infections. Older children can learn about bacteria and viruses. The importance of washing hands (including appropriate demonstration) cannot be overstated in elementary and preschool classrooms.

Other aspects of hygiene such as covering the mouth while coughing and covering the nose while sneezing, not sharing cups, practicing clean bathroom habits, showering and bathing, and, in older children, using deodorants, antiperspirants, and facial cleansers should be included in the curriculum.

Substance Abuse

Beginning substance abuse education early provides students with the knowledge and support they need to avoid addiction and other mental health challenges later in life. The key concept to elementary substance abuse education is **personal autonomy.** While elementary students aren't prepared to understand the psychological or chemical details about how drugs affect the body, they are capable of understanding that substances can cause harm. Teaching students to recognize everyday drugs, resist peer pressure, and understand that *they* have control over their own body prepares the student to avoid substance abuse later in life.

Elementary students ought to be familiar with three common types of drugs:

- Alcohol
- Cigarettes/vapes
- Pills

Recognizing these substances as drugs helps students understand that their use affects how the body works. Alcohol, cigarettes, and vapes–which contain nicotine or THC—are common in everyday life. Understanding what they are often reduces a child's curiosity in these adult behaviors. Likewise, medicines in pill form are readily available in most households. Elementary students are capable of understanding that a medicine may be helpful if they're sick, but can be harmful if they're healthy or take too much. Learning to only take pills when prescribed by a doctor or given by a trusted adult reduces the risk of substance abuse.

The biggest cause of substance abuse is **peer pressure.** Effective substance abuse education builds up a student's sense of personal autonomy, which empowers them to say no to peers when feeling pressured to try drugs. Exercises that bolster a student's self-esteem, practice refusing drugs, and identify positive and negative uses of drugs all contribute to the student's education. Teaching students to refuse drugs and supporting their sense of well-being will help children avoid substance abuse later in life.

Communicable Disease

Humans appear to be the kings of nature, but unfortunately, disease can strike. Some protists (like the malaria-causing paramecium), fungi (yeast), and bacteria (strep) can make humans sick and can even be deadly.

The human body has an arsenal to help fight illness. Skin and the acid in our stomach are inhospitable to all sorts of disease-causing agents (pathogens) and fight them off without even trying. Eyebrows, eyelashes, nose hair, and cilia (tiny hairs) in the respiratory system trap any germs and prevent them from getting inside. Mucus is a defense to trap germs, which is why the human body overproduces it when sick—it acts like a spider web that catches germs, and when a person coughs or sneezes, the germs are expelled and unable to cause harm. If, however, the pathogen gets past these barriers, then the body has to start fighting them off. Inflammation and swelling, though annoying, actually help by increasing blood flow to an injured or infected area. Blood carries white blood cells that eat and destroy germs. Fevers are actually a body's natural response to killing pathogens.

If the germ is still not killed off, then the body makes massive amounts of white blood cells. One type of blood cell, the **plasma B-cell**, is particularly helpful because it makes structures called **antibodies**, little proteins that tag pathogens so that the other white blood cells can easily find and destroy them. Other types of white blood cells include **T-cells**, which destroy the pathogen as well as infected cells.

This picture shows how antibodies work:

The **antigen** on the germ is the part that attaches to cells in our body and destroys them. Think of the antigen like the key that attaches to a protein on the outside of our cell, tricking the cell to let it in. The antibody perfectly binds to the antigen (the key), making it so that the germ cannot open and enter our cells. And the immune system produces killer T-cells that eat these tagged pathogens.

An amazing thing about antibodies is that they are completely fashioned to match each germ they come across. And antibodies stay circulating in blood so that if they ever encounter the disease again, they can tag it for destruction and block its harmful effects, making a person immune to the pathogen.

For this reason, scientists have developed vaccines, which can save lives. For example, **polio** is a disease that attacks the brain and spinal cord, causing paralysis and death. The vaccine for polio is given to children. It is given in the inactive form of the virus (dead virus) but it still carries the same antigen. A person vaccinated will develop antibodies that are exactly matched to the polio antigens, so if they ever encounter polio in real life, the immune system will eradicate it before it can do any damage.

When a person gets infected and their body starts making massive amounts of antibodies and killer cells, they can feel sick due to the energy expended to create such an army. Usually, after a few days, the body effectively fights off the germ, and life goes back to normal. In the case of bacterial infections that don't resolve themselves, antibiotics (bacteria killers) can be taken to help the body fight the germs. Antibiotics, unfortunately, don't help with viruses.

Interestingly enough, antibiotics were discovered by accident in 1928 by **Alexander Fleming**. He was performing research of an entirely different nature when he noticed mold had killed the cells he was trying to study. Upon further investigation, he realized that the effect of the mold was reproducible and effectively killed a variety of bacteria. His discovery laid groundwork for a new field of medicine, which targeted the destruction of bacteria. Since then, a variety of antibiotics have been developed, and some of them are uniquely designed for different diseases. Biological research is critical for disease prevention because bacteria are always changing, and there is a need to continually improve the antibiotics already available.

Early childhood educators should be able to incorporate health and physical education concepts into the classroom for the overall health, wellness, and growth of their students. Physical activity is especially important at young ages, and children need at least sixty minutes of moderate to vigorous physical activity daily according to the U.S. Surgeon General's Recommendations. There are five components of health-related physical fitness: cardiovascular fitness, muscular strength, muscular endurance, flexibility, and body composition. All five areas should be addressed in physical education classes. With cardiovascular training, as the heart enlarges, the volume of the chambers increase, allowing for a greater stroke volume and cardiac output. This also enables the heart to be more efficient, with a resultant lowering of the resting and submaximal exercise heart rate and blood pressure, which increases the body's exercise duration and intensity tolerance. Blood volume—both in terms of plasma and hemoglobin—increases oxygen-carrying capacity and lactic acid metabolism improves, which allows the aerobic system to more effectively metabolize substrates for usable energy. Muscle glycogen storage, another important form of energy storage in the body, also increases. Vasculature increases as well, improving the blood perfusion of muscles.

Other positive results of physical fitness include increased bone mineral density, improvements in body composition, and neural adaptations. Resistance training, even with body weight alone (such as squats and push-ups), affords strength, power, and coordination improvements and leads to greater efficiency of the anaerobic metabolic systems. Nervous system adaptations occur quickly with training as motor units (connections between the spine and other muscles throughout the body) become conditioned to activate more quickly and more often. As a greater number of motor units activate together and coordinate with each other, a higher percentage of fibers in a muscle contract simultaneously, increasing strength. Over time, muscle fibers increase in size and bone mineral density increases in load-bearing bones. Flexibility training increases elasticity and resting length of muscle and connective tissues and joint range of motion (ROM) before the stretch reflex is initiated (muscle spindle adaptation), reducing injury risk.

Health education – even beginning at preschool ages – has been shown to have a significant positive impact on an individual for maintaining healthy behaviors as an adolescent and adult. Preschool children who receive high-quality physical and health education may have improved nutrition and exercise habits and are more likely to receive routine medical and dental care as adults. Early childhood educators can start laying the groundwork for a lifetime of healthier behaviors and attitudes by fostering an environment of enjoyment of physical activity, an understanding of nutrition and hydration, and methods of disease and injury prevention.

Educators can talk with older children about the types, causes, and characteristics of chronic, degenerative, communicable, and non-communicable diseases, as well as ways to detect and prevent them. Students can learn about modifiable risk factors for various diseases and conditions such as diabetes, coronary artery disease, cardiovascular disease, and obesity.

Science as a Human Endeavor

In addition to learning about bacteria and viruses to save lives, an example of how increased scientific knowledge has helped society can be seen in the field of botany. **Flowers** are the reproductive structure of plants and are very complex structures that allow plants to create genetic diversity.

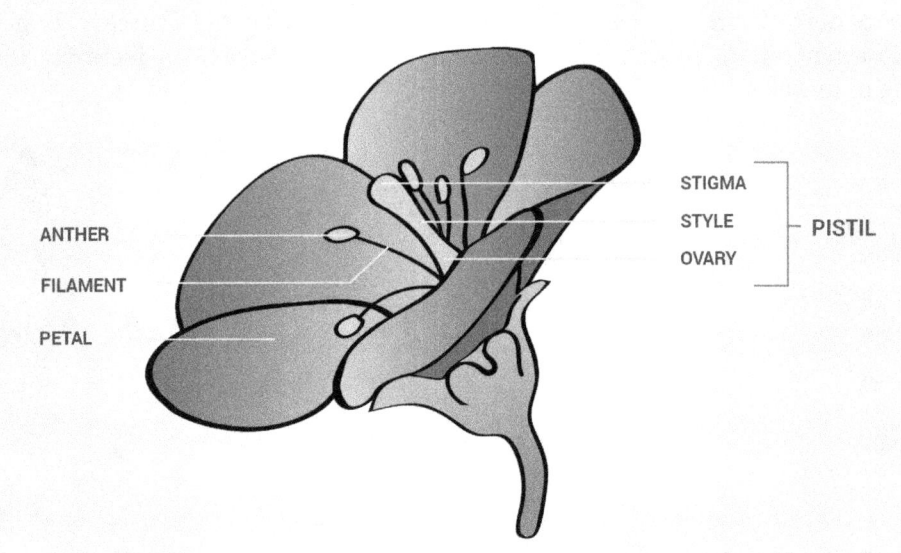

Scientists have determined the purpose for all of a flower's many parts:

- The **stamen** contains the pollen-holding **anther** (pollen is plant sperm) and the **filament** that holds it high.

- The **pistil** contains the sticky **stigma** at the top to which pollen sticks; the **style**, which holds up the stigma; and the **ovary**, or egg that will eventually be fertilized.

- The petals are colored and even have infrared patterns we cannot see to attract pollinators like birds and bees.

Note how structure aids function in the flower: the pollen is lightweight and easily attaches to pollinators. The stigma is sticky and easily catches the pollen. The petals are beautiful landing pads designed to attract different animals.

Scientists are using their knowledge of flowers and genetics to genetically engineer flowers. They are working on creating pollen-free flowers that are easy on people with allergies, blue roses, and other flower varieties that don't exist in nature, and even glow-in-the-dark flowers by introducing foreign DNA.

Other botanists are also genetically engineering plants that provide our food, which is much more controversial, as many are worried about the consequences of consuming genetically modified organisms (GMOs). Some think GMOs are wonderful because they can provide massive amounts of food at low costs, while others fear introducing foreign food into the biosphere will alter ecosystems.

Science as Inquiry

As scientists have been able to visualize and decode DNA, they are also able to predict diseases. **Karyotypes** are pictures of individual's chromosomes, and even before birth, abnormalities such as Down syndrome (an extra chromosome 21) can be detected.

Down syndrome karyotype

Adults can have blood tests to test their alleles and see if they have cancer-causing (or other disease-causing) genes. Being aware of possible diseases helps people to prevent and treat them.

As scientists ask more questions about disease detection, prevention, and treatment, quality of life continues to increase. For example, type 1 diabetes occurs when a person's pancreas fails to make insulin, and it is a deadly disease if left untreated. A few decades ago, scientists found a way to synthetically create insulin, and now diabetics can have long and prosperous lives.

Research and Process of Science

One little change can disrupt an entire ecosystem. For example, in Hawaii, North American ducks were brought for hunting purposes, but they've endangered the native duck species. One new non-native organism can cause a natural species to become extinct.

Another danger to an ecosystem is human activity. As the human population grows and technology advances, our energy needs are polluting the atmosphere. And there are no doubts that global temperatures are climbing, which can change ecosystem dynamics. Increases in oil spills and ocean pollution is destroying aquatic ecosystems. Chopping down trees for wood as well as building parking lots and buildings is decimating terrestrial ecosystems. With these changes, biodiversity will dramatically drop. The list of endangered species continues to grow, and eventually many will become extinct. Altering populations of ecosystems can have dramatic effects.

Livestock overgrazing is also detrimental to the environment. If farms don't monitor grazing animals, plants simply lose the ability to rebound, often resulting in death. The lack of producers in an ecosystem, the start of the food chain, will have disastrous consequences for the entire community.

Research is important so that society can minimize activities that interfere with ecosystems. Developing non-renewable energy (such as wind, solar, and geothermal), deliberately planning a grazing schedule to prevent overgrazing, and protecting endangered species all should be primary focuses of research.

Scientific research always starts as a question, followed by a hypothesis, data collection, and conclusions. Conclusions lead to further questions, repeating the process.

This was the case with the study of insect development. Long ago, scientists noticed a strange phenomenon in insects, which we now know is a process called **metamorphosis**.

Science

There are two types of metamorphosis in insects: incomplete metamorphosis, which has three stages, and complete metamorphosis, which has four stages.

Incomplete Metamorphosis: Grasshoppers	Complete Metamorphosis: Butterflies and Beetles
• Egg • Nymph: a mini-adult with no wings • Adult: how the organism will look for the rest of its life	• Egg • Larva: a wormy, six legged, massive eater • Pupa: a larva encased in a hard shell that dramatically develops and changes in appearance • Adult: how the organism will look for the rest of its life

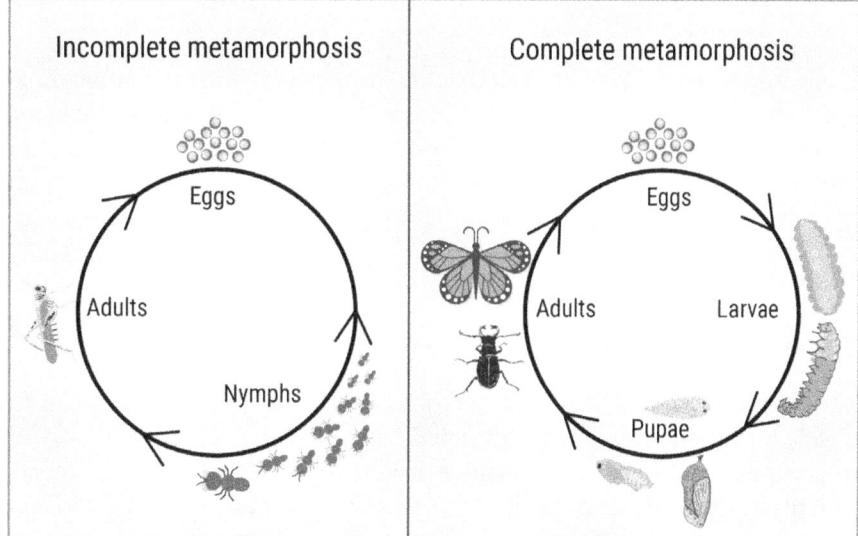

Insight into metamorphosis developed over centuries of research and goes through the scientific process, as shown below.

Problem/Question: What's happening to these insects that makes them look completely different from their younger selves?

Hypothesis: The prevailing hypotheses that were researched over the years were:

- These different creatures are from two different organisms.
- The worm-like creature is a younger version of the adult creature.

Data collection: A biologist named **Swammerdam** in the 1600s rejected the popular belief that the caterpillar and the butterfly were different organisms. Using observations from microscopic data, he confirmed that an insect (but not all insects) could go through an intermediate larval stage. Fossil evidence also confirmed the development of some insects through a larval stage. Scientists have even found genetic and protein differences from organisms that go through incomplete metamorphosis and complete metamorphosis. The insects with larval stage have a specific gene required for the process as well as differences in hormone production.

Conclusion: There is a complete metamorphosis cycle for many insects with larval and pupa stages between the egg and adult.

New problem: Why do insects go through complete metamorphosis?

New hypothesis: Complete metamorphosis is an adaptation. The intermediate "pupa egg" state between the larva and the adult stage arose so the juvenile and adult population don't compete for food, ensuring greater overall survival.

Physical Science

Structure of Matter

In the physical sciences, it is important to break things down to their simplest components in order to truly understand why they act and react the way they do. It may seem burdensome to separate out each part of an object or to diagram each movement made by an object, but these methods provide a solid basis for understanding how to accurately depict the motion of objects and then correctly predict their future movements.

Everything around us is composed of different materials. To properly understand and sort objects, we must classify what types of materials they comprise. This includes identifying the foundational properties of each object such as its reaction to chemicals, heat, water, or other materials. Some objects might not react at all and this is an important property to note. Other properties include the object's physical appearance or any magnetic properties. Being able to sort and classify objects is the first step to understanding them.

- **Matter**: anything that has mass and takes up space.

- **Substance**: a type of matter that cannot be separated out into new material through a physical reaction.

- **Elements**: substances that cannot be broken down by either physical or chemical reactions. Elements are the most basic form of matter and are grouped by identified properties using the Periodic Table. The periodic table groups elements based on similar properties. Metallic elements, inert elements, and transition elements are a few categories used to organize elements on the periodic table. New elements are added as they are discovered or created, and these newer elements tend to be heavier, fall into the metal section of the periodic table, and are often unstable. Examples of elements include carbon, gold, and helium.

- **Atoms**: the building blocks of all elements. Atoms are the smallest particles of matter that retain their identities during chemical reactions. Atoms have a central nucleus that includes positively charged protons, and neutrons, which carry no charge. Atoms are also surrounded by electrons that carry a negative charge. The amount of each component determines what type of atom is formed when the components come together. For example, two hydrogen atoms and one oxygen atom can bond together to form water, but the hydrogen and oxygen atoms still remain true to their original identities.

- **Mass**: the measure of how much of a substance exists in an object. The measure of mass is not the same as weight, area, or volume.

Physical and Chemical Properties
Both physical and chemical properties are used to sort and classify objects:

Physical properties: refers to the appearance, mass, temperature, state, size, or color of an object or fluid; a physical change indicates a change in the appearance, mass, temperature, state, size or color of an object or fluid.

Science

Chemical properties: refers to the chemical makeup of an object or fluid; a chemical change refers to an alteration in the makeup of an object or fluid and forms a new solution or compound.

<u>Changes of States</u>
A **reversible change** (physical change) is the changing of the size or shape of an object without altering its chemical makeup. Examples include the heating or cooling of water, change of state (solid, liquid, gas), the freezing of water into ice, or cutting a piece of wood in half.

When two or more materials are combined, it is called a **mixture**. Generally, a mixture can be separated out into the original components. When one type of matter is dissolved into another type of matter (a solid into a liquid or a liquid into another liquid), and cannot easily be separated back into its original components, it is called a **solution**.

States of matter refers to the form substances take such as solid, liquid, gas, or plasma. **Solid** refers to a rigid form of matter with a flexed shape and a fixed volume. A rock is a solid because it has a fixed shape and volume. **Liquid** refers to the fluid form of matter with no fixed shape and a fixed volume. Water is a liquid because it has a set volume, but not a set shape; therefore, you could pour it into different containers of different shapes, as long as they were large enough to contain the existing volume of the water. **Gas** refers to an easily compressible fluid form of matter with no fixed shape that expands to fill any space available. Finally, **plasma** refers to an ionized gas where electrons flow freely from atom to atom. Oxygen is a gas. Oxygen does not have a set volume or a set shape; therefore, it could expand or contract to fill a container or even a room. Gases in fluorescent lamps become plasma when electric current is applied to them.

Matter can change from one state to another in many ways, including through heating, cooling, or a change in pressure. Changes of state are identified as:

- **Melting**: solid to liquid
- **Sublimation**: solid to gas
- **Evaporation**: liquid to gas
- **Freezing**: liquid to solid
- **Condensation**: gas to liquid
- **Non-reversible change** (chemical change): When one or more types of matter change and it results in the production of new materials. Examples include burning, rusting, and combining solutions. If a piece of paper is burned it cannot be turned back into its original state. It has forever been altered by a chemical change.

Forces and Motion

People have been studying the movement of objects since ancient times, sometimes prompted by curiosity, and sometimes by necessity. On Earth, items move according to specific guidelines and have motion that is fairly predictable. In order to understand why an object moves along its path, it is important to understand what role forces have on influencing an object's movements. The term **force** describes an outside influence on an object. Force does not have to refer to something imparted by another object. Forces can act upon objects by touching them with a push or a pull, by friction, or without touch like a magnetic force or even gravity. Forces can affect the motion of an object.

In order to study an object's motion, the object must be locatable and describable. When locating an object's position, it can help to locate it relative to another known object, or put it into a frame of reference. This phrase means that if the placement of one object is known, it is easier to locate another object with respect to the position of the original object.

The measurement of an object's movement or change in position (x), over a change in time (t) is an object's speed. The measurement of speed with direction is **velocity**. A "change in position" refers to the difference in location of an object's starting point and an object's ending point. In science, the Greek letter **Delta**, Δ, represents a change.

Equation:

$$velocity\ (v) = \frac{\Delta x}{\Delta t}$$

Position is measured in meters, and time is measured in seconds. The standard measurement for velocity is meters/second (m/s).

$$\frac{\text{meters}}{\text{second}} = \frac{m}{s}$$

The measurement of an object's change in velocity over time is an object's **acceleration**. **Gravity** is considered to be a form of acceleration.

Equation:

$$acceleration\ (a) = \frac{\Delta v}{\Delta t}$$

Velocity is measured in meters/second and time is measured in seconds. The standard measurement for acceleration is meters/second² (m/s²).

$$\frac{\frac{\text{meters}}{\text{second}}}{\text{second}} = \frac{\text{meters}}{\text{second}^2} = \frac{m}{s^2}$$

For example, consider a car traveling down the road. The speed can be measured by calculating how far the car is traveling over a certain period of time. However, since the car is traveling in a direction (north, east, south, west), the distance over time is actually the car's velocity. It can be confusing, as many people will often interchange the words speed and velocity. But if something is traveling a certain distance, during a certain time period, in a direction, this is the object's velocity. Velocity is speed with direction.

The change in an object's velocity over a certain amount of time is the object's acceleration. If the driver of that car keeps pressing on the gas pedal and increasing the velocity, the car would have a change in velocity over the change in time and would be accelerating. The reverse could be said if the driver were depressing the brake and the car was slowing down; it would have a negative acceleration, or be decelerating. Since acceleration also has a direction component, it is possible for a car to accelerate without changing speed. If an object changes direction, it is accelerating.

Motion creates something called **momentum**. This is a calculation of an object's mass multiplied by its velocity. Momentum can be described as the amount an object wants to continue moving along its current course. Momentum in a straight line is called **linear momentum**. Just as energy can be transferred and conserved, so can momentum.

For example, a car and a truck moving at the same velocity down a highway will not have the same momentum, because they do not have the same mass. The mass of the truck is greater than that of the car, therefore the truck will have more momentum. In a head-on collision, the vehicles would be expected to slide in the same direction of the truck's original motion because the truck has a greater momentum.

Science

The amount of force during a length of time creates an **impulse**. This means that if a force acts on an object during a given amount of time, it will have a determined impulse. However, if the length of time can be extended, the force will be less, due to the conservation of momentum.

Consider another example: when catching a fast baseball, it helps soften the blow of the ball to follow through, or cradle the catch. This technique is simply extending the time of the application of the force of the ball, so the impact of the ball does not hurt the hand. As a final example, if a martial arts expert wants to break a board by executing a chop from their hand, they need to exert a force on a small point on the boards, extremely quickly. If they slow down the time of the impact from the force of their hand, they will probably injure their hand and not break the board.

Newton's Three Laws of Motion

Sir Isaac Newton spent a great deal of time studying objects, forces, and how an object's motion responds to forces. Newton made great advancements by using mathematics to describe the motion of objects and to predict future motions of objects by applying his mathematical models to situations. Through his extensive research, Newton is credited for summarizing the basic laws of motion for objects here on Earth. These laws are as follows:

First Law

The first law is the **law of inertia**. An object in motion remains in motion, unless acted upon by an outside force. An object at rest remains at rest, unless acted upon by an outside force. Simply put, inertia is the natural tendency of an object to continue along with what it is already doing; an outside force would have to act upon the object to make it change its course. This includes an object that is sitting still. The inertia of an object is relative to its momentum.

Example: If a car is driving at a constant speed in a constant direction (also called a constant velocity), it would take a force in a different direction to change the path of the car. Conversely, if the car is sitting still, it would take a force greater than that of friction from any direction to make that stationary car move.

Second Law

The force (F) on an object is equal to the mass (m) multiplied by the acceleration (a) on that object. **Mass** (m) refers to the amount of a substance and **acceleration** (a) refers to a rate of velocity over time. In the case of an object falling on Earth, the value of gravity will be placed in for acceleration (a). In the case of an object at rest on Earth, gravity is placed in for acceleration (a), and the force calculated by $F = ma$ is called **weight** (W). It is important to discern that an object's mass (measured in kilograms, kg) is not the same as an object's weight (measured in Newtons, N). Weight is the mass times the gravity.

Example: The gravity on the Earth's Moon is considerably less than the gravity on Earth. Therefore, the weight of an object on the Earth's Moon would be considerably less than the weight of the object on Earth. In each case, a different value for acceleration/gravity would be used in the equation $F = ma$. Mass is used to calculate weight, and they are not the same.

Example: If a raisin is dropped into a bowl of pudding, it would make a small indentation and stick in the pudding a bit, but if a grapefruit is dropped into the same bowl of pudding, it would splatter the pudding out of the bowl and most likely hit the bottom of the bowl. Even though both items are accelerating at the same rate (gravity), the mass of the grapefruit is larger than that of the raisin; therefore, the force with which the grapefruit hits the bowl of pudding is considerably larger than the force from the raisin hitting the bowl of pudding.

Third Law

The third law of motion states that for every action there is an equal and opposite reaction. If someone pounds a fist on a table, the reactionary force from the table causes the person to feel a sharp force on the fist. The magnitude of the force felt on the fist increases the harder that they pound on the table. It should be noted that action/reaction pairs occur simultaneously. As the fist applies a force on the table, the table instantaneously applies an equal and opposite force on the fist.

Example: Imagine a person is wearing ice skates on ice and attempts to push on a heavy sled sitting in front of them. They will be pushed in the direction opposite of their push on the sled; the push the skater is experiencing is equal and opposite to the force they are exerting on the sled. This is a good example of how the icy surface helps to lessen the effects of friction and allows the reactionary force to be more easily observed.

Forces are anything acting upon an object either in motion or at rest; this includes friction and gravity. These forces are often depicted by using a force diagram or free body diagram. A **force diagram** shows an object as the focal point, with arrows denoting all the forces acting upon the object. The direction of the head of the arrow indicates the direction of the force. The object at the center can also be exerting forces on things in its surroundings.

Equilibrium

If an object is in constant motion or at rest (its acceleration equals zero), the object is said to be in **equilibrium**. It does not imply that there are no forces acting upon the object, but that all of the forces are balanced in order for the situation to continue in its current state. This can be thought of as a "balanced" situation.

Note that if an object is resting on top of a mountain peak or traveling at a constant velocity down the side of that mountain, both situations describe a state of equilibrium.

Falling Objects

Objects falling within the Earth's atmosphere are all affected by gravity. Their rate of acceleration will be that of gravity. If two objects were dropped from a great height at the exact same time, regardless of mass, theoretically, they should hit the ground at the same time. This is due to gravity acting upon them at the same rate. In actuality, if this were attempted, the shape of the objects and external factors such as air resistance would affect their rates of fall and cause a discrepancy when each lands.

Consider the traditional illustration of this principle: a feather and a rock are released at the same time in regular air versus being released at the same time in a vacuum. In the open atmosphere, the feather would slowly loft down to the ground, due to the effects of air resistance, while the rock would quickly drop to the ground. If the feather and the rock were both released at the same time in a vacuum, they would both hit the bottom at the same time. The rate of fall is not dependent upon the mass of the item or any external factors in a vacuum (there is no air resistance in a vacuum); therefore, all that would be affecting the rate of fall would be gravity. Gravity affects every object on the Earth with the same rate of acceleration.

Circular Motion

An **axis** is an invisible line on which an object can rotate. This is most easily observed with a toy top. There is actually a point (or rod) through the center of the top on which the top can be observed to be spinning. This is called the axis.

When objects move in a circle by spinning on their own axis, or because they are tethered around a central point (also an axis), they exhibit circular motion. Circular motion is similar in many ways to linear (straight line) motion; however, there are a few additional points to note. A spinning object is always accelerating because it is always changing direction. The force causing this constant acceleration on or around an axis is called **centripetal force** and is often associated with centripetal acceleration. Centripetal force always pulls toward the axis of rotation. An imaginary reactionary force, called **centrifugal force**, is the outward force felt when an object is undergoing circular motion. This reactionary force is not the real force; it just feels like it is there. This has also been referred to as a "**fictional force**." The true force is the one pulling inward, or the centripetal force.

The terms centripetal and centrifugal are often mistakenly interchanged. If the centripetal force acting on an object moving with circular motion is removed, the object will continue moving in a straight line tangent to the point on the circle where the object last experienced the centripetal force. For example, when a traditional style washing machine spins a load of clothes in order to expunge the water from the load, it spins the machine barrel in a circle at a high rate of speed. A force is pulling in toward the center of the circle (centripetal force). At the same time, the wet clothes, which are attempting to move in a straight line, are colliding with the outer wall of the barrel that is moving in a circle. The interaction between the wet clothes and barrel wall causes a reactionary force to the centripetal force and expel the water out of the small holes that line the outer wall of the barrel.

Conservation of Angular Momentum

An object moving in a circular motion also has momentum; for circular motion it is called **angular momentum**. This is determined by rotational inertia and rotational velocity and the distance of the mass from the axis of rotation or center of rotation. When objects are exhibiting circular motion, they also demonstrate the conservation of **angular momentum**, meaning that the angular momentum of a system is always constant, regardless of the placement of the mass. Rotational inertia can be affected by how far the mass of the object is placed with respect to the center of rotation (axis of rotation). The larger the distance between the mass and the center of rotation, the slower the rotational velocity. Conversely, if the mass is closer to the center of rotation, the rotational velocity increases. A change in one affects the other, thus conserving the angular momentum. This holds true as long as no external forces act upon the system.

For example, an ice skater spinning on one ice skate extends their arms out for a slower rotational velocity. When the skater brings their arms in close to their body (or lessens the distance between the mass and the center of rotation), their rotational velocity increases and they spin much faster. Some skaters extend their arms straight up above their head, which causes an extension of the axis of rotation, thus removing any distance between the mass and the center of rotation and maximizing their rotational velocity.

Another example is when a person selects a horse on a merry-go-round: the placement of their horse can affect their ride experience. All of the horses are traveling with the same rotational speed, but in order to travel along the same plane as the merry-go-round turns, a horse on the outside will have a greater linear speed, due to it being farther away from the axis of rotation. Another way to think of it is that an outside horse has to cover a lot more ground than a horse on the inside, in order to keep up with the rotational speed of the merry-go-round platform. Thrill seekers should always select an outer horse.

Energy

The term **energy** typically refers to an object's ability to perform work. This can include a transfer of heat from one object to another, or from an object to its surroundings. Energy is usually measured in Joules. There are two main categories of energy: renewable and non-renewable.

- **Renewable**: energy produced from the exhaustion of a resource that can be replenished. Burning wood to produce heat, then replanting trees to replenish the resource is an instance of using renewable energy.

- **Non-renewable**: energy produced from the exhaustion of a resource that cannot be replenished. Burning coal to produce heat would be an example of a non-renewable energy. Although coal is a natural resource that is mined or harvested from the earth, it cannot be regrown or replenished. Other examples include oil and natural gas (fossil fuels).

Temperature is measured in degrees Celsius (°C) or Kelvin (°K). Temperature should not be confused with heat. **Heat** is a form of energy: a change in temperature or a transfer of heat can also be a measure of energy. The amount of energy measured by the change in temperature (or a transfer) is the measure of heat.

Transfer and Conservation of Energy
Heat energy (thermal energy) can be transferred through the following ways:

Conduction
Conduction is the heating of one object by another through the actual touching of molecules, in order to transfer heat across the objects involved. A spiral burner on an electric stovetop heats from one molecule touching another to transfer the heat via conduction.

Convection
Heat transfer due to the movement/flow of molecules from areas of high concentration to ones of low concentration. Warmer molecules tend to rise, while colder molecules tend to sink. The heat in a house will rise from the vents in the floor to the upper levels of the structure and circulate in that manner, rising and falling with the movement of the molecules. This molecular movement helps to heat or cool a house and is often called **convection current**.

Radiation
The Sun warms the Earth through **radiation** or radiant energy. Radiation does not need any medium for the heat to travel; therefore, the heat from the Sun can radiate to the Earth across space.

Greenhouse Effect
The Sun transfers heat into the Earth's atmosphere through radiation traveling in waves. The atmosphere helps protect the Earth from extreme exposure to the Sun, while reflecting some of the waves continuously within the atmosphere, creating habitable temperatures. The rest of the waves are meant to dissipate out through the atmosphere and back into space. However, humans have created pollutants and released an overabundance of certain gasses into the Earth's atmosphere, causing a layer of blockage. So, the waves that should be leaving the atmosphere continue to bounce back upon the Earth repeatedly, thus contributing to global warming. This is a negative effect from the extra re-radiation of the Sun's energy and causes planetary overheating.

This additional warming is not something easily or quickly reversed. Because the rate of reflection within the atmosphere only multiplies the more a light wave is bounced around, it will take a concerted effort to undue past reflectance and stop future reflectance of the light waves in the Earth's atmosphere. Once the re-reflectance occurs, it duplicates exponentially, along with the additional compounding of more waves. Each degree the atmospheric temperature increases has a profound effect on the delicate balance of our planet, including the melting of polar ice caps, the rise of tidal currents—which cause strong weather systems—and the depletion of specific ecosystems necessary to sustain certain species of animals or insects, to name a few.

Energy can be harnessed to operate objects, and this energy is obtained from various sources such as electricity, food, gasoline, batteries, wind, and sun. For example, wind turbines out in a field are turned by the natural power of the wind. The turbines then store that energy internally in power cells; that stored energy can be used to power the lights on a farm or run machinery.

Conservation of Energy

There is a fundamental law of **thermodynamics** (the study of heat and movement) called **Conservation of Energy**. This law states that energy cannot be created or destroyed, but rather energy is transferred to different forms involved in a process. For instance, a car pushed beginning at one end of a street will not continue down that street forever; it will gradually come to a stop some distance away from where it was originally pushed. This does not mean the energy has disappeared or has been exhausted; it means the energy has been transferred to different mediums surrounding the car.

The frictional force from the road on the tires dissipates some of the energy, the air resistance from the movement of the car dissipates some of the energy, the sound from the tires on the road dissipates some of the energy, and the force of gravity pulling on the car dissipates some of the energy. Each value can be calculated in a number of ways including measuring the sound waves from the tires, measuring the temperature change in the tires, measuring the distance moved by the car from start to finish, etc. It is important to understand that many processes factor into such a small situation, but all situations follow the conservation of energy.

Types of Energy

Potential energy (gravitational potential energy, or *PE*) is stored energy, or energy due to an object's height above the ground. **Kinetic energy** (*KE*) is the energy of motion. If an object is moving, it has some amount of kinetic energy.

Consider a rollercoaster car sitting still on the tracks at the top of a hill. The rollercoaster has all potential energy and no kinetic energy. As it travels down the hill, the energy transfers from potential energy into kinetic energy. At the bottom of the hill, where the car is going the fastest, it has all kinetic energy, but no potential energy. If energy losses to the environment (friction, heat, sound) are ignored, the amount of potential energy at the top of the hill equals the amount of kinetic energy at the bottom of the hill.

Mechanical Energy

Mechanical energy is the sum of the potential energy plus the kinetic energy in a system, minus energy lost to non-conservative forces. Often, the effects of non-conservative forces are small enough that they can be ignored. The total mechanical energy of a system is conserved or always the same. The amount of potential energy and the amount of kinetic energy can vary to add up to this total, but the total mechanical energy in the situation remains the same.

$$ME = PE + KE$$

Mechanical Energy = Potential Energy + Kinetic Energy

An illustration of a rollercoaster going down a hill demonstrates this point. At the top of the hill a label of $ME = PE$ describes the rollercoaster, halfway down the hill the label $ME = \frac{1}{2}PE + \frac{1}{2}KE$ describes the rollercoaster, and at the bottom of the hill, $ME = KE$ describes the rollercoaster.

Remember, energy can transfer or change forms, but it cannot be created or destroyed. This transfer can take place through waves (including light waves and sound waves), heat, impact, etc. The rollercoaster at the top of a hill has a measurable amount of potential energy, and when it rolls down the hill, it converts most of that energy into kinetic energy. There are still additional factors like friction and air resistance working on the rollercoaster and dissipating some of the energy, but energy transfers in every situation.

Simple Machines

The use of simple machines can help by requiring less force to perform a task with the same result. This is also referred to as **mechanical advantage**.

Trying to lift a child into the air to pick an apple from a tree would require less force if the child was placed on the end of a teeter-totter and the adult pushed the other end of the teeter-totter down, in order to elevate the child to the same height to pick the apple. In this instance, the teeter-totter is a lever and provides a mechanical advantage to make the job easier.

Interactions of Energy

Electricity

Electrostatics is the study of electric charges at rest. A charge comes from an atom having more or fewer electrons than protons. If an atom has more electrons than protons, it has a negative charge. If an atom has fewer electrons than protons, it has a positive charge. It is important to remember that opposite charges attract each other, while like charges repel each other. So, a negative attracts a positive, a negative repels a negative, and similarly, a positive repels a positive. Just as energy cannot be created or destroyed, neither can charge; charge is transferred. This transfer can be done through touch.

If a person wears socks and scuffs their feet across carpeting, they are transferring electrons to the carpeting through friction. If that person then goes to touch a light switch, they will receive a small shock, which is the electrons transferring from the switch to their hand. The person lost electrons to the carpet, which left them with a positive charge; therefore, the electrons from the switch attract to the person for the transfer. The shock is the electrons jumping from the switch to the person's finger.

Another method of charging an object is through induction. **Induction** is when a charged object is brought near, but not touched to, a neutral conducting object. The charged object will cause the electrons within the conductor to move. If the charged object is negative, the electrons will be induced away from the charged object and vice versa.

Yet another way to charge an object is through polarization. **Polarization** can be achieved by simply reconfiguring the electrons on an object. If a person were to rub a balloon on their hair, the balloon would then stick to a wall. This is because rubbing the balloon causes it to become negatively charged and when the balloon is held against a neutral wall, the negatively charged balloon repels all of the wall's electrons, causing a positively charged surface on the wall. This type of charge would be temporary, due to the massive size of the wall, and the charges would quickly redistribute.

Electric Current

Electrical current is the process by which electrons carry charge. In order to make the electrons move so that they can carry a charge, a change in voltage must be present. On a small scale, this is demonstrated through the electrons travelling from the light switch to a person's finger in the example where the person scuffed their socks on a carpet. The difference between the switch and the finger caused the electrons to move. On a larger and more sustained scale, this movement would need to be more controlled. This can be achieved through batteries/cells and generators. Batteries or cells have a chemical reaction that takes place inside, causing energy to be released and a charge to be able to move freely. Generators convert mechanical energy into electric energy.

If a wire is run from touching the end of a battery to the end of a light bulb, and then another is run from touching the base of the light bulb to the opposite end of the original battery, the light bulb will light up. This is due to a complete circuit being formed with the battery and the electrons being carried across the voltage drop (the two ends of the battery). The appearance of the light from the bulb is the visible heat caused by the friction of the electrons moving through the filament.

Electric Energy

Electric energy can be derived from a number of sources including coal, wind, sun, and nuclear reactions. Electricity has numerous applications, including being able to transfer into light, sound, heat, or magnetic forces.

Magnetism

Magnetic forces can occur naturally in certain types of materials. If two straight rods are made from iron, they will naturally have a negative end (pole) and a positive end (pole). These charged poles react just like any charged item: opposite charges attract and like charges repel. They will attract each other when set up positive to negative, but if one rod is turned around, the two rods will repel each other due to the alignment of negative to negative and positive to positive.

These types of forces can also be created and amplified by using an electric current.

The relationship between magnetic forces and electrical forces can be explored by sending an electric current through a stretch of wire, which creates an electromagnetic force around the wire from the charge of the current, as long as the flow of electricity is sustained. This magnetic force can also attract and repel other items with magnetic properties. Depending upon the strength of the current in the wire, a smaller or larger magnetic force can be generated around this wire. As soon as the current is cut off, the magnetic force also stops.

Magnetic Energy

Magnetic energy can be harnessed, or controlled, from natural sources or from a generated source (a wire carrying electric current). Magnetic forces are used in many modern applications, including the creation of super-speed transportation. Super-magnets are used in rail systems and supply a cleaner form of energy than coal or gasoline.

Sound and Light Energy

Light and sound travel in waves and both are forms of energy. The transmittance of a sound wave produced when plucking a guitar string sends vibrations at a specific frequency through the air, resulting in one's ear hearing a specific note or sets of notes that form a chord. If the same guitar is plugged into an electric amplifier, the strength of the wave is increased, producing what is perceived as a "louder" note. If a glass of water is set on the amplifier, the production of the sound wave can also be visually observed in the vibrations in the water. If the guitar were being plucked loudly enough and in great succession, the force created by the vibrations of the sound waves could even knock the glass off of the amplifier.

Waves can travel through different mediums. When they reach a different material (i.e., light traveling from air to water), they can bend around and through the new material. This is called **refraction**.

If one observes a straw in half a glass of water from above, the straw appears to be bent at the height of the water. The straw is still straight, but the observation of light passing from air to water (different materials) makes the straw seem as though it bends at the water line. This illusion occurs because the human eye can perceive the light travels differently through the two materials. The light might slow down in one material, or refract or reflect off of the material, causing differences in an object's appearance.

In another example, imagine a car driving straight along a paved road. If one or two of the tires hit the gravel along the side of the road, the entire car will pull in that direction, due to the tires in the gravel now traveling slower than the tires on the paved road. This is what happens when light travels from one medium to another: its path becomes warped, like the path of the car, rather than traveling in a straight line. This is why a straw appears to be bent when the light travels from water to air; the path is warped.

When waves encounter a barrier, like a closed door, parts of the wave may travel through tiny openings. Once a wave has moved through a narrow opening, the wave begins to spread out and may cause interference. This process is called **diffraction**.

Science as an Endeavor, Process, and Career

People of all cultures around the world utilize science in order to explore questions and find solutions to problems. The systematic process of designing, conducting, and analyzing experiments is universally known and respected. These processes are time-consuming and require specific knowledge and skills. Therefore, the pursuit of science is its own career path, with many smaller paths for each respective area of study (i.e., life sciences, chemical sciences, physical sciences). Of course, each of those paths splits into even more refined areas and requires much study and dedication. Men and women alike pursue scientific questions; some are driven by pure curiosity and others are compelled by finding a faster, or even a more economical way, of performing a task or producing an object.

Not all ideas, methods, or results are popular or accepted by society. Thus, the pursuit of science is often riddled with controversy. This has been an underlying theme since the early days of astronomical discovery. Copernicus was excommunicated from his religious establishment when he announced the belief that the sun, not the Earth, was the controlling body of the heavens known to humans at the time. Despite his having documented observations and calculations, those opposed to his theory could not be convinced. Copernicus experienced great ridicule and suffering due to his scientific research and assertions. In addition, other scientists have faced adverse scrutiny for their assertions including Galileo, Albert Einstein, and Stephen Hawking. In each case, logical thought, observations, and calculations have been used to demonstrate their ideas, yet opposition to their scientific beliefs still exists.

The possibilities for careers involving science range from conducting research, to the application of science and research (engineering), to academia (teaching). All of these avenues require intensive study and a thorough understanding of the respective branch of science and its components. An important factor of studying and applying science is being able to concisely and accurately communicate knowledge to other people. Many times this is done utilizing mathematics or even through demonstration. The necessity of communicating ideas, research, and results brings people from all nationalities together. This often lends to different cultures finding common ground for research and investigation, and opens lines of communication and cooperation.

Science as Inquiry

Scientific questions can be derived from a multitude of sources including observation, experience, or even just wondering how something is made or works. In order to answer these questions, experiments should be designed and conducted to try to achieve a solution. At the end of an experiment, there often is no clear solution and a new experiment must be designed to test the same question. If a sound, logical solution is reached through experimentation, then it must be repeatable, by the experimenter and any other person wishing to test this solution. This entire process is commonly referred to as the **scientific method**.

A question or situation exists, a **hypothesis** (or a well-educated guess) is formulated, an **experiment** is designed to test this guess, a prediction is made as to what the outcome might be based upon research, and a conclusion is formed (either the guess was correct or not). This simple method is repeated over and over, as much as necessary for each question, idea, or proposed investigation.

An experiment must be carefully designed to include concerns for safety, use of proper instrumentation for measurement, systematic methods of documentation or data collection, appropriate mathematics for analysis of data and for the interpretation to draw valid conclusions. These conclusions must be explainable and verifiable by an outside source.

The importance of having an independent party test a solution is one of the critical parts of scientific inquiry. This ensures an experiment is free from bias, truly repeatable, and documentable to multiple sources. Without this confirmation, people could make erroneous claims and cause disastrous results. There would be no order to the inquiry of science.

In scientific experimentation, safety, respect for living things, and the effect on an environment must be acknowledged and protected, as necessary. There exist universal rules for research in order to preserve these underlying tenets. Most researchers or facilities that demonstrate an adherence to these rules garner the most support from others in the scientific community when accepting ideas.

Research

Part of the process of scientific inquiry is researching a problem or question. Before an experiment can be designed, proper research should be conducted into the question. The initial question needs to be well formed and based in logical reasoning. A literature review should be conducted on existing material pertaining to the subject in question, and confirmation of any experimentation on the question that has been conducted prior should be made. If prior experimentation exists, what were the results obtained and were any conclusions drawn from those results? In addition, research should be done on all possible information regarding the initial question, the experiment, how to investigate the question, and what tools will be necessary to draw conclusions and explain any findings. Just as an experiment must be unbiased, so should any research regarding the experiment. All sources of information need to be proven reliable and accredited. For instance, a person's account of their opinion on a situation does not constitute as a valid source for research. Sources should be free of opinion or speculation.

During experimentation, research should be conducted with appropriate mechanisms for observation and measurement. Knowing the proper tools and units for accurately measuring a volume or a mass is a fundamental skill of research. Researchers also need to be held to standards of ethics and honesty. The independent repetition of an experiment helps to ensure this level of accountability. Often, the most reliable resources are those of accredited experimenters, universities, and other research laboratories. In order for such sources to publish information, they should demonstrate strict adherence to scientific methods, precise measurements for observations, and specific mathematical reporting.

It is often common for different scientists in the same place, or even separate countries, to be conducting experiments to test the same hypothesis. This does not always lead to a race to see who finishes first, but it can lead to cooperative research and shared accolades if the results prove successful. Awards for research, discoveries, and scientific application are often used by the scientific community to show appreciation for advancements in science.

Unifying Process of Science

Following the scientific method, and keeping to the standards of proper research and reporting, lends to easier communication of data and results. When information can be conveyed to multiple audiences in a manner of common understanding (i.e., mathematics), it increases the possibilities for the use of such information. Having other scientists understand an idea can also lead to further experimentation and discovery in that area. This leads to the further organization of information and a deeper understanding of our universe.

It is more systematic to group, sort, and organize information for commonalities in order to increase understanding. The organization of groups can also serve as a reference point when attempting to identify other members of that group. For instance, a newly discovered type of rock can be compared to known rocks and then better categorized as to its uses or properties, based upon how it appears and responds in experiments, when measured against known rocks. This occurs regularly when varying crystal rock structures are developed for use in super-cooled or super-conductive experiments because certain properties are more useful with regard to conduction and strength. In order to have knowledge and access to this type of variation of information, societies are formed and people from all over the world find ways to communicate and share in the scientific endeavor.

The communication of research can further questions and explorations across the world. This common goal of reaching new discoveries or uses for the application of science can bring people together. Oftentimes, the quest for scientific discovery is spawned by competition or the race to create something before another society or country. Examples of this include the race to explore space, the race for nuclear armaments, and the race to create and cure strains of deadly bacteria. In these situations, the urge to push scientific discovery ahead may not be for the most humanitarian motives; however, oftentimes these research prompts result in accidental discoveries that can solve other problems. The discoveries of vaccinations, stronger materials such as plastics, and cleaner forms of energy through superconducting crystals have all been accidental discoveries along the way of competitive scientific research. Whatever the motive for scientific discovery, it can be seen as a common thread across many nations with a potential to create unity through its demand for structure and organization.

Practice Quiz

1. How many daughter cells are formed from one parent cell during meiosis?
    a. One
    b. Two
    c. Three
    d. Four

2. What is the total mechanical energy of a system?
    a. The total potential energy
    b. The total kinetic energy
    c. Kinetic energy plus potential energy
    d. Kinetic energy minus potential energy

3. What does the Lewis dot structure of an element represent?
    a. The outer electron valence shell population
    b. The inner electron valence shell population
    c. The positioning of the element's protons
    d. The positioning of the element's neutrons

4. Which rock is formed from cooling magma underneath the Earth's surface?
    a. Extrusive sedimentary rocks
    b. Sedimentary rocks
    c. Igneous rocks
    d. Metamorphic rocks

5. Which of the following is most abundant in the Earth's atmosphere?
    a. Carbon dioxide
    b. Oxygen
    c. Nitrogen
    d. Water

See answers on the next page.

Answer Explanations

1. D: Meiosis has the same phases as mitosis, except that they occur twice—once in meiosis I and once in meiosis II. During meiosis I, the cell splits into two. Each cell contains two sets of chromosomes. Next, during meiosis II, the two intermediate daughter cells divide again, producing four total haploid cells that each contain one set of chromosomes.

2. C: In any system, the total mechanical energy is the sum of the potential energy and the kinetic energy. Either value could be zero, but it still must be included in the total. Choices *A* and *B* only give the total potential or kinetic energy, respectively. Choice *D* gives the difference between the kinetic and potential energy.

3. A: A Lewis Dot structure shows the alignment of the valence (outer) shell electrons and how readily they can pair or bond with the valence shell electrons of other atoms to form a compound. Choice *B* is incorrect because the inner shell does not help us understand how likely an atom is to bond with another atom. The positioning of protons and neutrons concerns the nucleus of the atom, which again would not relate to the likelihood of bonding.

4. C: Igneous rocks are formed from the cooling of magma, both on and below the Earth's surface, which are classified as extrusive and intrusive, respectively. Sedimentary rocks are formed from deposition and cementation on the surface, and metamorphic rocks are formed from the transformation of sedimentary or igneous rocks through heat and pressure.

5. C: Nitrogen is the most abundant element in the atmosphere at 78%. Carbon dioxide and water don't make up a large percentage. Oxygen makes up only 21% of the atmosphere.

Practice Test #1

Reading and Language Arts

1. What area of study involves mechanics, usage, and sentence formation?
    a. Word analysis
    b. Spelling conventions
    c. Morphemes
    d. Phonics

2. How do the majority of high-frequency sight words differ from decodable words?
    a. They do not rhyme.
    b. They do not follow the alphabetic principle.
    c. They do not contain onsets.
    d. They contain rimes.

3. Reading fluency involves what key areas?
    a. Accuracy, rate, and prosody
    b. Accuracy, rate, and consistency
    c. Prosody, accuracy, and clarity
    d. Rate, prosody, and comprehension

4. Which of the following is a pre-reading strategy used to support comprehension?
    a. Skimming the text for content
    b. Summarizing the text effectively
    c. Organizing the main ideas and supporting details
    d. Clarifying unfamiliar ideas in the text

5. Which mode of writing aims to inform the reader objectively about a particular subject or idea and typically contains definitions, instructions, or facts within its subject matter?
    a. Argumentative
    b. Informative
    c. Narrative
    d. Descriptive

6. Which sentence is written in second-person point of view?
    a. I went down the road, hoping to catch a glimpse of his retreating figure.
    b. You, my dear reader, can understand loss and grief, too.
    c. He left her standing there, alone to face the world.
    d. There's nothing wrong with Margaret.

7. Which of the following parts of a book could help a reader to find a specific word or concept they are looking for?
    a. Bibliography
    b. Appendix
    c. Preface
    d. Glossary

Practice Test #1

8. Which of the following describes the organizational pattern of chronological or sequence order?
   a. Text organized by describing a dilemma and a possible solution
   b. Text organized by observing the consequences of an action
   c. Text organized by the timing of events or actions
   d. Text organized by analyzing the relative placement of an object or event

9. A student can say a few letters, can name animals and make animal sounds, but holds a book upside down. What area of reading is the student struggling in?
   a. Phonemic awareness
   b. Phonological awareness
   c. Print awareness
   d. Phoneme-grapheme correspondence

10. Which option best exemplifies an author's use of alliteration and personification?
    a. Her mood hung about her like a weary cape, very dull from wear.
    b. It shuddered, swayed, shook, and screamed its way into dust under hot flames.
    c. Driving past the still, silent house always sent a shiver down his spine.
    d. At its shoreline, visitors swore they heard the siren call of the cliffs above.

11. A teacher gives a group of students the word "can" and asks them to come up with rhyming words. The students respond with "ban", "tan" and "fan". Which of the following methods did they MOST LIKELY use to come up with their answer?
    a. Blending
    b. Substitution
    c. Deletion
    d. Decoding

12. In the word "tap", the "t" is considered the:
    a. Onset
    b. Rime
    c. Blend
    d. Segment

13. Which phrase best completes the definition of a *memoir*?
    a. A historical account of a person's life written by one who has intimate knowledge of the person's life
    b. A non-fictional account of a person's entire life
    c. A fictional account about a famous person
    d. A nonfictional account about a famous person without factual reference

14. What is a phoneme?
    a. A word
    b. A relationship between a letter and a sound
    c. An individual sound
    d. A consonant

15. Which word serves as the best example of the poetic device onomatopoeia?
    a. Crackle
    b. Eat
    c. Provide
    d. Walking

16. Which of the following is NOT true of word walls?
    a. They promote strategic spelling, vocabulary development, common letter combinations, and common morphological units.
    b. They help students sort words they know, want to know, and have learned.
    c. They are useful during the phonetic stage of spelling development.
    d. They group words that share common consonant-vowel patterns or letter clusters.

17. Every week, Cindy volunteers time at the local shelter. She always has a smile on her face, and she always talks to others with kindness and patience. Considering that her current job is very taxing, that two of her three children are still in diapers, and that her husband, Steve, the old curmudgeon, is the opposite of her in temperament, it's amazing that no one has ever seen her angry.

Based on the context in this passage, the best substitute for *curmudgeon* would be:
    a. Stingy
    b. Surly
    c. Scared
    d. Shy

The next question is based on the following passage.

> Annabelle Rice started having trouble sleeping. Her biological clock was suddenly amiss, and she began to lead a nocturnal schedule. She thought her insomnia was due to spending nights writing a horror story, but then she realized that even the idea of going outside into the bright world scared her to bits. She concluded she was now suffering from heliophobia.

18. Which of the following most accurately describes the meaning of the underlined word in the sentence above?
    a. Fear of dreams
    b. Fear of sunlight
    c. Fear of strangers
    d. Anxiety spectrum disorder

19. What does a Developmental Reading Assessment mainly assess students for?
    a. Reading comprehension
    b. Reading speed
    c. Phoneme-grapheme correspondence
    d. Contextual strategies

20. Which of the following is a primary source?
    a. A critic's summary and review of a new book on the life of Abraham Lincoln
    b. A peer-reviewed scientific journal's table of contents
    c. A personal journal from a commander during World War II
    d. An encyclopedia entry discussing the Industrial Revolution

21. Which of the following involves using the root word to understand the meaning of a larger word?
    a. Word maps
    b. Prosody
    c. Structural analysis
    d. Metacognition

22. What are the three interconnected indicators of reading fluency?
    a. Phonetics, word morphology, and listening comprehension
    b. Accuracy, rate, and prosody
    c. Syntax, semantics, and vocabulary
    d. Word exposure, phonetics, and decodable skills

23. Which of the following methods BEST supports fluent reading at the passage level?
    a. Timed reading exercises
    b. Word walls
    c. Phonemic awareness
    d. Sight word practice

The next two questions are based on the timeline of the life of Alexander Graham Bell.

24. Which of the following is the event that occurred fourth on the timeline?
    a. Helped found National Geographic Society
    b. Developed a metal detector
    c. Moved to Canada
    d. Started a school for the deaf

25. Which one of the following events occurred most recently?
    a. Bell's invention of the telephone
    b. Bell's founding of the school
    c. Bell's birth
    d. Bell's move to Canada

26. When students identify the phonemes in spoken words, they are practicing which of the following?
    a. Sound blending
    b. Substitution
    c. Rhyming
    d. Segmentation

27. Phonological awareness is best assessed through which of the following?
    a. Identification of rimes or onsets within words
    b. Identification of letter-sound correspondences
    c. Comprehension of an audio book
    d. Writing samples

28. Print awareness includes all EXCEPT which of the following concepts?
    a. The differentiation of uppercase and lowercase letters
    b. The identification of word boundaries
    c. The proper tracking of words
    d. The spelling of sight words

29. Sharon is a first-grade teacher who assigned her students a rhyming project to come up with three words that rhyme with "cat". One of her students returned the project with the words "dog", "hi", and "to". The teacher realizes that the student is struggling with which of the following skills:
    a. Phonological awareness
    b. Phoneme deletion
    c. Phoneme blending
    d. Directionality

30. Which of the following sentences has an error in capitalization?
    a. The East Coast has experienced very unpredictable weather this year.
    b. My Uncle owns a home in Florida, where he lives in the winter.
    c. I am taking English Composition II on campus this fall.
    d. There are several nice beaches we can visit on our trip to the Jersey Shore this summer.

31. Which of the following sentences uses correct punctuation?
    a. Carole is not currently working; her focus is on her children at the moment.
    b. Carole is not currently working and her focus is on her children at the moment.
    c. Carole is not currently working, her focus is on her children at the moment.
    d. Carole is not currently working her focus is on her children at the moment.

32. Which of these examples is a compound sentence?
    a. Alex and Shane spent the morning coloring and later took a walk down to the park.
    b. After coloring all morning, Alex and Shane spent the afternoon at the park.
    c. Alex and Shane spent the morning coloring, and then they took a walk down to the park.
    d. After coloring all morning and spending part of the day at the park, Alex and Shane took a nap.

33. Which of these examples shows INCORRECT use of subject-verb agreement?
    a. Neither of the cars are parked on the street.
    b. Both of my kids are going to camp this summer.
    c. Any of your friends are welcome to join us on the trip in November.
    d. Each of the clothing options is appropriate for the job interview.

34. Which example shows correct comma usage for dates?
    a. The due date for the final paper in the course is Monday, May 16, 2016.
    b. The due date for the final paper in the course is Monday, May 16 2016.
    c. The due date for the final project in the course is Monday, May, 16, 2016.
    d. The due date for the final project in the course is Monday May 16, 2016.

35. Which of the following passages best displays clarity, fluency, and parallelism?
    a. Ernest Hemingway is probably the most noteworthy of expatriate authors. Hemingway's concise writing style, void of emotion and stream of consciousness, had a lasting impact, one which resonates to this very day. In Hemingway's novels, much like in American cinema, the hero acts without thinking, is living in the moment, and is repressing physical and emotional pain.
    b. Ernest Hemingway is probably the most noteworthy of expatriate authors since his concise writing style is void of emotion and stream of consciousness and has had a lasting impact on Americans which has resonated to this very day, and Hemingway's novels are much like in American cinema. The hero acts. He doesn't think. He lives in the moment. He represses physical and emotional pain.
    c. Ernest Hemingway is probably the most noteworthy of authors. His concise writing style, void of emotion and consciousness, had a lasting impact, one which resonates to this very day. In Hemingway's novels, much like in American cinema, the hero acts without thinking, lives in the moment, and represses physical and emotional pain.
    d. Ernest Hemingway is probably the most noteworthy of expatriate authors. His concise writing style, void of emotion and stream of consciousness, had a lasting impact, one which resonates to this very day. In Hemingway's novels, much like in American cinema, the hero acts without thinking, lives in the moment, and represses physical and emotional pain.

36. The teacher writes the letters "s" "t" "a" "k" and "e" on the board and asks students to chorus the word, to which they correctly answer "stake". Then, the teacher asks the students to chorus "stake" again, but without the /s/ sound, but many students have trouble and mispronounce the new word. The teacher notes that the class is struggling with which of the following concepts?
    a. Phoneme substitution
    b. Phoneme deletion
    c. Phoneme-grapheme correspondence
    d. Blending

37. Based on the words *transfer*, *transact*, *translation*, and *transport*, what is the meaning of the prefix *trans*?
    a. Separation
    b. All or everywhere
    c. Forward
    d. Across, beyond, or over

38. An antibiotic is prescribed to eliminate bacterial infections; someone who is antisocial ignores society and laws. Based on these two definitions, the Latin prefix *anti-* would most likely mean:
    a. Reduce
    b. Revolt
    c. Oppose
    d. Without

39. *Conform* means to adjust one's behavior to better fit in with social norms. *Inform* means to communicate new knowledge to another. Based on these definitions, the Latin suffix *-form* most likely means:
    a. Match
    b. Relay
    c. Negate
    d. Shape

40. Ms. Brown has just finished a lesson introducing the lowercase letter "b" to her students. Which of the following is the best letter to introduce in her next lesson?
    a. Lowercase "d"
    b. Lowercase "v"
    c. Lowercase "p"
    d. Lowercase "s"

41. A student can follow the directions "sit down, get out a pencil and two pieces of paper". However, when asked a question, she doesn't respond. Which type of language skills does the student have?
    a. Expressive
    b. Basic
    c. Receptive
    d. Auditory

42. What is the method called that teachers use before and after reading to improve critical thinking and comprehension?
    a. Self-monitoring comprehension
    b. KWL charts
    c. Metacognitive skills
    d. Directed reading-thinking activities

The next question is based on the following passage.

> A famous children's author recently published a historical fiction novel under a pseudonym; however, it did not sell as many copies as her children's books. In her earlier years, she had majored in history and earned a graduate degree in Antebellum American History, which is the time frame of her new novel. Critics praised this newest work far more than the children's series that made her famous. In fact, her new novel was nominated for the prestigious Albert J. Beveridge Award but still isn't selling like her children's books, which fly off the shelves because of her name alone.

43. Which one of the following statements might be accurately inferred based on the above passage?
    a. The famous children's author produced an inferior book under her pseudonym.
    b. The famous children's author is the foremost expert on Antebellum America.
    c. The famous children's author did not receive the bump in publicity for her historical novel that it would have received if it were written under her given name.
    d. People generally prefer to read children's series over historical fiction.

44. A student spells *eagle* as *EGL*. This student is performing at which stage of spelling?
    a. Conventional
    b. Phonetic
    c. Semi phonetic
    d. Transitional

45. What is the most valuable strategy for helping children understand new words?
    a. Phonics instruction
    b. Pre-teaching
    c. Self-monitoring
    d. Context clues

46. Context clues assist vocabulary development by providing:
    a. A knowledge of roots, prefixes, and suffixes that are used to determine the meaning of a word
    b. Information within the sentence that surrounds an unknown word and is used to determine the word's meaning
    c. Content learned in previous grades that serves as a bridge to the new term
    d. Background knowledge to fill in a missing word within a sentence

47. Samantha is in second grade and struggles with fluency. Which of the following strategies is likely to be most effective in improving Samantha's reading fluency?
    a. The teacher should encourage Samantha to stop and sound out the words she is unfamiliar with while reading.
    b. The teacher should have Samantha read multiple grade-level passages one time each.
    c. The teacher should review the different types of genres with Samantha before she begins reading.
    d. The teacher should have Samantha read one grade-level passage multiple times.

48. The assassination of Archduke Franz Ferdinand of Austria is often ascribed as the cause of World War I. However, the assassination merely lit the fuse in a combustible situation since many of the world powers were in complicated and convoluted military alliances. For example, England, France, and Russia entered into a mutual defense treaty seven years prior to World War I. Even without Franz Ferdinand's assassination
_____

Which of the following most logically completes the passage?
    a. a war between the world powers was extremely likely.
    b. World War I never would have happened.
    c. England, France, and Russia would have started the war.
    d. Austria would have started the war.

The next question is based on the following passage.

> In 2015, 28 countries, including Estonia, Portugal, Slovenia, and Latvia, scored significantly higher than the United States on standardized high school math tests. In the 1960s, the United States consistently ranked first in the world. Today, the United States spends more than $800 billion on education, which exceeds the next highest country by more than $600 billion. The United States also leads the world in spending per school-aged child by an enormous margin.

49. If these statements above are factual, which of the following statements must be correct?
    a. Outspending other countries on education has benefits beyond standardized math tests.
    b. The United States' education system is corrupt and broken.
    c. The standardized math tests are not representative of American academic prowess.
    d. Spending more money does not guarantee success on standardized math tests.

50. Philadelphia is home to some excellent walking tours where visitors can learn more about the culture and rich history of the city of brotherly love.

    What are the adjectives in the preceding sentence?

    a. Philadelphia, tours, visitors, culture, history, city, love
    b. Excellent, walking, rich, brotherly
    c. Is, can, learn
    d. To, about, of

51. The realtor showed _____ and _____ a house on Wednesday afternoon.

Which of the following pronoun pairs should be used in the blanks above?
    a. she, I
    b. she, me
    c. me, her
    d. her, me

52. Which of the following examples uses correct punctuation?
    a. Recommended supplies for the hunting trip include the following: rain gear, a large backpack, hiking boots, a flashlight, and non-perishable foods.
    b. I left the store, because I forgot my wallet.
    c. As soon as the team checked into the hotel; they met in the lobby for a group photo.
    d. None of the furniture came in on time: so they weren't able to move into the new apartment.

53. Which of the following sentences shows correct word usage?
    a. Your going to have to put you're jacket over their.
    b. You're going to have to put your jacket over there.
    c. Your going to have to put you're jacket over they're.
    d. You're going to have to put your jacket over their.

54. A teacher notices that when students are talking to each other between classes, they are using their own unique vocabulary words and expressions to talk about their daily lives. When the teacher hears these non-standard words that are specific to one age or cultural group, what type of language is she listening to?
    a. Slang
    b. Jargon
    c. Dialect
    d. Vernacular

55. Structural analysis would be the most appropriate strategy in determining the meaning of which of the following words?
    a. Extra
    b. Improbable
    c. Likely
    d. Wonder

56. Which of the following is true of using citations in a research paper?
    a. If a source is cited in the bibliography, it is not necessary to cite it in the text as well.
    b. In-text citations differ in format from bibliographic citations.
    c. Students should learn one standard method of citing sources.
    d. Books and articles need to be cited, but websites and multimedia sources do not.

57. Which of the following is true regarding the integration of source material to maintain the flow of ideas in a paper?
    a. There should be at least one quotation in every paragraph.
    b. If a source is paraphrased instead of being directly quoted, it is not necessary to include a citation.
    c. An author's full name must be used in every signal phrase.
    d. In-text citations should be used to support the paper's argument without overwhelming the student's writing.

Questions 58-62 are based on the following passage:

The Middle Ages were a time of great superstition and theological debate. Many beliefs were developed and practiced, while some died out or were listed as heresy. Boethianism is a Medieval theological philosophy that attributes sin to gratification and righteousness with virtue and God's providence. Boethianism holds that sin, greed, and corruption are means to attain temporary pleasure, but they inherently harm the person's soul as well as other human beings.

In *The Canterbury Tales,* we observe more instances of bad actions punished than goodness being rewarded. This would appear to be some reflection of Boethianism. In the "Pardoner's Tale," all three thieves wind up dead, which is a result of their desire for wealth. Each wrongdoer pays with their life, and they are unable to enjoy the wealth they worked to steal. Within his tales, Chaucer gives reprieve to people undergoing struggle, but he also interweaves stories of contemptible individuals being cosmically punished for their wickedness. The thieves idolize physical wealth, which leads to their downfall. This same theme and ideological principle of Boethianism is repeated in the "Friar's Tale," in which the summoner character attempts to gain further wealth by partnering with a demon. The summoner's refusal to repent for his avarice and corruption leads to the demon dragging his soul to Hell. Again, we see the theme of the individual who puts faith and morality aside in favor for a physical prize. The result, of course, is that the summoner loses everything.

The examples of the righteous being rewarded tend to appear in a spiritual context within the *Canterbury Tales*. However, there are a few instances where we see goodness resulting in physical reward. In the "Prioress's Tale," we see corporal punishment for barbarism and a reward for goodness. The Jews are punished for their murder of the child, giving a sense of law and order (though racist) to the plot. While the boy does die, he is granted a lasting reward by being able to sing even after his death, a miracle that marks that the murdered youth led a pure life. Here, the miracle represents eternal favor with God.

Again, we see the theological philosophy of Boethianism in Chaucer's *The Canterbury Tales* through acts of sin and righteousness and the consequences that follow. When pleasures of the world are sought instead of God's favor, we see characters being punished in tragic ways. However, the absence of worldly lust has its own set of consequences for the characters seeking to obtain God's favor.

58. What would be a potential reward for living a good life, as described in Boethianism?
    a. A long life sustained by the good deeds one has done over a lifetime
    b. Wealth and fertility for oneself and the extension of one's family line
    c. Vengeance for those who have been persecuted by others who have a capacity for committing wrongdoing
    d. God's divine favor for one's righteousness

59. What might be the main reason why the author chose to discuss Boethianism through examining *The Canterbury Tales*?
    a. *The Canterbury Tales* is a well-known text.
    b. *The Canterbury Tales* is the only known fictional text that contains use of Boethianism.
    c. *The Canterbury Tales* presents a manuscript written in the medieval period that can help illustrate Boethianism through stories and show how people of the time might have responded to the idea.
    d. Within each individual tale in *The Canterbury Tales*, the reader can read about different levels of Boethianism and how each level leads to greater enlightenment.

60. What "ideological principle" is the author referring to in the middle of the second paragraph when talking about the "Friar's Tale"?
    a. The principle that the act of ravaging another's possessions is the same as ravaging one's soul
    b. The principle that thieves who idolize physical wealth will be punished in an earthly sense as well as eternally
    c. The principle that fraternization with a demon will result in one losing everything, including their life
    d. The principle that a desire for material goods leads to moral malfeasance punishable by a higher being

61. Which of the following words, if substituted for the word *avarice* in paragraph two, would LEAST change the meaning of the sentence?
    a. Perniciousness
    b. Pithiness
    c. Covetousness
    d. Precariousness

62. Based on the passage, what view does Boethianism take on desire?
    a. Desire does not exist in the context of Boethianism.
    b. Desire is a virtue and should be welcomed.
    c. Having desire is evidence of demonic possession.
    d. Desire for pleasure can lead toward sin.

Questions 63-68 are based upon the following passage:

Four score and seven years ago our fathers brought forth on this continent, a new nation, conceived in Liberty, and dedicated to the proposition that all men are created equal.

Now we are engaged in a great civil war, testing whether that nation, or any nation so conceived and so dedicated, can long endure. We are met on a great battle-field of that war. We have come to dedicate a portion of that field, as a final resting place for those who here gave their lives that that nation might live. It is altogether fitting and proper that we should do this.

But, in a larger sense, we can not dedicate—we can not consecrate—we can not hallow—this ground. The brave men, living and dead, who struggled here, have consecrated it, far above our poor power to add or detract. The world will little note, nor long remember what we say here, but it can never forget what they did here. It is for us the living, rather, to be dedicated here to the unfinished work which they who fought here have thus far so nobly advanced. It is rather for us to be here dedicated to the great task remaining before us—that from these honored dead we take increased devotion to that cause for which they gave the last full measure of devotion—that we here highly resolve that these dead shall not have died in vain—that this nation, under God, shall have a new birth of freedom—and that government of the people, by the people, for the people, shall not perish from the earth.

Excerpt from Abraham Lincoln's Address Delivered at the Dedication of the Cemetery at Gettysburg, November 19, 1863

63. The best description for the phrase *four score and seven years ago* is which of the following?
    a. A unit of measurement
    b. A period of time
    c. A literary movement
    d. A statement of political reform

Practice Test #1

64. What is the setting of this text?
    a. A battleship off of the coast of France
    b. A desert plain on the Sahara Desert
    c. A battlefield in North America
    d. The residence of Abraham Lincoln

65. Which war is Abraham Lincoln referring to in the following passage?

    Now we are engaged in a great civil war, testing whether that nation, or any nation so conceived and so dedicated, can long endure.

    a. World War I
    b. The War of the Spanish Succession
    c. World War II
    d. The American Civil War

66. What message is the speaker trying to convey through this address?
    a. The audience should perpetuate the ideals of freedom that the soldiers died fighting for.
    b. The audience should honor the dead by establishing an annual memorial service.
    c. The audience should form a militia that would overturn the current political structure.
    d. The audience should forget the lives that were lost and discredit the soldiers.

67. Which rhetorical device is being used in the following passage?

    ...we here highly resolve that these dead shall not have died in vain—that this nation, under God, shall have a new birth of freedom—and that government of the people, by the people, for the people, shall not perish from the earth.

    a. Antimetabole
    b. Antiphrasis
    c. Anaphora
    d. Epiphora

68. What is the effect of Lincoln's statement in the following passage?

    But, in a larger sense, we can not dedicate—we can not consecrate—we can not hallow—this ground. The brave men, living and dead, who struggled here, have consecrated it, far above our poor power to add or detract.

    a. His comparison emphasizes the great sacrifice of the soldiers who fought in the war.
    b. His comparison serves as a reminder of the inadequacies of his audience.
    c. His comparison serves as a catalyst for guilt and shame among audience members.
    d. His comparison suggests that the dedication ceremony was inappropriate.

69. Julia Robinson, an avid photographer in her spare time, was able to capture stunning shots of the local wildlife on her last business trip to Australia.

   Which of the following is an adjective in the preceding sentence?

   a. Time
   b. Capture
   c. Avid
   d. Photographer

70. When it gets warm in the spring, _____ and _____ like to go fishing at Cobbs Creek.

   Which of the following word pairs should be used in the blanks above?

   a. me, him
   b. he, I
   c. him, I
   d. he, me

71. At last night's company function, in honor of Mr. Robertson's retirement, several employees spoke kindly about his career achievements.

   In the preceding sentence, what part of speech is the word *function*?

   a. Adjective
   b. Adverb
   c. Verb
   d. Noun

72. Which of the examples uses the correct plural form?
   a. Tomatos
   b. Analysis
   c. Cacti
   d. Criterion

73. The identification of morphemes within words occurs during the instruction of what?
   a. Structural analysis
   b. Syllabic analysis
   c. Phonics
   d. The alphabetic principle

74. In which of the following sentences does the word *part* function as an adjective?
   a. The part Brian was asked to play required many hours of research.
   b. She parts ways with the woodsman at the end of the book.
   c. The entire team played a part in the success of the project.
   d. Ronaldo is part Irish on his mother's side of the family.

Practice Test #1

75. Which of the following is the complete subject of the following sentence? All of Shannon's family and friends helped her to celebrate her 50th birthday at Café Sorrento.
    a. Family and friends
    b. All
    c. All of Shannon's family and friends
    d. Shannon's family and friends

76. Which of the following examples correctly uses quotation marks?
    a. "Where the Red Fern Grows" was one of my favorite novels as a child.
    b. Though he is famous for his roles in films like "The Great Gatsby" and "Titanic," Leonardo DiCaprio never won an Oscar until 2016 for his work in "The Revenant".
    c. Sylvia Plath's poem "Daddy" will be the subject of this week's group discussion.
    d. "The New York Times" reported that many fans are disappointed in some of the trades made by the Yankees this off-season.

77. Which of the following sentences shows correct word usage?
    a. It's often been said that work is better then rest.
    b. Its often been said that work is better then rest.
    c. It's often been said that work is better than rest.
    d. Its often been said that work is better than rest.

78. Syntax is best described as what?
    a. The arrangement of words in sentences
    b. The study of language meaning
    c. The study of grammar and language structure
    d. The proper formatting of a written text

79. Which of the following examples is a compound sentence?
    a. Shawn and Jerome played soccer in the backyard for two hours.
    b. Marissa last saw and spoke to Elena this morning.
    c. The baby was sick, so I decided to stay home from work.
    d. Denise, Kurt, and Eric went for a run after dinner.

80. Which of the following sentences uses correct subject-verb agreement?
    a. There is two constellations that can be seen from the back of the house.
    b. At least four of the sheep needs to be sheared before the end of summer.
    c. Lots of people were auditioning for the singing competition on Saturday.
    d. Everyone in the group have completed the assignment on time.

Mathematics

1. Which of the following numbers has the greatest value?
    a. 1.43785
    b. 1.07548
    c. 1.43592
    d. 0.89409

2. The value of 6 × 12 is the same as:
    a. 2 × 4 × 4 × 2
    b. 7 × 4 × 3
    c. 6 × 6 × 3
    d. 3 × 3 × 4 × 2

3. Which of the following values is the largest?
    a. 0.45
    b. 0.096
    c. 0.3
    d. 0.313

4. What is the value of b in this equation?

$$5b - 4 = 2b + 17$$

    a. 13
    b. 24
    c. 7
    d. 21

5. In 2015, it was estimated that there were 7,350,000,000 people living on Earth. Express this value in scientific notation.
    a. 7.35×10^7
    b. 7.35×10^9
    c. 73.5×10^8
    d. 73.5×10^9

6. Express the following in decimal form:

$$\frac{3}{5} \times \frac{7}{10} \div \frac{1}{2}$$

    a. 0.042
    b. 84%
    c. 0.84
    d. 0.42

7. What is the product of two irrational numbers?
    a. Irrational
    b. Rational
    c. Irrational or rational
    d. Complex and imaginary

8. The number −4 can be classified as which of the following?
    a. Real, rational, integer, whole, natural
    b. Real, rational, integer, natural
    c. Real, rational, integer
    d. Real, irrational

Practice Test #1

9. 20 is 40% of what number?
   a. 50
   b. 8
   c. 200
   d. 5,000

10. What is the product of the following expressions?

$$(4x - 8)(5x^2 + x + 6)$$

   a. $20x^3 - 36x^2 + 16x - 48$
   b. $6x^3 - 41x^2 + 12x + 15$
   c. $20x^3 + 11x^2 - 37x - 12$
   d. $2x^3 - 11x^2 - 32x + 20$

11. What is the solution for the following equation?

$$\frac{x^2 + x - 30}{x - 5} = 11$$

   a. $x = -6$
   b. There is no solution.
   c. $x = 16$
   d. $x = 5$

12. Simplify $(1.2 \times 10^{12}) \div (3.0 \times 10^8)$ and write the result in scientific notation.
   a. 0.4×10^4
   b. 4.0×10^4
   c. 4.0×10^3
   d. 3.6×10^{20}

13. Give a numerical expression for the following: "Six less than three times the sum of twice a number and one."
   a. $2x + 1 - 6$
   b. $3x + 1 - 6$
   c. $3(x + 1) - 6$
   d. $3(2x + 1) - 6$

14. What is $4 \times 7 + (25 - 21)^2 \div 2$?
   a. 512
   b. 36
   c. 60.5
   d. 22

15. What value of x would solve the following equation?

$$9x + x - 7 = 16 + 2x$$

   a. $x = -4$
   b. $x = 3$
   c. $x = \frac{9}{8}$
   d. $x = \frac{23}{8}$

16. Arrange the following numbers from least to greatest value:

$$0.85, \frac{4}{5}, \frac{2}{3}, \frac{91}{100}$$

a. $0.85, \frac{4}{5}, \frac{2}{3}, \frac{91}{100}$

b. $\frac{4}{5}, 0.85, \frac{91}{100}, \frac{2}{3}$

c. $\frac{2}{3}, \frac{4}{5}, 0.85, \frac{91}{100}$

d. $0.85, \frac{91}{100}, \frac{4}{5}, \frac{2}{3}$

17. Keith's bakery had 252 customers go through its doors last week. This week, that number increased to 378. Express this increase as a percentage.
    a. 26%
    b. 50%
    c. 35%
    d. 12%

18. Simplify the following fraction:

$$\frac{\left(\frac{5}{7}\right)}{\left(\frac{9}{11}\right)}$$

a. $\frac{55}{63}$

b. $\frac{7}{1,000}$

c. $\frac{13}{15}$

d. $\frac{5}{11}$

19. Which of the following is the correct order of operations that could be used on a difficult math problem that contained grouping symbols?
    a. Parentheses, Exponents, Multiplication & Division, Addition & Subtraction
    b. Exponents, Parentheses, Multiplication & Division, Addition & Subtraction
    c. Parentheses, Exponents, Addition & Multiplication, Division & Subtraction
    d. Parentheses, Exponents, Division & Addition, Subtraction & Multiplication

Practice Test #1

20. This chart indicates how many sales of CDs, vinyl records, and MP3 downloads occurred over the last year. Approximately what percentage of the total sales was from CDs?

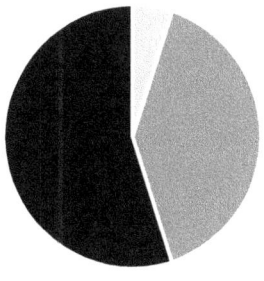

Total sales of vinyl records, CDs, and MP3 downloads (in millions)

Vinyl ▨ CD ■ MP3

   a. 55%
   b. 25%
   c. 40%
   d. 5%

21. Express $\frac{54}{15}$ as a mixed number, reduced to lowest terms.
   a. $3\frac{3}{5}$
   b. $3\frac{1}{15}$
   c. $3\frac{3}{54}$
   d. $3\frac{1}{54}$

22. Express $8\frac{3}{7}$ as an improper fraction.
   a. $\frac{11}{7}$
   b. $\frac{21}{8}$
   c. $\frac{5}{3}$
   d. $\frac{59}{7}$

23. $52.3 \times 10^{-3} =$
   a. 0.00523
   b. 0.0523
   c. 0.523
   d. 523

24. A teacher cuts a pie into 6 equal pieces and takes one away. What topic would she be introducing to the class by using such a visual?
    a. Decimals
    b. Addition
    c. Fractions
    d. Measurement

25. The total perimeter of a rectangle is 36 cm. If the length is 12 cm, what is the width?
    a. 3 cm
    b. 12 cm
    c. 6 cm
    d. 8 cm

26. What is the probability of rolling a 6 at least once in two rolls of a die?
    a. $\frac{1}{3}$
    b. $\frac{1}{36}$
    c. $\frac{1}{6}$
    d. $\frac{11}{36}$

27. If the point $(-3, -4)$ is reflected over the x-axis, what new point does it make?
    a. $(-3, -4)$
    b. $(3, -4)$
    c. $(3, 4)$
    d. $(-3, 4)$

28. The graph shows the position of a car over a 10-second time interval. Which of the following is the correct interpretation of the graph for the interval 1 to 3 seconds?

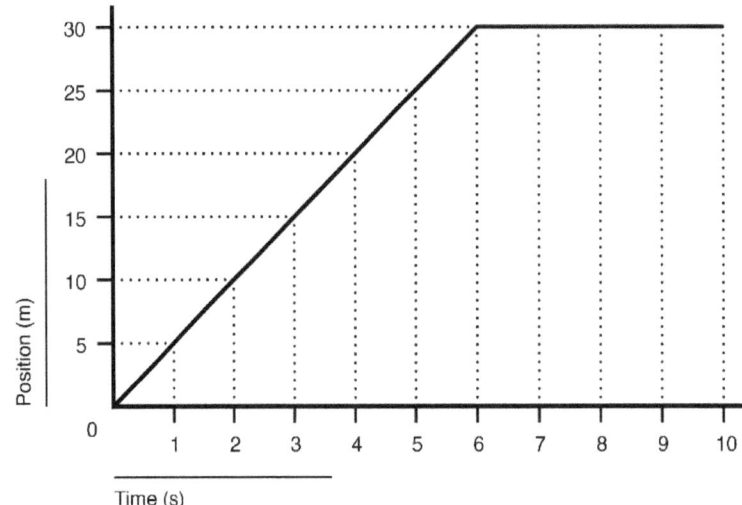

a. The car remains in the same position.
b. The car is traveling at a speed of 5 m/s.
c. The car is traveling up a hill.
d. The car is traveling at 5 mph.

29. An equilateral triangle has a perimeter of 18 feet. The sides of a square have the same length as the triangle's sides. What is the area of the square?
    a. 6 square feet
    b. 36 square feet
    c. 256 square feet
    d. 1,000 square feet

30. A cube has sides that are 7 inches long. What is the cube's volume?
    a. 49 in^3
    b. 343 in^3
    c. 294 in^3
    d. 28 in^3

31. A right triangle has a hypotenuse of 10 inches, and one leg is 8 inches. How long is the other leg?
    a. 6 in
    b. 18 in
    c. 80 in
    d. 13 in

32. Five students take a test. The scores of the first four students are 80, 85, 75, and 60. If the median score is 80, which of the following could NOT be the score of the fifth student?
    a. 60
    b. 80
    c. 85
    d. 100

33. If Sarah reads at an average rate of 21 pages in 4 nights, how long will it take her to read 140 pages?
    a. 6 nights
    b. 26 nights
    c. 8 nights
    d. 27 nights

34. Johnny earns $2,334.50 from his job each month. He pays $1,437 for monthly expenses and saves the rest. Johnny is planning a vacation in 3 months that he estimates will cost $1,750 total. How much will Johnny have left over from 3 months of saving once he pays for his vacation?
    a. $948.50
    b. $584.50
    c. $852.50
    d. $942.50

35. Kimberley earns $10 an hour babysitting, and after 10 p.m., she earns $12 an hour. The time she works is rounded to the nearest hour for pay purposes. On her last job, she worked from 5:30 p.m. to 11:00 p.m. In total, how much did Kimberley earn on her last job?
   a. $45
   b. $57
   c. $62
   d. $42

36. Which of the following is the best description of the relationship between x and y?

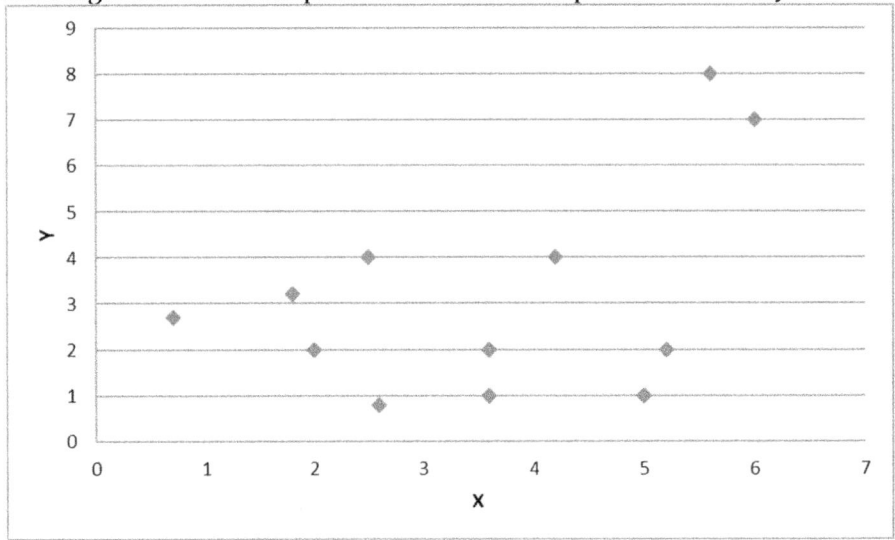

   a. The data has normal distribution.
   b. x and y have a negative relationship.
   c. x and y have no apparent relationship.
   d. x and y have a positive relationship.

37. What type of function is modeled by the values in the following table?

x	$f(x)$
1	2
2	4
3	8
4	16
5	32

   a. Linear
   b. Exponential
   c. Quadratic
   d. Cubic

38. Which of the following is a factor of both $x^2 + 4x + 4$ and $x^2 - x - 6$?
    a. $x - 3$
    b. $x + 2$
    c. $x - 2$
    d. $x + 3$

39. If $4x - 3 = 5$, what is the value of x?
    a. 1
    b. 2
    c. 3
    d. 4

40. A ball is drawn at random from a ball pit containing 8 red balls, 7 yellow balls, 6 green balls, and 5 purple balls. What's the probability that the ball drawn is yellow?
    a. $\frac{1}{26}$
    b. $\frac{19}{26}$
    c. $\frac{7}{26}$
    d. 1

Social Studies

1. An elementary teacher is planning a social studies lesson on individuals who have had an important historical influence on the state of Georgia. All EXCEPT which of the following individuals should be discussed in this lesson?
    a. Andrew Jackson
    b. John White
    c. William T. Sherman
    d. Booker T. Washington

2. What is NOT a responsibility for citizens of democracy?
    a. To stay aware of current issues and history
    b. To avoid political action
    c. To actively vote in elections
    d. To understand and obey laws

Question 3 is based on the following passage:

> We hold these truths to be self-evident, that all men are created equal, that they are endowed by their Creator with certain unalienable Rights, that among these are Life, Liberty and the pursuit of Happiness.—That to secure these rights, Governments are instituted among Men, deriving their just powers from the consent of the governed,—That whenever any Form of Government becomes destructive of these ends, it is the Right of the People to alter or to abolish it, and to institute new Government, laying its foundation on such principles and organizing its powers in such form, as to them shall seem most likely to effect their Safety and Happiness.
>
> Prudence, indeed, will dictate that Governments long established should not be changed for light and transient causes; and accordingly all experience hath shown that mankind are more disposed to suffer, while evils are sufferable, than to right themselves by abolishing the forms to

which they are accustomed. But when a long train of abuses and usurpations, pursuing invariably the same Object evinces a design to reduce them under absolute Despotism, it is their right, it is their duty, to throw off such Government and to provide new Guards for their future security.

Excerpt from the United States Declaration of Independence, adopted July 4, 1776

3. What is the main purpose of the excerpt?
    a. Provide a justification for revolution when the government infringes on "certain inalienable rights"
    b. Provide specific evidence of the "train of abuses"
    c. Provide an argument why "all Men are created equal"
    d. Provide an analysis of the importance of "life, liberty, and the pursuit of happiness"

4. Which member of British parliament convinced King George II in 1732 to colonize the area that is now Georgia with individuals from Britain's overflowing debtor prisons?
    a. James Oglethorpe
    b. Button Gwinnett
    c. George Walton
    d. Lyman Hall

5. A fourth-grade teacher is having students work in small groups to research and present about historical figures instrumental in leading the charge for discussion at the Constitutional Convention held in Philadelphia in 1787. Which of the following gentlemen would NOT be assigned to a group for this project?
    a. George Washington
    b. Alexander Hamilton
    c. Thomas Jefferson
    d. James Madison

6. A text read in a third-grade classroom is introducing readers to an American Indian tribe that led a nomadic lifestyle and lived in teepees that were easily moved from place to place. In which region did this tribe likely live?
    a. Plains
    b. Southwest
    c. Eastern
    d. Northwest

7. What was Britain's first permanent settlement in North America?
    a. Plymouth, Massachusetts
    b. Roanoke, Virginia
    c. Jamestown, Virginia
    d. L'Anse Meadows, Newfoundland

8. Fourth-grade students are creating timelines with landmark events of the American Revolution. Under which of the following events should they notate as where the first shot took place?
    a. At the Boston Massacre
    b. During the Boston Tea Party
    c. On Lexington Green
    d. At the Battle of Trenton

9. How many times has the US Constitution been amended in order to accommodate changes and updates?
   a. 14
   b. 18
   c. 21
   d. 27

10. Which type of map illustrates the world's climatological regions?
    a. Topographic map
    b. Conformal projection
    c. Isoline map
    d. Thematic map

11. In which manner is absolute location expressed?
    a. The cardinal directions (north, south, east, and west)
    b. Through latitudinal and longitudinal coordinates
    c. Location nearest to a more well-known location
    d. Hemispherical position on the globe

12. Which of these is NOT a true statement about culture?
    a. Culture derives from the beliefs, values, and behaviors of people in a community.
    b. All people are born into a certain culture.
    c. Cultures are stagnant and cannot be changed.
    d. Culture can be embedded within families, schools, businesses, social classes, and religions.

13. Latitudinal lines are used to measure distance in which direction?
    a. East to west
    b. North to south
    c. Between two sets of coordinates
    d. In an inexact manner

14. Which of the following statements most accurately describes the Achaemenid Empire in Persia until the fourth century BC?
    a. Islam was the official religion.
    b. Achaemenid emperors constructed the entire Silk Road network.
    c. The Achaemenid Empire successfully conquered Greece.
    d. None of the above

15. The Silk Roads caused which of the following?
    a. Spread of Buddhism from India to China
    b. The devastation of European economies
    c. Introduction of the Bubonic Plague to the New World
    d. The Great War

16. What caused the end of the Western Roman Empire in 476 AD?
    a. Invasions by Germanic tribes
    b. The Mongol invasion
    c. The assassination of Julius Caesar
    d. Introduction of Taoism in Rome

17. Which of the following statements most accurately describes the Mongol Empire?
    a. The Mongol army was largely a cavalry force.
    b. Mongol rulers did not tolerate other religions.
    c. Mongol rulers neglected foreign trade.
    d. The Mongol Empire is known for its discouragement of literacy and the arts.

18. Renaissance scholars and artists were inspired by which classical civilization?
    a. Ancient Greece
    b. Ancient Egypt
    c. The Zhou Dynasty
    d. The Ottoman Empire

19. Which of the following was a consequence of increasing nationalism in Europe in the 1800s?
    a. The unification of Spain
    b. The unification of France
    c. Increasing competition and tension between European powers
    d. More efficient trade between nations

20. Which of the following led to the American Revolutionary War?
    a. The Stamp Act
    b. The Boston Massacre
    c. The Boston Tea Party
    d. All of the above

21. Which feature differentiates a state from a nation?
    a. Shared history
    b. Common language
    c. Population
    d. Sovereignty

22. Which of the following was a consequence of World War II?
    a. The collapse of British and French empires in Asia and Africa
    b. A communist revolution in Russia
    c. The end of the Cold War
    d. The death of Franz Ferdinand, the Archduke of Austria

23. Which best describes ethnic groups?
    a. Subgroups within a population who share a common history, language, or religion
    b. Divisive groups within a nation's boundaries seeking independence
    c. People who choose to leave a location
    d. Any minority group within a nation's boundaries

24. In recent years, agricultural production has been affected by which of the following?
    a. The prevalence of biotechnology and GMOs
    b. Weaker crop yields due to poor soil
    c. Plagues of pests, which have limited food production
    d. Revolutions in irrigation, which utilize salinated water

25. Which of the following is true of political boundaries?
    a. They have remained static for centuries.
    b. They are generally visible on Earth.
    c. They are constantly changing.
    d. They are never disputed among nations.

26. Which of the following is the subgroup of economics that studies large-scale economic issues such as unemployment, interest rates, price levels, and national income?
    a. Microeconomics
    b. Macroeconomics
    c. Scarcity
    d. Supply and demand

27. Which kind of market does NOT involve government interventions or monopolies while trades are made between suppliers and buyers?
    a. Free
    b. Command
    c. Gross
    d. Exchange

28. Which is NOT an indicator of economic growth?
    a. GDP (gross domestic product)
    b. Unemployment
    c. Inflation
    d. Theory of the firm

29. Which of the following consequences did NOT result from the discovery of the New World in 1492 AD?
    a. Proof that the world was round instead of flat
    b. The deaths of millions of Native Americans
    c. Biological exchange between Europe and the New World
    d. The creation of new syncretic religions

30. Which of the following was NOT a consequence of industrialization in Europe during the 1800s?
    a. The birth of the working class
    b. The expansion of European empires in Africa and Asia
    c. Improved transportation and economic efficiency
    d. The reduction of child labor

31. Which check does the legislative branch possess over the judicial branch?
    a. Appoint judges
    b. Call special sessions of Congress
    c. Rule legislation unconstitutional
    d. Determine the number of Supreme Court judges

32. Which of the following is NOT included in the Bill of Rights?
    a. Freedom to assemble
    b. Freedom against unlawful search
    c. Freedom to vote
    d. Reservation of non-enumerated powers to the states or the people

33. The United States elects the president by which of the following ways?
    a. Popular majority vote
    b. Plurality vote
    c. Electoral College
    d. Party list system

Question 34 is based on the following passage:

Hand in hand with this we must frankly recognize the overbalance of population in our industrial centers and, by engaging on a national scale in a redistribution, endeavor to provide a better use of the land for those best fitted for the land. The task can be helped by definite efforts to raise the values of agricultural products and with this the power to purchase the output of our cities. It can be helped by preventing realistically the tragedy of the growing loss through foreclosure of our small homes and our farms. It can be helped by insistence that the Federal, State, and local governments act forthwith on the demand that their cost be drastically reduced. It can be helped by the unifying of relief activities which today are often scattered, uneconomical, and unequal. It can be helped by national planning for and supervision of all forms of transportation and of communications and other utilities which have a definitely public character. There are many ways in which it can be helped, but it can never be helped merely by talking about it. We must act and act quickly.

Finally, in our progress toward a resumption of work we require two safeguards against a return of the evils of the old order; there must be a strict supervision of all banking and credits and investments; there must be an end to speculation with other people's money, and there must be provision for an adequate but sound currency.

Excerpt from President Franklin D. Roosevelt's Inaugural Address, March 4, 1933

34. Which of the following best describes President Roosevelt's underlying approach to government?
    a. Government must be focused on redistribution of land.
    b. Government must "act and act quickly" to intervene and regulate the economy.
    c. Government must exercise "strict supervision of all banking."
    d. Government must prevent the "growing loss through foreclosure."

35. In the American election system, where do the candidates ultimately receive the nomination from their party?
    a. At the primary
    b. At the caucus
    c. At the debates
    d. At the party convention

36. Which part of the legislative process differs in the House and the Senate?
    a. Who may introduce the bill
    b. How debates about a bill are conducted
    c. Who may veto the bill
    d. What wording the bill contains

37. Which of the following is the primary problem with map projections?
    a. They are not detailed.
    b. They do not include physical features.
    c. They distort areas near the poles.
    d. They only focus on the Northern Hemisphere.

38. All of the following are negative demographic indicators EXCEPT which of the following?
    a. High infant mortality rates
    b. Low literacy rates
    c. High population density
    d. Low life expectancy

39. Which of the following is NOT a factor in a location's climate?
    a. Latitudinal position
    b. Elevation
    c. Longitudinal position
    d. Proximity to mountains

40. What is the term for the ability of a ruling body to influence the actions, behavior, and attitude of a person or group of people?
    a. Politics
    b. Power
    c. Authority
    d. Legitimacy

41. Which of the following is a function of a nation after it has been formed rather than a shared characteristic that would be helpful in the formation of a nation?
    a. Culture and traditions
    b. History
    c. Sovereignty
    d. Beliefs and religion

42. The central government established under the Articles of Confederation held which of the following powers?
    a. The power to impose taxes
    b. The power to declare war
    c. The power to regulate trade
    d. The power to enforce laws enacted by Congress

43. What was a consequence of the industrialization that followed the Civil War?
    a. Decreased immigration
    b. Increased urbanization
    c. Decreased socioeconomic inequality
    d. Increased rights for workers

44. Which of the following best describes how the Treaty of Versailles contributed to the outbreak of World War II?
    a. It forced Germany to assume responsibility for all damage incurred during the war and pay billions of dollars in reparations.
    b. It failed to adequately end the violence of World War I.
    c. It left large tracts of territory unclaimed by any nation-state.
    d. It created the League of Nations.

Question 45 is based on the following passage:

> Now, therefore I, Abraham Lincoln, President of the United States, by virtue of the power in me vested as Commander-in-Chief, of the Army and Navy of the United States in time of actual armed rebellion against the authority and government of the United States, and as a fit and necessary war measure for suppressing said rebellion...
>
> And by virtue of the power, and for the purpose aforesaid, I do order and declare that all persons held as slaves within said designated States, and parts of States, are, and henceforward shall be free; and that the Executive government of the United States, including the military and naval authorities thereof, will recognize and maintain the freedom of said persons.
>
> Excerpt from President Abraham Lincoln's Emancipation Proclamation, January 1, 1863

45. How does President Lincoln justify freeing the slaves in designated areas of the South?
    a. Emancipation is necessary since slavery is evil.
    b. Emancipation is necessary to boost the morale of the North.
    c. Emancipation is necessary to punish for the South seceding from the Union.
    d. Emancipation is necessary to strengthen the war effort of the North.

46. Federalism describes the relationship between the federal government and which of the following?
    a. The people
    b. State governments
    c. The branches of government
    d. The Constitution

47. The case of *Brown v. Board of Education* reversed what landmark Supreme Court doctrine?
    a. Judicial review doctrine
    b. Public safety exception
    c. Due process doctrine
    d. Separate but equal doctrine

48. All EXCEPT which of the following are true of an area with an extremely high population density?
    a. Competition for resources is intense.
    b. Greater strain on public services exists.
    c. More people live in rural areas.
    d. More people live in urban areas.

49. Which of the following characteristics best defines a formal region?
    a. Homogeneity
    b. Diversity
    c. Multilingualism
    d. Social mobility

50. The process of globalization can best be described as what?
    a. The integration of the world's economic systems into a singular entity
    b. The emergence of powerful nations seeking world dominance
    c. The absence of nation-states who seek to control certain areas
    d. Efforts to establish a singular world government for the world's citizens

Practice Test #1

51. What is the name of the central bank that controls the value of money in the United States?
   a. Commodity Reserve
   b. Central Reserve
   c. Federal Reserve
   d. Bank Reserve

52. How is economic growth measured?
   a. By the rise in the inflation of a country
   b. By the amount of reserves that a country holds
   c. By the amount of exports that a country has
   d. By the GDP of a country

53. A developing nation is more likely to have which of the following?
   a. Complex highway networks
   b. Higher rates of subsistence farmers
   c. Stable government systems
   d. Little economic instability

54. Which constitutional amendment gave women the right to vote in the United States?
   a. 15th
   b. 18th
   c. 19th
   d. 21st

55. What consequences did the Great Migration have?
   a. It led to conflict with Native Americans in the West in the 1800s.
   b. It led to increased racial tension in the North in the early 1900s.
   c. It led to increased conflict with Mexican immigrants in the 1900s.
   d. It led to increased conflict with Irish and German immigrants in the 1800s.

Science

1. An ecosystem that normally has moderate summers with high rainfall is experiencing a heat wave and a drought. How does this affect the rate of photosynthesis of the producers in this ecosystem?
   a. The decrease in transpiration from the high heat and the drop in rainfall decreases the number of chloroplasts, so photosynthesis rates decrease.
   b. The increase in transpiration from the high heat and the drop in rainfall results in less water. Since photosynthesis creates water, the rate increases to meet increased water demands.
   c. Increased temperature increases the number of mitochondria, so photosynthesis rates increase.
   d. The increase in transpiration from the high heat and the drop in rainfall results in less water available for photosynthesis. The rate decreases.

Practice Test #1

2. A farmer grows all of his tomato plants by vegetative propagation. He finds that one clone produces tomatoes that sell much better than any other clone. He then uses this clone to plant his entire field. Two years later a fungus wipes out his entire crop. What could the farmer have done to prevent this?

   I. Plant tomatoes that sell poorly. They are more resistant to fungus.
   II. Plant a variety of tomatoes. Genetic variation would have left some of the crop less susceptible to the fungus.
   III. Plant a variety of crops. Plants other than tomatoes might not be affected by the fungus.

   a. Choice I only
   b. Choice II only
   c. Choice I or III
   d. Choice II or III

3. What object in the solar system becomes dim during a lunar eclipse?
   a. Sun
   b. Earth
   c. Moon
   d. Earth and Moon

4. Which statement about white blood cells is true?
   a. B cells are responsible for antibody production.
   b. White blood cells are made in the white/yellow cartilage before they enter the bloodstream.
   c. Platelets, a special class of white blood cell, function to clot blood and stop bleeding.
   d. The majority of white blood cells only activate during the age of puberty, which explains why children and the elderly are particularly susceptible to disease.

5. Which locations in the digestive system are sites of chemical digestion?
   1. Mouth
   2. Stomach
   3. Small Intestine

   a. II only
   b. III only
   c. II and III only
   d. I, II, and III

6. What is the theory that certain physical and behavioral survival traits give a species an evolutionary advantage?
   a. Gradualism
   b. Evolutionary advantage
   c. Punctuated equilibrium
   d. Natural selection

7. Which of the following structures is unique to eukaryotic cells?
   a. Cell walls
   b. Nuclei
   c. Cell membranes
   d. Organelles

8. Which cellular organelle is used for digestion to recycle materials?
    a. The Golgi apparatus
    b. The lysosome
    c. The centrioles
    d. The mitochondria

9. Which of the following leads to diversity in meiotic division but not mitotic division?
    a. Tetrad formation
    b. Disassembly of the mitotic spindle
    c. Extra/fewer chromosomes due to nondisjunction
    d. Fertilization by multiple sperm

10. The Sun is a major external source of energy. Which of the following is the best demonstration of this?
    a. Flowers tend to bloom in the morning, after dawn.
    b. Large animals like bears do not need to eat food when hibernating.
    c. Deserts can reach scorching temperatures in daylight but subzero temperatures at night.
    d. The tides of the ocean are highly dependent on the movement of the Moon, the celestial body that is highly reflective to sunlight.

11. Which of the following describes a typical gas?
    a. Indefinite shape and indefinite volume
    b. Indefinite shape and definite volume
    c. Definite shape and definite volume
    d. Definite shape and indefinite volume

12. What information does a genotype give that a phenotype does not?
    a. The genotype necessarily includes the proteins coded for by its alleles.
    b. The genotype will always show an organism's recessive alleles.
    c. The genotype must include the organism's physical characteristics.
    d. The genotype shows what an organism's parents looked like.

13. Which statement is supported by the Punnett square below, if "T" = tall and "t" = short?

	T	t
T		
t		

    a. Both parents are homozygous tall.
    b. 100% of the offspring will be tall because both parents are tall.
    c. There is a 25% chance that an offspring will be short.
    d. The short allele will soon die out.

Practice Test #1

14. Which of the following is a chief difference between evaporation and boiling?
    a. Liquids boil only at the surface, while they evaporate equally throughout the liquid.
    b. Evaporating substances change from gas to liquid, while boiling substances change from liquid to gas.
    c. Evaporation happens in nature, while boiling is a man-made phenomenon.
    d. Evaporation can happen below a liquid's boiling point.

15. Which of the following is a special property of water?
    a. Water easily flows through phospholipid bilayers.
    b. A water molecule's oxygen atom allows fish to breathe.
    c. Water is highly cohesive which explains its high boiling point.
    d. Water can self-hydrolyze and decompose into hydrogen and oxygen.

16. A student believes that there is an inverse relationship between sugar consumption and test scores. To test this hypothesis, he recruits several people to eat sugar, wait one hour, and take a short aptitude test afterwards. The student will compile the participants' sugar intake levels and test scores. How should the student conduct the experiment?
    a. One round of testing, where each participant consumes a different level of sugar.
    b. Two rounds of testing: The first, where each participant consumes a different level of sugar, and the second, where each participant consumes the same level as they did in round 1.
    c. Two rounds of testing: The first, where each participant consumes the same level of sugar as each other, and the second, where each participant consumes the same level of sugar as each other but at higher levels than in round 1.
    d. One round of testing, where each participant consumes the same level of sugar.

17. Which of the following is a standard or series of standards to which the results from an experiment are compared?
    a. A control
    b. A variable
    c. A constant
    d. Collected data

18. What is the last phase of mitosis?
    a. Prophase
    b. Telophase
    c. Anaphase
    d. Metaphase

19. Which of the following is a type of boundary between two tectonic plates?
    a. Continental
    b. Oceanic
    c. Convergent
    d. Fault

20. Volcanic activity can occur in which of the following?
    a. Convergent boundaries
    b. Divergent boundaries
    c. The middle of a tectonic plate
    d. All of the above

21. Where is most of the Earth's weather generated?
    a. The troposphere
    b. The ionosphere
    c. The thermosphere
    d. The stratosphere

22. What type of cloud is seen when looking at the sky during a heavy rainstorm?
    a. High-clouds
    b. Altocumulus
    c. Stratus
    d. Nimbostratus

23. What is the largest planet in our solar system and what is it mostly made of?
    a. Saturn, rocks
    b. Jupiter, ammonia
    c. Jupiter, hydrogen
    d. Saturn, helium

24. Viruses belong to which of the following classifications?
    a. Domain Archaea
    b. Kingdom Monera
    c. Kingdom Protista
    d. None of the above

25. Considering a gas in a closed system that is kept at a constant volume, what will happen to the temperature if the pressure is increased?
    a. The temperature will stay the same.
    b. The temperature will decrease.
    c. The temperature will increase.
    d. The result cannot be determined with the information given.

26. According to Newton's three laws of motion, which of the following is true?
    a. Two objects cannot exert force on each other without touching.
    b. An object at rest has no inertia.
    c. The weight of an object is the same as the mass of the object.
    d. The weight of an object is equal to the mass of an object multiplied by the acceleration of gravity.

27. The Sun transferring heat to the Earth through space is an example of which of the following?
    a. Convection
    b. Conduction
    c. Induction
    d. Radiation

28. Which of the Earth's layers is thickest?
    a. The crust
    b. The shell
    c. The mantle
    d. The inner core

Practice Test #1

29. What is the process called in which one tectonic plate moves over another plate?
    a. Fault
    b. Diversion
    c. Subduction
    d. Drift

30. What is transpiration?
    a. Evaporation from moving water
    b. Evaporation from plant life
    c. Movement of water through the ground
    d. Precipitation that falls on trees

31. Which of the following will freeze last?
    a. Fresh water from a pond
    b. Pure water
    c. Seawater from the Pacific Ocean
    d. Seawater from the Dead Sea

32. Which of the following is true of glaciers?
    a. They form in water.
    b. They float.
    c. They form on land.
    d. They are formed from icebergs.

33. What is the broadest, or least specialized, classification of the Linnaean taxonomic system?
    a. Species
    b. Family
    c. Domain
    d. Phylum

34. Salts like sodium iodide (NaI) and potassium chloride (KCl) use what type of bond?
    a. Ionic bonds
    b. Disulfide bridges
    c. Covalent bonds
    d. London dispersion forces

35. Which of the following is unique to covalent bonds?
    a. Most covalent bonds are formed between the elements H, F, N, and O.
    b. Covalent bonds are dependent on forming dipoles.
    c. Bonding electrons are shared between two or more atoms.
    d. Molecules with covalent bonds tend to have a crystalline solid structure.

36. For any given element, an isotope is an atom with which of the following?
    a. A different atomic number
    b. A different number of protons
    c. A different number of electrons
    d. A different mass number

37. What is the electrical charge of the nucleus?
    a. A nucleus always has a positive charge.
    b. A stable nucleus has a positive charge, but a radioactive nucleus may be neutral with no charge.
    c. A nucleus is always neutral with no charge.
    d. A stable nucleus is neutral with no charge, but a radioactive nucleus may have a charge.

38. Which of the following is a representation of a natural pattern or occurrence that's difficult or impossible to experience directly?
    a. A theory
    b. A model
    c. A law
    d. An observation

39. Which statement is true regarding atomic structure?
    a. Protons orbit around a nucleus.
    b. Neutrons have a positive charge.
    c. Electrons are in the nucleus.
    d. Protons have a positive charge.

40. What is ionization energy?
    a. One-half the distance between the nuclei of atoms of the same element
    b. A measurement of the tendency of an atom to form a chemical bond
    c. The amount of energy needed to remove a valence electron from a gas or ion
    d. The ability or tendency of an atom to accept an electron into its valence shell

41. The process of breaking down large molecules into smaller molecules to provide energy is known as which of the following?
    a. Metabolism
    b. Bioenergetics
    c. Anabolism
    d. Catabolism

42. Which of the following inventions likely had the greatest improvement on the ability to combat nutrition deficiencies in developing countries?
    a. Food products fortified with dietary vitamins and minerals
    b. Integrated statistical models of fish populations
    c. Advances so that microscopes can use thicker tissue samples
    d. Refrigerated train cars for transportation of food

43. Which element's atoms have the greatest number of electrons?
    a. Hydrogen
    b. Iron
    c. Copper
    d. Iodine

44. A teacher presents a science lesson to her class of second graders about physical and chemical properties. After the lesson, students create posters that highlight examples of each. Which of the following would be included on the list of examples of chemical properties?
    a. Color
    b. Malleability
    c. Reactivity
    d. Luster

45. An elementary teacher is about to begin a new science unit of seasons and as a part of various activities to gauge students' background knowledge, he asks each student to share what they believe to be the difference between seasons and weather. The responses of four students are presented below. Which of these students is most accurate?
    a. Carter: Seasons depend on wind and heat patterns.
    b. Darrel: Weather depends on proximity to the sun.
    c. Gloria: Seasons are day-to-day weather.
    d. Dimitri: Weather involves the water cycle.

46. Which is the best way to teach the concept of day and night to early childhood students?
    a. Showing an animated PowerPoint
    b. Going outside and talking about the Sun's location
    c. Modeling with flashlights and tennis balls
    d. Reading a book where the Sun and Moon are friends

47. Why is Florida hotter than Alaska?
    a. Florida is next to the ocean.
    b. Florida is a peninsula.
    c. Alaska is farther from the equator.
    d. Alaska is larger than Florida.

48. Which of the following weather phenomena does NOT directly involve the water cycle?
    a. Hurricanes
    b. Tornadoes
    c. Snow
    d. Rain

49. Plate tectonic movement contributes to the Earth's topography by doing which of the following?
    a. Causing volcanoes
    b. Stimulating evaporation
    c. Forming deltas
    d. Stopping tornadoes

50. Which type of fossil is considered a "trace fossil"?
    a. Bone
    b. Footprint
    c. Shell
    d. Tooth

Answer Explanations #1

Reading and Language Arts

1. B: Spelling conventions is the area of study that involves mechanics, usage, and sentence formation. Mechanics refers to spelling, punctuation, and capitalization. Usage refers to the use of the various parts of speech within sentences, and sentence formation is the order in which the various words in a sentence appear. Generally speaking, word analysis is the breaking down of words into morphemes and word units in order to arrive at the word's meaning. Morphemes are the smallest units of a written language that carry meaning, and phonics refers to the study of letter-sound relationships.

2. B: The alphabetic principle relies on specific letter-sound correspondence. Although some high-frequency sight words are decodable, the majority of them are not. High-frequency sight words appear often in children's literature and are studied and memorized in order to strengthen a child's spelling and reading fluency. High-frequency sight words, as well as decodable words, may or may not rhyme and may or may not contain onsets and rimes.

3. A: Reading fluency involves how accurately a child reads each individual word within a sentence, the speed at which a child reads, and the expression the child applies while reading. Therefore, accuracy, rate, and prosody are the three key areas of reading fluency.

4. A: Skimming text for content is an important pre-reading strategy where readers identify important ideas and words without reading every line of the text. Summarizing text effectively, organizing main ideas and supporting details, and clarifying unfamiliar ideas in the text are all strategies to be used during or after reading a text.

5. B: The key word here is *inform*, which is the primary purpose of all informative modes. They contain facts, definitions, instructions, and other elements with the objective purpose of informing a reader—such as study guides, instruction manuals, and textbooks. Choice *A* is incorrect because an argumentative mode contains language that is subjective and is intended to persuade or to inform with a persuasive bias. Choice *C* is incorrect as a narrative mode is used primarily to tell a story and has no intention of informing, nor is the language inherently objective. Choice *D* is incorrect as descriptive modes possess no inherent intent to inform and are used primarily to describe.

6. B: The correct answer is Choice *B*, as the author is speaking directly to the reader and uses the pronoun *you*. Choice *A* uses first-person point of view, which uses the pronoun *I*. Choice *C* uses third-person point of view which utilizes pronouns such as *he*, *she*, or *we*. Choice *D* is unclear.

7. D: The glossary of a book is the best place to look for specific words and concepts. The appendix, bibliography, and preface of a book all serve other purposes than helping the reader look up specific words.

8. C: Chronological or sequence order is the organizational pattern that structures text to show the passage of time or movement through steps in a certain order. Choice *A* demonstrates the problem/solution structure. Choice *B* defines the cause/effect pattern. Choice *D* represents the spatial order structure.

9. C: The student doesn't understand print awareness because they are holding the book upside down. Print awareness is an understanding of how books and other print work, meaning that books should be held in the correct direction, print should be read left to right, and the reader should know how to turn pages.

Answer Explanations #1

10. B: Only Choice *B* uses both repetitive beginning sounds (alliteration) and personification—the portrayal of a building as a human crumbling under a fire. Choice *A* is a simile and does not utilize alliteration or the use of consistent consonant sounds for effect. Although Choice *C* does use alliteration, it does not use personification to describe the house. Choice *D* describes neither alliteration nor personification.

11. B: The students used substitution to come up with the rhyming words because they substituted the first letter "c" for other letters ("b", "t," and "f").

12. A: In the word "tap", the "t" is considered the onset (or initial consonant sound) and the "ap" is the rime (the letters that follow the onset).

13. A: A memoir is a historical account of a person's life written by one who has intimate knowledge of the person's life. Choice *B* is not applicable since it is the definition of an autobiography. Choice *C* strictly refers to fiction and is not applicable to nonfiction. Choice *D* indicates that a memoir is not based on historical fact. In many instances, it is.

14. C: A phoneme is the smallest unit of sound (for example, the phonogram "ph" represents the phoneme /f/). Choice *A*, a word, is typically composed of multiple phonemes. Choice *B* refers to phonics, and Choice *D* is a subtype of phoneme.

15. A: The correct answer is *crackle* as it is the only option that reflects the sound that the action would make. The other options do not.

16. B: Word walls are great tools for students as they learn to read, spell, and write. Because they help students pronounce unfamiliar words and provide visual contact with the word along with the auditory experience, they are particularly useful in the phonetic stage of spelling development. All the statements given are correct except Choice *B*, which describes KWL charts typically used for reading.

17. B: To arrive at the best answer, all the character traits for Cindy must be analyzed. She's described as *happy* ("always has a smile on her face"), *kind* ("volunteers at the local shelter"), and *patient* ("no one has ever seen her angry"). Since Cindy's husband is the opposite of her, these adjectives must be converted to antonyms. Someone who is *surly* is unhappy, rude, and impatient. *Stingy*, Choice *A*, is too narrow of a word. Someone could be happy and kind, for instance, but still be stingy. For Choice *C*, *scared*, to be plausible, the rest of the passage would need instances of Cindy being bold or courageous. *Shy*, Choice *D*, also doesn't match. Someone who is shy could still be happy, kind, and patient.

18. B: The passage indicates that Annabelle has a fear of going outside into the daylight. Thus *heliophobia* must refer to a fear of bright lights or sunlight.

19. A: A DRA mainly assesses students' reading comprehension skills along with their accuracy, rate, and prosody.

20. C: A primary source is an artifact, document, recording, or other source of information that is created at the time under study. Think of a primary source as the original representation of the information. In contrast, secondary sources make conclusions or draw inferences based on primary sources, as well as other secondary sources. Choice *C* is correct because a personal journal from World War II is a historical document and is, therefore, a primary source. Choice *A*, a critic's summary and review of a new book, is a secondary source. Choice *B*, a table of contents, is a secondary source, since it refers to other information. Choice *D* is also a secondary source.

21. C: Structural analysis is the concept of identifying the root words, base words, and affixes to help further understanding of larger words.

Answer Explanations #1

22. B: Key indicators of reading fluency include accuracy, rate, and prosody. Phonetics and decodable skills aid fluency. Syntax, semantics, word morphology, listening comprehension, and word exposure aid vocabulary development.

23. A: The best method for supporting fluent reading at the passage level is timed reading exercises. While all of the other answers help to improve students' general reading skills, timed reading exercises are best to encourage fluency.

24. D: This question is testing whether you realize how a timeline illustrates information in chronological order from left to right. "Started school for the deaf" is fourth on the timeline from the left, which means that it is the fourth event on the timeline. Thus, Choice D is the correct answer.

25. B: The founding of the school is the event listed farthest to the right of the events in the answer choices. This means it occurred most recently. Thus, Choice B is the correct answer.

26. D: Phoneme segmentation is the identification of all the component phonemes in a word. An example would be the student identifying each separate sound, /t/, /u/, and /b/, in the word *tub*. Choice A, sound blending, is the blending together of two or more sounds in a word, such as /ch/ or /sh/. Choice B, substitution, occurs when a phoneme is substituted within a word for another phoneme, such as substituting the sound /b/ in *bun* to /r/ to create *run*. Choice C, rhyming, is an effective tool to utilize during the analytic phase of phonics development because rhyming words are often identical except for their beginning letters.

27. A: Phonological awareness is best assessed through identification of rimes or onsets within words. Instruction of phonological awareness includes detecting and identifying word boundaries, onsets/rimes, syllables, and rhyming words.

28. D: Print awareness includes all the answer choices except the spelling of sight words. Print awareness includes Choice A, the differentiation of uppercase and lowercase letters, so that students can understand which words begin a sentence. Choice B, the identification of word boundaries, is also included in print awareness; that is, students should be made aware that words are made up of letters and that spaces appear between words, etc. Choice C, the proper tracking of words, is also included in print awareness, which is the realization that print is organized in a particular way, so books must be tracked and held accordingly.

29. A: The correct answer is phonological awareness, the understanding that words are made of multiple sounds working together, which aids with rhyming abilities. Phoneme deletion includes deleting letters or parts of a word, phoneme blending is the ability to blend letters to create words, and directionality is the ability to track words while reading.

30. B: In Choice B the word *Uncle* should not be capitalized because it is not functioning as a proper noun. If the word named a specific uncle, such as *Uncle Jerry*, then it would be considered a proper noun and should be capitalized. Choice A correctly capitalizes the proper noun *East Coast*, and does not capitalize winter, which functions as a common noun in the sentence. Choice C correctly capitalizes the name of a specific college course, which is considered a proper noun. Choice D correctly capitalizes the proper noun *Jersey Shore*.

31. A: Choice A is correct because it uses a semicolon to join the two independent clauses (clauses that could function as independent sentences). Choice B is incorrect because the conjunction is not preceded by a comma. A comma and conjunction should be used together to join independent clauses. Choice C is incorrect because a comma should only be used to join independent sentences when it also includes a coordinating conjunction such as *and* or *so*. Choice D does not use punctuation to join the independent clauses, so it is considered a fused (same as a run-on) sentence.

32. C: Choice C is a compound sentence because it joins two independent clauses with a comma and the coordinating conjunction *and*. The sentences in Choices B and D include one independent clause and one dependent clause, so they are complex sentences, not compound sentences. The sentence in Choice A has both a compound subject, *Alex and Shane*, and a compound verb, *spent and took*, but the entire sentence itself is one independent clause.

33. A: Choice A uses incorrect subject-verb agreement because the indefinite pronoun *neither* is singular and must use the singular verb form *is*. In Choice B, the pronoun *both* is plural and uses the plural verb form of *are*. The pronoun any can be either singular or plural. In Choice C, *any* is plural, so the plural verb form *are* is used. The pronoun *each* is singular and uses the singular verb form *is*, as seen in Choice D.

34. A: It is necessary to put a comma between the date and the year. It is also required to put a comma between the day of the week and the month. Choice B is incorrect because it is missing the comma between the day and year. Choice C is incorrect because it adds an unnecessary comma between the month and date. Choice D is missing the necessary comma between day of the week and the month.

35. D: This passage displays clarity (the author states precisely what he or she intended), fluency (the sentences run smoothly together), and parallelism (words are used in a similar fashion to help provide rhythm). Choice A lacks parallelism. When the author states, "the hero acts without thinking, is living in the moment, and is repressing physical and emotional pain," the words *acts*, *is living* and *is repressing* are in different tenses, and, consequently, jarring to one's ears. Choice B runs on endlessly in the first half ("Ernest Hemingway is probably the most noteworthy of expatriate authors since his concise writing style is void of emotion and stream of consciousness and has had a lasting impact on Americans which has resonated to this very day, and Hemingway's novels are much like in American cinema."). It demands some type of pause and strains the readers' eyes. The second half of the passage is choppy: "The hero acts. He doesn't think. He lives in the moment. He represses physical and emotional pain." For Choice C, leaving out *expatriate* is, first, vague, and second, alters the meaning. The correct version claims that Hemingway was the most notable of the expatriate authors while the second version claims he's the most notable of any author *ever*, a very bold claim indeed. Also, leaving out *stream of* in "stream of consciousness" no longer references the non-sequential manner in which most people think. Instead, this version sounds like all the characters in the novel are in a coma!

36. B: The correct answer is phoneme deletion, which is the ability to remove phonemes to create a new word. The students understood phoneme-grapheme correspondence and blending because they were able to read the original word but struggled to understand deletion. Phoneme substitution would have involved substituting a different phoneme for the "s" rather than removing it completely.

37. D: The prefix *trans* can mean across, beyond, over. Choices A, B, and C are incorrect because they are the meanings of other prefixes. Choice A is a meaning of the prefix *de*. Choice B is the meaning of the prefix *omni*. Choice C is one of the meanings of the prefix *pro*. The example words are helpful in determining the meaning of *trans*. All of the example words—*transfer*, *transact*, *translation*, and *transport*—indicate something being *across*, *beyond*, or *over* something else. For example, *translation* refers to text going across languages. If no example words were given, you could think of words starting with *trans* and then compare their meanings to try to determine a common definition.

38. C: *Oppose* makes sense in both instances. *Antibiotics* oppose *bacteria*, and *antisocial* people oppose *society*.

39. D: If *conform* means to adjust behavior, *shape* could replace *conform*, as if to say that the behavior was reshaped or modified. The same goes for *inform*. New information reshapes how one thinks about the world. Also, the word *shape* gives rise to the abstract idea that both behavior and knowledge are malleable, like modeling clay, and can be molded into new forms. Choice A (*match*) works for *conform* (matching to society), but it doesn't work for *inform* (one cannot *match* information to a person). Choice B (*relay*) doesn't work for *conform* (there's no way to pass on new behavior), but it does work for *inform*, as to pass on new information. Choice *C* (*negate*) works for neither *conform* (the behavior is not being completely cancelled out) nor *inform* (the information is not being rescinded).

40. D: The best choice of letter for her next lesson is "s". The lowercase "d" and "p" letters are too visually similar to "b", and "v" is too similar in letter sound. "S" is the best choice because it doesn't look or sound like "b".

41. C: Because the student can follow directions, but isn't able to verbally express herself, she has receptive language skills. Expressive language skills would include an ability to respond with words or gestures, and basic and auditory language skills are both fictitious answer choices.

42. D: Teachers use directed reading-thinking activities before and after reading to improve critical thinking and reading comprehension. Metacognitive skills are when learners think about thinking. Self-monitoring is when children are asked to think as they read and ask themselves if what they have just read makes sense. KWL charts help guide students to identify what they already know about a given topic.

43. C: We are looking for an inference—a conclusion that is reached on the basis of evidence and reasoning—from the passage that will likely explain why the famous children's author did not achieve her usual success with the new genre (despite the book's acclaim). Choice *A* is wrong because the statement is false according to the passage. Choice *B* is wrong because, although the passage says the author has a graduate degree on the subject, it would be an unrealistic leap to infer that she is the foremost expert on Antebellum America. Choice *D* is wrong because there is nothing in the passage to lead us to infer that people generally prefer a children's series to historical fiction. In contrast, Choice *C* can be logically inferred since the passage speaks of the great success of the children's series and the declaration that the fame of the author's name causes the children's books to "fly off the shelves." Thus, we can infer that she did not receive any bump from her name since she published the historical novel under a pseudonym, which makes Choice *C* correct.

44. B: The student is performing at the phonetic stage. Phonetic spellers will spell a word as it sounds. The speller perceives and represents all the phonemes in a word. However, because phonetic spellers have limited sight word vocabulary, irregular words are often spelled incorrectly.

45. B: Pre-teaching is the most valuable strategy for helping children understand new words. Educators select what they evaluate to be the unfamiliar words in the text and then introduce them to the class before reading. Educators using this method should be careful not to simply ask the children to read the text and then spell the new words correctly.

46. B: When using contextual strategies, students are indirectly introduced to new words within a sentence or paragraph. Contextual strategies require students to infer the meaning(s) of new words. Word meaning is developed by utilizing semantic and contextual clues of the reading in which the word is located.

47. D: The correct answer is Choice *D*, the teacher should have Samantha read the same passage multiple times to help her read accurately, smoothly, and fluently. Choice *A* is incorrect because fluency aims to reduce the amount of times a student stops while reading. Choice *B* is incorrect because fluency is best supported by practicing the same passage multiple times instead of changing the passage. Choice *C* is incorrect because understanding of genre doesn't affect fluency.

48. A: Choice *A* is consistent with the argument's logic. The argument asserts that the world powers' military alliances amounted to a lit fuse, and the assassination merely lit it. The main point of the argument is that any event involving the military alliances would have led to a world war. Choice *B* runs counter to the argument's tone and reasoning. It can immediately be eliminated. Choice *C* is also clearly incorrect. At no point does the

Answer Explanations #1

argument blame any single or group of countries for starting World War I. Choice *D* is incorrect for the same reason as Choice *C*, so it can be eliminated.

49. D: Outspending other countries on education could have other benefits, but there is no reference to this in the passage, so Choice *A* is incorrect. Choice *B* is incorrect because the author does not mention corruption. Choice *C* is incorrect because there is nothing in the passage stating that the tests are not genuinely representative. Choice *D* is accurate because spending more money has not brought success. The United States already spends the most money, and the country is not excelling on these tests. Choice *D* is the correct answer.

50. B: *Excellent* and *walking* are adjectives modifying the noun *tours*. *Rich* is an adjective modifying the noun *history*, and *brotherly* is an adjective modifying the noun *love*. Choice *A* is incorrect because all of these words are functioning as nouns in the sentence. Choice *C* is incorrect because all of these words are functioning as verbs in the sentence. Choice *D* is incorrect because all of these words are considered prepositions, not adjectives.

51. D: The object pronouns *her* and *me* act as the indirect objects of the sentence. If *me* is in a series of object pronouns, it should always come last in the series. Choice *A* is incorrect because it uses subject pronouns *she* and *I*. Choice *B* is incorrect because it uses the subject pronoun *she*. Choice *C* uses the correct object pronouns, but they are in the wrong order.

52. A: In this example, a colon is correctly used to introduce a series of items. Choice *B* places an unnecessary comma before the word *because*. A comma is not needed before the word *because* when it introduces a dependent clause at the end of a sentence and provides necessary information to understand the sentence. Choice *C* is incorrect because it uses a semi-colon instead of a comma to join a dependent clause and an independent clause. Choice *D* is incorrect because it uses a colon in place of a comma and coordinating conjunction to join two independent clauses.

53. B: Choice *B* correctly uses the contraction for *you are* as the subject of the sentence, and it correctly uses the possessive pronoun *your* to indicate ownership of the jacket. It also correctly uses the adverb *there*, indicating place. Choice *A* is incorrect because it reverses the possessive pronoun *your* and the contraction for *you are*. It also uses the possessive pronoun *their* instead of the adverb *there*. Choice *C* is incorrect because it reverses *your* and *you're* and uses the contraction for *they are* in place of the adverb *there*. Choice *D* incorrectly uses the possessive pronoun *their* instead of the adverb *there*.

54. A: *Slang* refers to non-standard expressions that are not used in elevated speech and writing. *Slang* tends to be specific to one group or time period and is commonly used within groups of young people during their conversations with each other. *Jargon* refers to the language used in a specialized field. The *vernacular* is the native language of a local area, and a *dialect* is one form of a language in a certain region. Thus, Choices *B*, *C*, and *D* are incorrect.

55. B: Structural analysis focuses on the meaning of morphemes. Morphemes include base words, prefixes, and word endings (inflections and suffixes) that are found within longer words. Students can use structural analysis skill to find familiar word parts within an unfamiliar word in order to decode the word and determine the definition of the new word. The prefix *im-* (meaning not) in the word *improbable* can help students derive the definition of an event that is not likely to occur.

56. B: In-text citations are much shorter and usually only include the author's last name, page numbers being referenced, and for some styles, the publication year. Bibliographic citations contain much more detailed reference information. Choice *B* is incorrect because citations are necessary both in the text and in a bibliography. Choice *C* is incorrect because there are several different citation styles depending on the type of

Answer Explanations #1

paper or article being written. Rather, students should learn when it is appropriate to apply each different style. Choice *D* is incorrect because all sources need to be cited regardless of medium.

57. D: The purpose of integrating research is to add support and credibility to the student's ideas, not to replace the student's own ideas altogether. Choice *A* is incorrect as the bulk of the paper or project should be comprised of the author's own words, and quotations and paraphrases should be used to support them. Outside sources should be included when they enhance the writer's argument, but they are not required in every single paragraph. Choice *B* is also incorrect because regardless of whether ideas are directly quoted or paraphrased, it is essential to always credit authors for their ideas. The use of the author's full name in every signal phrase is unnecessary, so Choice *C* is also incorrect.

58. D: The author explains that Boethianism is a Medieval theological philosophy that attributes sin to temporary pleasure and righteousness with virtue and God's providence. Other than Choice *D*, the choices listed are all physical things. While these could still be divine rewards, Boethianism holds that the true reward for being virtuous is God's favor. It is also stressed in the article that physical pleasures cannot be taken into the afterlife. Therefore, the best choice is *D*, God's favor.

59. C: Choices *A* and *B* are generalized statements, and we have no evidence to support Choice *B*. Choice *D* is very compelling, but it looks at Boethianism in a way that the author does not. The author does not mention different levels of Boethianism when discussing the tales, only that the concept appears differently in different tales. Boethianism also doesn't focus on enlightenment.

60. D: Choice *A* is incorrect; while the text does mention thieves ravaging others' possessions, it is only meant as an example and not as the principle itself. Choice *B* is incorrect for the same reason as *A*. Choice *C* is mentioned in the text and is part of the example that proves the principle, but it is also not the principle itself.

61. C: The word *avarice* most nearly means *covetousness*, an extreme desire for money or wealth. Choice *A* means evil or mischief and does not relate to the context of the sentence. Choice *B* is also incorrect, because *pithiness* means shortness or conciseness. Choice *D* is close because *precariousness* means *danger* or *instability*, which goes well with the context. However, we are told of the summoner's specific characteristic of greed, which makes Choice *C* the best answer.

62. D: Boethianism acknowledges desire as something that leads out of holiness, so Choice *A* is incorrect. Choice *B* is incorrect because in the passage, Boethianism is depicted as being wary of desire and anything that binds people to the physical world. Choice *C* can be eliminated because the author never says that desire indicates demonic possession.

63. B: It is apparent that Lincoln is referring to a period of time within the context of the passage because the sentence contains the words *years* and *ago*. Choices *A*, *C*, and *D* do not fit the language or context of the sentence and are therefore incorrect.

64. C: Lincoln's reference to "the brave men, living and dead, who struggled here" proves that he is referring to a battlefield. Choices *A* and *B* are incorrect, as a civil war is mentioned and not a war with France or a war in the Sahara Desert. Choice *D* is incorrect because it does not make sense to consecrate a President's ground instead of a battlefield ground for soldiers who died during the American Civil War.

65. D: Abraham Lincoln is a former president of the United States, and he referenced a "civil war" during his address.

66. A: The speaker is trying to convey that the audience should perpetuate the ideals of freedom that the soldiers died fighting for. Lincoln doesn't address any of the topics outlined in Choices *B*, *C*, or *D*. Therefore, Choice *A* is the correct answer.

67. D: Choice D is the correct answer because of the repetition of the word *people* at the end of the passage. Choice A, *antimetatabole*, is the repetition of words in a succession. Choice B, *antiphrasis*, is a form of denial of an assertion in a text. Choice C, *anaphora*, is the repetition that occurs at the beginning of sentences.

68. A: Choice A is correct because Lincoln's intention was to memorialize the soldiers who had fallen as a result of war as well as celebrate those who had put their lives in danger for the sake of their country. Choices B, C, and D are incorrect because Lincoln's speech was supposed to foster a sense of pride among the members of the audience while connecting them to the soldiers' experiences.

69. C: In Choice C, *avid* is functioning as an adjective that modifies the word photographer. *Avid* describes the photographer Julia Robinson's style. The words *time* and *photographer* are functioning as nouns, and the word *capture* is functioning as a verb in the sentence. Other words functioning as adjectives in the sentence include *local*, *business*, and *spare*, as they all describe the nouns they precede.

70. B: Choice B is correct because the pronouns *he* and *I* are in the subjective case. *He* and *I* are the subjects of the verb *like* in the independent clause of the sentence. Choices A, C, and D are incorrect because they all contain at least one objective pronoun (*me* and *him*). Objective pronouns should not be used as the subject of the sentence, but rather, they should come as an object of a verb. To test for correct pronoun usage, try reading the pronouns as if they were the only pronoun in the sentence. For example, *he* and *me* may appear to be the correct answer choices, but try reading them as the only pronoun.

He like[s] to go fishing...

Me like to go fishing...

When looked at that way, *me* is an obviously incorrect choice.

71. D: In Choice D, the word *function* is a noun. While the word *function* can also act as a verb, in this particular sentence it is acting as a noun as the object of the preposition *at*. Choices A and B are incorrect because the word *function* cannot be used as an adjective or adverb.

72. C: *Cacti* is the correct plural form of the word *cactus*. Choice A (*tomatos*) includes an incorrect spelling of the plural of *tomato*. Both Choice B (*analysis*) and Choice D (*criterion*) are incorrect because they are in singular form. The correct plural form for these choices would be *criteria* and *analyses*.

73. A: The identification of morphemes within words occurs during the instruction of structural analysis. Structural analysis is a word recognition skill that focuses on the meanings of word parts, or morphemes, during the introduction of a new word. Choice B, syllabic analysis, is a word analysis skill that helps students split words into syllables. Choice C, phonics, is the direct correspondence between and blending of letters and sounds. Choice D, the alphabetic principle, teaches that letters or other characters represent sounds.

74. D: In Choice D, the word *part* functions as an adjective that modifies the word *Irish*. Choices A and C are incorrect because the word *part* functions as a noun in these sentences. Choice B is incorrect because the word *part* functions as a verb.

75. C: *All of Shannon's family and friends* is the complete subject because it includes who or what is doing the action in the sentence as well as the modifiers that go with it. Choice A is incorrect because it only includes the simple subject of the sentence. Choices B and D are incorrect because they only include part of the complete subject.

Answer Explanations #1

76. C: Choice C is correct because quotation marks should be used for the title of a short work such as a poem. Choices A, B, and D are incorrect because the titles of novels, films, and newspapers should be placed in italics, not quotation marks.

77. C: This question focuses on the correct usage of the commonly confused word pairs of *it's/its* and *then/than*. *It's* is a contraction for *it is* or *it has*. *Its* is a possessive pronoun. The word *than* shows comparison between two things. *Then* is an adverb that conveys time. Choice C correctly uses *it's* and *than*. *It's* is a contraction for *it has* in this sentence, and *than* shows comparison between *work* and *rest*. None of the other answers choices use both of the correct words.

78. A: Syntax refers to the arrangement of words and phrases to form properly flowing sentences and paragraphs. Semantics has to do with language meaning. Grammar is a composite of all systems and structures utilized within a language and includes syntax, word morphology, semantics, and phonology. Cohesion and coherence of oral and written language are promoted through a full understanding of syntax, semantics, and grammar.

79. C: Choice C is a compound sentence because it joins two independent clauses—*The baby was sick* and *I decided to stay home from work*—with a comma and the coordinating conjunction *so*. Choices A, B, and D are all simple sentences, each containing one independent clause with a complete subject and predicate. Choices A and D each contain a compound subject, or more than one subject, but they are still simple sentences that only contain one independent clause. Choice B contains a compound verb (more than one verb), but it's still a simple sentence.

80. C: The simple subject of this sentence, the word *lots*, is plural. It agrees with the plural verb form *were*. Choice A is incorrect, because the simple subject *there*, referring to the two constellations, is considered plural. It does not agree with the singular verb form *is*. In Choice B, the plural subject *four* does not agree with the singular verb form *needs*. In Choice D, the singular subject *everyone* does not agree with the third person plural verb form *have*.

Mathematics

1. A: Compare each number after the decimal point to figure out which overall number is greatest. In Choices A (1.43785) and C (1.43592), both have the same tenths place (4) and hundredths place (3). However, the thousandths place is greater in Choice A (7), so it has the greatest value overall.

2. D: By rearranging and grouping the factors in Choice D, we can notice that $3 \times 3 \times 4 \times 2 = (3 \times 2) \times (4 \times 3) = 6 \times 12$, which is what we were looking for.

3. A: To figure out which value is the largest, look at the first nonzero digits. Choice B's first nonzero digit is in the hundredths place. The other three all have nonzero digits in the tenths place, so it must be Choice A, C, or D. Of these, Choice A's first nonzero digit is the largest.

4. C: To solve for the value of b, isolate the variable b on one side of the equation.

Start by moving the lower value of -4 to the other side by adding 4 to both sides:

$$5b - 4 = 2b + 17$$

$$5b - 4 + 4 = 2b + 17 + 4$$

$$5b = 2b + 21$$

Then subtract $2b$ from both sides:

$$5b - 2b = 2b + 21 - 2b$$

$$3b = 21$$

Then, divide both sides by 3 to get the value of b:

$$\frac{3b}{3} = \frac{21}{3}$$

$$b = 7$$

5. B: Scientific notation starts with a number between 1 and 10 and multiplies it by a power of 10, so we can eliminate Choices C and D because they do not start with a number between 1 and 10 (even though C does equal the number in the question). The exponent on the 10 tells us how many places to move the decimal point. To get from 7.35 to 7,350,000,000, we have to move the decimal point 9 places to the right, so the exponent must be 9. This gives us 7.35×10^9, which is Choice B.

6. C: The first step in solving this problem is expressing the result in fraction form. Multiplication and division are typically performed in order from left to right, but they can be performed in any order. For this problem, start with the division operation between the last two fractions. When dividing one fraction by another, invert—or flip—the second fraction and then multiply the numerators and denominators.

$$\frac{7}{10} \times \frac{2}{1} = \frac{14}{10}$$

Next, multiply the first fraction by this value:

$$\frac{3}{5} \times \frac{14}{10} = \frac{42}{50}$$

In this instance, to find the decimal form, multiply the numerator and denominator by 2 to get 100 in the denominator. In decimal form, this would be expressed as 0.84.

7. C: The product of two irrational numbers can be rational or irrational. Sometimes the irrational parts of the two numbers cancel each other out, leaving a rational number. For example, $\sqrt{2} \times \sqrt{2} = 2$ because the roots cancel each other out. Technically, the product of two irrational numbers is a complex number, because real numbers are a type of complex number. However, Choice D is incorrect because the product of two irrational numbers is not an imaginary number.

8. C: The terms "whole numbers" and "natural numbers" include all the ordinary counting numbers $(1, 2, 3, 4, 5, ...)$, and sometimes zero depending on the definition used, but no negative numbers. The term "integers" includes all those numbers, their negatives, and zero. So -4 is not a whole number or a natural number, but it is an integer. It is also rational because it can be written as a ratio of two integers $(-\frac{4}{1})$; all integers are rational. It is a real number because it does not have an imaginary component (symbolized by the letter i); all integers are real numbers.

9. A: Setting up a proportion is the easiest way to represent this situation. The proportion is $\frac{20}{x} = \frac{40}{100}$, and cross-multiplication can be used to solve for x. Here, $40x = 2,000$, so $x = 50$.

Answer Explanations #1

10. A: Finding the product means distributing one polynomial to the other so that each term in the first is multiplied by each term in the second. Then, like terms can be collected. Multiplying the factors yields the expression:

$$20x^3 + 4x^2 + 24x - 40x^2 - 8x - 48$$

Collecting like terms means adding the x^2 terms and adding the x terms. The final answer after simplifying the expression is:

$$20x^3 - 36x^2 + 16x - 48$$

11. B: We can try to solve the equation by factoring the numerator into:

$$(x + 6)(x - 5)$$

Since $(x - 5)$ is on the top and bottom, that factor cancels out. This leaves the equation $x + 6 = 11$. Solving the equation gives the answer $x = 5$. When this value is plugged into the equation, it yields a zero in the denominator of the fraction. Since this is undefined, there is no solution.

12. C: It may help to look at this problem as a fraction: $\frac{1.2 \times 10^{12}}{3.0 \times 10^8}$. We can calculate $\frac{1.2}{3} = 0.4$, and using the rules of exponents, we can see that:

$$\frac{10^{12}}{10^8} = 10^8 = 10^{(12-8)} = 10^4$$

This gives us an answer of 0.4×10^4, which is Choice A, but our answer is not yet in scientific notation because the first term, 0.4, is not between 1 and 10. We can rewrite 0.4×10^4, multiplying the first term by 10 and subtracting 1 from the exponent, which gives 4.0×10^3, Choice C.

13. D: We can work backwards to figure this out one step at a time. "Sum" means the result of addition, so "the sum of twice a number and one" can be written as $2x + 1$. Next, "three times the sum of twice a number and one" would be $3(2x + 1)$. Finally, "six less than three times the sum of twice a number and one" would be $3(2x + 1) - 6$.

14. B: To solve this correctly, keep in mind the order of operations with the mnemonic PEMDAS (Please Excuse My Dear Aunt Sally). This stands for Parentheses, Exponents, Multiplication & Division, Addition & Subtraction. Taking it step by step, start with the parentheses:

$$4 \times 7 + (4)^2 \div 2$$

Then, apply the exponent:

$$4 \times 7 + 16 \div 2$$

Multiplication and division are both performed next:

$$28 + 8$$

Then finally, addition:

$$28 + 8 = 36$$

Answer Explanations #1

15. D:

$9x + x - 7 = 16 + 2x$	Combine $9x$ and x.
$10x - 7 = 16 + 2x$	
$10x - 7 + 7 = 16 + 2x + 7$	Add 7 to both sides to remove the –7.
$10x = 23 + 2x$	
$10x - 2x = 23 + 2x - 2x$	Subtract $2x$ from both sides to move it to the other side of the equation.
$8x = 23$	
$\dfrac{8x}{8} = \dfrac{23}{8}$	Divide by 8 to get x by itself.
$x = \dfrac{23}{8}$	

16. C: For each fraction, we can divide the numerator by the denominator to find a decimal value. $\dfrac{4}{5} = 0.8$, $\dfrac{2}{3} \approx 0.67$, and $\dfrac{91}{100} = 0.91$. Ordering these from least to greatest gives us 0.67, 0.8, 0.85, and 0.91, which matches Choice C.

17. B: First, calculate the difference between the larger value and the smaller value:

$$378 - 252 = 126$$

To calculate this difference as a percentage of the original value, and thus calculate the percentage *increase*, divide 126 by 252 to get 0.5, then multiply by 100 to reach the percentage 50%, Choice B.

18. A: First, simplify the larger fraction by separating it into two. When dividing one fraction by another, remember to invert the second fraction and multiply, like so:

$$\dfrac{5}{7} \times \dfrac{11}{9}$$

The resulting fraction $\dfrac{55}{63}$ cannot be simplified further, so this is the answer to the problem.

19. 6. A: Order of operations follows PEMDAS: Parentheses, Exponents, Multiplication and Division from left to right, and Addition and Subtraction from left to right.

20. C: The total percentage of a pie chart equals 100%. CD sales make up less than half of the chart (50%) but more than a quarter (25%), and the only answer choice that meets these criteria is Choice C, 40%.

21. A: Divide 54 by 15:

$$15\overline{)54}\begin{array}{r}3\\-45\\\hline 9\end{array}$$

Answer Explanations #1

The result is 3 with a remainder of 9, which is equivalent to $3\frac{9}{15}$. Reduce the fraction $\frac{9}{15}$ for the final answer, $3\frac{3}{5}$.

22. D: The original number was $8\frac{3}{7}$. Multiply the denominator by the whole number portion. Add the numerator, and put the total over the original denominator.

$$\frac{(8 \times 7) + 3}{7} = \frac{59}{7}$$

23. B: Multiplying by 10^{-3} means moving the decimal point three places to the left, putting in zeros as necessary.

24. C: The teacher would be introducing fractions. If a pie was cut into 6 pieces, each piece would represent $\frac{1}{6}$ of the pie. If one piece was taken away, $\frac{5}{6}$ of the pie would be left over.

25. C: The formula for the perimeter of a rectangle is $P = 2L + 2W$, where P is the perimeter, L is the length, and W is the width. The first step is to substitute all of the data into the formula:

$$36 = 2(12) + 2W$$

Simplify by multiplying 2×12:

$$36 = 24 + 2W$$

Simplifying this further by subtracting 24 on each side gives:

$$36 - 24 = 24 - 24 + 2W$$

$$12 = 2W$$

Divide by 2:

$$6 = W$$

The width is 6 cm. Remember to test this answer by substituting this value into the original formula:

$$36 = 2(12) + 2(6)$$

26. D: If we roll a die twice, there are six possibilities for the first roll and six for the second roll, which gives $6 \times 6 = 36$ total possibilities. Now, how many ways are there to roll at least one 6? We could get a 6 & 1, or 6 & 2, or 6 & 3, or 6 & 4, or 6 & 5, or 6 & 6. Or, the 6 could come on the second roll; we could get a 1 & 6, or 2 & 6, or 3 & 6, or 4 & 6, or 5 & 6, or 6 & 6. Counting up all these possibilities, disregarding the duplicate 6 & 6 (since it appears in both lists), we find a total of 11 different ways to roll at least one 6. That means our event happens in 11 out of 36 possible rolls, so the probability is $\frac{11}{36}$.

27. D: When a point is reflected over an axis, the sign of at least one of the coordinates must change. When it's reflected over the x-axis, the sign of the y coordinate must change. The x-value remains the same. Therefore, the new point is $(-3, 4)$.

28. B: The car is traveling at a speed of 5 meters per second. On the interval from 1 to 3 seconds, the position changes by 10 meters. This is 10 meters in 2 seconds, or 5 meters in each second.

Answer Explanations #1

29. B: An equilateral triangle has 3 sides of equal length, so if the total perimeter is 18 feet, each side must be 6 feet long. A square with sides of 6 feet will have an area of $6^2 = 36$ square feet.

30. B: The formula for the volume of a cube is $V = s^3$. Substitute the side length of 7 in to get:

$$V = 7^3 = 343 \text{ in}^3$$

31. A: The Pythagorean theorem tells us that $8^2 + x^2 = 10^2$, where x is the unknown side. This simplifies to:

$$64 + x^2 = 100$$

$$x^2 = 100 - 64 = 36$$

$$x = \sqrt{36} = 6 \text{ inches}$$

32. A: Putting the scores in order from least to greatest, we have 60, 75, 80, and 85, as well as one unknown. The median is 80, so 80 must be the middle data point out of these five. Therefore, the unknown data point must be the fourth or fifth data point, meaning it must be greater than or equal to 80. The only answer that fails to meet this condition is 60.

33. D: This problem can be solved by setting up a proportion involving the given information and the unknown value. The proportion is:

$$\frac{21 \text{ pages}}{4 \text{ nights}} = \frac{140 \text{ pages}}{x \text{ nights}}$$

Cross-multiply to get $21x = 4 \times 140$. Solving this leaves $x \approx 26.67$. Since this is not an integer, round up to 27 nights because 26 nights would not give Sarah enough time to finish.

34. D: First, subtract $1,437 from $2,334.50 to find Johnny's monthly savings; this equals $897.50. Then, multiply this amount by 3 to find out how much he will have (in 3 months) before he pays for his vacation; this equals $2,692.50. Finally, subtract the cost of the vacation ($1,750) from this amount to find how much Johnny will have left: $942.50.

35. C: Kimberley worked 4.5 hours at the rate of $10/h and 1 hour at the rate of $12/h. The problem states that her time is rounded to the nearest hour, so the 4.5 hours would round up to 5 hours at the rate of $10/h.

$$(5 \text{ h}) \times (\$10/\text{h}) + (1 \text{ h}) \times (\$12/\text{h}) = \$50 + \$12 = \$62$$

36. C: The data points do not appear to form any sort of line, even approximately, as we would expect for a positive or negative relationship. They also do not form the characteristic bell-shaped curve of a normal distribution. No relationship is apparent.

37. B: The table shows values that are increasing exponentially. The differences between the inputs are the same, while the differences in the outputs are changing by a factor of 2. The values in the table can be modeled by the equation $f(x) = 2^x$.

38. B: To factor $x^2 + 4x + 4$, the numbers needed are those that add to 4 and multiply to 4. Therefore, both numbers must be 2, and the expression factors to:

$$x^2 + 4x + 4 = (x + 2)^2$$

Similarly, the second expression factors to $x^2 - x - 6 = (x - 3)(x + 2)$, so that they have $x + 2$ in common.

Answer Explanations #1

39. B: When solving for x, add 3 to both sides to get $4x = 8$. Then, divide both sides by 4 to get $x = 2$.

40. C: The sample space is made up of:

$$8 + 7 + 6 + 5 = 26 \text{ balls}$$

The probability of pulling each individual ball is $\frac{1}{26}$. Since there are 7 yellow balls, the probability of pulling a yellow ball is $\frac{7}{26}$.

Social Studies

1. B: John White does not have an important historical influence to the state of Georgia. White was the leader of the Roanoke colony founded under the authority of Sir Walter Raleigh in what was then called Virginia and later became North Carolina. White went back to England for supplies in 1587, and when he returned, all of the colonists had mysteriously disappeared.

2. B: To avoid involvement in political processes such as voting is antithetical to the principles of a democracy. Therefore, the principal responsibility of citizens is the opposite, and they should be steadily engaged in the political processes that determine the course of government.

3. A: Heavily influenced by the Enlightenment, the Declaration of Independence repudiated the colonies' allegiance to Great Britain. The main purpose of the excerpt is to justify the colonists' revolutionary stance due to Great Britain's tyranny and the role of consent in government to protect the natural rights of citizens. Choice *B* is incorrect because, although the excerpt alludes to abuses, the purpose isn't to list specific evidence. This occurs later in the Declaration of Independence. Choices *C* and *D* are supporting evidence for the main purpose.

4. A: James Oglethorpe convinced King George II to colonize the area that is now Georgia with individuals from Britain's overflowing debtor's prisons. Button Gwinnett, George Walton, and Lyman Hall were the three Georgians who signed the Declaration of Independence in 1776. Thus, Choices *B*, *C*, and *D* are incorrect.

5. C: At the time of the Constitutional Convention, Thomas Jefferson was in Paris serving as America's foreign minister to France. Therefore, he is not a good fit for this project. George Washington led the meeting, and Alexander Hamilton and James Madison set the tone for debate, rendering *A*, *B*, and *D* incorrect.

6. A: Plains Indians followed the buffalo across the prairies, living in tent-like teepees that were easily moved from place to place. Choice *B* is incorrect because Native Americans in the Southwest relied on farming for much of their food and built adobes, which are houses made out of dried clay or earth. Native Americans in the Eastern and Northwest sections of North America survived by hunting, gathering, farming, and fishing, and lived in wooden longhouses, plank houses, or wigwams. Thus, Choices *C* and *D* are incorrect.

7. C: Established in 1607, Jamestown, Virginia was the first permanent British settlement in the New World. Plymouth was founded a bit later in 1620 when a group of Pilgrims founded the first permanent European settlement in New England, making Choice *A* incorrect. Choice *B* is incorrect because although the Roanoke Colony was founded in 1585, it isn't considered permanent—the colony's leader, John White, went back to England for supplies two years later, and he returned to find that all of the colonists had mysteriously disappeared. Choice *D* is incorrect because L'Anse Meadows was an area in Newfoundland that was briefly settled by Scandinavian Vikings around 1000 AD.

Answer Explanations #1

8. C: The first shot took place on Lexington Green. When the British heard that colonists were stockpiling weapons, they sent troops to Concord to seize them. However, a group of approximately seventy Minutemen confronted the British soldiers on Lexington Green. British troops killed five protesting colonists during the Boston Massacre in 1770, but this is not considered the first shot of the Revolution. Thus, Choice *A* is incorrect. Choice *B* is incorrect because the Boston Tea Party was when colonists dumped 342 chests of expensive tea into the Boston Harbor in defiance of the tea tax. The Revolution had already started when the Battle of Trenton took place on December 25, 1776, making Choice *D* incorrect.

9. D: There are 27 amendments to the US Constitution. The 14th Amendment was adopted in 1868 to abolish slavery. The 18th Amendment was passed in 1919 and prohibited the production and sale of alcoholic beverages, but the 21st Amendment repealed it in 1933.

10. D: Thematic maps create certain themes in which they attempt to illustrate a certain phenomenon or pattern. The obvious theme of a climate map is the climates in the represented areas. Thematic maps are very extensive and can include thousands of different themes, which makes them quite useful for students of geography. Topographic maps, Choice *A*, are utilized to show physical features; conformal projections, Choice *B*, attempt to illustrate the globe in an undistorted fashion; and isoline maps, Choice *C*, illustrate differences in variables between two points on a map.

11. B: Latitudinal and longitudinal coordinates delineate absolute location. Absolute location provides an exact place on the globe through the latitude and longitude system. Cardinal directions (north, south, east, west), Choice *A*, are used in absolute location, but coordinates must be added in order to have an absolute location. Relative location, Choice *C*, describes a location as compared to another, better-known place. Absolute location is far more precise than simply finding the hemispherical position on the globe, Choice *D*.

12. C: Each statement about culture is correct except for Choice *C*. Cultures often will adapt to the settings in which they are found. Improvements in technology, changes in social values, and interactions with other cultures all contribute to cultural change.

13. B: Lines of latitude measure distance north and south. The equator is zero degrees, and the Tropic of Cancer is 23.5 degrees north of the equator. The distance between those two lines measures degrees north to south, as with any other two lines of latitude. Longitudinal lines, or meridians, measure distance east and west, even though they run north and south down the globe. Latitude is not inexact, in that there are set distances between the lines. Furthermore, coordinates can only exist with the use of longitude and latitude.

14. D: During the Achaemenid Empire, Persians practiced the Zoroastrian faith and worshipped two gods. Islam only came about one thousand years later. The Achaemenids built a Royal Road that stretched across their empire, but the Silk Roads expanded throughout Asia. The Achaemenids twice tried to conquer Greece but failed both times.

15. A: The Silk Roads were a network of trade routes between Asia and the Mediterranean. Merchants and Pilgrims traveled along the Silk Roads and brought new ideas and technologies, as well as trade goods. For example, Buddhism spread from India to China. Chinese technologies also spread westward, including gunpowder and the printing press. The Silk Roads also spread the Bubonic Plague to Europe, but it did not arrive in the New World until Columbus landed there in 1492.

16. A: Large numbers of Franks, Goths, Vandals, and other Germanic peoples began moving south in the 5th century AD. They conquered Rome twice, and the Western Roman Empire finally disintegrated. The Mongol invasion, Choice *B*, pushed westward in the 13th century, long after the western Roman Empire was gone. The assassination of Julius Caesar, Choice *C*, led to the end of the Roman Republic and the birth of the Roman Empire. Taoism never spread to Rome, making Choice *D* incorrect.

Answer Explanations #1

17. A: The Mongols were a nomadic people who trained as horsemen from a young age. They used their highly mobile army to build a huge empire in Asia, the Middle East, and Eastern Europe. Mongol rulers were relatively tolerant of other religions because they wanted to reduce conflict within their empire, making Choice *B* incorrect. They also encouraged trade because they produced few of their own goods, making Choice *C* incorrect. The Mongol rulers also encouraged literacy and appreciated visual art, making Choice *D* incorrect.

18. A: Renaissance scholars and artists sought to emulate classical Greek and Roman culture. They translated Greek and Roman political philosophers and literature. They also copied classical architecture. Europeans had little direct contact with China until the 13th century, which was long after the Zhou Dynasty collapsed, making Choice *C* incorrect. The Renaissance Era occurred within the continent of Europe and drew from other European styles, so nations of northern Africa and the Middle East, such as ancient Egypt and the Ottoman Empire, had little to no inspiration on Renaissance scholars and artists at that time. Therefore, Choices *B* and *D* are incorrect.

19. C: In the 1800s, nationalists in different parts of Europe encouraged their countrymen to take pride in their shared backgrounds. This led to tension between different nations, as each sought to increase its status and prestige. The French and British nearly came to blows in Africa, and nationalism ultimately led to World War I in 1914. France and Spain were unified several centuries before the 1800s.

20. D: All three events led to increasing tension and conflict between the colonists and the British government, which finally exploded at the Battle of Lexington and Concord in 1775. The Stamp Act of 1765 imposed a tax on documents. It was repealed after colonists organized protests. The Boston Massacre resulted in the death of five colonists in 1770. The Boston Tea Party was a protest in 1773 against a law that hurt colonial tea merchants. The British responded to the tea party by punishing the colony of Massachusetts, which created fear among the other colonies and united them against the British government.

21. D: Sovereignty is the feature that differentiates a state from a nation. Nations have no sovereignty, as they are unable to enact and enforce laws independently of their state. A state must possess sovereignty over the population of a territory in order to be legitimized as a state. Both a nation and a state must have a population, Choice *C*. Although sometimes present, shared history and common language are not requirements for a state, making Choices *A* and *B* incorrect.

22. A: Devastated by World War II, Britain and France were unable to maintain their empires. Japan and Germany were also weak, which left only the United States and USSR as superpowers. The Russian Revolution had occurred during World War I, in 1917, making Choice *B* incorrect. Ideological and economic conflict between the US and the USSR led to the start of the Cold War shortly after World War II ended, making Choice *C* incorrect. Choice *D* is also incorrect; the death of Franz Ferdinand marked the beginning of World War I.

23. A: Ethnic groups are simply a group of people with a religious, cultural, economic, or linguistic commonality. Although some ethnic groups throughout the world do engage in armed conflicts, the vast majority do not. Most ethnic groups tend to live in relative harmony with others with whom they share differences. Ethnic groups don't always choose to leave places; many have called certain locations home for centuries. Additionally, some ethnic groups actually make up the majority in some countries; they're not always minority groups.

24. A: The use of biotechnology and GMOs has increased the total amount of food on Earth and helped to sustain the Earth's growing population. However, many activists assert that scientists are creating crops that, in the long run, will be destructive to human health, even though not enough evidence exists to prove such an allegation. Agricultural production has not been affected by poorer soil, plagues of pests, or the use of saline for irrigation purposes.

Answer Explanations #1

25. C: Like the boundaries of the United States, political boundaries are constantly changing due to war (South Sudan), religious conflict (India and Pakistan, Israel, East Timor), and differing political ideologies (North and South Korea, reunification of Germany after the Cold War). The only constant with political boundaries is change. It is not possible to see manmade lines separating countries on Earth, unless they are natural boundaries. Additionally, boundaries are always under dispute, and they have not remained static for centuries.

26. B: Macroeconomics studies the economy on a large scale and focuses on issues such as unemployment, interest rates, price levels, and national income. Microeconomics studies more individual or small group behaviors such as scarcity or supply and demand. Scarcity is incorrect because it refers to the availability of goods and services. Supply and demand is also incorrect because it refers to the quantity of goods and services that is produced and/or needed.

27. A: A free market does not involve government interventions or monopolies while trading between buyers and suppliers. However, in a command market, the government determines the price of goods and services. Gross and exchange markets refer to situations where brokers and traders make exchanges in the financial realm.

28. D: The theory of the firm refers to the behavior that firms use to reach their desired outcome. GDP, unemployment, and inflation are all indicators that help determine economic growth.

29. A: Most scholars already knew the world was round by 1492. On the other hand, the arrival of Europeans in North and South America introduced deadly diseases that killed millions of native peoples. Europeans had developed immunity to diseases such as smallpox, while Native Americans had not. In addition, Europeans introduced a number of new plants and animals to the New World, but they also adopted many new foods as well, including potatoes, tomatoes, chocolate, and tobacco. Finally, Europeans tried to convert Native Americans to Christianity, but Native Americans did not completely give up their traditional beliefs. Instead, they blended Christianity with indigenous and African beliefs to create new syncretic religions.

30. D: The Industrial Revolution is one of the most important turning points in world history. The United States and Western Europe, especially Britain, were the first areas to industrialize. Steam engines were used to improve economic and transportation efficiency. They also gave western empires a military advantage over less developed countries in Asia and Africa. Finally, industrialization required large amounts of unskilled labor, which created the working class.

31. D: The Constitution granted Congress the power to decide how many justices should be on the court, and Congress first decided on six judges in the Judiciary Act of 1789. The Constitution granted the power to appoint judges and to call special sessions of Congress to the president. Only the Supreme Court may interpret the laws enacted by Congress and rule a law unconstitutional and subsequently overturn the law.

32. C: The first ten amendments to the Constitution are collectively referred to as the Bill of Rights. The Founding Fathers did not support universal suffrage, and as such, the Bill of Rights did not encompass the freedom to vote. The Fifteenth Amendment provided that the right to vote shall not be denied on the basis of race, color, or previous condition of servitude, and women did not receive the right to vote until passage of the Nineteenth Amendment. The other three answer choices are included in the Bill of Rights: the freedom to assembly is established in the First Amendment, the freedom against unlawful search is established in the Fourth Amendment, and the reservation of non-enumerated powers to the states or the people is established in the Tenth Amendment.

33. C: The President of the United States is elected by the Electoral College. The number of electors for each state depends on the state's total number of senators and representatives. The president must receive a majority

Answer Explanations #1

(270) of the electoral votes (538), and if this doesn't occur, the Twelfth Amendment empowers the House of Representatives to elect the president. Choices *A*, *B*, and *C* are different methods for electing candidates.

34. B: President Franklin D. Roosevelt introduced the New Deal, a series of executive orders and laws passed by Congress in response to the Great Depression. The excerpt describes how President Roosevelt intended to fight poverty by using the government's power to intervene and regulate the economy. Although Choices *A*, *C*, and *D* correctly identify specific activities referenced in the excerpt, they are specific examples of the underlying philosophy in action. The underlying philosophy is an active role for government in the nation's economic affairs.

35. D: The two major political parties hold conventions to nominate their presidential candidate. The delegates are awarded based on candidates' performance in the primary elections or caucuses vote at the party convention to select the nominee. Primaries and caucuses are the democratic contests held by each state to award their delegates. The candidates participate in debates on the campaign issues, but they do not receive the nomination at debates.

36. B: The process by which the House and Senate may debate a bill differs. In the House, how long a speaker may debate a bill is limited, while in the Senate, speakers may debate the bill indefinitely and delay voting on the bill by filibuster—a practice in which a speaker refuses to stop speaking until a majority vote stops the filibuster or the time for the vote passes. In both the House and the Senate, anyone may introduce a bill. Only the president of the United States may veto the bill, so neither the House nor Senate holds that power. Before the bill may be presented to the president to be signed, the wording of the bill must be identical in both houses. Another procedural difference is that the number of amendments is limited in the House but not the Senate; however, this does not appear as an answer choice.

37. C: Map projections, such as the Mercator Projection, are useful for finding positions on the globe, but they attempt to represent a spherical object on a flat surface. As a result, they distort areas nearest the poles, which misrepresent the size of Antarctica, Greenland, and other high latitudinal locations. Map projects can include great detail; some illustrate the physical features in an area, and most include both the northern and southern hemispheres.

38. C: Although it can place a strain on some resources, population density is not a negative demographic indicator. For example, New York City, one of the most densely populated places on Earth, enjoys one of the highest standards of living in the world. Other world cities such as Tokyo, Los Angeles, and Sydney also have tremendously high population densities and high standards of living. High infant mortality rates, low literacy rates, and low life expectancies are all poor demographic indicators that suggest a low quality of life for the citizens living in those areas.

39. C: Longitudinal position, or a place's location either east or west, has no bearing on the place's climate. In contrast, a place's latitudinal position, or its distance away from the direct rays of the Sun in the Tropics, greatly affects its climate. Additionally, proximity to mountains, which can block wind patterns, and elevation, which generally lowers temperature by three degrees for every one thousand feet gained, also impact climate.

40. B: Choice *B* is correct, as power is the ability of a ruling body to influence the actions, behavior, and attitude of a person or group of people. Choice *A* is incorrect, as politics is the process of governance typically exercised through the enactment and enforcement of laws over a community, such as a state. Although closely related to power, Choice *C* is incorrect, because authority refers to a political entity's justification to exercise power. Legitimacy is synonymous with authority, so Choice *D* is also incorrect.

41. C: Sovereignty is a characteristic of a nation that is self-governing, which can only happen after the nation has been formed. Choices *A*, *B*, and *D* are incorrect because, while there are no definitive requirements to form

Answer Explanations #1

a nation, they typically begin with a group of people bound by some shared characteristic. Examples include language, culture and traditions, history, beliefs and religion, homeland or geography, and ethnicity.

42. B: The Articles of Confederation were the first form of government adopted in the American colonies. Under the Articles of Confederation, the central government (the Continental Congress) was granted very limited powers, rendering it largely ineffective. Although the choices describe what would appear to be basic functions of government, the central government could only declare war.

43. B: Industrialization directly caused an increase in urbanization. Factories were located near cities to draw upon a large pool of potential employees. Between 1860 and 1890, the urbanization rate increased from about 20 percent to 35 percent. The other three choices are factually incorrect. Immigration increased during industrialization, as immigrants flooded into America to search for work. Socioeconomic problems plagued the period due to the unequal distribution of wealth and the social ills caused by rapid urbanization. Labor unrest was common as unions advocated for workers' rights and organized national strikes.

44. A: The Treaty of Versailles contained a clause that required Germany to assume responsibility for damages incurred during the conflict. Thus, the Treaty ordered Germany to pay $31.4 billion, the equivalent of $442 billion in 2017. World War I ravaged the German economy, and the country couldn't afford the war debt. The resulting poverty contributed to the rise of the Nazi Party, leading to World War II.

45. D: President Lincoln issued the Emancipation Proclamation to free the slaves in the Confederacy, allowing the institution to continue in states and territories that didn't secede. The excerpt justifies the decision as a "fit and necessary war measure for suppressing said rebellion." Therefore, per the excerpt, emancipation was necessary to strengthen the war effort for the North. Choice *C* is the second-best answer, but the excerpt supports the contention that emancipation was part of an active war effort, rather than merely a punishment. Choices *A* and *B* are incorrect because nothing in the excerpt describes the evil of slavery or the effect of emancipation on morale in the North.

46. B: In the US, the powers of government are divided between the federal and state governments. Choice *A* is incorrect because federalism does not refer to a relationship between the federal government and the people. Instead, the federal government interacts with the people through their state governments. Choice *C* is incorrect because the relationship between the branches of the federal government is defined by a system of checks and balances, not federalism. Choice *D* is incorrect because the Constitution lays out the system of federalism, but federalism does not describe the relationship between the federal government and the Constitution.

47. D: *Brown v. Board of Education* set the stage for the fight for civil rights throughout the United States and was the first true rebuff to segregation. It overturned the separate but equal doctrine laid out in the Plessy v. Ferguson Supreme Court case. on Supreme Court case. Choice *A* is incorrect because the doctrine of judicial review was established one hundred years earlier and has never been overturned. Choice *B* is incorrect because the public safety exception has to do with Miranda Rights. Choice *C* is incorrect because the due process doctrine doesn't apply here.

48. C: Population density, which is the total number of people divided by the total land area, generally tends to be much higher in urban areas than rural ones. This is true due to high-rise apartment complexes, sewage and freshwater infrastructure, and complex transportation systems, allowing for easy movement of food from nearby farms. Consequently, competition among citizens for resources is certainly higher in high-density areas, as are greater strains on infrastructure within urban centers.

49. A: Homogeneity, or the condition of similarity, is the unifying factor in most formal regions. Regions have one or more unifying characteristics, such as language, religion, history, or economic similarities, which make

Answer Explanations #1

the area a cohesive formal region. A good example is the Southern United States. In contrast, diversity and multilingualism, Choices *B* and *C*, are factors that may cause a region to lose homogeneity and be more difficult to classify as a region. Also, social mobility, Choice *D*, is a distractor that refers to one's ability to improve their economic standing in society and is not related to formal regions.

50. A: Globalization has put students and workers in direct conflict with one another despite their relative level of physical separation. For example, students who excel in mathematics and engineering may be recruited by multinational firms who want the best talent for their business despite where they are educated. Furthermore, products produced in other nations are also in competition with global manufacturers to ensure quality craftsmanship at an affordable price. Globalization does not refer to world domination, an absence of nation-states, or a singular world government.

51. C: The Federal Reserve is the bank of banks. A commodity is the value of goods such as precious metals. While "Central Reserve" and "Bank Reserve" may sound like good options, the term "bank reserve" refers to the amount of money a bank deposits into a central bank, and "Central Reserve" is simply a fictitious name.

52. D: The GDP is used to measure an economy's growth. The inflation of a country doesn't tell us anything about their growth. A country may hold a lot of money in reserves but this does not tell us if they are growing or not. The same can be said for having a lot of exports. It doesn't indicate that an economy is necessarily growing.

53. B: Developing nations tend to have higher levels of impoverished citizens. As a result, many of their citizens must rely on subsistence farming, or producing enough food to feed their families, in order to survive. In contrast, developed nations tend to produce surpluses of food and very few, if any, of its citizens engage in subsistence farming. Developing nations are less likely to have complex highway systems, stable governments, and economic stability due to financial pressures.

54. C: The 19th Amendment gave women the right to vote. The 15th Amendment, Choice *A*, gave African Americans the right to vote. The 18th Amendment, Choice *B*, introduced alcohol prohibition. The 21st Amendment, Choice *D*, repealed prohibition.

55. B: More than one million African Americans in the South went north in search of jobs during and after World War I. The Great Migration led to increased racial tension as black and white Americans competed for housing and jobs in northern cities. The Great Migration also led to the Harlem Renaissance.

Science

1. D: Water is essential for photosynthesis. Increasing temperatures increase transpiration and drought conditions result in less water available for photosynthesis. The rate of photosynthesis will decrease.

2. D: Genetic variety in a species allows them to be more resistant to stresses. Having genetic diversity increases resilience. Growing multiple strains of tomatoes or multiple types of crops could protect the farm.

3. C: During a lunar eclipse, the Sun and Moon are on opposite sides of the Earth. They line up so that the Sun's light that normally illuminates the Moon is blocked by the Earth. This causes the Moon to become dim. Sunlight can still be seen, Choice *A*, and the Earth does not become dark, Choices *B* and *D*.

4. A: When activated, B cells create antibodies against specific antigens. White blood cells are generated in red and yellow bone marrow, not cartilage. Platelets are not a type of white blood cell and are typically cell fragments produced by megakaryocytes. White blood cells are active throughout nearly all of one's life and have not been shown to specially activate or deactivate because of life events like puberty or menopause.

5. D: Mechanical digestion is physical digestion of food by tearing it into smaller pieces using force. This occurs in the stomach and mouth. Chemical digestion involves chemically changing the food and breaking it down into small organic compounds that can be utilized by the cell to build molecules. The salivary glands in the mouth secrete amylase that breaks down starch, which begins chemical digestion. The stomach contains enzymes such as pepsinogen/pepsin and gastric lipase which chemically digest protein and fats, respectively. The small intestine continues to digest protein using the enzymes trypsin and chymotrypsin. It also digests fats with the help of bile from the liver and lipase from the pancreas. These organs act as exocrine glands because they secrete substances through a duct. Carbohydrates are digested in the small intestine with the help of pancreatic amylase, gut bacterial flora and fauna, and brush border enzymes like lactose. Brush border enzymes are contained in the towel-like microvilli in the small intestine that soak up nutrients.

6. D: Charles Darwin developed the theory of natural selection, which explains the evolutionary process. He postulated that heritable genetic differences could aid an organism's chance of survival in its environment. The organisms with favorable traits pass genes to their offspring, and because they have more reproductive success than those that do not contain the adaptation, the favorable gene spreads throughout the population. Those that do not contain the adaptation often extinguish, so their genes are not passed on. In this way, nature "selects" for the organisms that have more fitness in their environment. Birds with bright-colored feathers and cacti with spines are examples of "fit" organisms.

7. B: The structure exclusively found in eukaryotic cells is the nucleus. Animal, plant, fungi, and protist cells are all eukaryotic. DNA is contained within the nucleus of eukaryotic cells, and they also have membrane-bound organelles that perform complex intracellular metabolic activities. Prokaryotic cells (archaea and bacteria) do not have a nucleus or other membrane-bound organelles and are less complex than eukaryotic cells.

8. B: The cell structure responsible for cellular storage, digestion, and waste removal is the lysosome. Lysosomes are like recycle bins. They are filled with digestive enzymes that facilitate catabolic reactions to regenerate monomers. The Golgi apparatus is designed to tag, package, and ship out proteins destined for other cells or locations. The centrioles typically play a large role only in cell division when they ratchet the chromosomes from the mitotic plate to the poles of the cell. The mitochondria are involved in energy production and are the powerhouses of the cell.

9. A: Crossing over, or genetic recombination, is the rearrangement of chromosomal sections in tetrads during meiosis, and it results in each gamete having a different combination of alleles than other gametes. The disassembly of the mitotic spindle happens only after telophase and is not related to diversity. While nondisjunction does cause diversity in division and is highly noticeable in gametes formed through meiosis, it can also happen through mitotic division in somatic cells. Although an egg being fertilized by multiple sperm would lead to interesting diversity in the offspring (and possibly fraternal twins), this is not strictly a byproduct of meiotic division.

10. C: Deserts' temperatures are extremely hot in the day and cold at night because of the warming effects of the sun's solar rays, so this is the best example of the sun's energy. Although some flowers do tend to bloom after dawn, this is probably due to day/night cycles regulated by the presence of light rather than intense amounts of energy. Hibernating animals tend to use large repositories of stored nutrients as energy sources rather than relying on the sun's energy, and they may in fact be in caves or hidden underground to shelter them from the Sun or weather. The tides are more dependent on the Moon due to its gravity rather than any effects its albedo moonlight may have.

11. A: Gases like air will move and expand to fill their container, so they are considered to have an indefinite shape and indefinite volume. Liquids like water will move and flow freely, so their shapes change constantly, but they do not change volume or density on their own. Solids change neither shape nor volume without external forces acting on them, so they have definite shapes and volumes.

12. B: Since the genotype is a depiction of the specific alleles that an organism's genes code for, it includes recessive genes that may or may not be otherwise expressed. The genotype does not have to name the proteins that its alleles code for; indeed, some of them may be unknown. The phenotype is the physical, visual manifestations of a gene, not the genotype. The genotype does not necessarily include any information about the organism's physical characteristics. Although some information about an organism's parents can be obtained from its genotype, its genotype does not actually show the parents' phenotypes.

13. C: One in four offspring (or 25%) will be short, so all four offspring cannot be tall. Although both of the parents are tall, they are hybrid or heterozygous tall, not homozygous. Although it may seem intuitive that the short allele will be expressed by lower numbers of the population than the tall allele, it still appears in 75% of the offspring (although its effects are masked in 2/3 of those). Besides, conditions could favor the recessive allele and kill off the tall offspring.

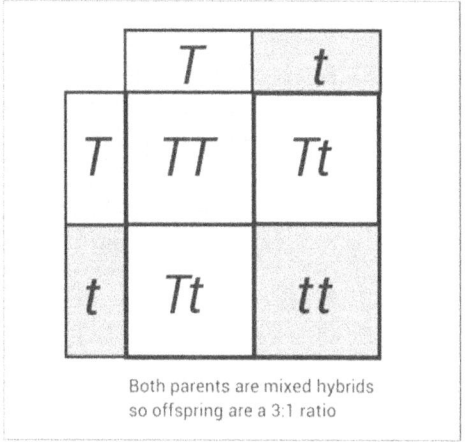
Both parents are mixed hybrids so offspring are a 3:1 ratio

14. D: Evaporation takes place at the surface of a fluid while, boiling takes place throughout the fluid. The liquid will boil when it reaches its boiling or vaporization temperature, but evaporation can happen due to a liquid's volatility. Volatile substances often coexist as a liquid and as a gas, depending on the pressure forced on them. The phase change from gas to liquid is condensation, and both evaporation and boiling take place in nature.

15. C: Water's polarity lends it to be extremely cohesive and adhesive; this cohesion keeps its atoms very close together. Because of this, it takes a large amount of energy to boil its liquid form. Phospholipid bilayers are made of nonpolar lipids; water, a polar liquid, cannot easily flow through it. Cell membranes use proteins called aquaporins to solve this issue and let water flow in and out. Fish breathe by capturing dissolved oxygen through their gills. Water can self-ionize, wherein it decomposes into a hydrogen ion (H+) and a hydroxide ion (OH-), but it cannot self-hydrolyze.

16. C: To gather accurate data, the student must be able compare a participant's test score from round 1 with their test score from round 2. The differing levels of intellect among the participants means that comparing participants' test scores to those of other participants would be inaccurate. This requirement excludes Choices A and D, which involve only one round of testing. The experiment must also involve different levels of sugar consumption from round 1 to round 2. In this way, the effects of different levels of sugar consumption can be seen on the same subjects. Thus, Choice B is incorrect because the experiment provides for no variation of sugar consumption. Choice C is the correct answer because it allows the student to compare each participant's test score from round 1 with their test score from round 2 after different levels of sugar consumption.

17. A: A control is the component or group in an experimental design that isn't manipulated—it's the standard against which the resultant findings are compared, so Choice A is correct. A variable is an element of the experiment that is able to be manipulated, making Choice B false. A constant is a condition of the experiment

Answer Explanations #1

outside of the hypothesis that remains unchanged in order to isolate the changes in the variables; therefore, Choice C is incorrect. Choice D is false because collected data are simply recordings of the observed phenomena that result from the experiment.

18. B: During telophase, two nuclei form at each end of the cell and nuclear envelopes begin to form around each nucleus. The nucleoli reappear, and the chromosomes become less compact. The microtubules are broken down by the cell, and mitosis is complete. The process begins with prophase as the mitotic spindles begin to form from centrosomes. Prometaphase follows, with the breakdown of the nuclear envelope and the further condensing of the chromosomes. Next, metaphase occurs when the microtubules are stretched across the cell and the chromosomes align at the metaphase plate. Finally, in the last step before telophase, anaphase occurs as the sister chromatids break apart and form chromosomes.

19. C: Convergent plate boundaries occur where two tectonic plates collide together. The denser oceanic plate will drop below the continental plate in a process called subduction.

20. D: Volcanic activity can occur both at fault lines and within the area of a tectonic plate at points called hot spots. Volcanic activity is more common at fault lines because of cracks that allow the mantle's magma to more easily escape to the surface.

21. A: The troposphere is the layer of the atmosphere where the majority of the activity that creates weather conditions experienced on Earth occurs. The ozone layer is in the stratosphere; this is also where airplanes fly.

22. D: Stratus clouds are also grey, but nimbostratus clouds are the low clouds that appear during stormy weather. The other choices are usually seen on fair-weather days.

23. C: Jupiter is the largest planet in the solar system, and it is primarily composed of hydrogen and helium. Ammonia is in much lower quantity and usually found as a cloud within Jupiter's atmosphere.

24. D: Viruses are not classified as living organisms. They are neither prokaryotic or eukaryotic; therefore, they don't belong to any of the answer choices.

25. C: According to the ideal gas law ($PV = nRT$), if volume is constant, the temperature is directly related to the pressure in a system. Therefore, if the pressure increases, the temperature will increase in direct proportion. Choice A would not be possible, since the system is closed and a change is occurring, so the temperature will change. Choice B incorrectly exhibits an inverse relationship between pressure and temperature, or $P = 1/T$. Choice D is incorrect because even without actual values for the variables, the relationship and proportions can be determined.

26. D: According to Newton's second law of motion, $F = m \times a$. Weight is the force resulting from a given situation, so the mass of the object needs to be multiplied by the acceleration of gravity on Earth: $W = m \times g$.

Choice A is incorrect because, according to Newton's law of universal gravitation, all objects exert some force on each other, which is based on their distance from each other and their masses. This is seen in planets, which affect each other's paths and those of their moons. Choice B is incorrect because an object in motion or at rest can have inertia; inertia is the resistance of a physical object to changing its state of motion. Choice C is incorrect because the mass of an object is a measurement of how much substance there is to the object, while the weight is gravity's effect on the mass.

27. D: Radiation can be transmitted through electromagnetic waves and needs no medium to travel; it can travel in a vacuum. This is how the Sun warms the Earth, and it typically applies to large objects with great amounts of heat or objects that have a large difference in their heat measurements. Choice A, convection, involves atoms or molecules traveling from areas of high concentration to those of low concentration and transferring energy or

Answer Explanations #1

heat with them. Choice *B*, conduction, involves the touching or bumping of atoms or molecules to transfer energy or heat. Choice *C*, induction, deals with charges and does not apply to the transfer of energy or heat. Choices *A*, *B*, and *C* need a medium in which to travel, while radiation requires no medium.

28. C: The mantle is the Earth's thickest layer; it holds most of the Earth's material. The crust is thin, and the inner core is also small compared to the mantle. There is no such thing as Earth's shell.

29. C: Subduction occurs when one plate is pushed down by another. A fault is where two plates meet. Diversion occurs when two plates move apart. *Drift* isn't a term used with tectonic plates.

30. B: Transpiration is water that evaporates from pores in plants called stomata. Evaporation of moving water is still called evaporation. Infiltration is the process of water moving into the ground, and precipitation that falls on trees is called canopy interception.

31. D: Water with a higher salinity has more dissolved salt and a lower freezing point. Water from the Dead Sea has the highest salinity of the answer choices.

32. C: Glaciers are formed only on land and constantly move because of their own weight. Icebergs are formed from glaciers, and they float.

33. C: In the Linnaean system, organisms are classified as follows, moving from few and general similarities to comprehensive and specific similarities: domain, kingdom, phylum, class, order, family, genus, and species. A popular mnemonic device to remember the Linnaean system is "Dear King Philip Came Over For Good Soup."

34. A: Salts are formed from compounds that use ionic bonds. Disulfide bridges are special bonds in protein synthesis which hold the protein in their secondary and tertiary structures. Covalent bonds are strong bonds formed through the sharing of electrons between atoms and are typically found in organic molecules like carbohydrates and lipids. London dispersion forces are fleeting, momentary bonds which occur between atoms that have instantaneous dipoles but quickly disintegrate.

35. C: Covalent bonds are special because they share electrons between multiple atoms. Most covalent bonds are formed between the elements H, F, N, O, S, and C, while hydrogen bonds are formed nearly exclusively between H and either O, N, or F of other molecules. Covalent bonds may inadvertently form dipoles, but this does not necessarily happen. For instance, dipoles do not form with similarly electronegative atoms, like carbon and hydrogen. Crystal solids are typically formed by substances with ionic bonds like the salts sodium iodide and potassium chloride.

36. D: An isotope of an element has an atomic number equal to its number of protons, but a different mass number because of the additional neutrons. Even though there are differences in the nucleus, the behavior and

Answer Explanations #1

properties of isotopes of a given element are identical. Atoms with different atomic numbers also have different numbers of protons and are different elements, so they cannot be isotopes.

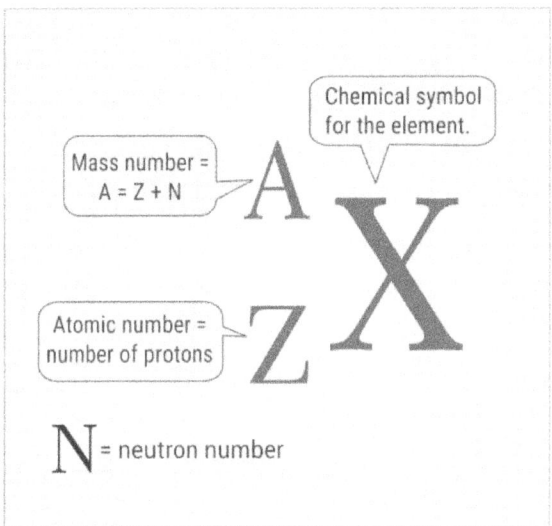

37. A: The neutrons and protons make up the nucleus of the atom. The nucleus is positively charged due to the presence of the protons. The negatively charged electrons are attracted to the positively charged nucleus by the electrostatic or Coulomb force; however, the electrons are not contained in the nucleus. The positively charged protons create the positive charge in the nucleus, and the neutrons are electrically neutral, so they have no effect. Radioactivity does not directly have a bearing on the charge of the nucleus.

38. B: Models are representations of concepts that are impossible to experience directly, such as the 3D representation of DNA, so Choice *B* is correct. Choice *A* is incorrect because theories simply explain why things happen. Choice *C* is incorrect because laws describe how things happen. Choice *D* is false because an observation analyzes situations using human senses.

39. D: An atom is structured with a nucleus in the center that contains neutral neutrons and positive protons. Surrounding the nucleus are orbiting electrons that are negatively charged. Choice *D* is the only correct answer.

40. C: The qualitative definition of ionization energy is the amount of energy needed to remove the most loosely bound valence electron from a gaseous atom or molecule to form a cation. Choice *A* refers to atomic radius, Choice *B* refers to electronegativity, and Choice *D* refers to electron affinity. All four of these properties follow trends on the periodic table.

41. D: Catabolism is the process of breaking down large molecules into smaller molecules to release energy for work. Carbohydrates and fats are catabolized to provide energy for exercise and daily activities. Anabolism synthesizes larger molecules from smaller constituent building blocks. Bioenergetics and metabolism are more general terms involving overall energy production and usage.

42. A: Many foods from developed countries are grown from plants which have been processed or bioengineered to include increased amounts of nutrients like vitamins and minerals that otherwise would be lost during manufacturing or are uncommon to the human diet. White rice, for example, is typically enriched with niacin, iron, and folic acid, while salt has been fortified with iodine for nearly a century. These help to prevent nutrition deficiencies. While it can be useful for fisheries to maintain models of fish populations so that they don't overfish their stock, this is not as immediately important to nutrition as are fortified and enriched foods. Although innovations to microscopes could lead to improved healthcare, this also has no direct effect on nutrition deficiency. Refrigerated train carts were historically a crucial invention around Civil War times and

Answer Explanations #1

were used to transport meat and dairy products long distances without spoiling, but dietary deficiencies could be more easily remedied by supplying people with fortified foods containing those nutrients rather than spoilable meats.

43. D: Iodine has the greatest number of electrons at 53 electrons. The number of electrons increases in elements going from left to right across the periodic table. Hydrogen, Choice *A*, is at the top left corner of the periodic table, so it has the fewest electrons (one electron). Iron has 26 electrons, copper has 29 electrons, Choices *B* and *C*, respectively.

44. C: Chemical properties describe the behavior of substances, while physical properties describe their appearance. Reactivity is a behavior, and therefore it's the correct answer.

45. D: Dimitri is correct because weather involves the water cycle. The other suggestions (and thus, answer choices) reflect misunderstandings. Weather itself changes day-to-day, and it depends on wind and heat patterns, while seasons depend on proximity to the Sun. Weather patterns such as rain and snow definitely involve the water cycle, so Choice *D* is the correct answer.

46. C: Early childhood educators should know that PowerPoint isn't an effective teaching method, and while going outside is fun, without modeling, the activity will be meaningless. The book idea would not be an effective teaching tool in this case because it's unable to model nearness, closeness, and general location. Modeling is the best option.

47. C: Climate has nothing to do with the size or shape of a state; it relates to exposure to the Sun. Places closer to the equator are hotter, so the answer is Choice *C*.

48. B: Hurricanes and rain are liquid precipitation, and snow is solid precipitation. Tornadoes only involve wind, so Choice *B* is the correct answer.

49. A: Plate tectonics involve movement in the Earth's crust that exposes areas for volcanic activities. Plates have nothing to do with evaporation or delta formation; both of those processes involve the water cycle. Plate movement also has nothing to do with tornados and wind movement.

50. B: Trace fossils are evidence of an organism as opposed to the remains of an organism. Bones, shells, and teeth were all once part of an organism and are true fossils.

Practice Tests #2, #3, & #4

To keep the size of this book manageable, save paper, and provide a digital test-taking experience, the 2nd through the 4th practice tests can be exclusively found online. Scan the QR code or go to this link to access it:

studyguideteam.com/online387/prax7001

The first time you access the tests, you will need to register as a "new user" and verify your email address.

If you have any issues, please email support@testprepbooks.com.

Index

1765 Quartering Act, 172
1787 Constitution of the United States, 180
A Five-Finger Retell Activity, 46
Abiotic, 232
Abraham Lincoln, 174, 180, 262, 271, 288, 303
Academic Language, 95
Acceleration, 246, 247, 248, 249, 321
Accuracy, 40, 100, 101, 260, 263
Active Learning, 73
Acute Angle, 132
Acute Triangle, 136
Adaptive Radiation, 227
Adjective, 101
Advanced Literacy Stage, 18
Affixes, 28, 29
Aftershocks, 216
Alexander Fleming, 239
Alexander Hamilton, 174, 282, 311
Alexander the Great, 191
Algebraic Expression, 118, 119, 120, 121, 123
Alleles, 226, 242, 291, 319
Allies, 175, 192
Alliteration, 17, 59
Alphabetic Principle, 21
American Revolution, 172, 173, 177, 178, 282
Analytic, 299
Anchor Charts, 78
Andrew Jackson, 172, 174, 281
Angiosperm, 209
Angle, 55, 130, 131, 132, 135, 136, 139, 144, 145, 200, 217
Angular Momentum, 249
Animals, 231
Annotation, 79
Antagonist, 53
Anther, 241
Antibodies, 238, 239, 318
Antigen, 238
Apollo 11, 176
Apollo Missions, 176
Apothem, 145, 146
Appositives, 37
Aqueducts, 191
Arc of a Circle, 144
Archaebacteria, 230
Archduke Ferdinand of Austria, 192

Area, 24, 25, 97, 112, 113, 140, 141, 142, 143, 144, 145, 146, 147, 149, 150, 152, 153, 154, 179, 182, 190, 206, 228, 238, 244, 255, 257, 260, 282, 288, 297, 302, 310, 311, 315, 317
Area Model, 112, 113
Area of a Square, 142
Area of a Trapezoid, 145
Area of a Two-Dimensional Figure, 140
Argumentative, 87, 297
Arithmetic Sequence, 127, 128
Articles of Confederation, 173, 178, 180, 182, 287
Associative Property of Addition and Multiplication, 110
Asteroid, 211
Asthenosphere, 202, 207
Aswan Dam, 188
Atlas, 183
Atmosphere, 200, 203, 205, 206, 209, 212, 213, 214, 215, 222, 242, 248, 249, 250, 251, 258, 259, 320
Atomic Bomb, 176
Atoms, 244, 322
ATP, 224
Auditory Learning, 73
Autobiography, 52, 87
Autotrophs, 218, 220, 223, 230, 231
Axon, 221
Babylon, 191
Background Knowledge, 36, 38, 42, 43, 44, 45, 46
Bar Graph, 166, 167
Barter System, 194
Base, 17, 102, 103, 115, 138, 139, 140, 141, 142, 143, 145, 146, 148, 149, 153, 229, 254
Base Words, 29
Bathymetry, 184
Battle of Gettysburg, 180
Battle of New Orleans, 174
Big Bang Theory, 209
Bill of Rights, 173, 180, 285, 314
Bills, 178, 179, 224
Binary Fission, 224, 225
Binomial, 121, 230
Binomial Nomenclature, 230
Biographies and Autobiographies, 52
Biography, 20, 52
Biosphere, 200, 201, 209, 231, 232, 241
Black Hole, 211

Blending, 15, 16, 31
Blizzards, 206
Bolshevik Revolution In 1917, 175
Book of the Dead, 191
Boston Tea Party, 173, 177, 282, 284, 313
Box Plot, 162, 163, 164, 167
Box-and-Whisker Plot, 162
Brain, 221, 223, 229, 238
Brown Dwarfs, 211
Buzz Aldrin, 176
Caliphs, 190
Cambrian Explosion, 209
Canyons, 208
Capital, 25, 194
Capsule, 220
Carbon-12, 210
Carbon-14, 210
Carolus Linnaeus, 230
Cartesian Plane, 150
Cause, 61, 65, 69, 77, 173, 177, 178, 205, 206, 208, 213, 216, 227, 238, 242, 249, 251, 253, 255, 256, 267, 270, 297, 317, 319
Cause and Effect Relationship, 69
Cause/Effect, 64
Cell Membranes, 220
Cells, 218, 220, 222, 224, 225, 226, 229, 230, 231, 238, 239, 251, 254, 258, 259, 290, 318, 319
Cenozoic Era, 209
Center of a Data, 161
Central Or Major Characters, 53
Centrifugal Force, 249
Centripetal Force, 249
Chance, 168
Characters, 53
Charles Darwin, 226, 227
Chemical Properties, 202, 245, 296
Chitin, 231
Chlorophyll, 223
Chloroplasts, 218, 220, 223
Choices, 195, 199, 259, 300, 302, 303, 304, 305, 311, 313, 315, 316, 317, 318, 320, 321, 323
Christianity, 192
Christopher Columbus, 171
Chromosomes, 220, 224
Chronological/Sequence Order, 64
Cinder Volcanoes, 207
Circumference, 143
Civil Rights Movement, 175, 176, 177, 178, 198, 199
Civil War, 174, 177, 180, 271, 287, 303, 323

Clean Water Act of 1972, 176
Climate, 82, 182, 189, 206, 232, 287, 312, 315
Clouds, 204, 205, 293
Code of Hammurabi, 191
Coherent Writing, 98
Cold War, 175, 176, 188, 192, 284, 314
Collaborative Learning, 72
Collinear, 129
Comedy, 52
Comet, 211
Command System, 196, 197
Commander-In-Chief, 178
Commensalism, 233
Common Difference, 127, 128
Common Ratio, 128
Communication, 71, 80
Communism, 175, 192, 197
Commutative Property of Addition, 110
Comparison/Contrast, 64
Competition, 192, 217, 227, 233, 257, 273, 284, 317
Complex Sentences, 94
Composing a Number, 102
Composing Fractions, 109
Composite Number, 117
Composite Volcanoes, 207
Compound Sentences, 94
Compound-Complex Sentences, 95
Concave, 135
Condensation, 245
Conduction, 250, 293
Cone, 121, 139, 207
Confederate States of America, 174
Conflict, 54
Congress, 173, 178, 179, 180, 181, 198, 285, 287, 314, 316
Congruent, 138, 139, 147, 148, 149
Connotations, 59
Conservation of Energy, 251
Consonant Blend, 27, 91
Consonant Digraphs, 27
Constant, 121, 126, 127, 182, 209, 223, 247, 248, 249, 292, 314, 320, 321
Constitution, 173, 177, 178, 179, 180, 182, 288, 314
Constitutional Convention In 1787, 173
Content, 20, 32, 40, 52, 70, 72, 77, 80, 91
Content-Specific, 91
Contextual Strategies, 36, 37
Continental Army, 173
Continental Drift, 217
Continents, 171, 183, 184, 185, 190, 217

Index

Convection, 208, 213, 250, 321
Convection Current, 250
Conventional Stage, 91
Convergent Boundary, 208
Conversational Language, 95
Convex, 135, 206
Coordinate Plane, 150, 151, 152
Coplanar, 129
Corresponding Terms, 128
Countries, 183
Covalent Bonds, 201, 294, 322
Creative Writing, 57
Crescent Moon, 215
Cuneiform Tablets, 191
Cylinder, 138, 139
Cytokinesis, 224
Cytoplasm, 220, 224
Cytoskeleton, 220, 229
Declaration of Independence, 177, 179, 180, 311
Decodable Words, 31, 97, 260, 297
Decoding, 26, 87
Decomposing a Number, 102
Deflation, 195, 197
Degrees, 132, 144, 184, 250, 312
Deletions, 16
Delta, 246
Deltas, 208
Denominator, 107, 108, 109, 113, 114, 116, 117, 307, 309
Dependent, 94, 95, 122, 163, 164, 168, 179, 226, 249, 291, 294, 300, 302, 319
Derivational Suffixes, 29
Description, 64
Descriptive Statistics, 158
Dialects, 95
Diameter, 143
Diction, 78
Differentiated Instruction, 47, 77
Diffraction, 255
Digital Literacy, 71, 72, 73
Digital Sources, 82
Digital Tools, 80
Directionality, 19
Discussion, 72, 73, 78
Distance Learning, 73
Distributive Property, 111, 119, 120
Divergent Boundary, 208
DNA, 209, 218, 220, 222, 224, 225, 226, 229, 241, 318, 322
DNA Replication, 224
Dolch Word List, 31
Domain-Specific Languages, 95
Dominant Allele, 226
Doppler Radar, 217
Dot Plot, 166
Double Bar Graph, 166
Dr. Edward Fry, 31
Dr. Edward William Dolch, 31
Drama, 52
Dynamic Characters, 53
Dysfluency, 40, 42
Early Intermediate Literacy Stage, 18
Earth, 156, 176, 200, 201, 202, 203, 204, 205, 206, 207, 208, 209, 210, 211, 212, 213, 214, 215, 216, 232, 247, 255, 258, 259, 274, 285, 290, 293, 296, 314, 315, 321
Eclipses, 215
Editing Step, 79
Effects, 57, 76, 80, 177, 179, 188, 189, 193, 195, 196, 238, 242, 248, 249, 251, 319, 320
Elastic Rebound, 216
Electoral College System, 179
Electric Energy, 254
Electrical Current, 254
Electrostatics, 253
Elements, 74, 76, 244
Elliptic Orbit, 212
Emancipation Proclamation, 180
Empress of China, 172
Encoding, 26, 87
End Rhyme, 51, 52
Energy, 222, 223, 250, 251, 253, 254, 255
Entrepreneurship, 194, 196
Equation, 116, 118, 119, 121, 122, 123, 124, 125, 129, 143, 144, 157, 170, 224, 247, 274, 275, 306, 307, 308, 311
Equator, 184, 206, 213, 296, 312
Equiangular Polygons, 135
Equilateral Polygons, 135
Equilateral Triangle, 136, 310
Equilibrium, 195, 248, 290
Era of Good Feelings, 174
Erosion, 206, 207, 208
Estates-General, 197
Ethos, 96
Eubacteria, 230
Eukaryotes, 218, 220, 223, 230
Evaporation, 203, 292, 296, 319, 321, 323
Executive Branch, 173, 178, 181
Expanded Form, 102
Experiment, 256, 257, 292, 320

Index

Explicitly, 26, 41, 44, 88
Expository, 85, 86
Faces, 138, 139, 140, 141, 147, 148
Factors of a Number, 117
Fall, 15, 162, 164, 205, 206, 214, 226, 244, 249, 264
Farewell Address, 180
Federal Aid Highway Act of 1956, 175
Federal Government, 178, 179, 180, 197
Feedback, 69, 77
Fertile Crescent, 190
Fictional Force, 249
Figurative Language, 57
Filament, 241, 254
First, 308
First Person, 55, 65, 297
First Trophic Level, 233
Flagellum, 220
Flash Cards, 32, 34
Flat Character, 53
Flowers, 240, 291
Focus, 22, 23, 40, 56, 63, 83, 96, 97, 98, 171, 176, 177, 180, 216, 264, 287, 303
Food Webs, 233
Force, 173, 175, 176, 177, 192, 216, 245, 247, 248, 249, 251, 253, 254, 255, 284, 318, 321, 322
    Forces, 245, 248, 254
Force Diagram, 248
Formative Assessment, 69
Formative Assessments, 96, 98
Formulas, 121, 122
Fossils, 210
Fractions, 107, 109, 113, 114, 278
Franklin D. Roosevelt, 175
Freezing, 205, 245
Freshwater, 201, 317
Front, 29, 119, 120, 148, 206, 248
Fry Graph, 34
Fry's Formula, 34, 35
Fungi, 231
G1 Phase, 224
G2 Phase, 224
Gametes, 225, 319
Gap, 162
Gas, 245
General Circulation, 206
General Cornwallis, 173
General George Washington, 173
Genotype, 226, 291, 319
Genres, 99

Genus, 230
Geology, 201
Geometric Sequence, 127, 128
George Washington, 173, 180, 282, 311
Gettysburg Address, 180
Gibbous Moon, 215
Gilded Age, 174
Glucose, 222, 223, 224, 233
Graphemes, 21, 41
Graphic Organizers, 46, 48
Gravity, 246, 249
Great Depression, 175, 192
Gregor Mendel, 226
Hail, 205
Headings, 66, 86
Heat, 209, 250
Henry Ford, 175
Herbert Spencer, 226
Heterotrophs, 222, 223, 230, 231
Hieroglyphs, 191
Hippocratic Oath, 191
Histograms, 162, 167
Homo Sapiens, 230
House of Representatives, 178, 315
Hurricanes, 206, 296
Hydrosphere, 200, 201
Hyperlinks, 67, 77
Hyphen, 100, 101
Hypothesis, 217, 242, 244, 256, 257, 292, 320
Identity Property of Addition, 110
Identity Property of Multiplication, 110
Impulse, 247
Independent Clause, 94, 95, 300, 302, 304, 305
Induction, 253, 293
Industrial Revolution, 174, 196, 262, 314
Industrialization, 174, 176, 187, 189, 193, 195, 285, 287, 314, 316
Inferences, 60, 61, 158, 298
Inferential Comprehension, 60
Infixes, 29
Inflation, 161, 195, 197, 289, 314, 317
Inflectional Suffixes, 29
Informational Text, 52, 63, 64
Informational Texts, 77
Informational Writing, 86
Integer, 102, 117, 274
    Integers, 107, 113
Intermediate Literacy Stage, 18
Internal Rhyme, 51, 52

Index

International Date Line, 184
Inverse Operations, 104, 105, 106, 112, 123
Inverse Property of Addition, 110
Inverse Property of Multiplication, 110
Irregular Words, 32, 33, 90, 301
Isosceles Triangle, 136
James Madison, 173, 282, 311
Jim Crow, 174, 181
    Jim Crow Laws, 181
Judaism, 190, 192
Judicial Branch, 179, 285
July 4, 1776, 179, 282
Karyotypes, 241
Kinesthetic Learning, 73
Kinetic Energy, 251, 258
King George III, 180
King Louis XIV, 196, 197
Kurtosis, 162
KWL Charts, 46, 48, 298
Kyoto Protocol, 193
Labor, 40, 194, 285, 314
Laissez-Faire, 196
Land, 171, 172, 174, 187, 189, 194, 200, 204, 208, 217, 220, 286, 294, 317, 321
Language, 14, 15, 16, 21, 22, 23, 25, 30, 53, 54, 57, 58, 60, 61, 74, 75, 76, 82, 91, 93, 94, 95, 96, 97, 98, 190, 193, 230, 268, 284, 297, 302, 303, 313, 316, 317
Language Acquisition, 22, 74
Language Comprehension, 43
Lava, 206, 207, 208
Law of Demand, 195
Law of Inertia, 247
Law of Supply, 195
League of Nations, 174, 181, 192, 288
Legislative Branch, 178, 179, 285
Letter Recognition, 20
Level of Meaning, 36
Lexile Text Measures, 35
Like Terms, 119
Line, 51, 111, 124, 125, 129, 130, 131, 132, 143, 145, 150, 152, 163, 165, 166, 167, 175, 184, 213, 215, 224, 247, 249, 255, 269
Line Graph, 165, 167
Line Plot, 166, 167
Line Segment, 131, 132
Linear Equations, 123
Linear Inequalities, 123
Linear Momentum, 247
Linear Relationships, 125, 126
Linear Term, 121
Liquid, 245
Listening Comprehension, 42
Literal Comprehension, 59
Literary Analysis, 61
Literary Elements, 52
Literary Nonfiction, 52
Lithification, 207
Lithosphere, 201, 202, 207, 208
Local Governments, 179
Location, 54, 93, 102, 129, 150, 151, 179, 182, 187, 246, 283, 284, 287, 296, 312, 315, 323
Logos, 96
Longitude, 184
Low Tide, 216
Loyalists, 173
Lunar Eclipse, 215, 290, 318
Luster, 201
M Phase, 224, 225
Macroeconomics, 194
Magnetic Energy, 254
Magnetic Forces, 254
Main Idea, 62, 63, 66, 67, 68, 69, 77, 260
Malcolm X, 175
Mantle, 202, 206, 208, 293, 320, 321
Market System, 196, 197
Martin Luther King Jr, 175, 177, 181, 199
Martin Luther King Jr., 175, 177, 181, 199
Mass, 154, 156, 244, 247
Matter, 244, 245
Mean, 61, 158, 159, 160, 161, 186, 251, 265
Measures of Central Tendency, 158, 159
Mechanical Advantage, 253
Mechanical Energy, 251
Mechanics, 25, 97, 297
Median, 158, 159, 160, 161, 162, 163, 279
Meiosis, 225, 258, 259, 319
Melting, 245
Mercantilism, 196, 197
Meridians, 184, 312
Mesopotamia, 190, 191
Mesosphere, 200
Mesozoic Era, 209
Metamorphosis, 228, 242, 243, 244
Meteor, 212
Meteorite, 212
Meteoroid, 211
Meteorologists, 217
Meteorology, 217

Index

Meter, 52
Microeconomics, 194
Middle, 14, 29, 51, 75, 84, 131, 158, 159, 160, 200, 213, 224, 270, 292
Milky Way, 211
Minerals, 194, 201, 206, 210, 295, 323
Mitochondria, 218, 220, 223
Mixture, 84, 245
Mode, 158, 159, 160, 161, 260, 297
Mode of a Data Set, 160
Momentum, 246, 247, 249
Monera, 230, 293
Money, 154, 195
Monomial, 121
Monopolies, 195, 196, 197, 285
Monotheism, 192
Mood, 59, 61, 261
Moons, 212, 215, 321
Morphemes, 23, 260, 297, 302
Morphological Maps, 38
Morphology, 28, 100, 101
Multiples of a Given Number, 117
Multisensory Approach, 32
Mutualism, 233
Myelin, 221
Narrative Writing, 87
Narratives, 86, 177
Narrator, 53, 55
National Aeronautics and Space Administration (NASA), 176
National Association for the Advancement of Colored People (NAACP), 177
Native American Tribes, 172, 177, 179, 187
Natural Phenomena, 187
Natural Resources, 187, 190, 194, 195, 227
Neil Armstrong, 176, 212
Nerve, 221, 229
Net, 139, 140, 141
Neuron, 221, 229
Neutron Star, 211
New Deal, 175, 178
New Moon, 215, 216
New Spain, 171
Nile River, 188, 191
Non-Decodable, 32
Non-Print Sources, 43
Non-Renewable, 250
Nonrenewable Resources, 194, 195
Non-Reversible Change, 245

Northwest Ordinance of 1787, 173
Nuclear Fission, 203, 208
Nuclear Fusion, 203
Nucleus, 200, 203, 218, 220, 224, 244, 295, 318, 320, 322
Nullification, 179
Number Line, 111, 113, 124, 150, 166, 169
Objective Point of View, 55
Obtuse Angle, 132
Obtuse Triangle, 136
Omniscient, 55
Ones, 100
One-to-One Correspondence, 19
Onset, 16
Opinion Pieces, 87
Opposites, 110
Order of Importance, 64
Ordered Pair, 151, 152, 164, 165
Organ Systems, 221, 222
Organic Products, 195
Organism, 210, 218, 220, 221, 223, 225, 226, 228, 229, 232, 233, 242, 243, 291, 318, 319
Organize, 48
Organs, 221, 222, 318
Origin, 23, 150, 152
Ottoman Empire, 171, 192, 198, 199, 284, 313
Outliers, 158, 159
Ovary, 241
Paleontology, 209
Paleozoic Era, 209
Paper Money, 195
Parallel Lines, 130
Parallelogram, 137, 145
Parallels, 184
Paraphrasing, 82
Parasitism, 233
Parenthetical Elements, 37
Pathos, 96
PEMDAS, 110, 307
Percent, 114, 115, 116, 118, 158, 161, 166, 168, 200, 201, 220, 233, 316
Perimeter, 139, 141
Perimeter of a Square, 142
Persuasive, 66, 82, 87, 99, 297
Persuasive Text, 52
Persuasive Writing, 85, 87
Phenotype, 226, 291, 319
Phoneme, 41, 87, 261, 298, 299
Phoneme-Grapheme Correspondence, 24

Index

Phonemic Awareness, 14, 21, 41, 88
Phonetic Stage, 88, 89, 262, 298, 301
Phonics, 21, 260, 266
Phonics Instruction, 27
Phonological Awareness, 14, 23, 264, 299
Photosynthesis, 213, 222, 223, 224, 289, 317
Photosynthesizers, 231
Physical Properties, 245
Pi, 143
Pictograms, 191
Picture Walk, 45, 75
Pie Chart, 166
Pistil, 241
Place, 54, 75, 83, 93, 96, 97, 102, 103, 104, 112, 113, 118, 129, 144, 160, 174, 182, 209, 216, 220, 223, 229, 252, 254, 257, 270, 282, 302, 305, 311, 315, 319
Places, 101
Plagiarizing, 82
Planning, 83
Plants, 213, 220, 222, 223, 231, 233, 290
Plasma, 238, 245
Plasma B-Cell, 238
Plot, 45, 46, 53, 54, 55, 59, 61, 65, 75, 76, 85, 86, 87, 152, 161, 163, 166, 167, 269
Poetry, 51, 55
Point, 25, 55, 56, 61, 62, 65, 66, 69, 74, 80, 83, 86, 97, 102, 103, 113, 124, 126, 129, 130, 131, 138, 143, 150, 151, 152, 153, 158, 159, 160, 161, 162, 165, 176, 201, 202, 205, 206, 246, 247, 248, 249, 252, 257, 292, 297, 301, 305, 309, 321
Point of View, 55, 56, 62, 65, 80, 86, 97, 297
Polarization, 254
Polio, 238
Polis, 191
Polygon, 132, 135, 138, 139, 141, 145, 146, 147
Polyhedrons, 138
Polymorphs, 201
Population, 158, 172, 178, 179, 183, 191, 195, 196, 197, 227, 232, 242, 244, 258, 284, 286, 288, 313, 314, 315, 318, 319
Potential Energy, 251
Potomac, 172
Power of 10, 103, 104
Preamble, 180
Precommunicative Writing, 88
Predator-Prey Relationships, 233
Predictable Structures, 35
Prefix, 101
Prefixes, 29, 302

President, 173, 174, 178, 179, 180, 286, 303, 314, 315
President Eisenhower, 175
President Theodore Roosevelt, 176
President Woodrow Wilson, 174
Primary Sources, 82, 198, 199
Prime [Greenwich] Meridian, 184
Prime Factorization, 117
Prime Number, 117
Print, 18, 19, 20, 264, 299
Print Awareness, 18, 19, 264, 299
Print Sources, 82
Prism, 138, 139, 141, 148, 149, 150
Probability, 129, 167
Problem/Solution, 64
Prokaryotes, 218, 220, 223, 225, 230
Proportion, 114, 115, 116, 157, 307, 310, 321
Prose, 52
Prosody, 40, 260
Protagonist, 53
Protein Enzymes, 229
Proton, 200
Pyramid, 138, 140, 194
Quadrant I, 151
Quadrant II, 151
Quadrant III, 151
Quadrant IV, 151
Quadrilaterals, 137
Qualitative Measures, 35
Quantitative Measures, 34
Radiation, 176, 203, 213, 227, 250, 321
Rain, 205, 296
Rainbow Writing, 32
Rainforest, 206
Range of a Data Set, 159
Rate, 40, 115, 260
Ratio, 107, 113, 114, 115, 116, 128
Ratio Pieces, 114
Rational Number, 107, 108, 111, 113, 306
Ray, 130, 131
Readability Formulas, 34
Reading Comprehension, 43, 45
Reading Fluency, 26, 40, 41, 42, 260, 263, 297, 299
Receptor Protein, 229
Recessive Allele, 226, 291, 319
Reciprocal Numbers, 110
Reciprocal Phonological Skills, 26
Recombination, 226, 319
Rectangle, 112, 122, 133, 134, 137, 139, 140, 141, 142, 147, 150, 162, 278, 309

Recursively, 26
Red Dwarfs, 211
Red Giant, 211
Refraction, 255
Region, 140, 171, 182, 184, 190, 192, 282, 288, 302, 317
Register, 95
Regular Polygon, 135, 145
Relationship, 100
Remainder, 107, 113
Renewable, 250
Renewable Resources, 194, 195
Research, 65, 74, 76, 81, 82, 83, 95, 96, 203, 217, 239, 242, 243, 247, 255, 256, 257, 268, 272, 282, 303
Resource, 65, 82, 187, 194, 195, 196, 250
Respiration, 222, 223, 224
Return Sweeping, 19
Reversible Change, 245
Revision Step, 78
Revisions, 83, 97
Revolutionary War, 173
Rhombus, 137
Rhyme, 14, 16, 260, 297
Ribosomes, 220
Richter Scale, 216
Right Angle, 130, 132, 141, 145, 148
Right Rectangular Prism, 147, 148, 149, 150
Right Triangle, 136, 146
Rime, 16
Riparian Customs, 187
RNA, 222, 229
Roman Empire, 191, 192, 198, 199, 313
Root Word, 29
Root Words, 29
Rounding Numbers, 104
Royal Ice Cream Parlor, 178
S Phase, 224
Sand Dunes, 209
Scalene Triangle, 136
Scarcity, 195, 285, 314
Scatter Plot, 163, 164, 165
Schwa, 28
Scientific Method, 256, 257
Seawater, 201
Second Continental Congress, 179
Second Person Point of View, 55
Second Trophic Level, 233
Secondary Sources, 82, 198
Segmenting, 16, 28, 31, 88
Seismic Waves, 216

Seismology, 216
Semantic Organizers, 18, 50
Senate, 178, 286, 315
Sensory Neurons, 229
Setting, 41, 44, 45, 46, 53, 59, 85, 87
Sexual Reproduction, 225, 226
Shield Volcanoes, 206
Sidebars, 67
Sides of the Angle, 131
Sight Words, 31, 33, 41, 264, 299
Signal Words, 69
Silent Reading Fluency, 40
Simple Sentences, 94
Sir Isaac Newton, 247
Skim, 36, 65
Sleet, 205
Snow, 206, 296
Solar Eclipse, 216
Solid, 133, 134, 138, 139, 140, 201, 202, 203, 206, 244, 245, 294
Solution, 118, 123, 124, 125, 245, 256, 261, 275, 297, 307
Spanish-American War In 1898, 174
Spatial Order, 64
Speaker, 53
Species, 186, 187, 209, 220, 226, 227, 229, 230, 232, 233, 242, 251, 290, 317
Spelling, 25, 97, 260, 297
Spelling Development, 88
Sphere, 138, 183
Spread of a Data Set, 161
Sputnik, 176, 217
Sputnik Satellite, 176
Square, 132, 137, 140, 141, 142, 143, 147, 150, 279, 291, 310
Stamen, 241
Stamp Act of 1765, 172, 313
Stars, 211
State Governments, 179, 288
States of Matter, 245
Statistics, 56, 65, 158
Steve Jobs, 176
Steve Wozniak, 176
Stigma, 241
Stomata, 203, 321
Storyboards, 46
Straight Angle, 132
Strata, 209
Stratosphere, 200, 293, 320
Structural Analysis, 37, 268, 272, 302, 304

Index

Structure, 65, 200, 218
Study of Informational Text, 61
Style, 57, 58, 83, 96, 97, 172, 193, 241, 249, 265, 303, 304
Sublimation, 245
Substance, 244
Substitutions, 16
Suffixes, 29, 302
Summarize, 42, 43, 44, 46, 79
Summarizing, 62, 260
Summarizing for Others, 63
Summative Assessments, 96, 98
Supernovas, 211
Supply, 195, 285, 314
Supporting Details of Texts, 67
Supreme Court, 179, 182, 198, 285, 288, 314, 316
Surface Area, 140, 141, 148
Surface Area of a Three-Dimensional Figure, 140
Surface Area of the Prism, 141, 148
Swammerdam, 243
Syllabic Analysis, 272
Syllabication, 30
Syllabication Patterns, 30, 31
Syllable, 15, 16, 30
    Syllables, 14, 15, 16, 17
Systematically, 26, 88
T-Cells, 238
Teacher-Led Practice, 87
Temperature, 250
Tenth Amendment, 179, 180, 315
Term, 119, 120, 121, 128, 129, 178, 190, 245, 250, 267, 287, 307, 321
Tetrahedron, 138
Theory, 65, 209, 217, 226, 227, 255, 290, 295
Theory of Adaptation, 227
Theory of Natural Selection, 226
Thermodynamics, 251
Thermosphere, 200, 293
Thesis Statement, 87
Third Person, 55, 65
Third Person Limited, 55
Third Person Omniscient, 55
Third Person Point of View, 55
Third Trophic Level, 233
Thomas Jefferson, 174, 282, 311
Three-Dimensional Shapes, 133
Timed-Reading, 41
Timed-Repeated Readings, 42
Tissue, 221, 295

Tone, 56, 59
Topography, 183, 189, 208, 296
Tories, 173
Tornadoes, 206, 296
Tragedy, 52
Trait, 226
Transcription, 229
Transform Boundaries, 208
Transitional Terms, 65
Transpiration, 203, 321
Transport Protein, 229
Trapezoid, 137, 145
Treaty of Paris of 1783, 173
Treaty of Versailles, 192, 288
Triangles, 136, 142
Trinomial, 121
Triple Entente, 198, 199
Troposphere, 200, 205, 206, 293
Two-Dimensional Shapes, 132, 134
Unicellular, 220, 230
Union of Soviet Socialist Republics, 175
Unit Fraction, 109
Unit Rates, 115
United Nations, 178, 192, 193
Universal Design for Learning, 23
Uracil, 229
Usage, 25, 65, 97, 98, 260, 264, 268, 273, 297, 304, 305, 323
Variable, 116, 118, 119, 120, 121, 122, 123, 124, 125, 129, 157, 163, 164, 167, 179, 292, 306, 320
Velocity, 246, 247, 248, 249
Venn Diagrams, 46, 48
Vertex, 131, 132, 138, 139, 140, 141
Vertex of the Angle, 131
Vice President, 178
Viruses, 220, 293, 321
Visual Aids, 48, 56, 68, 74
Visual Learning, 73
Vocabulary, 33, 35, 39
Volcanoes, 206, 207, 209, 296
Volume of a Solid, 148
Voting Rights Act of 1965, 175
Water Cycle, 203, 206, 296, 323
Weathering, 206, 207
Weight, 156, 247, 321
White Dwarf, 211
Whole Numbers, 113, 117
Woodrow Wilson's Fourteen Points, 181
Word Analysis, 23, 297

Index

Word Families, 16, 28, 32
Word Maps, 38
Word Recognition, 41
Word Walls, 89, 298
Word Webs, 18, 38, 50
Words, 18, 39
Worksheets, 32

Wright Brothers, 176
Writing Clarity, 98
Written Expression, 78
X-Axis, 150, 152, 163, 164, 278
Y-Axis, 150, 151, 152, 163, 164, 165
Yeast, 231, 238
Zygote, 226

Dear Praxis Elementary Education Test Taker,

Thank you again for purchasing this study guide for your Praxis Elementary Education exam. We hope that we exceeded your expectations.

Our goal in creating this study guide was to cover all of the topics that you will see on the test. We also strove to make our practice questions as similar as possible to what you will encounter on test day. With that being said, if you found something that you feel was not up to your standards, please send us an email and let us know.

We would also like to let you know about other books in our catalog that may interest you.

Praxis Social Studies

This can be found on Amazon: amazon.com/dp/1628457686

Praxis English Language Arts

amazon.com/dp/1628458895

Praxis General Science

amazon.com/dp/1628458550

Praxis Mathematics

amazon.com/dp/1628458496

Praxis Core Study Guide

amazon.com/dp/1637759819

We have study guides in a wide variety of fields. If the one you are looking for isn't listed above, then try searching for it on Amazon or send us an email.

Thanks Again and Happy Testing!
Product Development Team
support@testprepbooks.com

Online Resources

Included with your purchase are multiple online resources. This includes the practice tests in an interactive format and a convenient study timer to help you manage your time.

Scan the QR code or go to this link to access this content:

studyguideteam.com/online387/prax7001

The first time you access the page, you will need to register as a "new user" and verify your email address.

If you have any issues, please email support@testprepbooks.com.

Thank you for letting us be a part of your studying journey!